LABOR
LAW and
PUBLIC
POLICY

KF
3369
.W9

LABOR
LAW and
PUBLIC
POLICY

Ronald A. Wykstra
COLORADO STATE UNIVERSITY

Eleanour V. Stevens
COLORADO STATE UNIVERSITY

THE ODYSSEY PRESS   *New York*

201723

Copyright © 1970 by Western Publishing Company, Inc.
Published by The Odyssey Press, a division of Western Publishing Company, Inc.
All rights reserved
Printed in the United States
Library of Congress Catalog Card Number: 73-100366
A 0 9 8 7 6 5 4 3 2 1

CONTENTS

v

3

4

5

6

PREFACE

Judicial control has had a great deal of influence on the growth of labor movements, management relations, and utilization of human resources. Labor-management practices require an understanding of the legal boundaries of the area in which labor and management may function in the conduct of their activities for goal achievement. This text is designed to provide a concise but complete view of the evolution of labor legislation and public policy applied to manpower. In order to do this, the authors have included the historical sources from which the law and public policy evolved. Also taken into account is the legislation that was used to control labor activities prior to the passage of laws designed exclusively for dealing with labor disputes. Contemporary issues and problems receive the most detailed attention in this volume. In order to illustrate applications of the law to real-life situations, leading cases and Supreme Court opinions have been included, thus allowing a more complete understanding of the public policy process. National Labor Relations Board decisions, judicial decisions, and actual laws are included in original form to allow maximum use of the "case" approach as a complement to the authors' narrative. Every effort has been made to keep chapters to a palatable length while providing complete coverage of topics considered, with the hope that the instructor and reader may use those additional supplements deemed most applicable to his own individual needs.

Special attention and separate chapter treatment have been given to national emergency strikes, the weapons of conflict, collective bargaining, public employees, and manpower policy and human resource management. This volume also contains appendices that include the body of major legislative enactments which are referred to in the text. The availability of this material allows those who wish to study the law in greater detail to do so.

The objective of the authors has been to develop a meaningful and complete volume that will provide the student, the practitioner, and the professor with a complete and concise text for a contemporary insight and understanding of the industrial relations scene.

Many people provided valuable assistance to the authors. Mrs. William James, Mrs. Marvin Shipley, and Mary Ann Reid provided valuable clerical assistance and Mr. William Lacey, a student in the College of Business, provided research assistance for which we are grateful. We are deeply grateful to Miss Kay Kilburn and Miss Ruth L. Roberts who typed the manuscript and performed other valuable clerical duties.

This volume represents a joint effort on the part of the authors and the responsibility for the inclusion of material is, therefore, jointly shared. Any opinions expressed are those of the authors and in no way reflect those of any institution or organization with whom the authors have been or are associated.

Ronald A. Wykstra
Eleanour V. Stevens

LABOR
LAW and
PUBLIC
POLICY

1

INTRODUCTION TO LABOR LAW

The Context of Labor Legislation

Civilized mankind has used a variety of techniques to create order and organized efforts in economic affairs including slavery, custom, and law. Labor law is one dimension of an institutional system of social control embracing labor-capital relationships. Control by law may be a tardy mechanism for recasting economic interrelationships because of the delayed deliberation in a democratically oriented system. At the same time, it is frequently suggested that labor law is reasonably dynamic and responsive to changing social and economic forces; i.e., it is a result, for the most part, in contrast to a cause or initiating force. Moreover, legal institutions related to laws concerning labor-capital relationships initially were derivative of other more firmly established fields of law, although this is less the case with the passage of time. Therefore, it is appropriate to direct attention to the socioeconomic circumstances leading to the development of labor law as well as to its historical course and present content.

1

It is staggering to the imagination to contemplate the hundreds of thousands of economic-oriented tasks a modern society must see to their end in an organized fashion. On the one hand, man is imbued with a fiercely independent and selfish nature. At the same time, it is only because he is a socially cooperative being that perpetuation and progress of the human environment is maintained. Excessive numbers of men constructing and supplying too many automobiles or too few beans may lead to hopeless chaos. In short, imbalance in an infinite number of activities in the product or resource market could lead to a state of perpetual confusion. Breakdown of the economic system is an omnipresent threat derived from man's unpredictability and an expanding environment of economic interrelationships in a world of uncertainty. The decision of too many or too few to seek or supply a quantity of goods, services, and specific tasks leads to constant changes and adjustments rippling outward to all of the interdependent parts of the whole of economic organization, including the markets for products and resources. One might very well maintain ". . . society's existence hangs by a hair." [1]

ECONOMIC ORGANIZATION OF SOCIETIES

How then is order embedded in a seemingly chaotic state of affairs? Early history reveals that in certain civilizations, custom and tradition handed down from parent to sibling or state to the individual tended to preserve established patterns of economic behavior. The use of authoritarianism is likewise a means of acquiring an "order" in economic affairs that is not uncommon. Edicts of a supreme power, augmented by enforcement, may shape the community of man and order its social and economic behavior. Laws may be utilized as a supplementary means of determining courses of action or for restraining choice and behavior which emanates from this custom or command. Both custom and command rule dominate the time dimension of civilized man's organized state of economic affairs.

Within the last few centuries a third system of organization, the market system, has emerged as a guide in the game of organized economic life. The paradox of the "rules" of the market system game is that each participant allegedly furthers the well-being of his cohabitants by pursuing his own ends first. It is alleged that the consequent pitting of individual skills against the skills of others assures the com-

[1] Robert L. Heilbroner, *The Worldly Philosophers* (New York: Simon and Schuster, Inc., 1953), p. 7.

munity of more nearly and rapidly approaching optimal solutions in playing the economic game. Abandonment of the comfortable security of dictate or tradition is an astonishing and revolutionary answer to the age-old question of socioeconomic organization. The rules of this new game not only were different in form but also in kind, number, and complexity. During the late seventeenth and early eighteenth centuries, workers increasingly recognized that their interests were quite different from those of their superiors engaged in organizing labor and capital in a viable pattern of production. The expansion of markets resulted in master workmen becoming engrossed in such matters as buying raw materials and labor at the best obtainable prices, stocking them for future use, organizing them in the most profitable combinations, and planning the production of goods for stock and for sale in the market. The then developing entrepreneur class came into competition with other masters who were also producing goods for similar purposes. For these activities, the master needed more capital than ever before, and he needed to produce better goods more cheaply than those with whom he was competing. The master had become a businessman; the journeyman became a worker. No longer did the master work at the bench himself; no longer could those who worked at the trade believe that in a matter of years they, too, would automatically become masters. Two separate economic groups gradually emerged, and their differences were emphasized by technological change, customarily referred to as the Industrial Revolution. With increasing specialization and the division of labor, business units became much larger and the worker became less independent. The result was that a large portion of the population became employees with little realistic hope that they would ever achieve any other status. Consequently, different concepts of law and order cognizant of the changing mode of production, the potential collusion inspired by common association, and a desire for increased individual freedom began to replace the dissolving chains of custom and authoritarian bondage.

It is hardly surprising that laws ultimately had to reckon with the circumstance of man's labor, which effort sustains his very being. Expansion of the absolute size and complexity of law follows from its application to an increasingly interdependent community of workers subject to an environment of uncertainty. The relationship of employee and employer became less and less personal, and the worker was increasingly forced to seek employment in the industrial sector, face his problems personally and collectively, and somehow reconcile his differences with the employer.

The transition from tradition and command to a market system of organization was not accomplished without certain duress. The pursuit of personal gain from organized economic activity and exchange was not readily accepted. History is replete with instances of men's being tried and chastised for the "heinous crime" of making profit and the "sin of avarice." [2] Heilbroner cites numerous instances in his intriguing account of the history of economic ideas.[3] The trial, 200-pound fine, and "repentence" of the Reverend Robert Keane of Boston for having earned sixpence on the shilling is but one of numerous possible examples. The Privy Council of England denied a patent for an innovative stocking frame and ordered the "disruptive contraption" outlawed in 1623. In France, the importation and trading of illegal calico cloth (which allegedly was undermining the textile industry) resulted in some 750 persons being hanged, broken on the wheel, or sentenced to the galleys. The Button-makers' Guild succeeded in persuading the indignant French government to forbid and fine the tailors for making cloth buttons in the late seventeenth century. The profit potential served as a vehicle that prompted more innovation and added to the dynamic character of the engaging market economy. The early bitterness and resistance to the operation and growth of the market economy, with its inherent innovations and disruptions, were exceeded only by the pervasiveness of this force. Ultimately, the eruption of the market form of socioeconomic organization and the gradual decay of tradition and command were sustained. The philosophical framework that emerged in justification of the market economy lent support to individualism and the concept of laissez-faire. This was advantageous to the growth of enterprise in the product market, but the philosophy retarded organized efforts in the resource market as far as labor was concerned.

Why Labor Law?

Serfdom grudgingly gave way to the worker and proletariat classes, and guild masters and lords gradually assumed the tasks of applying and organizing factors of production and reaping the rewards of the dense jungle of the market economy which persisted in

[2] The concept of the profit motive is by no means universal even today, just as it was not completely acceptable a scant three centuries ago in most western civilizations, including the early colonies of the United States. To advocate such activity often was viewed as covetous, corrupt, and blasphemous behavior inspired by Satan himself.

[3] Heilbroner, *op. cit.*, pp. 10–18.

rearing its pervasive and ubiquitous influence. Business became more highly organized and institutionalized as the concept and acceptance of private property rights was promulgated. Change, reform, innovation, and even the cloth button eventually prevailed in the product market. Concurrent with the destruction of the old order and localized rules and regulations was the gradual spatial extension of organized groups and the application of common weights, monies, distance measurements, and laws. The gradual emergence of the market economy was both a cause and a result of adventure and exploration, larger national political units, and the decay of medieval religious domination. The gradual assimilation of diverse cultures and numerous revolutionary inventions now regarded as mundane (e.g., paper money) are also related to the extension of the market's influence.

That the process of change and resistance to varying market relationships is not yet complete is obvious to all but utopian observers of even the most modern economies. Indeed, this resistance and change furnished the very setting for modern laws governing commerce or labor. The notion that a collective struggle for gain might ultimately lend cohesion to an economy was viewed as worldly and sheer madness in the Old World, in part because the concept of factors of production was not understood three or four centuries ago. Labor in those times had no content or market as we know it today. Rather, this agent of production was born and obligated to the Lord's land. Land itself was the primary basis for community organization, protection, sustenance, and the center of social life for the nobleman. Capital, while obviously extant, sought security, certainty, and preservation—not risk, uncertainty, and potential depletion.[4]

With the birth and acceptance of the commercial system of socioeconomic organization, now called capitalism, came a need to focus more clearly on the economic dimensions of life. Religious, social, and political policy and philosophy had dominated law and intellectual thought in the past. Conflict between labor and capital was quickly thrust to the fore, however, and a system of conflict resolution was required. The now seemingly ancient, but then new, struggle between capital and labor was born in a setting of mounting dynamic social and economic pressures that culminated in a dynamic but repressive pattern of early labor law. The older statute and common laws governing master-servant and craft guild-journeymen relationships were forced to accommodate change—belatedly perhaps, but ultimately even the law must change.

---

[4] A problem shared by the less developed world even today.

Adam Smith, one of the earliest philosophers to divert his attention to the economics of labor, succinctly perceived the process of social and economic change in *The Wealth of Nations*. Smith observed:

> In that original state of things, which precedes both the appropriation of land and the accumulation of stock, the whole produce of labour belongs to the labourer. But this original state of things in which the labourer enjoyed the whole produce of his own labour, could not last beyond the accumulation of stock. As soon as land becomes private property the landlord demands a share of almost all the produce which the labourer can either raise, or collect from it. The produce of almost all other labour is liable to the like deduction of profit. In all arts and manufacture the greater part of the workmen stand in need of a master to advance them the materials of their work, and their wages and maintenance till it be completed. . . . What are the common wages of labour, depends everywhere upon the contract usually made between these two parties, whose interests are by no means the same. The workmen desire to get as much, the masters to give as little as possible. The former are disposed to combine in order to raise, the latter in order to lower the wages of labour.
>
> It is not, however, difficult to foresee which of the two parties must, upon all ordinary occasions, have the advantage in the dispute, and force the other into a compliance with their terms. The masters, being fewer in number, can combine more easily; and the law, besides, authorizes, or at least does not prohibit their combinations, while it prohibits those of working men. We have no acts of Parliament against combining to lower the price of work, but many against combining to raise it. In all such disputes, the masters can hold out much longer. . . .
>
> We rarely hear, it has been said, of the combinations of masters, though frequently of those of working men. But whoever imagines, upon this account, that masters rarely combine, is as ignorant of the world as of the subject. Masters are always and everywhere in a sort of tacit, but constant and uniform combination, not to raise the wages of labour above their actual rate. . . . We seldom, indeed, hear of this combination, because it is the usual, and one may say, the natural state of things which nobody ever hears of. Masters too sometimes enter into particular combinations to sink the wages of labour even below this rate. These are always conducted with the utmost silence and secrecy, till the movement of execution, and when the workingmen yield, as they sometimes do,

without resistance, though severely felt by them, they are never heard of by other people. Such combinations, however, are frequently resisted by a contrary defensive combination of the workmen; who sometimes too, without any provocation of this kind, combine of their own accord to raise the price of labour. . . .[5]

It is obvious from Smith's entire account of the political economy nearly two centuries ago, that the "invisible hand" in the resource market was beset with travail and imperfections. It is likewise true from other accounts, that the wages and conditions of labor in the early emerging industrial environment were barbaric and abhorrent by modern-day standards. The socioeconomic order of the intellect differed greatly on all accounts from reality, much as it does today, and resistance to change existed in the labor market in terms as real and as devastating as the above-noted resistance to emerging capitalism in product markets. Casual observation of the circumstances of labor and life in the factory system bears out the cruelty, passion, and bestiality of the functioning of the "laws of the market" that Adam Smith so panoramically perceived in his penetrating analyses. Competition, as a regulator of a way of doing economic things, became subject to and a part of institutional forces. Laws, the business institution, the institution of government, and (much later) the institution of organized labor were both shaped by and have formed the market system we know today.

The institutions of government and labor constitute the subject of this inquiry into labor and legal policy. Our attention will be directed to the development and application of laws that sometimes supported, sometimes supplemented, and at other times supplanted the "laws" of the market. In a word, we are concerned with the laws of the institution of government that aid in resolving human resource problems in the market system. Some of this law has affected the physical conditions and economic security of labor; much of it has contributed to a system of resolution of the conflict between capital and labor now formalized into an industrial democracy; and some of it has broached the more general problem of manpower management in the aggregate. Taken in its entirety, labor law furnishes a skeletal framework for the study of human capital, including the trade union as an institutional force in the market system.

[5] Adam Smith, *The Wealth of Nations* (New York: Random House, Inc.), selected quotations from pp. 64–67.

The Nature of Labor Law

The labor law of modern times that regulates, directs, and protects the participants in the labor-management struggle is complex and relatively new. But it was, and continues to be, formed in a reasonably logical progression stemming from and constantly conforming to changing economic and social pressures. By any standard, labor law today is of pivotal interest to labor, management, and the public. A reasonably adequate understanding and appreciation for its successes and its inadequacies in coping with the complex economic environment demands more historical perspective. Labor legislation does not affect industrial relations piecemeal, even though it sometimes appears to have been impregnated into a society with a resounding, thunderous clap at one point in time. Labor law normally follows previous warnings of impending change that have appeared on the horizon, even though its initial application may dramatically change previously ordered relationships. Labor law is an integral part of a historical socioeconomic whole, reflecting the sweeping transition of life from a near-primitive cottage system to a factory system through which the worker lost ownership of and control over the instruments of production. As new technology changed ways of producing things, rural to urban transitions changed modes of living and laws of coexistence. Labor law, by its very nature, is highly personalized in its origins as well as its consequences, often reflecting competing interest group desires, all of which must be telescoped into one workable set of relationships. Fundamentally, it is alive in its impact on the business enterprise, its effects on members of interest groups, and its social consequences. Because of the impact on society and the nature and origins of labor law, we cannot be unconcerned with where we have been and where we now stand in the area of government regulation of labor-management relationships. It quickly becomes apparent that labor law is a changing force on society; this contributes to the need for perspective as well as continuing interest in this field of study.

TYPES OF LABOR LAW

Labor law is a complex set of relationships originating in private, federal, and state sources of power. In some cases, federal and state originated labor law is administered and interpreted in the judicial branch of the government. In other instances, initial interpretive power is vested in established agencies of the government subject to verification by the courts. In addition to the numerous bodies and procedures for applying and interpreting labor law, the purposes of labor law are diverse. Furthermore, some labor laws may be all-encompassing while others are quite specific. Whenever laws are developed and applied in the field of labor, their impact may be compounded through multiple objectives, forms of control, and sources of authority. The potential for legal conflict thus arises, and while some laws must yield, others take precedence.

The concern of most of that which is now regarded as labor law is with labor-management relations. The rights, duties, and restraints on both parties are determined through the development and application of the law. Other kinds of legislation exist; law concerned with worker protection, sometimes termed "class" legislation, is a case in point. The regulation of wages, hours, and conditions of work is of the "protective" type. While the bulk of our interest is in labor relations law, we cannot ignore legislation relating to the conditions of labor and manpower management in more general terms. Like labor relations law, protective or class legislation and manpower management law reflect the socioeconomic pressures exerted on lawmaking bodies. The purpose of all labor law is to establish certain rules for the improved functioning of human capital in an industrial environment. It is a planned and cohesive action by society in which sociological, psychological, economic, and political forces act as determinants. In short, labor law has considerable spillover content into other areas of human behavior and social relationships. This spillover acts as a feedback system to the existing body of law, i.e., as a guiding device to newly emerging law. Law remains essential to labor relations as it etches out the broad policies and detailed framework of labor-management relationships. Labor law cannot help but be intertwined and interdependent with related dimensions of life, both in its origination and in its application.[6] It is, therefore, helpful to appreciate these interrelationships and integrate the study of labor law into a broader understanding of the development of social and economic systems. Indeed, this is necessary for a complete understanding of labor and the development of legal policy.

[6] As an illustration, consider the depression of the 1930's. Failure to be cognizant of the depression background—politically, sociologically, and economically—only distorts and renders incomplete one's understanding of the labor law of that period.

The diversity of labor law in origin and application reflects the fact that there are numerous "types" of law applying to labor. The major types are (1) criminal law, (2) civil law, (3) case or common law, (4) statutory law, (5) constitutional law, (6) protective law, (7) administrative agency law, and (8) private law. Each deserves further clarification.

Criminal law is a code of specified public policy for which punitive reprisals and remedial action are taken on.behalf of the public sector to maintain the general welfare of a nation. Criminal codes of law are a reflection of the values and moral principles of society. Aside from some activities involving serious forms of violence, the type of violation of criminal law most directly related to labor relations is contempt of court. Persons willfully ignoring or disobeying an order of the court, such as an injunction, can be prosecuted under criminal law for contempt of court.

Civil law pertains to individual relationships between two or more parties whose claims are in conflict. The purpose of civil law is the preservation of equity in interpersonal relationships. Equity law is a form of jurisprudence sometimes administered and interpreted by the regular courts and at other times through tribunals distinct from the normal judicial process. The system of equity jurisprudence is designed to provide relief under circumstances in which normal court action might fail to provide adequate redress. Parties seeking redress normally must be prepared to demonstrate that there is no alternative remedy at law, as currently structured, that affords adequate protection. If such a claim is deemed justifiable, monetary judgments may be levied or injunctive relief (court orders prohibiting certain acts) may be granted. When injunctive relief is granted, a party is prohibited from continuing to act in the manner complained of because it will continue to damage the plaintiff. Failure to adhere to a court order to desist from injuring the plaintiff may result in a contempt of court charge against the party inflicting harm.

Common law is created by courts through historical decisions that set precedents for future cases of a similar nature. Most of the early law applying to labor in England as well as in the United States was of the common law variety. Such law derives its authority from tradition and usage as it is reflected in the past judgments or decrees of courts. The judiciary either recognizes an act as being legal and thus affirms continued practice, or deems it illegal and denies continued practice. Various kinds of activities for which no existing laws apply may be subject to court interpretation and evaluation. This, of course, can give the judicial authorities considerable latitude in setting patterns of acceptable social behavior according to their beliefs and economic philosophy. Any time that legislators have not formalized public policy through the passage of laws within their jurisdiction, common law interpretation by judicial authorities establishes the legality of patterns of acceptable behavior. This leaves considerable room for vague, varying, and sometimes nebulous interpretation and application of common law. Historically, the prevailing Anglo-American common-law philosophy has supported concepts of private property and freedom of enterprise, leaving it to the legislative authorities to curb any abuses or excesses. In the case of organized labor, much of the early conflict between labor and capital was deemed in violation of the property rights of the capital class, hence common law hindered the development and functioning of the trade union.

Statutory law. The action of legislative bodies formalized into statutory law is subject to ratification periodically by the voting electorate. Statutory law thus serves as a crystallization of public policy. It may be judged legal in subsequent court decisions, or it may be deemed to conflict with previously established law (e.g., constitutional law) that takes precedence over statutory legislation. Again, decisions by the judicial branch of government may validate or invalidate statutory legislation in this context. In addition, statutory law is frequently subject to interpretation and application by the court; this action may or may not correspond to the intent of the legislative body. In certain instances, statutory labor law has been interpreted in a way not intended by the legislative body in the United States. Statutory legislation can originate at the federal, state, or local level. Normally, federal statutory legislation and the rights guaranteed by the Constitution take precedence over state law, unless jurisdiction is ceded by the federal government to a state or local body. For the most part, statutory labor law at the federal level has been for the prevention and settlement of interstate conflicts between labor and management. On the other hand, state statutory law is more concerned with police problems raised by labor disputes, such as violence, trespass, etc. In cases where state law conflicts with a right guaranteed by the Constitution or existing statutory legislation at the federal level, the state law is declared illegal by the courts. State and local statutes are also subject to court interpretation and application; they may ultimately be ruled upon by the Supreme Court of the United States. Law originating at the state level of government is often of a "grass roots" nature. It is not uncommon to find federal legislation in the area of labor relations preceded by a previously enacted state law, although this is not a universally valid generalization.

Constitutional law. The legal pinnacle in the United States is the

Constitution, and it is particularly important in the field of labor, largely because other kinds of law (e.g., common and statutory) are based upon or derive their power from constitutional law. Requirements, rights, and conditions denoted in constitutional provisions cannot be infringed upon by any form of law unless the Constitution itself is amended. Just as decisions by the United States Supreme Court constitute a pervasive type of law in the judiciary branch, constitutional law represents a general form of law in the legislative branch of government.

Protective law refers to statutory enactments and court decisions that relate, for the most part, to conditions of work and the protection of labor in the interest of the general welfare. A large portion of protective labor law historically is concerned with specific issues that relate to various "classes" of labor, such as women, children, hours, or wages of work. More recently, a considerable body of protective labor law has evolved that relates to aggregative problems of manpower (e.g., unemployment and poverty) in a broader context of economic growth and security. Simultaneous to and, in some instances, prior to the passage of protective laws at the federal level, states have passed legislation related to working conditions and circumstances.

Administrative agency law. Until the 1930's the law of labor relations was largely of the common law variety. Since then, a considerable amount of statutory law has evolved in the area of labor relations, collective bargaining, and class protection. With the rapid expansion of statutory labor relations law came an urgent need for considerable interpretation and application in countless numbers of cases. To accommodate the increased legal load, administrative agencies have been established. These agencies are often given authority to interpret and apply law and develop ancillary rules and procedures at the operational level. Some of the law of administrative agencies is considered to be binding, while some is subject to subsequent interpretive rulings from judicial authorities. One of the most prominent of the administrative agencies currently creating agency law is the National Labor Relations Board. Laws of this kind are more concerned with administration than establishing policy or setting precedents. These latter duties normally are left to the legislature and courts. Administrative agency law may exist at the federal, state, and local level, and it is of increasing importance as a bellwether reflection of pressing socioeconomic concerns.

Private law has evolved as the institutions of business and labor have congealed their differences and been subjected to an increasing amount of government regulation in the last few decades. Labor and management assume a lawmaking function whenever they come to agreement upon the circumstances or conditions of their relationship. Normally, this takes the form of a collectively agreed upon contract that represents the culmination of a bargaining process. Such a contract establishes ground rules for behavior between the two parties as well as stipulating working conditions, wages, and the procedure for settling small but irritating and frequent grievances. Such agreements cannot conflict with other labor law, and if private law does not conform, publicly derived labor law has precedence. Private labor law itemizes employer-employee relations in minute detail, covering many of the fine points of labor-management relations. Public labor law acts as a stabilizing and conditioning force on the provisions stipulated in private agreements. With increasing frequency, controversies that arise within the established pattern of private law that cannot be settled by the parties to a dispute are referred to a third party for settlement. In some cases, agreement to arbitrate a dispute is provided for in the private law that governs the relationships of labor and management. Decisions of a third party are binding and enforceable upon the parties agreeing to arbitration. Such action, of course, removes the decision-making power from the hands of the parties in conflict and is not normally popular with either party. Mediation and conciliation procedures are likewise provided for under public and private law to promote the resolution of disputes between labor and management. These latter procedures are designed to clarify issues and assist the conflicting groups in reaching a final decision. As such, mediation or conciliation is not a compelling or binding process but rather purely advisory.

ECONOMICS AND LABOR LAW

The various types of law noted previously relate to the economic system in time and place. Of these eight types of law, none are unrelated to the economics of labor-management relations, although protective laws differ in that they must be recognized in labor-management agreements but do not affect the procedural, behavioral, or conflict aspects of labor relations. These various types of labor law slowly emerged with the historical movement away from a chattel system of organizing human resources that characterized the Egyptian, Roman, and feudalistic socioeconomic systems. For the most part, the varied kinds of existing labor laws are an outgrowth of a few major economic transition points in the economic history of modern man. Chief among these are (1) the gradual dissolution of command and custom as a way of organizing and ordering human resources, and replacement of this authority by a market system; and (2) recognition of the manipulative ability, imperfections, and impersonal characteristics inherent in the market economy.

While the former has been given brief consideration, there are certain major economic transitions during the emergence of the market economy that have led to various types of labor law and establishment of the sources of authority for these laws in the United States. This dynamic economic background certainly must include the transition from a rural, agricultural society to a complex, industrial, and urbanized environment. One part of these pressures was that of the trade union as an agent of social and economic reform that began nearly a century before the Civil War. The rapid growth of industrial capitalism with the attendant economic crises, immigration bulge, inventions, and innovations are also critical ingredients in the broader economic background from which labor law emerged. Conditions of work and the labor-capital structure of the economy became a matter of social concern. Working life was generally unpleasant by today's standards, and even in these times physical conditions, hours, wages, and economic insecurity were matters of employee and employer contention. The pressures for various forms of public control and intervention were not easily or readily heard on all occasions, and violence and work disruption sometimes characterized the struggle. With the calamity of the Great Depression of the 1930's, labor law, which had so far retained a conservative and property orientation, veered abruptly in new directions. These directions favored the aspirations of organized labor for a short period, and the trade union emerged as an irrevocable institution in the economy. Changes in the present economic system continue to shape labor law by giving birth to previously unrecognized social issues and values. The post-World War II movement towards a less permissive economic environment for organized labor reflects these economic dynamics. The increasing public concern for poverty, discrimination, and manpower utilization now being reflected in labor law is another illustration of dynamic change as this nation enters the decade of the 1970's. The sources and limitations for authority to legally alter labor relations and broach labor problems therefore constitute an important background to labor law per se.

Labor Law: Sources and Limitations of Authority

Labor law can be traced back to the ancient world and, in some respects, is as old as the written word itself. In more recent times, the origins of labor law stem from the feudal system of land ownership and serfdom that made the common laborer a subject of his lord. The major source of labor law and its limitations is vested in court and constitutional authority. Other secondary sources of labor law are borrowed from related legal doctrines (e.g., the Anglican Church).

COMMON LAW

In early England the kings established Privy Councils in which the king's "men" set up statutory law to complement the court's common law. Craft guilds of the medieval and emerging market economy also had a hand in shaping law. Organizations of craftsmen established rules and procedures governing the length and terms of apprenticeship (e.g., seven years, for the most part). Likewise, the church, which was so dominant throughout the medieval period of history, was a direct source of law and an indirect influence on much of the law of the land. Early in the English labor movement, the judicial branch was important as an interpretive and administrative authority on points of common and statutory law. The source of power of authority for common law developed by the judiciary was a constitutionally derived power, often subject to the appointive jurisdiction of the executive branch of government. The common law evolving from judicial rulings and interpretations was a reflection of the judiciary's concept of "proper" relationships. Common law ultimately derives authority from constitutional provision or executive mandate. The English heritage of common law had an important influence on American labor law.

CONSTITUTIONAL LAW

The second major source of labor law, and by far the most important today, is the Constitution. Major labor legislation (e.g., the Fair Labor Standards Act) is a reality today because of delegated powers in the Constitution as interpreted, ultimately, by the courts. The importance of constitutional law is not only that it establishes a framework for common law rulings, but in addition it stipulates certain rights that are guaranteed to all citizens. These rights have been the subject of extended litigation in the area of labor and legal policy.

The federal government has only those powers delegated to it by the states. All power not delegated to the federal government is reserved as a right of the sovereign state and the people. Three clauses of the Constitution have played a prominent role in the evolution and application of American labor law: (1) the interstate commerce clause, (2) the due process clause of the Fifth and Fourteenth Amendments, and (3) the guarantee of free speech as stated in the First Amendment. In addition, the power to tax is a delegated and significant power of the federal government, although it has not been widely used in labor relations.[7] Other less important sources of federal government power sparingly applied in labor law include the right to make and enforce any laws necessary for carrying out all powers delegated to the federal government by the state; the power of eminent domain contracted by the people to their government to provide for the greatest good for the largest number; the right of proprietorship (e.g., ability to operate a postal system); the right of the guardianship of the people; and the preservation of the peace in areas of authority delegated to the federal government (e.g., interstate commerce).

Interstate commerce. The Constitution enumerates this power of Congress in Section 8 of Article I, which states that Congress has authority ". . . to regulate commerce with foreign Nations, and among the several States, and with the Indian Tribes." The activities of the federal government have ranged far and wide under the "commerce power," which has furnished the basis for important legislation such as the National Labor Relations Act and the Fair Labor Standards Act. Court interpretations of the commerce power have not been invariant over time, however. In the process of grafting Anglo-Saxon common law into American labor relations and later adding statutory laws, court interpretations of the interstate commerce clause have broadened considerably. In spite of the fact that there is often a legal lag in court interpretations of law and socioeconomic philosophy, the federal government's ability to use this power has been very flexible throughout the history of the United States. Generally speaking, the court has changed its interpretation of this power from the initial concept of "goods in commerce" to a concept of manufactured goods that are capable of "affecting the flow" of interstate commerce.[8] Consequently, the regulatory power stipulated in Article I, Section 8, is considerably more inclusive today since it is not based upon a literal interpretation of the Constitution. The combined forces of changing judicial decisions and dynamic statutory law as an expression of the social will of the people have been permitted to broaden. An umbrella of legality has been furnished for regulation over such diverse matters as protective legislation, the relationships and rights of labor

---

[7] An attempt to regulate child labor through the power to tax was ruled illegal by the Supreme Court in the case of *Bailey* v. *Drexell Furniture Co.*, 259 U.S. 20 (1922).

[8] One of the earlier attempts to deal with the inter- and intrastate commerce issue can be found in *Gibbons* v. *Ogden*, 9 Wheat, 1 (1824).

and management, and the extent to which the federal government should be actively involved in the process of collective bargaining.

Throughout most of the nineteenth century, the interstate commerce clause was a subject of controversy among political and economic interest groups. During this period, most of the economic issues related to the commerce clause dealt with conflicting attitudes about relative national and state government powers. Between the late nineteenth century and the mid-1930's, a conservative judicial majority rigidly controlled the extent to which the federal government could derive power from the commerce clause to shape socioeconomic conditions in the fast-emerging industrialized economy. Primary attention was devoted to the extent to which the commerce clause restricted the state power of commercial regulation. Not only was it necessary to demarcate the nebulous areas of interstate and intrastate commerce, but questions also arose as to what specific activities were involved in the power to regulate. While the conservative courts did recognize some need to regulate business, it was seldom known *ex ante* that any given statutory labor legislation would meet with the approval of the court. Judicial ambivalence and constitutional flexibility created an environment of considerable uncertainty in the area of labor law. The ideological composition of the Supreme Court varied, and distinctions between invalid and valid regulation under the commerce clause were often of the hairsplitting variety that reflected the biases of members of a particular tribunal.

In the 1930's, a composite of pressures began to appear in American society and their impact on the court, including Roosevelt's threat to "pack" the court, resulted in a broader and more liberal interpretation of the interstate commerce clause. This finally gave the federal government broader authority to regulate under the commerce clause. Henceforth, judicial discretion and interpretation gave way to more authoritative statutory legislation in establishing policies and restraints to labor-management relations. Whereas the court had previously been sensitive about government intrusion into a free labor market and had often invalidated welfare and pro-labor legislation, it now permitted such legislation to pass the barrier of constitutionality. The industrial relations system outlined by the labor laws we have today is due in no small part to this turnabout in the 1930's that centered upon a liberalized concept of the power of the federal government to regulate commerce. Thereafter, it was possible for social policy to be reflected in a larger measure in constitutionally acceptable statutory law.

Due process. Only those powers delegated by sovereign states comprise the domain of the federal government. The state thus has police power except where it has delegated this power to the federal government. This power includes all authority necessary to use government to administer and enforce a web of rules in the interest of the general welfare. Such power is an indefinite authorization to the state to regulate in the interest of the health, safety, and welfare of society at large, except that the federal government has a precedent police power to uphold its express and implied constitutional power. In the last part of the nineteenth century, some states enacted regulatory measures designed to curb what were regarded as business excesses under the authority of their police powers. Similarly, a large number of state labor statutes have been passed on the subjects of collective bargaining and the working conditions of labor. In the Constitution, Section 1 of the Fourteenth Amendment says that a state shall not ". . . deprive any person of life, liberty, or property without due process of law. . . ." [9]

Until the latter part of the nineteenth century, the due process clause was interpreted in a procedural context; that is, it was regarded as referring to legal procedures and not matters of substance. With the advent of business and labor laws passed by the states under their police power around the turn of the century, the court began to reinterpret the due process clause to also include matters of substance. The court held that the Fourteenth Amendment imposed certain limitations of substance as well as procedure on state law. This new interpretation, frequently referred to as the "Field Doctrine," permitted the Supreme Court to find many of the emerging state labor regulations in violation of the due process clause unless the reasonableness of state laws could be established. The judiciary thus saw its task in part as passing upon the wisdom of legislative enactments by the state.[10] For a period of several decades, a largely intolerant judiciary viewed much of the state-initiated regulation of labor markets under their police power as unreasonable legislation in conflict with the substantive content of the due process clause. Thus, a post-Civil War amendment to the Constitution that was initially in-

[9] The wording is very similar to that of the Fifth Amendment, which restricts the federal government in a similar manner.

[10] Rejection of the "Field Doctrine" occurred in the case of *Munn* v. *Illinois*, 94 U.S. 113 (1876), and early Supreme Court adherence to substantive interpretation of the due process clause can be found in *Chicago, Milwaukee, and St. Paul Railway Company* v. *Minnesota*, 134 U.S. 418 (1889).

tended to protect the rights of freed slaves served to retard the passage of a considerable amount of state labor legislation designed to enhance the conditions of the working man. In a minority of instances, the Supreme Court regarded the exercise of state police powers as reasonable in the protection of workers in a weak bargaining position (e.g., children or workers employed in excessively hazardous industries). A return to procedural interpretation of the due process clause began in the 1930's and, by 1937, the vogue of substantive interpretations had died. For the most part, the due process clause currently is not interpreted as giving the federal judiciary a license to judge the wisdom of state legislation, although limits upon the use of police powers by states do exist.[11]

Free speech. The constitutional guarantee of freedom of speech and certain prohibitions of state activity interfering with related freedoms (e.g., peaceable assembly) is another important source of authority and limitation to labor law. The guarantee is contained in the First Amendment, and prohibition against state interference is contained in the Fourteenth Amendment, each of which has been applied to restrain state regulation of labor-related activities (e.g., picketing). While a full treatment of the issue will be postponed until later, it is worth noting again that a dynamic judicial philosophy had a profound influence on the activity and progress of labor-management relations in terms of the guarantee of free speech. Picketing, for example, is one of the major communications media of a striking union. Both the content and objective of a picketing effort are important in that either may be peaceful or violent, legal or illegal. Violent picketing, however, is not protected even by the most liberal judiciary tribunals. Determination of peaceful picketing (which is legal) as compared to illegal picketing is a nebulous area. After the passage of the Norris-La Guardia Act in 1932, which limited the applicability of federal injunctions against labor union activities, state courts enjoined picketing on certain occasions under a variety of circumstances. The court initially appeared to treat picketing as a form of free speech protected by the First Amendment of the Constitution in a series of cases initiated in 1937.[12] By 1950 the Supreme Court completed a re-

[11] Movement away from the substantive and back to the procedural interpretation of the due process clause was consummated in the case of *West Coast Hotel* v. *Parrish,* 300 U.S. 379 (1936).

[12] See the remarks of Justice L. D. Brandeis in *Senn* v. *Tile Layers' Protective Union,* 301 U.S. 468, 57S. CT. 857 (1936) and *Thornhill* v. *Alabama,* 310 U.S. 88, 60S. CT. 736 (1939).

treat when they recognized the potential coercion inherent in picketing and the legitimacy of states to limit picketing activity under circumstances where the public interest was at stake.[13]

SATELLITE SOURCES OF LABOR LAW

A considerable amount of labor law is drawn from other fields of law for its substance, procedure, and ultimate source. The law of contract, for example, undergirds private labor law as contained in collective agreements between labor and management. The law of equity is invoked when injunctions (court orders) are requested and granted or denied. The circumstances peculiar to tort (civil) law may be invoked, and the law of damages may determine compensation. State constitutions are another source of labor law, as are enactments and rulings of federal or state bodies that are delegated authority in specified areas. These latter quasi-legislative and judicial agencies have become increasingly important in the determination of labor-management conflict issues, particularly in administration and surveillance. The power of evidentiary review and review as to matters of law still remains under the authority of courts, however.

Certainly, the above account of constitutional and common law sources and limitations gives a firm impression of the flexibility of the law, both as it is interpreted by the courts and as stated in the Constitution. In principle, this reflects what is so necessary in a dynamic society; namely, any consensus of public policy established in the form of law must reflect the economic dynamics and social needs of the time. Changes in the economic and industrial environment have been complemented by a dynamic legal environment. These two circumstances have interacted with the passage of time to produce the viable character of labor law that we know today.

Concluding Comments

This first chapter has stressed the various forms of economic organization for a society in terms of the relationships between labor and capital. The now commonplace acceptance of a market system was not immediately fused into economic patterns of behavior. The critical property of the transition from a command and custom economy

[13] The decision of the Supreme Court upholding the action of a Wisconsin court in *Vogt* v. *Teamsters*, 354 U.S. 284, 77S. CT. 31 (1956) is indicative of the changing viewpoint of the Supreme Court on this matter.

to a market economy was the dynamic economic environment which was mirrored by the laws and rules governing labor and capital relationships.

Several types of labor law that are recognizable include criminal, civil, common, statutory, constitutional, protective, administrative agency, and private law. The major sources of authority for labor laws and the limitations to these same powers and laws are the result of court interpretation. Major constitutional provisions that are sources of labor law include the interstate commerce, due process, and freedom of speech clauses. While labor law is a specialized type of law, it is also derivative in nature in that it was borrowed from other forms and sources of law.

The content of public policy as it applies to labor relations in the chapters that follow is presented both in conventional textbook narrative form and in the form of major cases decided by the courts. Much of the earlier legal policy concerned with labor relations is derivative of common law. Common law is founded on the principle of *stare decisis*, deciding similar cases in the same way. The American judicial process is also based upon the adversary principle in which there are two viewpoints to each case. Counsel for each side attempts to convince the trial and appellate courts that the law and facts on an issue favor his cause. By the time a case is heard by the appellate court (e.g., Supreme Court), much of the original factual content has been sifted out and reshaped by the stresses of the judicial processes. What remains is that information relevant to the issues selected for appeal, and evidence that meets requirements of proof and rules of evidence germane to the appeal. Justices for the appellate court summarize the issues, facts, argument of counsel, and legal principles applicable to the case in reasoning to a decision. Although the *stare decisis* principle governs this process, the individual nuances of each case require that courts deal with litigant and social pressures in a flexible manner that is also consistent with the continuity of prior law.

Because of fine legal distinctions, the specificity of issue, and subtle reasoning, a unique framework is created for each case. Therefore, the study of selected cases in their original language and form is very valuable. Sweeping generalizations about each case must be avoided; careful attention to the reasoning of the court is a prerequisite to a full understanding of each decision. Through the study and briefing of individual cases, the student can participate intellectually in the issues of the day instead of relying solely on the passive receipt of information from instructor and author. Study of the original case provides a reader with an opportunity to think in concrete terms; it accustoms him to see and work through the problems facing the court; and it sharpens his ability to critically evaluate a decision and sense the issues involved. Reading a case can also produce a fuller comprehension of the historic evolution of labor law and policy. In this way, a firmer grasp of the problems, procedures, and principles may be obtained, and a sense for the dynamic relationships inherent in labor and manpower policy can be cultivated. Common law is a process whereby a set of practices by which disputes are defined, heard, and decided yield rules or principles affecting future litigants. Because policies and laws are a creation of man, they are fallible. Therefore, doubts, objections, and questions need to be expressed and evaluated. The study of original cases helps develop this critical reasoning process.

For these reasons, it is appropriate to "brief" selected cases presented in original form. A brief is nothing more than an organized and thoroughly presented summary of a case. While the length and form of a brief is not a measure of its adequacy, there are certain characteristics exhibited in a good brief. They are:

1. *Identification:* this includes identifying the case name and date, the court deciding the case, and the action or relief sought.

2. *Parties:* the complainants and defendants in a case must be identified, and the judicial processes in prior trial or appellate courts, if any, must be noted.

3. *Background:* the relevant background facts to the primary issue(s) being heard by the court should be explained.

4. *Arguments of counsel:* a summary of the arguments of counsel for the complainant and the defendant is presented.

5. *Court decision:* it is necessary to state the decision of the court and the authority (e.g., common law, logic, etc.) cited by the court.

6. *Dissenting opinion:* the argument(s) advanced, if any, by dissenting members of the court.

7. *Evaluation:* presentation of the reader's appraisal of the decision in terms of its legal basis and justification on social, economic, and legal grounds.

Appraising each case that follows in the manner suggested above can improve the understanding of labor and public policy gained by the student in subsequent chapters.

The next three chapters present a chronology of legal policy in a period extending through the 1920's, which was repressive as far as organized labor was concerned. The social and economic changes that were occurring throughout this period irrevocably sowed the seeds of discontent that seemingly erupted in the evolution of a permissive legal policy during the Depression, the topic of Chapters 5 through 7. One of the most significant legal developments in labor relations during the 1930's was passage of the National Labor Relations Act in 1935, also known as the Wagner Act. Chapter 6 is a study of this legislation, and the major issues that relate to formalizing the legality of labor-management relations and collective bargaining in this period are discussed in subsequent chapters. With the closing of world-wide hostilities in the mid-1940's a new era emerged, dominated by concern for the stake the public held in labor relations. Chapters 8 through 11 discuss the emergence of post-war labor policy, chiefly the Taft-Hartley Act of 1947 and the Landrum-Griffin Act of 1959. This legislation redressed the balance of power between labor and capital and affirmed the recognizable interest of society in labor relations by thrusting government more directly to the forefront. The panorama of labor policy presented in Chapters 1 to 11 that was decades in the making is a product of the issues and weapons of conflict between labor and management. The final two chapters trace the development of labor problems and policy in relation to the public sector. Chapter 12 is concerned with public employees and public policy in the labor-management arena. The historical development of laws related to working conditions (e.g., hours and overtime) is the topic of Chapter 13. This chapter also discusses public policy in relation to human resources and socioeconomic problems such as economic opportunity, insecurity, poverty, and unemployment.

APPENDIX 1

The Language of Industrial Relations

The content of Chapter I contains certain terms that are not commonly encountered by students. To facilitate the comprehension of labor law, it is helpful to review some of this terminology formally because the language of industrial relations is to some extent a specialized language.* While it would be redundant as well as impossi-

---

* A more detailed presentation of some of the terminology common to labor law may be found in Commerce Clearing House, *Labor Law Course* (New York: Commerce Clearing House, Inc., 1970), pp. 299–328.

ble to identify a significant portion of the vocabulary of labor law, there are a few terms which by virtue of their common usage are worthy of defining prior to a more detailed examination of labor law. They are as follows:

Agency shop—a union security arrangement where nonmembers as well as members pay union fees as a condition of employment.

Anti-injunction act—the Norris-La Guardia Act restricting the use of injunctions issued by federal courts.

Arbitration—a hearing and determination of a labor-management controversy by a third party whose decision is binding.

Area-wide contract—a collective bargaining agreement covering a geographic area, industry sector, or occupational classification.

Bargaining rights—legally defined rights of labor and management stipulated by statutory law.

Bargaining unit—an employee group that has been appropriately designated as a unit for collective bargaining.

Blacklist—a list of employees circulated by employers identifying workers sympathetic to or active in the labor union movement.

Boulwareism—a bargaining philosophy of presenting one "take it or leave it" offer which was popularized by General Electric, Inc.

Boycott—a concerted refusal to deal with an employer or handle the goods an employer produces.

Brotherhood—a term used to describe the collective association of workers as a union.

Business agent—a union officer charged with general administration of union affairs in business and labor relations.

Cease-and-desist order—an order by the National Labor Relations Board to cease conducting a labor practice that is illegal.

Checkoff—a union security arrangement where union dues are automatically deducted from members' pay checks by management.

Clayton Act—an amendment (1914) to the Sherman Act that was thought to relieve legal pressures exerted against organized labor.

Closed shop—a type of union security that obligates employers to hire only union members.

Commerce clause—the constitutional provision that affords Congress jurisdictional authority to regulate a labor dispute if it has an effect on interstate commerce.

Common law—rulings formulated by court decisions that are viewed as law because of the precedence such judicial rulings establish.

Compulsory unionism—employment that is conditional upon securing membership in a labor union.

Conspiracy doctrine—a common law doctrine applied to labor that views organization and combination as a criminal or civil conspiracy.

Cooling-off period—a period of time specified in statutory law that must elapse before strike or lockout activities may resume.

Craft union—a union normally restricted to members having a particular craft or skill.

Economic strike—a strike over wages, hours, or terms of employment other than those protesting unfair labor practices.

Employer associations—organized groups of employers who band together for mutual strength.

Fair Labor Standards Act—the federal law establishing hour and wage requirements and employment conditions.

Featherbedding—seeking payment for work that is not necessary or is not done, or payment for more work than is accomplished.

Federal Mediation and Conciliation Services—the federal agency that maintains a list of individuals available to help reconcile labor disputes.

Federation—an international level of union organization representing affiliated local and international unions.

Grievance procedures—an established process for settling disputes during the period of administration of a contract.

Hot cargo clause—a clause specified in union contracts with management that permits employees to refuse to work or handle goods shipped from a nonunion employer or an employer plant listed on a union unfair list.

Industrial union—a union whose membership is based on a particular industry.

Informational picketing—picketing to inform and publicize a labor dispute.

Injunction—a court order that either restrains action or directs that certain action be taken which is backed by the court's authority to hold disobedient parties in contempt of court.

International union—a union comprised of several local unions.

Journeyman—a worker fully qualified in a craft.

Jurisdictional dispute—a dispute between two or more unions over which union shall represent a group of employees in the collective bargaining process.

Labor dispute—an employer and employee disagreement over the terms and conditions of employment.

Landrum-Griffin Act—the Labor-Management Reporting and Disclosure Act passed in 1959 that imposes administrative and procedural controls on unions and further stipulates national emergency strike procedures.

Local union—the smallest and most basic organizational unit for the labor union.

Lockout—an employer shutdown of a plant to discourage union activity or enforce employer demands.

Maintenance of membership—the form of union security that binds a union member to continued affiliation for the duration of a contract unless the member resigns within a stipulated period.

Master agreements—usually geographic or industry-wide contracts dealing with major contractual terms.

National emergency strike provisions—labor disputes deemed critical to the national safety and welfare are subject to special controls under current labor legislation.

No man's land—an area of interstate labor disputes for which no official form of settlement was provided by labor law in the early post-World War II era.

No raiding pact—an agreement between rival unions not to organize workers within the jurisdiction or control of another union.

No strike clause—a contractual agreement not to strike during the period covered by the labor contract.

Open shop—a place of employment not requiring union membership as an employment condition.

Organizational picketing—picketing designed to persuade employees to certify a union as its bargaining agent.

Pattern bargaining—collective bargaining based on the principle of applying similar terms and demands to a number of employees across industries, regions, or occupations.

Picketing—union patrolling near employer premises to publicize and communicate the existence of a conflict with the employer.

Plaintiff—the party bringing a case to court.

Preferential hiring—a union security arrangement where union members are hired on a preferential basis to meet labor demands of employers.

Raiding—a union policy of attempting to obtain affiliation of workers currently members of a rival union.

Recognition picketing—picketing to persuade an employer to recognize a union as the workers' bargaining agent.

Reopening clause—a contractual clause in a labor agreement providing for renegotiation under certain conditions during the term of contractual agreement.

Representation process—the process of certifying who, or which union(s), will be certified to represent employees.

Right-to-work laws—state laws prohibiting compulsory union membership as a condition for the retention of employees.

Scab—a worker who refuses to join striking workers or one who crosses a picket line.

Secondary boycott—a union refusal to deal with parties neutral to a primary labor dispute that is designed to bring greater pressure on the primary employer.

Secondary strike—a strike called against one employer for the purpose of bringing pressure on a second employer with whom the union is disputing.

Seniority—the granting of preferences to employees on the basis of length of employment.

Shop steward—the union member designated to represent workers in a shop.

Stranger picketing—picketing by persons other than firm employees.

Sweetheart contract—an agreement between union officials and employers intended to enrich or further the interests of union and management officials at the expense of the rank and file union member.

Taft-Hartley Act—the 1947 Labor-Management Relations Act that regulates labor relations and stipulates protectional conditions for management.

Unfair practices—union and employer practices designated by law to be unfair and therefore illegal.

Union shop—a form of union security in which employees must join a union within a stipulated period of time.

Wagner Act—the National Labor Relations Act passed in 1935 that established the basic framework of American labor relations law and created the National Labor Relations Board.

Wildcat strike—a strike that is not officially authorized by the union.

Yellow-dog contract—an employer-originated agreement between a worker and the employer, stipulating that the employee will not join or does not now belong to a union.

2

CONSPIRACY LAWS
AND INJUNCTIONS

The story of the early development of organized American labor is the first of a three-act drama. The initial oppressive era was followed by a brief period of liberality towards the union, followed in turn by a very modest return to conservatism in the form of greater government involvement. The background to early American labor law spans centuries and continents, deriving a wealth of precedent from the legal heritage of the English. As far as the early American labor law movement is concerned, the period of repression started in the mid-eighteenth century, and did not end until the early twentieth century. Initially, outright repression and open hostility to organized labor was the mode. Hostility eroded slowly, but a grudging tolerance accompanied by restrictive legal devices continued to hamper growth of the union movement. It has only been very recently that major barriers to organized labor were removed. The account that follows reiterates the process of repression and slowly eroding hostil-

29

ity through the development and application of legal constraints to organized American labor.

The English Common Law Heritage

ECONOMIC CONDITIONS AND ENGLISH LABOR

During the fourteenth century, the English labor force was reduced numerically by the bubonic plague. In the year of the Black Death (1348) and immediately thereafter, wages rose dramatically in England as commerce expanded and surviving workers clamored for higher wages and better working conditions.[1] The craft and merchant guilds also maintained rigid control over journeymen and apprentices, frequently through centuries-old statutory and common laws. This emergency was accompanied by the increasing vociferousness of worker guilds and countered by the passage of the Ordinances of Laborers in 1349. The Ordinances were followed two years later by the passage of a more comprehensive labor code, the Statute of Laborers.[2] These statutes tried to reduce labor's power by making the labor agreement or "contract" unique from other contracts. For example, the Statute of Laborers forbade enticing away another man's worker by offering higher wages, stipulated or fixed wages, and compelled workers to work, in addition to regulating other terms of the labor contract.

In the decades following the Statutes inspired by the Black Death, extensions and revisions occurred in the evolving English labor code, culminating in the Elizabethan Statute of Laborers in 1562.[3] It established extensive codes fixing the price of labor, laws regarding labor mobility to relieve the pressure on urban centers, and established price and quality standards to control craft and merchant guilds. The "criminal" and "civil" conspiracy doctrines, which held that the *combined* action of workers to raise wages and better their conditions was illegal, also became a significant part of the larger body of Anglo-American common and statutory law for a considerable period of time.

[1] See for example, A. Hayes, *A Political and Cultural History of Modern Europe* (New York: The Macmillan Co., 1936).

[2] 23 Edw. III, C.C. 1, 2 (1349); and 25 Edw. 3, St. 1 (1351) respectively.

[3] 5 Eliz. C. 4 (1562). Accounts of this period can be found in Sidney and Beatrice Webb, *The History of Trade Unionism, rev. ed.* (New York: Longmans, Green, Inc., 1935), pp. 6–26.

The historical transition from alternating labor codes to the medieval protectionism of the craft guilds and finally to a laissez faire environment is partially demonstrated by the events surrounding the Woolen Cloth Weavers Act of 1750. Prior to the passage and repeal of the Weavers Act, the House of Commons had periodically responded to wage-earner association pressures to maintain "customary" wages, support apprentice regulations, and suppress innovations "disruptive to the trade." The House of Commons had frequently prohibited manifestations of the "new" capitalistic competition (e.g., innovations such as the gig-mill). In the Weavers case, Parliament initially succumbed to the clothiers who assailed the Lords with arguments for freedom of contract to replace the fixed-wage rates. Less than two decades later, Parliament would not even receive the workers' petition protesting the evils done to their traditional livelihood through the adaptation of the spinning jenny. Parliament had no choice but to ultimately abolish medieval guild regulations, ignore their pressures, and endorse the emerging capitalist class or bear the penalty of arresting the growing export trade. The search for protection against skill degradation by the ex-artisan classes and Adam Smith's intellectual rationalization of the emerging laissez faire system are inextricably interwoven and headed the market economy towards obvious triumph by the eighteenth century.

With the decline of the guild system in the seventeenth and eighteenth centuries, organization of workers into trade unions appeared as the artisans gradually lost ownership of and control over the instruments of production. As the Webbs have indicated, the divorce of capital and labor preceded the factory system by a century, although the factory system intensified the division of classes.[4] Between the Black Death era and the more permanent organization of workers into associations or trade unions in the eighteenth century, the command and custom rules of socioeconomic organization were being wrenched away and supplanted by the market environment.[5]

Seemingly prompted by adverse economic and legal developments that resulted in the labor contract being treated differently than other contracts, worker combinations appeared with increasing frequency. Their grievances were real—deterioration of the circumstances of work through larger and more formal concentrations of capital which simultaneously increased the productivity of labor enormously. The

[4] Webb, *op. cit.*

[5] An interesting account of the economic transformation of England can be found in G. H. Perris, *The Industrial History of Modern England* (New York: Holt, Rinehart, and Winston, Inc., 1914).

needs of organized labor were not to be met, however, until the late nineteenth and early twentieth centuries' discovery and implementation of factory legislation and collective bargaining in the form of labor relations law.

THE CONSPIRACY DOCTRINE

Worker organizations were frequently prosecuted for combining to raise wages, and the courts gradually developed the doctrine that such combined action was a criminal conspiracy. Use of the English common-law conspiracy doctrine as a union restraining device is apparent in a decision rendered in 1721 by the King's tribunal in *Rex* v. *Journeymen Tailors of Cambridge,* where the jurists concluded that "every man may work at what price he pleases, but a combination not to work under certain prices is an indictable offense." [6] The court recognized the tailors' individual rights to refuse to accept conditions and wages of work, but held that a conspiracy to combine for this reason was a common crime in itself. Parliament reaffirmed the decision of the Bench in subsequent suppressive legislation (The Combination Acts) directed at organized unions. [7] In the case of the tailors, their offense was an illegal combination to do collectively what one individual could legally attempt to accomplish, and it was not until 1875 that labor was relieved of the criminality stigma by Parliamentary edict in England. [8]

The doctrine of civil conspiracy replaced that of criminal conspiracy in the latter nineteenth-century English labor movement when a "double standard" developed in English common law. In championing the cause of free enterprise, the House of Lords sanctioned combinations in the product market that were constructed by business institutions. Such, however, was not the case in the labor or resource market. As one labor law scholar has observed, the English courts evolved a trilogy of decisions through a highly inconsistent reasoning process. [9] In *Mogul Steamship Company* v. *McGregor, Gow and Co.,* a combination of shipping lines between the Far East and England

[6] 8 Mod. 10 (1721).

[7] 39 Geo. 3, C. 81 (1799), and 40 Geo. 3, C. 106v (1800).

[8] The Conspiracy and Protection Act, 38 and 39 Vict., C. 86, Sec. 3 (1875) also broadened the restrictive limitations imposed on picketing in the Combination Acts.

[9] The full account of the "trilogy" thesis summarized here can be found in C. O. Gregory, *Labor and the Law,* 2nd Ed. (New York: W. W. Norton and Co., 1961), Ch. II.

intentionally eliminated plaintiff Mogul's business by kickbacks to shippers using the combinations' lines and by refusing to handle the goods of any firm patronizing the plaintiff's firm.[10] The plaintiff sued for damages and sought an injunction against future action of this type on the basis that a civil conspiracy was committed. The House of Lords ruled in the *Mogul* case that:

(1) the combination had intentionally ruined the new company (and thereby suppressed competition), but this was not actionable because justification in the form of the bitter war of competition existed.

(2) the combination of capital for purposes of trade and competition did not fall under the indictable conspiracy heading.

This appeared on the surface to be a favorable development in principle insofar as the union movement was concerned. In the case of *Allen* v. *Flood,* the boilermakers (represented by Allen) were sued by one of two shipwrights (Flood) who were not inclined to join the workers' association.[11] Flood was subsequently discharged as a result of union pressure upon the employer. After considerable legal deliberation, the House of Lords approved the action of Allen in behalf of the trade as lawful as well as consistent with the previously rendered common law, i.e., the *Mogul* decision. The Bench charged society with enacting legislation if the decision of the judiciary was deemed inappropriate, since common law precedent demanded this decision. But the House of Lords was not done yet!

Shortly thereafter, the House of Lords reversed its position completely in *Quinn* v. *Leathem.*[12] Leathem, the employer, was subjected to secondary boycott pressures by Quinn and the union when he refused to replace his workers with members of the meat workers' union. After moving through the lower courts, the House of Lords affirmed an earlier judgment against Quinn and the union that gave damages to the employer, Leathem. The court held that the worker combination was without justifiable objective and was intended to harm the employer's trade. The Lords ruled that the union was guilty of civil conspiracy resulting from a combination inflicting illegal harm. In short, the court appears to have interpreted the law to suit its own concept of propriety in the *Quinn* labor conspiracy case, which resulted in treatment precisely counter to that ruled upon in

[10] H. L., A. C. 25 (1892).
[11] H. L., A. C. 1 (1898).
[12] H. L., A. C. 495 (1901).

the *Mogul* business conspiracy case. Thus a "double standard" existed in England until the civil conspiracy doctrine was outlawed in the Trade Disputes Act of 1906.[13] Even though the Conspiracy and Protection Act of 1875 had removed the previously restrictive criminal conspiracy doctrine used against labor in England, the labor movement was constrained soon thereafter by the new definition of civil conspiracy.

Early Attitudes Toward Labor in the United States

THE LEGAL SETTING

Early American labor law took a chapter from British history in that the organization of labor was considered to be a conspiracy. The American courts followed the precedent set by England and adopted the conspiracy doctrine early in dealing with labor organizations. Conspiracy as applied to labor established the principle that what could be done legally by an individual could not necessarily be done legally by a group. For example, an individual could quit a job or bargain to increase wages, but a group could not legally do the same thing. The simple threat of a conspiracy to combine became sufficient to make the combination illegal. This became particularly significant later as the employer needed only to show a *threat* of combined action to obtain relief through an injunction, one of the employer's chief weapons in combating labor organization around the turn of the century. The elements of the conspiracy doctrine were later extended to financial liability on the part of labor organizations in the United States. Conspirators (i.e., leaders and members of the organization) were legally held liable for damages. These legal principles were predicated on the philosophy that any organization whose purpose was to change the economic worth of labor was interfering with the "natural" operation of basic economic forces. Furthermore, concerted efforts to increase wages were often deemed to be an inappropriate invasion of employer rights, which could jeopardize a firm's competitive position.

Throughout most of the nineteenth century, the labor union movement in America was inhibited by the use of (1) the conspiracy doctrine adapted from English common law, and (2) injunctive relief given by the courts, allegedly in the interests of equity. It will be recalled that injunctions normally consisted of orders imposed upon or-

[13] 6 Edw. VII, C. 239 (1906).

ganized labor to fulfill a given act or refrain from taking a course of action. Thus, the conviction of unions for the commission of crimes, awards of adverse monetary judgments against unions for committing either criminal or civil conspiracy, and injunctive restraints against worker behavior all served to control the growth of organized labor.

The common law of the United States was based upon legal precedent established in this country and in England, the most notable of which was the conspiracy doctrine. In this nation, however, labor-management problems normally were confined to local areas, and, as a consequence, state courts established a considerable body of precedent law. State courts applied individual and sometimes conflicting versions of the common law. In the United States, the legal attitude toward labor organizations was relaxed first and most forcefully in a decision rendered by Justice Shaw of Massachusetts, who pointed out that labor organizations were not necessarily criminal per se. Shaw observed that there could be good labor organizations as well as bad ones, depending on (1) their purpose and (2) the means used to achieve that purpose.[14] This position will be examined in detail shortly.

LABOR ORGANIZATIONS

Organized "worker societies" conducted strike activities in pursuit of their objectives on infrequent occasions. One of the earliest recorded labor disputes occurred in 1741 when the New York bakers struck against government-established prices.[15] It is generally alleged that the first American trade union was organized in 1794 in Philadelphia. The Philadelphia Cordwainers conducted strikes in 1799 against a proposed wage cut and another in the early 1800's. During this same period of time, numerous workers' societies appeared among the major crafts (e.g., the printers, tailors, hatters, and carpenters), but in most cases their existence was very short indeed. The limited amount of overt union activity that was pursued by worker societies in the eighteenth and early nineteenth centuries normally was directed at correction of very specific short-term economic grievances. At this time, unions were primarily organizations confined to small regional labor market areas whose members were, for the most part, highly skilled workers. Mass-production industries were nonexistent, and the

[14] 14 Metcalf, 111, 45 Massachusetts (1842).
[15] U.S. Department of Labor, "Report on Strikes and Lockouts," *Third Annual Report*, 1887, pp. 1029–1030.

workers' societies served fraternal purposes as well as those objectives now associated with the major purposes of labor unions. Their concern was largely with preserving a closed shop, apprentice regulations, better wages, and shorter hours. Collective bargaining, as we know it today, was virtually nonexistent. Rather, union activities usually involved establishing wage and work regulations and insisting that the employer meet these conditions. Needless to say, the absence of any means for collectively resolving disputes short of sheer economic power contributed to the unpopular view of organized labor.

Criminal Conspiracy

The adoption of the English philosophy of laissez-faire and the grafting of English common law to the legal system in this country was firmly established at the beginning of the nineteenth century. By this time, the Philadelphia Cordwainers was a relatively well-established fraternal society, whose origins stemmed from a Boston trade guild chartered in the new world colony of Massachusetts Bay in 1648.[16] The journeymen shoemakers were relatively well-organized, and upon establishing a price for their labor they would notify the masters of this price, and a turnout (strike) would occur if the price was not met. On two occasions (1798 and 1804), the Journeymen's Society conducted a turnout and their wage demands were met.

THE CORDWAINER CONSPIRACY

In 1805, a strike was conducted by the Philadelphia Cordwainers in response to a reduction in the price paid workers by the master. During the strike, George Pullis and seven fellow journeymen were arrested on a preliminary complaint. This broke the strike of the union. Proprietary interests in Philadelphia viewed the heightened activities of workers' societies with some alarm, and in 1806 the eight previously-arrested bootmakers were indicted and charged with the crime of a combination and conspiracy to raise wages.[17] Members of

[16] See Elias Lieberman, *Unions Before the Bar* (New York: Harper and Brothers, 1950), Chapter I, for an excellent account of the Cordwainers.

[17] An excellent account of the Philadelphia Cordwainers and numerous other criminal conspiracy trials can be found in John R. Commons and Associates, *Documentary History of American Industrial Society* (Cleveland: The Arthur H. Clark Co., 1910), Vols. 3 and 4. The Cordwainers' case is described in Volume 3, p. 59 ff.

the Cordwainers' Society were charged with a criminal conspiracy to prevent other bootmakers from working for wages below the rate that the Society had set. In the trial, Recorder Moses Levy chastised Pullis and his fellow workers for combining to do what each of them as individuals had a perfect right to do. Levy contended that the law did not permit a combination of workers to pursue objects beneficial to themselves or to injure those who did not join their society; the jury found Pullis and his seven fellow journeymen "guilty of a combination to raise their wages." The ruling on the case of the Philadelphia Cordwainers established a precedent followed shortly thereafter by reconfirmation in another case involving the Journeymen Cordwainers decided in New York in 1809.[18] Between 1806 and 1842, some nineteen conspiracy trials of record occurred in various states across the nation. These trials and frequent convictions severely inhibited aggressive union activity and helped account for the short life-span of most early labor organizations.

In most of these conspiracy convictions, it was unnecessary to find the union illegal as a combination per se. Rather, conviction often rested upon finding either the means or the objectives of the workers' society to be unlawful and conspiratorial in nature. The conspiracy doctrine was therefore a very effective method for controlling the activities of trade unions. First, this doctrine rested upon the power of numbers, declaring concerted action illegal even though such action was legal if pursued by the individual. The very act of conspiring to combine was also held illegal. Finally, persons who acted in concert to effect an illegal purpose were held responsible for these acts when carried out by any member combination. During subsequent clashes between employees and employers, a great deal of protection was afforded employer property rights by the judiciary through the use of the conspiracy doctrine. The property background of judges was not normally in sympathy with combinations of working men who were viewed as interfering with the "natural laws" of the market economy. Indeed, some state legislatures passed conspiracy laws to support the common law.

A legal "double standard" also existed in the United States in that the courts did not find business combinations illegal on the grounds that entrepreneurial combinations permitted a business to engage in activities substantially greater than those that could be conducted alone. In the case of the Journeymen Cordwainers:

[18] *People* v. *James Melvin* (Yates Se. Cas. 114) (1809).

. . . the defense further showed that the Master Cordwainers (the employer association) who were behind the prosecution of these eight boot- and shoe-makers themselves had combined in a society for the purpose of maintaining prices and other mutual protections for themselves, as shown by the journal of the proceeding of the Masters' Society which contained the record of their first meeting held in April, 1789. Their rules included the following: (1) The subscribers were to hold four stated general meetings in every year. Absentees to pay a fine of 1s. 6d. (2) Members were to consult for the general good of the trade, and determine upon the most eligible means to prevent irregularities in the same. . . . (5) No person should be elected a member of the society who offered for sale any boots, shoes, etc., in the public market of that city, or advertised the price of his work in any of the public papers or handbills, so long as he continued in these practices. (6) All fines and penalties to be paid, or for neglect, after notice, to be considered as an unworthy member, and accordingly excluded from the society.[19]

Needless to say, this evidence did not sway the decision and while such practices are less conspicuously identified today, numerous professional associations still "suggest" standards of a similar nature (e.g., the American Medical Association), which the public equates with economic control by a union.

THE HUNT CASE

The anti-union ruling in the Cordwainers' decision and subsequent convictions understandably were not popular with the labor movement. One solution to this problem that was sought was more effective labor organizations. In 1827, several unions in Philadelphia joined forces and formed a Mechanics Union of Trade Associations as a city federation. This federation also sponsored one of the first newspapers in the labor movement. Subsequently, city associations were organized in Boston, New York, and Baltimore. A year later, in 1828, the Philadelphia Association gave birth to the Workingman's Party, one of the first labor parties in the United States. After the demise of the Mechanics Union of Trade Associations in 1832, the first national attempt was made to unite all unions in the form of the National Trade Union in 1834. The financial panic of 1837 wiped out this first attempt at national organization.

The precedent established in the *Cordwainers* case, which upheld

[19] Lieberman, *op. cit.*, p. 10.

the legality of the conspiracy doctrine applied to labor as an illegal combination, was overturned in the *Commonwealth* v. *Hunt* case of 1842.[20] The now famous *Hunt* case involved a very active union of shoemakers in Massachusetts. In 1840, the Boston Journeymen Shoemakers' Society organized what we now know as a closed shop and successfully requested the discharge of a nonmember employee. As a consequence of this, Hunt and six other members of the society were later charged with and convicted of conspiracy in a lower-court ruling in Boston. Upon appeal to the Massachusetts Supreme Court, the conviction was reversed. The decision of Chief Justice Shaw in the *Hunt* case established the very important precedent that the simple act of combination in and of itself did not constitute the formation of an unlawful organization. Chief Justice Shaw's observation resulted in the union's being judged on the basis of the legality of its motives or intent and the legal status of the means or techniques employed to achieve these ends.

The incident that prompted this highly significant ruling was seemingly innocent enough. A member of the Boston Journeymen Shoemakers' Society, one Jeremiah Horne, twice breached the Society's rules for accepting work without the Society's knowledge and was fined. Upon his refusal to pay the second fine and secure his membership in good standing, his discharge was requested by the Society. The employer complied as demanded. Horne lodged his complaint with Samuel Parker, the District Attorney in Boston who had indicted Hunt and six other members of the Society for criminal conspiracy in 1840. The lower court convicted Hunt *et al.* for committing an unlawful criminal conspiracy against the Commonwealth. The ruling occurred in spite of the fact that the defense drew a curious but pointed analogy between the Society's setting of fees and the practices of the Boston Bar, which had established rules fixing minimum fees consistent with what should be "honorably" received.[21]

As Justice Shaw saw this case, when it reached the Appellate Court in 1842, the combination did not have an illegal purpose in the form of a closed-shop objective, and their peaceful threat to not work for the employer did not constitute an illegal means. Consequently, the Supreme Court of Massachusetts overruled the earlier guilty verdict found by the Municipal Court of Boston, presided over by Judge Peter Thatcher.[22] In his decision, Justice Shaw noted that ". . . in

[20] 4 Metcalf, 111, 45 Massachusetts (1842).

[21] Lieberman, *op. cit.*, pp. 7–21.

[22] Among the precedents cited in this decision were the *Cordwainers* case and *People* v. *Fisher* (14 Wendel 9 N. W. 1835). In the latter case, Judge Savage of New York had reaffirmed the *Cordwainers* decision that a

order to charge all those who become members of an association with the guilt of criminal conspiracy, it must be averred and proved that the actual, if not the avowed object of the association was criminal. . . ." This point was not supported by the facts of the *Hunt* case. Shaw also noted that ". . . the legality of such an association will therefore depend upon the means to be used for its accomplishment." [23] This decision, then, without giving direct sanction to a variety of union activities (e.g., strikes or picketing), did eliminate the application of criminal conspiracy rulings against combined action simply because it was a combination. Criminality of union activity was henceforth to be judged by the nature and purpose of acts—not mere acts in combination.

The opinion of Chief Justice Shaw on this historic case follows:

COMMONWEALTH v. JOHN HUNT AND OTHERS: 1842
(4 *Metcalf, 111, 45 Mass.*)

The Supreme Judicial Court of Massachusetts; opinion of Chief Justice Shaw:

. . . We have no doubt, that by the operation of the constitution of this Commonwealth, the general rules of the common law, making conspiracy an indictable offence, are in force here, and that this is included in the description of laws which had, before the adoption of the constitution, been used and approved in the Province, Colony, or State of Massachusetts Bay, and usually practised in the courts of law. . . . The general rule of the common law is, that it is a criminal and indictable offence, for two or more to confederate and combine together, by concerted means, to do that which is unlawful or criminal, to the injury of the public, or portions or classes of the community, or even to the rights of an individual. This rule of law may be equally in force as a rule of the common law, in

combination of workers to raise wages was a conspiracy. Justice Shaw's decision overturned these previous precedents.

[23] Justice Shaw was not plowing completely new ground. In *Commonwealth* v. *Carlisle*, a group of employees attempted to apply the criminal conspiracy doctrine to employers who had combined to reduce wages. The employers were found not guilty by Chief Justice Gibson of Pennsylvania, however, since their acts were not prompted by an improper motive. Justice Gibson observed that ". . . where the act to be done and the means of accomplishing it are lawful, and the object to be attained is meritorious, combination is not conspiracy." See Brightly, Rep. 36, Pa. N.P. (1821).

England and in this Commonwealth; and yet it must depend upon the local laws of each country to determine, whether the purpose to be accomplished by the combination, or the concerted means of accomplishing it, be unlawful or criminal in the respective countries. All those laws of the parent country, whether rules of the common law, or early English statutes, which were made for the purpose of regulating the wages of laborers, the settlement of paupers, and making it penal for any one to use a trade or handicraft to which he had not served a full apprenticeship—not being adapted to the circumstances of our colonial condition—were not adopted, used or approved, and therefore do not come within the description of the laws adopted and confirmed by the provision of the constitution already cited. . . .

But the rule of law, that an illegal conspiracy, whatever may be the facts which constitute it, is an offence punishable by the laws of this Commonwealth, is established as well by legislative as by judicial authority. . . . Without attempting to review and reconcile all the cases, we are of opinion, that as a general description, though perhaps not a precise and accurate definition, a conspiracy must be a combination of two or more persons, by some concerted action, to accomplish some criminal or unlawful purpose, or to accomplish some purpose, not in itself criminal or unlawful, by criminal or unlawful means. We use the terms criminal or unlawful, because it is manifest that many acts are unlawful, which are not punishable by indictment or other public prosecution; and yet there is no doubt, we think, that a combination by numbers to do them would be an unlawful conspiracy, and punishable by indictment. . . .

But yet it is clear, that it is not every combination to do unlawful acts, to the prejudice of another by a concerted action, which is punishable as conspiracy. . . .

With these general views of the law, it becomes necessary to consider the circumstances of the present case, as they appear from the indictment itself, and from the bill of exceptions filed and allowed. . . .

The first count set forth, that the defendants, with divers others unknown, on the day and at the place named, being workmen, and journeymen, in the art and occupation of bootmakers, unlawfully, perniciously and deceitfully designing and intending to continue, keep up, form, and unite themselves, into an unlawful club, society and combination, and make unlawful by-laws, rules and orders among themselves, and thereby govern themselves and other workmen, in the said art, and unlawfully and unjustly to extort great sums of money by means thereof, did unlawfully assemble and meet together, and being so assembled, did unjustly and corruptly conspire, combine, confederate and agree together, that none of them should thereafter, and that none of them would, work for any master or person whatsoever, in the said art,.mystery and occupation, who should employ any workman or journeyman, or other person, in the said art, who was not a member of said club, society or combination, after notice given him to discharge such workman, from the employ of such master. . . .

Stripped then of these introductory recitals . . . the averment is this; that the defendants and others formed themselves into a society, and agreed not to work for any person, who should employ any journeyman or other person, not a member of such society, after notice given him to discharge such workman.

The manifest intent of the association is, to induce all those engaged in the same occupation to become members of it. Such a purpose is not unlawful. It would give them a power which might be exerted for useful and honorable purposes, or for dangerous and pernicious ones. If the latter were the real and actual object, and susceptible of proof, it should have been specially charged. Such an association might be used to afford each other assistance in times of poverty, sickness and distress; or to raise their intellectual, moral and social condition; or to make improvement in their art; or for other proper purposes. Or the association might be designed for purposes of oppression and injustice. But in order to charge all those, who become members of an association, with the guilt of a criminal conspiracy, it must be averred and proved that the actual, if not the avowed object of the association, was criminal. An association may be formed, the declared objects of which are innocent and laudable, and yet they may have secret articles, or an agreement communicated only to the members, by which they are banded together for purposes injurious to the peace of society or the rights of its members. Such would undoubtedly be a criminal conspiracy, on proof of the fact, however meritorious and praiseworthy the declared objects might be. The law is not to be hoodwinked by colorable pretences. It looks at truth and reality, through whatever disguise it may assume. But to make such an association, ostensibly innocent, the subject of prosecution as a criminal conspiracy, the secret agreement, which makes it so, is to be averred and proved as the gist of the offence. (But when an association is formed for purposes actually innocent, and afterwards its powers are abused, by those who have the control and management of it, to purposes of oppression and injustice, it will be criminal in those who thus misuse it, or give consent thereto, but not in the other members of the association.) In this case, no such secret agreement, varying the objects of the association from those avowed, is set forth in this count of the indictment.

Nor can we perceive that the objects of this association, whatever they may have been, were to be attained by criminal means. The means which they propose to employ, as averred in this count, and which, as we are now to presume, were established by the proof, were, that they would not work for a person, who, after due notice, should employ a journeyman not a member of their society. Supposing the object of the association to be laudable and lawful, or at least not unlawful, are these means criminal? The case supposes that these persons are not bound by contract, but free to work for whom they please, or not to work, if they so prefer. In this state of things, we cannot perceive, that it is criminal for men to agree together to exercise their own acknowledged rights, in such a manner as best to subserve their own interests. One way to test this is, to consider the effect of such an agreement, where the object of the association is acknowledged on all hands to be a laudable one. Suppose a class of workmen, impressed with the manifold evils of intemperance, should agree with each other not to work in a shop in which ardent spirit was furnished, or not to work in a shop with any one who used it, or not to work for an employer, who should, after notice, employ a journeyman who habitually used it. The consequences might be the same. A workman, who should still persist in the use of ardent spirit, would find it more difficult to get employment; a master employing such an one might, at times, experience inconvenience in his work, in losing the services of a skilful but intemperate workman. Still it seems to us, that as the object would be lawful, and the means not unlawful, such an agreement could not be pronounced a criminal conspiracy. . . .

The second count, . . . alleges that the defendants, with others unknown, did assemble, conspire, confederate and agree together, not to work for any master or person who should employ any workman not being a member of a certain club, society or combination, called the Boston Journeymen Bootmakers' Society, or who shall break any of their by-laws, unless such workmen should pay to said club, such sum as should be agreed upon as a penalty for the breach of such unlawful rules, &c; and that by means of said conspiracy they did compel one Isaac B. Wait, a master cordwainer to turn out of his employ one Jeremiah Horne, a journeyman boot-maker, &c. in evil example, &c. So far as the averment of a conspiracy is concerned, all the remarks made in reference to the first count are equally applicable to this . . . It sets forth no illegal or criminal purpose to be accomplished, nor any illegal or criminal means to be adopted for the accomplishment of any purpose. . . .

The third count, reciting a wicked and unlawful intent to impoverish one Jeremiah Horne, and hinder him from following his trade as a bootmaker, charges the defendants, with others unknown, with an unlawful conspiracy, by wrongful and indirect means, to impoverish said Horne and to deprive and hinder him, from his said art and trade and getting his support thereby, and that, in pursuance of said unlawful combination, they did unlawfully and indirectly hinder and prevent, and greatly impoverish him . . . The same thing may be said of all competition in every branch of trade and industry; and yet it is through that competition, that the best interests of trade and industry are promoted. It is scarcely necessary to allude to the familiar instances of opposition lines of conveyance, rival hotels, and the thousand other instances, where each strives to gain custom to himself, by ingenious improvements, by increased industry, and by all the means by which he may lessen the price of commodities, and thereby diminish the profits of others. We think, therefore, that associations may be entered into, the object of which is to adopt measures that may have a tendency to impoverish another, that is, to diminish his gains and profits, and yet so far from being criminal or unlawful, the object may be highly meritorious and public spirited. . . .

The fourth count avers a conspiracy to impoverish Jeremiah Horne, without stating any means; and the fifth alleges a conspiracy to impoverish employers, by preventing and hindering them from employing persons, not members of the Bootmakers' Society; and these require no remarks, which have not been already made in reference to the other counts. . . .

It appears by the bill of exceptions, that it was contended on the part of the defendants, that this indictment did not set forth any agreement to do a criminal act, or to do any lawful act by criminal means, and that the agreement therein set forth did not constitute a conspiracy indictable by the law of this State, and that the court was requested so to instruct the jury. This the court declined doing, but instructed the jury that the indictment did describe a confederacy among the defendants to do an unlawful act, and to effect the same by unlawful means—that the society, organized and associated for the purposes described in the indictment, was an unlawful conspiracy against the laws of this State, and that if the jury believed, from the evidence, that the defendants or any of them had engaged in such confederacy, they were bound to find such of them guilty.

In this opinion of the learned judge, this court, for the reasons stated, cannot concur. . . .

While the "go" signal seems to have been flashed for unions in the *Hunt* decision, the judiciary retained considerable power over the labor movement by ruling upon the legality of ends and means. The courts of various states applied common law doctrine to specific cases in diverse ways, as only the vagueness and uncertainty of common law permitted. Various decisions found certain acts and objectives (e.g., strikes and a closed shop) legal or illegal—depending on the prevailing statutory law and existing judicial and political philosophies. Some states went further and validated portions of the conspiracy doctrine through statutory law. The conspiracy doctrine was applied with decreasing frequency and increasing complexity after 1842, however. The legality of certain weapons of labor-management conflict (e.g., boycotts, strikes, picketing, and union-shop security provisions) became immersed in a crazy quilt of diverse court-made laws, as the judiciary sought fine distinctions between "lawful" and "unlawful" means and ends.

Gradually, the courts validated the legitimacy of direct strikes for better wages and working hours. Other weapons of labor-management conflict were less readily accepted. In *Vegelahn* v. *Guntner*, for example, a case in which the Massachusetts court upheld an order forbidding peaceful picketing in 1896, Justice Holmes eloquently defended the union's right to combine, free of conspiracy charges, in his oft-quoted dissent:

One of the eternal conflicts out of which life is made up is that between the effort of every man to get the most he can for his services, and that of society, disguised under the name of capital, to get his services for the least possible return. Combination on the one side is patent and powerful. Combination on the other is the necessary and desirable counterpart, if the battle is to be carried on in a fair and equal way.[24]

The volume and effectiveness of the conspiracy force died in the mid-nineteenth century, however, in response to (1) increasing labor movement pressures, (2) local and sometimes radical protest and re-form movements in the decades around the Civil War, and (3) bitter entanglements over legal means and ends. Concerts of socioeconomic pressure became more commonplace on many fronts, and blatant denial of group action to one singled-out institution simply could not be maintained. This did not mean, however, that those in sympathy with the cause of labor were successful in altering the balance of economic power in favor of the labor movement. The vitality and spirit of capitalism were caught up in the process of large-scale industrialization and hardening of the class lines after the Civil War. The property right ideology persisted by forging new and even more effective tools of legal combat, such as the injunction. Along with the yellow-dog contract, injunction virtually made the unions' right to organize meaningless as the nineteenth century was drawing to a close.

THE RISING TIDE OF UNIONISM

The organized labor movement took some halting steps after the dehydration of the National Trade Union in 1837 and Justice Shaw's landmark decision in 1842. Economic prosperity, along with nominal relaxation of some legal impediments to organized labor, established a more favorable environment for organization. By 1870, some thirty national unions had emerged. A second attempt at national unification of the labor movement was attempted in 1866 when the National Labor Union was formed. While its initial purposes tended to be economic, the movement soon gravitated toward social and political objectives. Subsequently, the labor union advocates in the group who were more interested in economic objectives than social reform dropped from its ranks. By 1872, the National Labor Union ceased to exist as an effective organization. Immediately thereafter, however, one of the more spectacular attempts at a unified labor movement occurred. Starting in Philadelphia as a secret society, the Knights of

[24] 167 Massachusetts 92 (1896).

Labor gradually grew in membership to over two-thirds of a million workers by 1886. This movement permitted affiliation of both craft and unskilled industrial workers. In addition, the Knights of Labor was vitally interested in political and social affairs and reform. In spite of the fact that the Knights were successful in conducting several strikes, they too ultimately failed, in part because of an ill-fated association with the Haymarket Riots in Chicago in 1886. Also contributing to the demise of the Knights was ideological division in the form of reformist elements and craft-industrial strife that appeared within the movement.

During the closing decade of the nineteenth century, labor was in a constant state of turmoil in the United States. This was the era of the long strike, which was closely followed by the Molly Maguire riots in the coal industry that resulted in the conviction of 24 members of the Miners' and Laborers' Benevolent Association. Upon conviction, ten of the 24 were executed. As the nation sunk deep into the throes of the depression of 1873, one of the most violent and significant upheavals in the labor movement occurred in the Railway Strike of 1877. The strike spread throughout many major urban centers in the East, and culminated in control by the militia. On one occasion, mob rule was rampant in the city of Pittsburgh after some 600 militia killed 26 people while breaking up a strike. Activities such as these terrified propertied interests, and many states enacted conspiracy laws aimed at labor uprisings. This unsettled period in which the National Labor Union and the Knights of Labor emerged and then died also included the Haymarket Riots in Chicago that ended in the death of more than a dozen people and convictions for murder and death sentences for seven of eight men tried for inciting to riot. This era of violence immediately preceded the organization in 1881 of a federation of craft unions that ultimately resulted in the American Federation of Labor. The labor movement experienced only moderate and sporadic relief in its struggle for survival, however, as gains were restricted to modest ones through the increasing use of injunctions.

Injunctive Relief and Contractual Interference

EFFECTIVENESS OF INJUNCTIONS

With the gradual withering away of the criminal conspiracy doctrine, the American judiciary followed the existing English pattern of controlling unpopular activities of the labor movement by awarding monetary judgments to employers who complained of tort actions.

Judgments for damages were relatively ineffective, however, in curbing activities of the labor movement, since the leaders and members often were unable to pay the judgments. Moreover, awards for damages were hardly adequate redress for the large losses allegedly sustained by employers due to strikes and boycotts. The American system of jurisprudence quickly and adeptly adopted the English concept of a tort liability. Because statutory law at this time did not provide a system of labor-management conflict resolution, the courts necessarily had to resolve disputes arising when labor and management did collide, which was relatively frequent. In both the United States and England, equity courts developed preventive devices to deal with cases in which monetary awards were deemed inadequate as a redress of a grievance. Such was alleged to be the case insofar as union damage to employer property rights was concerned.

For a case in equity in which injunctive relief is granted, a court issues an order charging that the union does, or refrains from doing, something. If the union fails to obey the court order, the union and its leadership can be held in contempt of court. Contempt of court is punishable under criminal law and, as a consequence, injunctive relief became an important and effective device in restraining the labor movement. Although the courts in England granted injunctive relief only in instances where there was tangible evidence of damage or threat to physical property, the American courts went further. Judges in the United States became increasingly prone to issue injunctions when there was only modest evidence of threatened or actual irreparable damage to the business of an employer.

The legal rationale for injunctive relief was based very simply on the allegation that certain activities of the labor union were sufficient to inflict injury for which monetary damages were insufficient. Since the judicial branch interpreted denial of the intangible property right to do business as a damage to property, relief usually was granted to the employer. Numerous court restraining orders were issued after the first use of the injunction against labor in the 1880's.

The injunction was effective in part because failure to obey the work restraining order resulted in an automatic contempt of court decree, a criminal offense punishable by imprisonment, fine, or both. In addition, the effectiveness of the injunction was due to the speed with which a temporary restraining order could be applied to "break" a strike. In most cases, the request for a temporary restraining order was immediately granted. Moreover, very frequently the temporary injunction was issued under circumstances in which no representative of the group being enjoined (i.e., the union) was present. This *ex parte* injunction normally was followed by a preliminary hearing at which time the judge issuing the restraining order would decide if a permanent injunction should be granted. The *ex parte* injunction was a very effective device for immediately breaking the intensity and momentum of striking unions. Frequently, little or no examination of witnesses occurred, and one judge normally rendered the decision. Injunctions often were vaguely worded, in many cases not even identifying the individuals being restrained specifically. Not only was the wording of injunctions frequently nebulous, but the scope often was very sweeping. In one instance, a barber who, in sympathy with the activities of the labor union, put a sign in his shop stating that "scabs" would not be served, was held in *contempt* of court.[25] By the time a hearing could be held and a permanent injunction ruled upon, the employer frequently had sufficient time to both break the strike and discharge union sympathizers and otherwise undermine organization of his plant. The union on the other hand was helpless, for violation of the restraining order was held as contempt of court. Thus, a liberal interpretation of property rights of employers that widened the scope of injunctive relief, *ex parte* issuance of injunctions, and all-encompassing wording resulted in continued demoralization of the labor union movement.

YELLOW-DOG CONTRACTS

Another effectively used device designed to curb the activities of organized labor at the turn of the twentieth century was the yellow-dog contract. Applicants for employment were frequently required by employers to sign a contract as a condition of employment in which the employee agreed not to become or remain a member of a union. This strengthened the hand of the employer considerably in his pursuit of an open shop.[26] The significance of the yellow-dog contract derived from the fact that, so long as such contractual arrangements were declared legal, attempts to organize workers when the worker had signed a contract were declared deliberate and illegal attempts on the part of the union to cause a breach of contract. Such action, of course, was enjoinable by the courts. Because of judiciary enforcement of yellow-dog contracts, organized labor made several attempts to pass state statutes outlawing

[25] H. R. Northrup and Gordon L. Bloom, *Government and Labor* (Homewood, Illinois: Richard D. Irwin, Inc., 1963), p. 18.

[26] The term "yellow dog" was used by unionists who referred to workers willing to sign such contracts as "yellow dogs."

the yellow-dog contract (e.g., Kansas). Congress enacted a federal anti-yellow-dog contract law relating to the railroad industry containing similar provisions.[27] The Supreme Court initially held that such legislation was in violation of the Fifth and Fourteenth Amendments to the Constitution, which guarantee freedom of contract as a right of property. The employer therefore had the very powerful combined weapons of the yellow-dog contract and injunctive relief with which to control the labor organization as the nineteenth century was closing.

THE PULLMAN-DEBBS SKIRMISH

The use of injunctions in labor disputes was relatively moderate in the 1880's, but became widespread in the United States after the Pullman Strike of 1895 which sanctioned the use of injunctions.[28] Eugene V. Debbs, a locomotive fireman and a militant member of the Brotherhood of Locomotive Firemen, led this strike. Debbs, with the assistance of a few other stalwart individuals, organized the American Railway Union in 1893 which admitted all workers of the railroad to membership, regardless of occupation. When the president of the Great Northern Railroad cut the wages of laborers who were members of the American Railway Union in 1894, Debbs led his union on strike. In spite of the fact that an injunction was issued against the newly-formed American Railway Union, Debbs *et al.* ultimately forced the Great Northern Railroad to yield. As a consequence, the prestige and membership of Debbs and his union increased substantially.

As a result of wage cuts during the depression of 1893 which adversely affected Pullman Company business, Pullman workers became aroused and affiliated with the American Railway Union. The workers organized a grievance committee, and members of this committee were fired by George Pullman. The workers immediately voted to strike.[29] George Pullman, president and originator of the Pullman Palace Car Company, notified Pullman strikers that the Company would be closed indefinitely; he persistently argued that there was

[27] The Erdman Act, passed in 1898.

[28] In re Debbs, 158 U.S. 564 (1895).

[29] Pullman had discharged three members of the union grievance committee who were attempting to reconcile differences over wage cuts and rental fees in the so-called "model company town" which the Pullman Company owned.

nothing to negotiate with the union. After hearing several appeals from the Pullman strikers, Debbs finally ordered the entire American Railway Union out on a sympathy strike during late June, 1894. During this period, the American Railway Union would not inspect, haul, or switch Pullman cars on any railroad. In the meantime, George Pullman had secured the support of a Railroad Employers Association known as the General Managers Association. The Association ordered that cars carrying the mail be attached to Pullman cars, and they also ordered the discharge of men refusing to haul Pullman cars. The General Managers Association then called upon the United States government for deputy marshals to inspect the movement of the mails and protect employer property. Nearly 4,000 deputy marshals were hired somewhat indiscriminately to act as United States agents and employees. In July of 1894, a complaint was lodged on behalf of the federal government at the suggestion of the Attorney General of the United States, R. B. Olney. Debbs and 16 other persons were charged with conspiracy to restrain and interfere with transportation of the mails and regular transportation. An injunction was issued against the union and its members, and immediately thereafter Attorney General Olney persuaded President Grover Cleveland to send four companies of federal troops to Chicago to enforce the injunction.

Both the troops and the injunction aroused the striking union members, who were legally restrained from conducting the strike and picketing. Olney moved quickly, had Debbs and other officers arrested, and seized all documents and papers of the union. Debbs offered to stop the Pullman boycott on the condition that all strikers except those convicted of a crime be rehired, but this plea for reinstatement was ignored by the General Managers Association. The next week Debbs was arrested again and charged with contempt of court for violating the injunction, and several hundred strikers were arrested on a variety of charges. This ended the railway strike, which was called off in September, 1894. Debbs and his fellow conspirators were sentenced to jail for terms ranging from three to six months in Woodstock County. The significance of the *Debbs* case is, first, that it represents a Supreme Court validation of the use of the injunction by the federal government in labor disputes. Secondly, Justice Brewer and his colleagues formally stretched the concept of "property rights" to include intangible property rights, such as employer-employee relationships.

Summary

The economic and legal conditions of the English working man were far from favorable in the era of industrialization. Adverse circumstances of work were made more severe by the adoption of a market process that eroded the protection and continuity established by century-old traditions and philosophies that guided man's economic life. Legally, workers desirous of common association were seriously hampered by the "conspiracy" doctrine, and it was not until the middle of the nineteenth century that the American worker was no longer subjugated to the "borrowed" common law conspiracy doctrine. The *Hunt* case is, indeed, a landmark decision because previous decisions reached by the courts in the *Cordwainer* and other conspiracy trials were reversed by it. The first 75 years of organized labor activities that preceded this landmark decision were not easy ones for the labor movement, however. Local unions and early attempts to create larger nationals or federations were very unsuccessful. The "localized" union effort was wiped out numerous times through combinations of financial crises, employer resistance, and government endorsed legal obstacles. Among these obstacles, the yellow-dog contract and court injunctions were of prime importance.

3

EARLY LABOR LAW: ANTI-TRUST LAWS AND THE COURTS

Even though criminal conspiracy charges did not represent an effective method of regimenting the labor movement after the *Hunt* decision, attempts to organize were thwarted in other ways, a fact demonstrated by our previous consideration of yellow-dog contracts and injunctions. A most formidable constraint was developed in 1890 with the passage of the Sherman Act, which was intended to control and destroy business monopoly power. The Clayton Act, which is discussed in the second section of this chapter, was designed to relieve organized labor prosecution under anti-trust law. The courts were very important in the interpretation and application of the Clayton Act, ultimately declaring its purpose to be invalid in the *Duplex, Coronado,* and *Bedford* decisions.

The Sherman Act: Era of Anti-Trust

Injunctions and yellow-dog contracts were not the only employer weapons that hampered labor organizations. With the advent of rapid industrialization immediately after the Civil War, concentrations of capital became very prevalent. Among the factors contributing to increasing size and concentration of industry were the development of scale technology, a growing and complex transportation system, increasing utilization of a formal corporate form of enterprise, and large fixed-investment requirements in many industries. Business combinations occurred in numerous forms, ranging from highly organized trusts to very loose associations or pools.[1] Major economic sectors were monopolized by business combinations in the American economy. Corporations were established to absorb formally competing business firms in an attempt to restrain price competition. The issues of monopoly power and anti-trust legislation were very evident in the election of 1888. After President Benjamin Harrison was elected, a bill was introduced by Senator Sherman of Ohio, and the Sherman Anti-Trust Act was enacted in 1890.[2] By Sherman's own admission, the Supreme Court was given the mandate to draw the precise line between lawful and unlawful combinations.

The integral part of the Sherman Act (reproduced in part in Appendix 3 A) with which we are concerned is contained in the first two sections, which read as follows:

SECTION 1: That every contract, combination in the form of trust or otherwise, or conspiracy, and restraint of trade or commerce among the several states or with foreign nations is hereby declared to be illegal.

SEC. 2: Every person who shall monopolize or attempt to monopolize, or combine or conspire with any other person or persons, to monopolize any part of the trade or commerce among the several states, or with foreign nations, shall be guilty of a misdemeanor . . . shall be punished by fine . . . or imprisonment.

[1] For additional treatment of anti-trust and the corporate enterprise see Hans B. Thorelli, *The Federal Anti-trust Policy* (Baltimore: The Johns Hopkins Press, 1955), pp. 72–93.

[2] The Sherman Act; 26 U.S. Stat. 209, 51st Congress, First Session, July, 1890.

Furthermore, Section 7 of the law made it possible for injured parties to sue for triple damages.

Whether Congress intended the Sherman Act to apply to union activities became an issue of great controversy. While the law itself does not speak to this point, congressional testimony preceding the passage of this bill does suggest that it was not the intent of Congress to include labor organizations even though exemption was not explicit.[3] In any event, it soon became obvious that another hurdle was placed before the labor movement.

DANBURY HATTERS AND UNION MONOPOLY

For nearly two decades after the passage of the Sherman Act, the court did not regard the activities of labor unions as being covered by the provisions of the Sherman Act. The initial Supreme Court test of the applicability of anti-trust legislation to organized labor came in the *Danbury Hatters* case in 1908.[4] Conflict arose in a dispute between the United Hatters Union, affiliated with the newly-established American Federation of Labor, and the Loewe Hat Company of Danbury, Connecticut. The hat-making trade was an abhorrent and injurious occupation in the nineteenth century, which probably contributed to the United Hatters' success in organizing workers. Workrooms were filled with steam and dust caused by dyeing and processing felt; nitrate of mercury acid was used to treat pelt-hair shavings prior to felt molding, and led to mercury poisoning; fumes that were released in pressing the felt caused teeth to fall out, palsy, and possible insanity. The United Hatters' Union was a relatively strong organization, having succeeded at most of the large felt hat manufacturers in the country at that time, but they had been unsuccessful in organizing the Loewe Company.

The union instituted a boycott against the Loewe Company and appealed to the public, union members, and distributors to boycott the product of an employer declared to be "unfair" by the union.[5] Loewe

[3] In congressional debates, Senator Sherman clearly indicated that his original bill was not intended to apply to labor or farm organizations. However, numerous other anti-trust bills introduced in this Congress did specify labor organization exemption whereas the Sherman Act failed to do so in its final form.

[4] *Loewe* v. *Lawlor*, 208 U.S. 274 (1908) and 235 U.S. 522 (1915).

[5] The Loewe Company was charged with retaining a 12- to 14-hour day and weekly pay of $13 compared to 8-hour days and $22 weekly wages in "fair" shops.

suffered a loss of business and then brought suit against the union under Section 7 of the Sherman Act. The Supreme Court ruled that Section 7 of Sherman did apply to the union and therefore granted triple damages to the Loewe Company. In its decision, the court stipulated that the Sherman Act made all contracts and combinations in restraint of trade illegal and it contained no exemptions. It further stipulated that the secondary boycott instituted by the union did affect interstate commerce and, as a consequence, union action fell under the stipulations contained in the Sherman Act.[6]

Justice Fuller presented the following opinion:

LOEWE v. LAWLOR: 1908
(*208 U.S. 274*)

The Supreme Court of the United States, Mr. Justice Fuller delivering the opinion:

This was an action brought in the circuit court for the District of Connecticut under Section 7 of the anti-trust act of July 2, 1890, . . . claiming threefold damages for injuries inflicted on plaintiffs by a combination or conspiracy declared to be unlawful by the act.

Defendants filed a demurrer to the complaint, assigning general and special grounds. The demurrer was sustained as to the first six paragraphs, which rested on the ground that the combination stated was not within the Sherman Act, and this rendered it unnecessary to pass upon any other questions in the case; and, upon plaintiffs declining to amend their complaint the court dismissed it with costs. . . .

The case was then carried by writ of error to the circuit court of appeals for the second circuit, and that court, desiring the instruction of this court upon a question arising on the writ of error, certified that question to this court. The certificate consisted of a brief statement of facts, and put the question thus: "Upon this state

[6] After ruling that the Sherman Act applied to the labor union, the Supreme Court remanded the case back to the lower courts for trial. Again in 1914 when the case reached the Supreme Court on appeal, the verdict of the lower courts was affirmed, including the award of nearly one-quarter of a million dollars to Loewe. The award of some one-quarter of a million dollars by the court to Loewe Manufacturing Company was not paid off until some 15 years after the strike had been initiated, and then only after the American Federation of Labor staged a mass appeal for funds to save the homes of 186 workers liable for damages.

of facts can plaintiffs maintain an action against defendants under Section 7 of the anti-trust act of July 2, 1890?". . . .

The question is whether, upon the facts therein averred and admitted by the demurrer, this action can be maintained under the anti-trust act. . . . The complaint averred that plaintiffs were manufacturers of hats in Danbury, Connecticut, having a factory there, and were then and there engaged in an interstate trade in some twenty states other than the state of Connecticut; that they were practically dependent upon such interstate trade to consume the product of their factory, only a small percentage of their entire output being consumed in the state of Connecticut; that, at the time the alleged combination was formed, they were in the process of manufacturing a large number of hats for the purpose of fulfilling engagements then actually made with consignees and wholesale dealers in states other than Connecticut, and that, if prevented from carrying on the work of manufacturing these hats, they would be unable to complete their engagements.

That defendants were members of a vast combination called The United Hatters of North America, comprising about 9,000 members and including a large number of subordinate unions, and that they were combined with some 1,400,000 others into another association known as The American Federation of Labor, of which they were members, whose members resided in all the places in the several states where the wholesale dealers in hats and their customers resided and did business; that defendants were "engaged in a combined scheme and effort to force all manufacturers of fur hats in the United States, including the plaintiffs, against their will and their previous policy of carrying on their business, to organize their workmen in the departments of making and finishing, in each of their factories, into an organization, to be part and parcel of the said combination known as The United Hatters of North America, or, as the defendants and their confederates term it, to unionize their shops, with the intent thereby to control the employment of labor in and the operation of said factories, and to subject the same to the direction and control of persons other than the owners of the same, in a manner extremely onerous and distasteful to such owners, and to carry out such scheme, effort and purpose by restraining and destroying the interstate trade and commerce of such manufacturers, by means of intimidation of and threats made to such manufacturers and their customers in the several states, of boycotting them, their product and their customers, using therefor [sic] all the powerful means at their command, as aforesaid, until such time as, from the damage and loss of business resulting therefrom, the said manufacturers should yield to the said demand to unionize their factories.

That the conspiracy or combination was so far progressed that out of eighty-two manufacturers of this country engaged in the production of fur hats, seventy had accepted the terms and acceded to the demand that the shop should be conducted in accordance, so far as conditions of employment were concerned, with the will of the American Federation of Labor; that the local union demanded of plaintiffs that they should unionize their shop under peril of being boycotted by this combination, which demand plaintiffs declined to comply with; that thereupon the American Federation of Labor, acting through its official organ and through its organizers, declared a boycott. . . .

The averments here are that there was an existing interstate traffic between plaintiffs and citizens of other states, and that, for the direct purpose of destroying such interstate traffic, defendants combined not merely to prevent plaintiffs from manufacturing articles then and there intended for transportation beyond the state, but also to prevent the vendees from reselling the hats which they had imported from Connecticut, or from further negotiating with plaintiffs for the purchase and intertransportation of such hats from Connecticut to the various places of destination. So that, although some of the means whereby the interstate traffic was to be destroyed were acts within a state, and some of them were, in themselves, as a part of their obvious purpose and effect, beyond the scope of Federal authority, still, as we have seen, the acts must be considered as a whole, and the plan is open to condemnation, notwithstanding a negligible amount of intrastate business might be affected in carrying it out. If the purposes of the combination were, as alleged, to prevent any interstate transportation at all, the fact that the means operated at one end before physical transportation commenced, and, at the other end, after the physical transportation ended, was immaterial.

Nor can the act in question be held inapplicable because defendants were not themselves engaged in interstate commerce. The act made no distinction between classes. It provided that "every" contract, combination, or conspiracy in restraint of trade was illegal. The records of Congress show that several efforts were made to exempt, by legislation, organizations of farmers and laborers from the operation of the act, and that all these efforts failed, so that the act remained as we have it before us. . . .

In our opinion, the combination described in the declaration is a combination "in restraint of trade or commerce among the several states," in the sense in which those words are used in the act, and the action can be maintained accordingly.

And that conclusion rests on many judgments of this court, to the effect that the act prohibits any combination whatever to secure action which essentially obstructs the free flow of commerce between the states, or restricts, in that regard, the liberty of a trader to engage in business.

The combination charged falls within the class of restraints of trade aimed at compelling third parties and strangers involuntarily not to engage in the course of trade except on conditions that the combination imposes; and there is no doubt that (to quote from the well-known work of Chief Justice Erle on Trade Unions)

"at common law every person has individually, and the public also has collectively, a right to require that the course of trade should be kept free from unreasonable obstruction."

But the objection here is to the jurisdiction, because, even conceding that the declaration states a case good at common law, it is contended that it does not state one within the statute. Thus, it is said, that the restraint alleged would operate to entirely destroy plaintiffs' business and thereby include intrastate trade as well; that physical obstruction is not alleged as contemplated; and that defendants are not themselves engaged in interstate trade.

We think none of these objections are tenable, and that they are disposed of by previous decisions of this court. . . .

Judgment reversed and case remanded with a direction to proceed accordingly.

The case of *Loewe* v. *Lawlor* was thus remanded back to lower courts for trial. In 1914, the case reached the Supreme Court again and Justice Holmes delivered the following opinion:

LOEWE v. LAWLOR: 1915
(235 U.S. 522)

The Supreme Court of the United States, opinion delivered by Mr. Justice Holmes:

. . . The substance of the charge is that the plaintiffs were hat manufacturers who employed nonunion labor; that the defendants were members of the United Hatters of North America and also of the American Federation of Labor; that in pursuance of a general scheme to unionize the labor employed by manufacturers of fur hats (a purpose previously made effective against all but a few manufacturers), the defendants and other members of the United Hatters caused the American Federation of Labor to declare a boycott against the plaintiffs and against all hats sold by the plaintiffs to dealers in other states, and against dealers who should deal in them; and that they carried out their plan with such success that they have restrained or destroyed the plaintiffs' commerce with other states. The case now has been tried, the plaintiffs have got a verdict and the judgment of the district court has been affirmed by the circuit court of appeals. . . .

The grounds for discussion under the statute that were not cut away by the decision upon the demurrer have been narrowed still further since the trial by the case of *Eastern States Retail Lumber Dealers' Asso.* v. *U.S.*, 23d U.S. 600. Whatever may be the law otherwise, that case establishes that, irrespective of compulsion or even agreement to observe its intimation, the circulation of a list of "unfair dealers," manifestly intended to put the ban upon those whose names appear therein, among an important body of possible customers, combined with a view to joint action and in anticipation of such reports, is within the prohibitions of the Sherman Act if it is intended to restrain and restrains commerce among the states.

It requires more than the blindness of justice not to see that many branches of the United Hatters and the Federation of Labor, to both of which the defendants belonged, in pursuance of a plan emanating from headquarters, made use of such lists and of the primary and secondary boycott in their effort to subdue the plaintiffs to their demands. The union label was used and a strike of the plaintiffs' employees was ordered and carried out to the same end, and the purpose to break up the plaintiffs' commerce affected the quality of the acts. . . . We agree with the circuit court of appeals that a combination and conspiracy forbidden by the statute were proved, and that the question is narrowed to the responsibility of the defendant for what was done by the sanction and procurement of the societies above named.

The court in substance instructed the jury that if these members paid their dues and continued to delegate authority to their officers unlawfully to interfere with the plaintiffs' interstate commerce in such circumstances that they knew or ought to have known, and such officers were warranted in the belief that they were acting in the matter within their delegated authority, then such members were jointly liable, and no others. It seems to us that this instruction sufficiently guarded the defendants' rights, and that the defendants got all that they were entitled to ask in not being held chargeable with knowledge as matter of law. It is a tax on credulity to ask anyone to believe that members of labor unions at that time did not know that the primary and secondary boycott and the use of the "We don't patronize" or "Unfair" list were means expected to be employed in the effort to unionize shops. Very possibly they were thought to be lawful. See *Gompers* v. *United States,* 233 U.S. 604. By the Constitution of the United Hatters the directors are to use "all the means in their power" to bring shops "not under our jurisdiction" "into the trade." The by-laws provide a separate fund to be kept for strikes, lockouts, and agitation for the union label. Members are forbidden to sell nonunion hats. The Federation of Labor, with which the Hatters were affiliated, had organization of labor for one of its objects, helped affiliated unions in trade disputes, and to that end, before the present trouble, had provided in its constitution for prosecuting and had prosecuted many what it called legal boycotts. Their conduct in this and former cases was made public, especially among the members, in every possible way. If the words of the documents, on their face and without explanation, did not authorize what was done, the evidence of what was done publicly and habitually showed their meaning and how they were interpreted. The jury could not but find that by the usage of the unions the acts complained of were authorized, and authorized without regard to their interference with commerce among the states. We think it unnecessary to repeat the evidence of the publicity of this particular struggle in the common newspapers and union prints, evidence that made it al-

most inconceivable that the defendants, all living in the neighborhood of the plaintiffs, did not know what was done in the specific
case. If they did not know that, they were bound to know the constitution of their societies, and at least well might be found to have
known how the words of those constitutions had been construed in
act. . . .

We need not repeat or add to what was said by the circuit
court of appeals with regard to evidence of the payment of dues
after this suit was begun. And, in short, neither the argument nor
the perusal of the voluminous brief for the plaintiffs in error shows
that they suffered any injustice, or that there was any error requiring the judgment to be reversed.

Thus, the *Danbury Hatters* case was one of the first in a series of numerous court decisions that defined the position of organized labor in
relation to anti-trust legislation. The decision jolted the union labor
movement, as they recognized that the court had read into statutory
law a provision detrimental to its cause. Needless to say, the union
movement was thwarted in the use of the boycott weapon under penalty of being responsible individually as members for damage awards.
As a consequence, the leaders of the labor movement became actively
involved in seeking legislation that would declare the union immune
from anti-trust law.

GOMPERS V. BUCK STOVE DECISION

Another dramatic anti-union decision was rendered in *Gompers* v.
Buck Stove that added more impetus to the unions' search for statutory legislation to remove them from the jurisdiction of anti-trust legislation.[7] In the *Gompers* decision, the American Federation of Labor
published a "do not patronize" list in its magazine. This incident
leading to the near imprisonment of the top leaders of the labor
movement started when the Buck Stove Company reestablished a 10-
hour day in early 1906, after some two years of operation on a 9-hour
day. The court in the District of Columbia enjoined the magazine on
the grounds that it constituted an illegal secondary boycott. The Supreme Court in its 1911 opinion found Gompers and other leaders
guilty of contempt of court for violating the injunction, although the
lower court's jail sentences were reversed.

The local union instituted a boycott and received the help of the

[7] 221 U.S. 418 (1911).

American Federation of Labor that publicized the company as an unfair employer. J. W. Van Cleave, the president of the company, was also president of the National Association of Manufacturers. With the assistance and encouragement of the latter group, as well as an employers association known as the American Anti-Boycott Association, Van Cleave charged the American Federation of Labor and certain of its leaders with an unlawful combination and conspiracy to destroy his business through the "we don't patronize" boycott list that appeared in the American Federationist. The request for injunctive relief was initiated in the Supreme Court of the District of Columbia, which granted relief and found the union defendants guilty. Subsequently, charges of criminal contempt of court were filed against Gompers and two other leaders of the American Federation of Labor for violating the injunction. Two days before Christmas in 1908 they were found guilty and sentenced to jail terms, the longest (12 months) being assessed against Gompers. The one year sentence to jail imposed against the leader of the American Federation of Labor severely upset the union movement. By the time the case reached the Supreme Court on first appeal in 1911, the initial disputants (the local Electrotypers' Union and Buck Stove Company) had negotiated a settlement, but the Anti-Boycott Association that had financed the costly litigation would not allow the case to be withdrawn by the company. Justice Holmes, in delivering the opinion of the court, found the defendants guilty but reversed the decision of contempt of court and the jail sentences on a technicality (expiration of the statute of limitations). Nevertheless, the constitutional guarantee of freedom of the press sought by the union in this case was thus denied, and the boycott as a union weapon of conflict was blunted.

The Clayton Act: Attempted Trade Union Relief

The *Danbury Hatters* and *Buck Stove* decisions spurred organized labor into direct legislative lobbying that resulted in the passage of the Clayton Act in 1914 (see Appendix 3 B). This statute was intended to amend the Sherman Act and clarify the position of organized labor under the Sherman Act as well as regulate the issuance of labor injunctions. The labor movement was elated upon passage of this act under President Woodrow Wilson's administration, but their joy was short-lived indeed. Hailed as labor's Magna Charta, the Clayton Act soon proved to do more damage than good because the court failed to extricate labor from the anti-trust cobweb as Congress seemingly ordered, and the Clayton Act made it possible for employers other than the government to obtain injunctive relief under the Sherman Act.

Two sections of the Clayton Act were directed towards labor and the anti-trust and injunction issues. Section 6 of this act declared that

> nothing in the anti-trust law forbids the operation of labor, agricultural or horticultural organizations. The law does not forbid nor restrict members of such organizations from carrying out lawful objectives. Neither such organizations nor their members are to be regarded as illegal combinations or conspiracies in restraint of trade under the anti-trust laws.

While these assertions appear on the surface to clearly establish the legal positions of organized labor, such was not the case. The interpretation of the Clayton Act and its applicability to labor rests upon the words "lawfully carrying out legitimate objectives." The court, of course, decided what was a lawful means and a legitimate objective. In other words, the Supreme Court could, and did, regard the union as guilty of an offense under the Sherman Act so long as the "lawful-legitimate" conditions were not met.

Section 20 of the Clayton Act prohibited issuing injunctions in instances involving a strike, boycott, or picketing activities in disputes between employees and employers concerning terms or conditions of employment. Unfortunately from the labor movement's point of view, Section 20 continued by stipulating that a restraining order or injunction could be granted if it was necessary to prevent irreparable injury to property or a property right for which no other appropriate remedy at law existed. This stipulation of conditions under which injunctions could be issued nullified the injunction-limiting intent apparent in the congressional passage of this legislation.

COURT EXTENSION OF ANTI-TRUST LEGISLATION

In spite of the passage of the Clayton Act, the use of the injunction became an even more popular employer weapon of conflict after 1914.[8] The Supreme Court grappled with the meaning of the Clayton Act as a modification of the earlier-passed Sherman Anti-Trust Act in three strategic court decisions. In the *Duplex, Coronado Coal Com-*

---

[8] One scholar has found that nearly 1900 requests for injunctive relief were heard between 1890 and 1931, and some 1750 such requests were granted. E. E. Witte, *The Government in Labor Disputes* (New York: McGraw-Hill Co., 1932), pp. 63–65.

pany, and *Bedford Cut Stone* cases, the Supreme Court reaffirmed the applicability of anti-trust legislation to the union, continued the imposition of triple damage awards against unions in violation of the Sherman Act, and actually extended the use of the injunction.[9] In the process of rendering these decisions, the court also established a "rule of reason" for labor organizations as they had done earlier in applying anti-trust legislation to corporate institutions.[10] This "rule of reason" meant that the court would take it upon itself to inquire into the conduct and motives in any labor-management dispute, and rule accordingly. This created what Justice Brandeis later argued was another "double standard" between labor and corporate institutions.

The Duplex v. Deering Decision. In rendering the decision on the first of these three important cases, the Court made a sharp distinction between primary and secondary boycotts. This distinction came out of the *Duplex* case, in which the court noted that a primary boycott is directed against the employer immediately involved in the dispute whereas the secondary boycott may be directed against persons dealing with the employer that is in dispute.

The optimistic view that the Clayton Act would in fact breathe new legal life into the labor union movement was quickly dispelled in the *Duplex* case. The Clayton Act, as the reader will recall, was designed to limit indiscriminate and blanket issuance of injunctions and to protect the union against prosecution under the Sherman Act. This was expected to be accomplished by specifically spelling out that the union movement was not an illegal combination in restraint of trade and that peaceful and legal labor-management disputes could not be enjoined. At the time of the *Duplex* case, only one of the four manufacturers of printing press equipment in the United States was unorganized. The Duplex Company maintained longer hours and lower wage scales than the organized shops. The unionized companies informed the International Association of Machinists that Duplex was presenting them with severe competition. The three organized companies also informed the union that unless labor standards were standardized within the industry, including those at the Duplex Company, the unionized companies would no longer negotiate with the

[9] *Duplex Printing Press Company* v. *Deering*, 254 U.S. 443 (1921); *United Mine Workers of America* v. *Coronado Coal Company*, 268 U.S. 595 (1925); and *Bedford Cut Stone Company* v. *Journeyman Stone Cutters' Association*, 274 U.S. 37 (1927).

[10] It should be noted that the Sherman Act was thus applied to corporate monopoly powers for which it was intended and not just labor organizations.

union. The union then called a strike at the Duplex plant, but only a handful of several hundred workers responded. A picket line was established, but it was unsuccessful in hindering Duplex operations. As a consequence, the union applied additional secondary economic pressures against Duplex by encouraging other locals of the union to refuse to handle Duplex presses.[11] The company immediately sought injunctive relief from the state of New York. In April of 1914, temporary relief was granted without a hearing (an *ex parte* injunction) until a trial could be held.

Some three years later, the temporary injunction was vacated by the lower court of New York when Justice Manton noted that the record did not show circumstances that warranted granting the injunction sought. Justice Manton stipulated that the strike was orderly and lawful and for a lawful purpose and the hardships caused the company were not sufficient to warrant injunctive relief. While moving through the United States Circuit Court of Appeals in 1918, the decision of the lower court was affirmed since the judicial tribunal ruled that the union activities, including the secondary boycott, were not in violation of the Sherman Act as amended by Section 20 of the Clayton Act. The company then appealed to the United States Supreme Court, where the decision was reversed and judgment was found against the union. Justice Pitney presented the following argument and opinion for the Supreme Court:

DUPLEX PRINTING PRESS COMPANY v. DEERING: 1921
(254 U.S. 443)

The Supreme Court of the United States, Mr. Justice Pitney delivering the majority opinion:

. . . Complainant is a Michigan corporation, and manufactures printing presses at a factory in Battle Creek, in that state, employing about 200 machinists in the factory in addition to 50 office employees, traveling salesmen, and expert machinists or road men who supervise the erection of the presses for complainant's customers at their various places of business. The defendants, who were brought into court and answered the bill, are Emil J. Deering and William Bramley, sued individually and as business agents and representatives of District No. 15 of the International Association

[11] E. J. Deering, who was a business agent for the International Association of Machinists, also attempted to prevent the Duplex Company from advertising its products at a New York commercial fair.

of Machinists, and Michael T. Neyland, sued individually and as business agent and representative of local Lodge No. 328, of the same association. The District Council and the lodge are unincorporated associations having headquarters in New York City, with numerous members resident in that city and vicinity. . . .

The jurisdiction of the Federal court was invoked both by reason of diverse citizenship and on the ground that defendants were engaged in a conspiracy to restrain complainant's interstate trade and commerce in printing presses, contrary to the Sherman Anti-Trust Act of July 2, 1890. . . . The suit was begun before, but brought to hearing after the passage of the Clayton Act of October 15, 1914. . . . Both parties invoked the provisions of the latter act, and both courts treated them as applicable. Complainant relied also upon the common law; but we shall deal first with the effect of the acts of Congress. . . .

Complainant conducts its business on the "open-shop" policy, without discrimination against either union or nonunion men. The individual defendants and the local organizations of which they are the representatives are affiliated with the International Association of Machinists, an unincorporated association having a membership of more than 60,000, and are united in a combination, to which the International Association also is a party, having the object of compelling complainant to unionize its factory, and enforce the "closed shop," the eight-hour day, and the union scale of wages, by means of interfering with and restraining its interstate trade in the products of the factory. Complainant's principal manufacture is newspaper presses of large size and complicated mechanism, varying in weight from 10,000 to 100,000 pounds, and requiring a considerable force of labor and a considerable expenditure of time . . . to handle, haul, and erect them at the point of delivery. These presses are sold throughout the United States and in foreign countries; and, as they are especially designed for the production of daily papers, there is a large market for them in and about the city of New York. They are delivered there in the ordinary course of interstate commerce, the handling, hauling, and installation work at destination being done by employees of the purchaser, under the supervision of a specially skilled machinist supplied by complainant. The acts complained of and sought to be restrained having nothing to do with the conduct or management of the factory in Michigan, but solely with the installation and operation of the presses by complainant's customers. None of the defendants is or ever was an employee of complainant, and complainant at no time has had relations with either of the organizations that they represent.

In August, 1913 (eight months before the filing of the bill), the International Association called a strike at complainant's factory in Battle Creek, as a result of which union machinists to the number of about eleven in the factory, and three who supervised the erection of presses in the field, left complainant's employ. But the defection of so small a number did not materially interfere with the operation of the factory, and sales and shipments in interstate commerce continued. The acts complained of made up the details of an elaborate program adopted and carried out by defendants and their organizations in and about the city of New York as part of a country-wide program adopted by the International Association, for the purpose of enforcing a boycott of complainant's product. The acts embraced the following, with others: Warning customers that it would be better for them not to purchase, or, having purchased, not to install, presses made by complainant, and threatening them with loss should they do so; threatening customers with sympathetic strikes in other trades; notifying a trucking company usually employed by customers to haul the presses not to do so, and threatening it with trouble if it should; inciting employees of the trucking company, and other men employed by customers of complainant, to strike against their respective employers, in order to interfere with the hauling and installation of presses, and thus bring pressure to bear upon the customers; notifying repair shops not to do repair work on Duplex presses; coercing union men by threatening them with loss of union cards and with being blacklisted as "scabs" if they assisted in installing the presses; threatening an exposition company with a strike if it permitted complainant's presses to be exhibited; and resorting to a variety of other modes of preventing the sale of presses of complainant's manufacture in or about New York City, and delivery of them in interstate commerce, such as injuring and threatening to injure complainant's customers and prospective customers, and persons concerned in hauling, handling, or installing the presses. In some cases the threats were undisguised; in other cases polite in form, but none the less sinister in purpose and effect. All the judges of the circuit court of appeals concurred in the view that defendants' conduct consisted essentially of efforts to render it impossible for complainant to carry on any commerce in printing presses between Michigan and New York; . . . The judges also agreed that the interference with interstate commerce was such as ought to be enjoined, unless the Clayton Act of October 15, 1914, forbade such injunction.

That act was passed after the beginning of the suit, but more than two years before it was brought to hearing. We are clear that the courts below were right in giving effect to it; the real question being, whether they gave it the proper effect. In so far as the act (a) provided for relief by injunction to private suitors, (b) imposed conditions upon granting such relief under particular circumstances, and (c) otherwise modified the Sherman Act, it was effective from the time of its passage, and applicable to pending suits for injunction. . . . The Clayton Act, . . . includes the Sherman Act in a definition of "anti-trust laws," and, . . . gives to private parties a right to relief by injunction in any court of the United States against threatened loss or damage by a violation of the Anti-Trust Laws, under the conditions and principles regulating the granting of such relief by courts of equity. Evidently this provision was intended to supplement the Sherman Act. . . .

The substance of the matters here complained of is an interference with complainant's interstate trade, intended to have coercive effect upon complainant, and produced by what is commonly known as a "secondary boycott;" that is, a combination not merely to refrain from dealing with complainant, or to advise or by peaceful means persuade complainant's customers to refrain ("primary boycott"), but to exercise coercive pressure upon such customers, actual or prospective, in order to cause them to withhold or withdraw patronage from complainant through fear of loss or damage to themselves should they deal with it.

As we shall see, the recognized distinction between a primary and a secondary boycott is material to be considered upon the question of the proper construction of the Clayton Act. But, in determining the right to an injunction under that and the Sherman Act, it is of minor consequence whether either kind of boycott is lawful or unlawful at common law or under the statutes of particular states. Those acts, passed in the exercise of the power of Congress to regulate commerce among the states, are of paramount authority, and their prohibitions must be given full effect irrespective of whether the things prohibited are lawful or unlawful at common law or under local statutes. . . . Such a restraint produced by peaceable persuasion is as much within the prohibition as one accomplished by force or threats of force; and it is not to be justified by the fact that the participants in the combination or conspiracy may have some object beneficial to themselves or their associates which possibly they might have been at liberty to pursue in the absence of the statute.

Upon the question whether the provisions of the Clayton Act forbade the grant of an injunction under the circumstances of the present case, the circuit court of appeals was divided; the majority holding that under Section 20, "perhaps in conjunction with Section 6," there could be no injunction. . . . Defendants seek to derive from them some authority for their conduct. As to Section 6, it seems to us its principal importance in this discussion is for what it does *not* authorize, and for the limit it sets to the immunity conferred. The section assumes the normal objects of a labor organization to be *legitimate* objects; and that such an organization shall not be held in itself—merely because of its existence and operation—to be an illegal combination or conspiracy in restraint of trade. But there is nothing in the section to exempt such an organization or its members from accountability where it or they depart from its normal and legitimate objects, and engage in an actual combination or conspiracy in restraint of trade. And by no fair or permissible construction can it be taken as authorizing any activity otherwise unlawful, or enabling a normally lawful organization to become a cloak for an illegal combination or conspiracy in restraint of trade, as defined by the Anti-Trust Laws.

Section 20 . . . regulates the granting of restraining orders and injunctions by the courts of the United States in a designated class of cases, with respect to (a) the terms and conditions of the relief and the practice to be pursued, and (b) the character of acts that are to be exempted from the restraint; and in the concluding words it declares (c) that none of the acts specified shall be held to be violations of any law of the United States. All its provisions are subject to a general qualification respecting the nature of the controversy and the parties affected. It is to be a "case between an employer and employees, or between employers and employees, or between employees, or between persons employed and persons seeking employment, involving, or growing out of, a dispute concerning terms or conditions of employment."

The first paragraph merely puts into statutory form familiar restrictions upon the granting of injunctions already established and of general application in the equity practice of the courts of the

United States. It is but declaratory of the law as it stood before. The second paragraph declares that "no such restraining order or injunction" shall prohibit certain conduct specified,—manifestly still referring to a "case between an employer and employees, . . . involving, or growing out of, a dispute concerning terms or conditions of employment," as designated in the first paragraph. It is very clear that the restriction upon the use of the injunction is in favor only of those concerned as parties to such a dispute as is described. The words defining the permitted conduct include particular qualifications consistent with the general one respecting the nature of the case and dispute intended; and the concluding words "nor shall any of the acts specified in this paragraph be considered or held to be violations of any law of the United States," are to be read in the light of the context, and mean only that those acts are not to be so held, when committed by parties concerned in "a dispute concerning terms or conditions of employment." If the qualifying words are to have any effect, they must operate to confine the restriction upon the granting of injunctions, and also the relaxation of the provisions of the anti-trust and other laws of the United States, to parties standing in proximate relation in a controversy such as is particularly described.

The majority of the circuit court of appeals appear to have entertained the view that the words "employers and employees," . . . should be treated as referring to "the business class or clan to which the parties litigant respectively belong:" and that, as there had been a dispute at complainant's factory in Michigan concerning the conditions of employment there,—a dispute created, it is said, if it did not exist before, by the act of the Machinists' Union in calling a strike at the factory,—Section 20 operated to permit members of the Machinists' Union elsewhere,—some 60,000 in number,—although standing in no relation of employment under complainant, past, present, or prospective, to make that dispute their own, and proceed to instigate sympathetic strikes, picketing, and boycotting against employers wholly unconnected with complainant's factory, and having relations with complainant only in the way of purchasing its product in the ordinary course of interstate commerce,—and this where there was no dispute between such employers and their employees respecting terms or conditions of employment.

We deem this construction altogether inadmissible. Section 20 must be given full effect according to its terms as an expression of the purpose of Congress; but it must be borne in mind that the section imposes an exceptional and extraordinary restriction upon the equity powers of the courts of the United States, and upon the general operation of the Anti-Trust Laws,—a restriction in the nature of a special privilege or immunity to a particular class, with corresponding detriment to the general public; . . .

Nor can Section 20 be regarded as bringing in all members of a labor organization as parties to a "dispute concerning terms and conditions of employment" which proximately affects only a few of them, with the result of conferring upon any and all members,— no matter how many thousands there may be, nor how remote from the actual conflict—those exemptions which Congress in terms conferred only upon parties to the dispute. That would enlarge . . . Section 20, which contains no mention of labor organizations, so as to produce an inconsistency with Section 6, which deals specifically with the subject and must be deemed to express the measure and limit of the immunity intended by Congress to be incident to mere membership in such an organization. At the same time it would virtually repeal by implication the prohibition of the Sherman Act, so far as labor organizations are concerned, notwithstanding repeals by implication are not favored; . . .

. . . The emphasis placed on the words "lawful" and "lawfully," "peaceful" and "peacefully," and the references to the dispute and the parties to it, strongly rebut a legislative intent to confer a general immunity for conduct violative of the Anti-Trust Laws, or otherwise unlawful. The subject of the boycott is dealt with specifically in the "ceasing to patronize" provision, and by the clear force of the language employed the exemption is limited to pressure exerted upon a "party to such dispute" by means of "peaceful and *lawful*" influence upon neutrals. There is nothing here to justify defendants or the organizations they represent in using either threats or persuasion to bring about strikes or a cessation of work on the part of employees of complainant's customers or prospective customers, . . . with the object of compelling such customers to withdraw or refrain from commercial relations with complainant, and of thereby constraining complainant to yield the matter in dispute. To instigate a sympathetic strike in aid of a secondary boycott cannot be deemed "peaceful and lawful" persuasion. In essence it is a threat to inflict damage upon the immediate employer, between whom and his employees no dispute exists, in order to bring him against his will into a concerted plan to inflict damage upon another employer who is in dispute with his employees. . . .

Complainant has a clear right to an injunction under the Sherman Act, as amended by the Clayton Act. . . . There should be an injunction against defendants and the associations represented by them. . . .

Mr. Justice Brandeis, in dissent, noted:

. . . May not all with a common interest join in refusing to expend their labor upon articles whose very production constitutes an attack upon their standard of living and the institution which they are convinced supports it? Applying common-law principles the answer should, in my opinion, be: Yes, if as matter of fact, those who so cooperate have a common interest.

The change in the law by which strikes once illegal and even criminal are now recognized as lawful was effected in America largely without the intervention of legislation. This reversal of a common-law rule was not due to the rejection by the courts of one principle and the adoption in its stead of another, but to a better realization of the facts of industrial life. It is conceded that, although the strike of the workmen in plaintiff's factory injured its business, the strike was not an actionable wrong, because the obvious self-interest of the strikers constituted a justification. . . . A single employer might, as in this case, threaten the standing of the whole organization and the standards of all its members; and when he did so the union, in order to protect itself, would naturally refuse to work on his materials wherever found. I have come to the conclusion that both the common law of a state and a statute of the United States declare the right of industrial combatants to push their struggle to the limits of the justification of self-interest. . . .

In this split decision, the Supreme Court noted that Section 6 of the Clayton Act failed to provide the union with legal immunities not provided prior to its passage. By this refusal on the part of the Supreme Court to recognize the existence of a union interest in cases involving nonunion employment, the court found that the Duplex Company had "a clear right to an injunction under the Sherman Act as amended by the Clayton Act." The wording of the Clayton Act required the union to lawfully carry out legitimate objectives, but the act did not stipulate that the unions were immune from liability when the means used resulted in restraint of trade. Consequently the union, which was regarded as only a nominally lawful institution by courts, was held in this instance to be an illegal combination in restraint of trade because it was exercising "illegal" secondary pressures.

It also will be recalled that Section 20 did not permit injunctions in disputes between employees and employers. The Supreme Court interpreted employers and employees narrowly in the *Duplex* decision, noting that none of the persons engaged in sympathy strikes or boycotts was a direct employee of the Duplex Company. As a consequence, an injunction could be issued legally. The decision of the Court was unchanged in spite of sharp criticism issued in the form of a dissenting opinion by Justice Brandeis that recognized employees of nonunion manufacturers to be of *immediate* and close interest to unionized workers. After the *Duplex* case, increased opposition to the union movement was generated, and more applications for injunctive relief on the part of employers were encouraged.

The Coronado Coal Case. Still a second and even more confusing decision, reaffirming the *Danbury Hatters* and *Duplex* decisions that found the union movement responsible to Sherman Act provisions was rendered in 1925 in the *Coronado Coal* cases. This dispute originated in the explosive coal country of Prairie Creek, Arkansas, in the same year that the Clayton Act was passed. One Franklin Bache, a mine engineer and operator, broke his contract with the United Mine Workers' Union in 1914. Bache had reluctantly signed with the union some three years earlier after the union had successfully defied the Southwestern Coal Operators' Association of Employers. Strikebreakers, guards, and United States marshals who were brought into the community precipitated several riots and other incidents that led to death and property destruction while they were protecting the Coronado Coal Company mines. The plaintiff consisted of nine associated coal companies who charged that they were engaged in interstate commerce and that the United Mine Workers had conspired to restrain commerce. The Union's action was alleged to have caused losses and damages amounting to over $400,000 which, under the Sherman Act, allowed a damage suit in the amount of 1.2 million dollars. After the case had moved through the lower courts, the plaintiff increased the amount of the damages sought, indicating that they had suffered losses totaling $740,000 for which 2.2 million dollars in triple damages was sought. The decision of the lower court resulted in an award to the plaintiff's combination of $720,000 for triple damages sustained with the assistance of Judge Elliot's "recommendation." [12] The union appealed the case.

[12] In his instructions to the jury, Judge Elliot noted that . . . "the court's opinion was that the Union's purpose in the complaint was unlawful." Lieberman, *op. cit.*, p. 149.

In 1922, the Supreme Court reversed the lower court's decision finding the union guilty, and thus denied the damages which the company had been awarded because of the alleged violation of the Sherman Act. To have ruled otherwise would have meant that almost any kind of strike activity would have fallen under the "indirect restraint of trade" concept, and Chief Justice Taft apparently realized that this bordered on areas outside of the federal jurisdiction. Thus, in spite of the fact that the court had ruled against the union in the *Danbury Hatters* case (which had directly affected commerce), the Court held in favor of United Mine Workers in this, the first *Coronado Coal* case.

A little more than a year after the 1922 decision of the Supreme Court, a second *Coronado* case was introduced. This time the company acquired the testimony of several witnesses, including former members of the union, who testified that the union had indeed intended to keep coal from reaching the interstate market. This testimony was critical, since the earlier Supreme Court decision had overruled the lower court's award for the company because it had not found evidence of intent to restrain interstate commerce. In 1925, the Supreme Court unanimously held in favor of the Company after admitting this new evidence. The union was found guilty of violating the Sherman Act, and the court therefore overruled its 1922 decision in the original Coronado case. No doubt triple damages would have been awarded, except for the fact that the participants in the case were worn out after the thirteen years of litigation and settled out of court for $27,500 in damages. As a consequence of the Coronado decision, however, the courts had left the door open for future judicial rulings in similar instances. Thus, the flexibility of judicial power continued to present a perplexing problem to the union movement and labor sympathizers.

The Bedford Cut Stone Decision. The *Bedford* case was also brought before the courts on the basis of violation of the anti-trust laws, and the consequences of this decision were to further restrain union organizing activity in the late 1920's. The Journeymen Stone Cutters' Association was a relatively old and unaggressive organization until about 1921. At that time, stone producers (then concentrated in Indiana) refused to continue to deal with the union and instituted a lockout. Some 24 companies combined forces and contrived to employ nonunion workers; then they organized these new employees into separate "Workers' Organizations" (company unions), and required any stonecutter to become a member of this organization as a condition of employment. Sympathetic boycott activities were initiated by the union because strike activities conducted by the original

union were ineffective. The Bedford Cut Stone Company was concerned about the possible loss of business because of the boycott activities, and it sought injunctive relief under Section 16 of the Clayton
Act.[13] After the lower court had denied injunctive relief, the company
appealed the case to the Supreme Court in 1927. The Supreme Court
reversed the decision of the Circuit Court of Appeals and ordered
that the injunction be granted after finding the union guilty of undue
and unreasonable restraint of trade. The court noted that the union
was a lawful organization and its purposes were lawful, but the
means employed (refusing to handle nonunion limestone shipped
from Indiana) was an illegal means of obtaining legal objectives. In
effect, the court ruled that effectiveness of a legal objective (a strike)
could not be enhanced by pursuing illegal means, in this instance secondary boycotting pressures.

Thus, the *Bedford* decision denied the right to union members to
refuse to work on goods produced by nonunion workers who had
been organized into an employer-dominated union. This was in direct
conflict and opposition to the objectives of the organized union movement. Perhaps most important, the *Bedford* decision validated the
awarding of injunctions to private parties under Section 16 of the
Clayton Act. It became quite apparent to organized labor that the
legal status of the movement had reached a new low in its search for
rights comparable to those granted to the employer. While Justice
Brandeis pointed out in his dissent in the *Bedford Cut Stone* decision
that the court held only *un*reasonable restraint of trade to apply to
business, this same interpretation was not made in disputes involving
labor. The *Duplex, Coronado,* and *Bedford* decisions typify the po-
tency of anti-trust laws and injunctions and give an indication of the
difficulty that the unions encountered in trying to function in the rapidly industrializing society of the early twentieth century. It seemed
very apparent to those associated with the labor movement that much
more direct congressional pressure was necessary than in the past.

Nevertheless, the labor movement had made some significant
strides since the close of the Civil War. Legislation had been enacted
on behalf of the union movement, and the American Federation of
Labor demonstrated a continuing viability during this half-century.
Member nationals of the American Federation of Labor were not experiencing very rapid growth, due in part to their ineptness in organizing an industrial labor force increasingly devoid of craft alliances as

[13] Section 16 of Clayton permitted private parties to apply for injunctions in instances restraining interstate commerce. The Sherman Anti-Trust
Act gave only the federal government authority to seek injunctions.

well as legal oppression. Indeed, certain legislation was on the books at the turn of the century that was suggestive of a better future—the topic to which we now turn our attention.

Summary

The second attempt to develop a national labor movement, The National Labor Union, met with failure a few years after the Civil War. Once again labor tried to organize nationally in conjunction with other social-reform advocates and failed as the Knights of Labor collapsed. The American Federation of Labor, which followed this failure, represented the first success at national unification. The combined forces of employers and the law hampered the movement, however, as injunctions, anti-trust laws, and yellow-dog contracts increased in use and efficacy. The trial and conviction of Eugene Debs *et al.* for violating an injunction in the Pullman strike highlighted new restraints on labor as we noted in Chapter II. Both the Hatters' Union and Sam Gompers (in the *Buck Stove* case) felt the brunt of the Sherman Anti-Trust Act in early instances of court treatment of unions as a labor "monopoly." This prompted organized labor to seek relief, and the Clayton Act was passed in 1914. Unfortunately, the courts did not remove the union from anti-trust prosecution as appears to have been the intent of Congress in the Clayton Act. Rather, the *Duplex, Coronado Coal,* and *Bedford Cut Stone* decisions all reaffirmed the applicability of anti-trust laws to the union, and extended the effectiveness of injunctions.

APPENDIX 3 A

The Sherman Anti-Trust Act
(*July 2, 1890, 51st Congress*)

SECTION 1 That every contract, combination in the form of trust or otherwise, or conspiracy, in restraint of trade or commerce among the several States, or with foreign nations, is hereby declared to be illegal: *Provided,* That nothing herein contained shall render illegal, contracts or agreements prescribing minimum prices for the resale of a commodity which bears, or the label or container of which bears, the trade mark, brand, or name of the producer or distributor of such commodity and which is in free and open competition with commodities of the same general class produced or distributed by others, when contracts or agreements of that description are lawful as applied to intrastate transactions, under any statute, law, or public policy now or hereafter in effect in any State, Territory, or the District of Columbia in which such resale is to be made, or to which the commodity is to be transported for such resale, and the making of such contracts or agreements shall not be an unfair method of competition under section 5, as amended and supplemented, of the Act entitled "An Act to create a Federal Trade Commission, to define its powers and duties, and for other purposes", approved September 26, 1914: *Provided further,* That the preceding proviso shall not make lawful any contract or agreement, providing for the establishment or maintenance of minimum resale prices on any commodity herein involved, between manufacturers, or between producers, or between wholesalers, or between brokers, or between factors, or between retailers, or between persons, firms, or corporations in competition with each other. Every person who shall make any contract or engage in any combination or conspiracy hereby declared to be illegal shall be deemed guilty of a misdemeanor, and, on conviction thereof, shall be punished by fine not exceeding fifty thousand dollars, or by imprisonment not exceeding one year, or by both said punishments, in the discretion of the court.

SEC. 2 Every person who shall monopolize, or attempt to monopolize, or combine or conspire with any other person or persons, to monopolize any part of the trade or commerce among the several States, or with foreign nations, shall be deemed guilty of a misdemeanor, and, on conviction thereof, shall be punished by fine not exceeding fifty thousand dollars, or by imprisonment not exceeding one year, or by both said punishments, in the discretion of the court.

.   .   .   .   .

SEC. 4 The several circuit courts of the United States are hereby invested with jurisdiction to prevent and restrain violations of this act; and it shall be the duty of the several district attorneys of the United States, in their respective districts, under the direction of the Attorney-General, to institute proceedings in equity to prevent and restrain such violations. Such proceedings may be by way of petition setting forth the case and praying that such violation shall be enjoined or otherwise prohibited. When the parties complained of shall have been duly notified of such petition the court shall proceed, as soon as may be, to the hearing and determination of the case; and pending such petition and before final decree, the court may at any time make such temporary restraining order or prohibition as shall be deemed just in the premises.

.   .   .   .   .

SEC. 7 Any person who shall be injured in his business or property by any other person or corporation by reason of anything forbidden or declared to be unlawful by this act, may sue therefore in any circuit court of the United States in the district in which the defendant resides or is found, without respect to the amount in controversy, and shall recover threefold the damages by him sustained, and the costs of suit, including a reasonable attorney's fee.

APPENDIX 3 B

The Clayton Anti-Trust Act
(October 15, 1914, 63rd Congress)

SECTION 1 That "antitrust laws," as used herein, include the Act entitled "An Act to protect trade and commerce against unlawful restraints and monopolies," approved July second, eighteen hundred and ninety; sections seventy-three to seventy-seven, inclusive, of an Act entitled "An Act to reduce taxation, to provide revenue for the Government, and for other purposes," of August twenty-seventh, eighteen hundred and ninety-four; an Act entitled "An Act to amend sections seventy-three and seventy-six of the Act of August twenty-seventh, eighteen hundred and ninety-four entitled 'An Act to reduce taxation, to provide revenue for the Government, and for other purposes'," approved February twelfth, nineteen hundred and thirteen; and also this Act.

"Commerce," as used herein, means trade or commerce, among the several States and with foreign nations, or between the District of Columbia or any Territory of the United States and any State, Territory, or foreign nation, or between any insular possessions or other places under the jurisdiction of the United States, or between any such possession or place and any State or Territory of the United States or the District of Columbia or any foreign nation, or within the District of Columbia or any Territory or any insular possession or other place under the jurisdiction of the United States: *Provided,* That nothing in this Act contained shall apply to the Philippine Islands.

The word "person" or "persons" wherever used in this Act shall be deemed to include corporations and associations existing under or authorized by the laws of either the United States, the laws of any of the Territories, the laws of any State, or the laws of any foreign country.

. . . . .

SEC. 6 That the labor of a human being is not a commodity or article of commerce. Nothing contained in the antitrust laws shall be construed to forbid the existence and operation of labor, agricultural, or horticultural organizations, instituted for the purposes of mutual help, and not having capital stock or conducted for profit, or to forbid or restrain individual members of such organizations, from lawfully carrying out the legitimate objects thereof; nor shall such organizations, or the members thereof, be held or construed to be illegal combinations or conspiracies in restraint of trade, under the anti-trust laws.

．　．　．　．　．

Sec. 16 Any person, firm, corporation, or association shall be entitled to sue for and have injunctive relief, in any court of the United States having jurisdiction over the parties, against threatened loss or damage by a violation of the antitrust laws, including sections two, three, seven and eight of this Act, when and under the same conditions and principles as injunctive relief against threatened conduct that will cause loss or damage is granted by courts of equity, under the rules governing such proceedings, and upon the execution of proper bond against damages for an injunction improvidently granted and a showing that the danger of irreparable loss or damage is immediate, a preliminary injunction may issue: *Provided,* That nothing herein contained shall be construed to entitle any person, firm, corporation, or association, except the United States, to bring suit in equity for injunctive relief against any common carrier subject to the provisions of the Act to regulate commerce, approved February fourth, eighteen hundred and eighty-seven, in respect of any matter subject to the regulation, supervision, or other jurisdiction of the Interstate Commerce Commission.

．　．　．　．　．

Sec. 20 That no restraining order or injunction shall be granted by any court of the United States, or a judge or the judges thereof, in any case between an employer and employees, or between employers and employees, or between employees, or between persons employed and persons seeking employment, involving, or growing out of, a dispute concerning terms or conditions of employment, unless necessary to prevent irreparable injury to property, or to a property right, of the party making the application, for which injury there is no adequate remedy at law, and such property or property right must be described with particularity in the application, which must be in writing and sworn to by the applicant or by his agent or attorney.

And no such restraining order or injunction shall prohibit any person or persons, whether singly or in concert, from terminating any relation of employment, or from ceasing to perform any work or labor, or from recommending, advising or persuading others by peaceful means so to do; or from attending at any place where any such person or persons may lawfully be, for the purpose of peacefully obtaining or communicating information, or from peacefully persuading any person to work or to abstain from working; or from ceasing to patronize or to employ any party to such dispute, or from recommending, advising, or persuading others by peaceful and lawful means so to do; or from paying or giving to, or withholding from, any person engaged in such dispute, any strike benefits or other moneys or things of value; or from peaceably assembling in a lawful manner, and for lawful purposes; or from doing any act or thing which might lawfully be done in the absence of such dispute by any party thereto; nor shall any of the acts specified in this paragraph be considered or held to be violations of any law of the United States.

4

A NEW ERA
HERALDED?

The railroad industry, so vital to the development of a viable national economy, became a focal point of labor unrest and impending change in public policy in the early 1800's. Defiance among organized railway employees intensified from 1860 to 1880 as the brotherhoods in the railroad industry became increasingly militant. A series of strikes in several industries was responsible for hundreds of deaths and more than ten million dollars in property damage as local and federal militia were pitted against the laboring masses, including miners, the unemployed, and railroad employees. The Railway Strike of 1877 was perhaps the most terrifying American labor upheaval in the nineteenth century.[1]

In the early 1900's, economic and social conditions were changing rapidly, as were previously held attitudes toward organized labor and the working man's position in the labor-management struggle. Widespread support for the labor movement developed as hatred mounted

[1] J. G. Rayback, *A History of American Labor* (New York: Free Press, 1966), p. 135.

against the railroads that were suspected of corruption, stock manipulation, and rate discrimination. Strikes in the railroad industry not only generated greater unity in the labor movement, but also lent impetus to the development of other social reform movements, including the development of state and national labor parties. Railroads became an early object of legislation because of their impact on interstate commerce, their existence as public monopolies, and their impact on the general welfare of the nation. Even though the Clayton Act failed to accomplish all that organized labor hoped it would, the early decades of the twentieth century set the stage for the more liberal treatment of unions. Key public policy developments in the railroad industry are examined in the following pages. A summary account of developing state legislation for labor relations in intrastate commerce follows the discussion of the railroad industry.

The Erdman Act

LEGISLATION AND THE RAIL INDUSTRY

The purpose of the Arbitration Act passed in 1888 was to provide a vehicle for voluntary arbitration and investigation of work stoppages through Presidentially appointed investigatory boards. The provisions of the Act were used rarely, partly because this legislative attempt lacked the requisite enforcement powers. Ten years later Congress passed the Erdman Act, a relatively progressive and innovative attempt to monitor disputes more directly and to moderately alter existing labor-management power relationships. Section 10 of the Erdman Act was particularly important because it outlawed the yellow-dog contract in the railway industry. Although the voluntary arbitration provisions of the Erdman Act were stronger than similar provisions in the earlier Arbitration Act, they were not widely used because of disinterest on the part of the carriers. The yellow-dog contract clause was a significant expression of public policy, in that the yellow-dog contract was an important weapon in restraining union organizing efforts.

In 1913, the Newlands Act was passed as an amendment to the Erdman Act and created a full-time Board of Mediation and Conciliation. Three years later, when operating employees of the railroad carriers refused to arbitrate their demand for an 8-hour day, President Wilson obtained passage of the Adamson Act (1916) which granted the 8-hour day to the brotherhoods. As soon as the United States entered World War I, the government took over the railroad industry. Special commissions were established to investigate labor demands, adjustment boards were created and empowered with settlement authority in matters of contract interpretation, and a permanent Railroad Administration was created, headed by a Director General of Railroads. During this period, carrier discrimination on the grounds of union affiliation was prohibited, pay discrimination against nonwhites was abolished, and the Railroad Administration enforced rigid seniority and craft classifications. At the end of World War I, the railroads were returned to private ownership under the Transportation Act of 1920, which also created a bipartisan nine-man Railroad Labor Board authorized to publicize the facts of labor disputes. The Board's limited power did little to resolve disputes between the brotherhoods and carriers. As the effects of the 1921 recession were translated into wage reductions for railroad workers, these disputes became increasingly serious. Employer-employee unrest was also heightened by the carriers' increasing interest in promoting company-dominated labor unions.

YELLOW-DOG CONTRACTS AND THE ADAIR DECISION

The American economy was highly vulnerable to labor relations problems in the railroad industry because of the vast amount of interstate commerce. The Big Four brotherhoods increasingly brought pressures to bear upon the railroads and government as the nineteenth century was nearing its close. The Pullman Strike, which occurred when the Louisville and National Railroad refused to permit union members to remain in its employ, exemplified the railroad problem. Refusal to retain union members was in direct violation of the anti-yellow-dog provision of the Erdman Act. The core centered around Harold Coppage, a fireman in the employ of the carrier, who was discharged by the railroad's representative, William Adair, for being a union member. Because Section 10 of the Erdman Act forbids threatening a worker with loss of employment or unjust discrimination because of union membership, the union attempted to indict Adair.

The *Adair* v. *United States* case reached the Supreme Court in 1908.[2] It was held that Section 10 of the Erdman Act was unconstitutional because it was inconsistent with the Fifth Amendment of the Constitution, which provides that no one shall be deprived of life, liberty, or the right of property without due process of law. Justice

[2] 208 U.S. 161 (1908).

Harlan, writing for the majority, declared that employers had the right to dispense with the services of employees for any reason, just as employees were free to contract with or leave the employ of any employer. According to Justice Harlan, this right was protected, in substance, by the due process clause. The court reasoned that Section 10 was invalid because it constituted a congressional infringement on the freedom of contract—an equal right of employer and employee. A second issue in the *Adair* decision involved the legality of legislative authorities to enact legislation on the basis of congressional power to regulate interstate commerce. On this point, the court recognized that Congress did have full authority over matters having a close and substantial connection with interstate commerce. However, Justice Harlan continued by noting that there was no legal connection between an employee's membership in a union and the functioning of interstate commerce. As a consequence, the court found Section 10 to be based upon the invalid exercise by Congress of the interstate commerce power as well as in violation of a constitutionally guaranteed freedom to make a labor contract. This early attempt on the part of Congress to use the commerce clause as a device for regulating industrial relations was invalidated by the Supreme Court's narrow interpretation of *direct* interstate commerce relations.[3] In short, the consequences of the *Adair* decision were unfavorable to continued organization of the railroad workers and the achievement of industrial peace on the rails. One contribution to the mounting conflict was the provincial concept of the labor-management contract in a property-right context, which preserved the inequality between employee-employer power. In addition, a narrow definition of interstate commerce imposed serious restraints upon efforts to improve and further regulate industrial relations problems through statutory law.

THE HITCHMAN COAL CASE

Legal sanction to the scheme whereby a worker was free to quit his job but was not free to keep his job *and* join a union retarded union organizing efforts, particularly in the regional and industry jurisdictions of the United Mine Workers. The *Adair* decision had invalidated public attempts to curb the use of the yellow-dog contract and, in this way, it established precedent for dealing with similar circumstances at the state level and in other industries. Later, the legality of

[3] It should be noted that the court held that only Section 10 of the Erdman Act was unconstitutional, and that the arbitration and mediation provisions remained in force.

private employer yellow-dog contracts was tested in the case of *Hitchman Coal and Coke Company* v. *Mitchell* in 1917.[4]

In the early 1900's, the West Virginia coal mines yielded a better quality of coke that was less costly to mine, giving firms in that area a competitive advantage over firms located in Illinois, Ohio, and Indiana. In 1906, the United Mine Workers called a strike against the West Virginia mine of the Hitchman Coal Co., then a major supplier to the Baltimore and Ohio Railroad. After enduring the strike for six weeks, the miners asked Hitchman for a settlement that was granted only on the terms that individuals would return to work without a union contract. The local union was then disbanded and a company-dominated union established. The United Mine Workers promptly dispatched a union organizer to Benwood, West Virginia, who began to reorganize the miners in 1907. While the company initially had no written individual contracts with the miners, they countered this new organizing effort of the United Mine Workers by seeking and obtaining an *ex parte* injunction against the union and its officers. Shortly thereafter, the Hitchman Company also asked employees to sign the following agreement:

> I am employed by and work for Hitchman Coal and Coke Company with the express understanding that I am not a member of the United Mine Workers of America and will not become so while an employee of Hitchman . . . and if at any time while I am employed by Hitchman Coal and Coke Company I want to become connected with the United Mine Workers of America, or any affiliated organization, I agree to withdraw from the employment of said Company. . . .[5]

In subsequent hearings and appeals, the injunction was upheld. Furthermore, the court broadened the coverage of the original restraining order, ultimately prohibiting the union from peaceful communication with Hitchman employees. This restraining order was in effect between 1907 and 1914. The lower court held union efforts to be conspiratorial and in breach of an employee-employer contract concerning conditions of employment. The Circuit Court of Appeals reversed the findings of the lower court that first heard the case. After seven years had elapsed, the union was judged by the Court of Appeals to have used lawful methods to secure a legal objective. The

[4] 245 U.S. 229 (1917).
[5] Lieberman, *op. cit.*, p. 87.

Hitchman Coal Company then appealed the case to the Supreme Court, which heard the case in 1917. The decision of the Court of Appeals of the Fourth District was reversed by the Supreme Court in a sharply split decision in favor of the Hitchman Coal Company. The highest court held that the Hitchman Coal Company had the right to form a contract making nonunion membership an employment condition, and that encouragement to join the union constituted inducements to breach a valid contract. The court majority opinion delivered by Justice Pitney also argued that the defendants were guilty of a combination injurious to the plaintiff; therefore, injunctive relief was the proper remedy at law. Justice Brandeis spoke for the minority opinion in a diametrically opposed dissent. Justice Brandeis observed that the ends and the means used by the union were lawful and the union was not guilty of inducing a breach of contract, since preparation to join the union did not constitute unlawful activity. The majority opinion, favoring Hitchman Coal as plaintiff and delivered by Justice Pitney, is recorded as follows:

HITCHMAN COAL COMPANY v. MITCHELL: 1917
(245 U.S. 229)

Mr. Justice Pitney speaking for the United States Supreme Court:

This was a suit in equity, commenced October 24, 1907, in the United States circuit (afterwards district) court for the northern district of West Virginia, by the Hitchman Coal and Coke Company. . . . At the time of the filing of the bill, and for a considerable time before and ever since, it operated its mine "nonunion," under an agreement with its men to the effect that the mine should be run on a nonunion basis, that the employees should not become connected with the Union while employed by plaintiff, and that if they joined it, their employment with plaintiff should cease. The bill . . . said defendants have unlawfully and maliciously agreed together, confederated, combined, and formed themselves into a conspiracy, to the purpose of which they are proceeding to carry out and are now about to finally accomplish, namely: To cause your orator's mine to be shut down, its plant to remain idle, its contracts to be broken and unfulfilled, until such time as your orator shall submit to the demand of the Union that it shall unionize its plant, and, having submitted to such demand unionize its plant by employing only Union men who shall become subject to the orders of the Union, etc. The general object of the bill was to obtain an injunction to restrain defendants from interfering with the relations existing between plaintiff and its employees in order to compel plaintiff to "unionize" the mine. . . .

That the plaintiff was acting within its lawful rights in employing its men only upon terms of continuing nonmembership in the United Mine Workers of America is not open to question. Plaintiff's repeated costly experiences of strikes and other interferences while attempting to "run union" were a sufficient explanation of its resolve to run "nonunion," if any were needed. The unorganized condition of the mines . . . was recognized as a serious interference with the purposes of the Union, particularly as it tended to keep the cost of production low; and, through competition with coal produced in the organized field, rendered it more difficult for operators there to maintain prices high enough to induce them to grant certain concessions demanded by the Union. . . . But neither explanation nor justification is needed. Whatever may be the advantages of "collective bargaining," it is not bargaining at all, in any just sense, unless it is voluntary on both sides. The same liberty which enables men to form unions, and through the Union to enter into agreements with employers willing to agree, entitles other men to remain independent of the union, and other employers to agree with them to employ no man who owes any allegiance or obligation to the Union. In the latter case, as in the former, the parties are entitled to be protected by the law in the enjoyment of the benefits of any lawful agreement they make. This court repeatedly has held that . . . this is a part of the constitutional rights of personal liberty and private property, not to be taken away even by legislation. . . . Plaintiff, having in the exercise of its undoubted rights established a working agreement between it and its employees, with the free assent of the latter, is entitled to be protected in the enjoyment of the resulting status, as in any other legal right. . . .

We turn to the matters set up by way of justification or excuse for defendants' interference with the situation existing at plaintiff's mine. It is suggested as a ground of criticism that plaintiff endeavored to secure a closed, nonunion mine through individual agreements with its employees. . . . It is a sufficient answer, in law, to repeat that plaintiff had a legal and constitutional right to exclude union men from its employ. But it may be worth while to say, in addition: first, that there was no middle ground open to plaintiffs; no option to have an "open shop" employing union men and nonunion men indifferently; it was the Union that insisted upon closed-shop agreements, requiring even carpenters employed about a mine to be members of the Union, and making the employment of any nonunion man a ground for a strike; and secondly plaintiff was in the reasonable exercise of its rights in excluding all union men from its employ: . . . The right of workingmen to form unions, and to enlarge their membership by inviting other workingmen to join . . . is freely conceded, provided the objects of the Union be proper and legitimate. . . . The cardinal error of defendants' position lies in the assumption that the right is so absolute that it may be exercised under any circumstances . . . whereas in truth it must always be exercised with reasonable regard for the conflicting rights of others. . . . Every Hitchman miner who joined Hughes' "secret order" and permitted his name to be entered upon Hughes' list was guilty of a breach of his contract of employment and acted a lie whenever thereafter he entered plaintiff's mine to work. . . . Mr. Pickett, the mine superintendent, had charge of employing the men, . . . and to each one who applied for employment he explained the conditions, which were that while the company paid the wages demanded by the Union and as much as anybody else, the mine was run nonunion and would continue so to run; that the company would not recognize the United Mine Workers of America; that if any man wanted to become a member of that Union he was at liberty to do so; but he could not be a member of it and remain in the employ of the Hitchman Company; that if he worked for the company he would have to work as a nonunion man. To this each man employed gave his assent, understanding that while he worked for the company he must keep out of the Union. . . . In addition to having this verbal understanding, each man has been required to sign an employment card expressing in substance the same terms.

But the facts render it plain that what the defendants were endeavoring to do at the Hitchman mine and neighboring mines cannot be treated as a bona fide effort to enlarge the membership of the Union. . . . Except as a means to the end of compelling the owners of these mines to change their method of operation, the defendants were not seeking to enlarge the Union membership.

In any aspect of the matter, it cannot be said that defendants were pursuing their object by lawful means. The question of their intentions—of their bona fides—cannot be ignored. . . . Of course, in a court of equity, when passing upon the right of injunction, damage threatened, irremediable by action at law, is equivalent to damage done. And we cannot deem the proffered excuse to be a "just cause or excuse," where it is based, as in this case, upon an assertion of conflicting rights that are sought to be attained by unfair methods, and for the very purpose of interfering with plaintiff's rights, of which defendants have full notice.

Another fundamental error in defendants' position consists in the assumption that all measures that may be resorted to are lawful if they are "peaceable,"—that is, if they stop short of physical violence, or coercion through fear of it. In our opinion, any violation of plaintiff's legal rights contrived by defendants for the purpose of inflicting damage, or having that as its necessary effect, is as plainly inhibited by the law as if it involved a breach of the peace. . . . There is no reason to doubt that if defendants had been actuated by a genuine desire to increase the membership of the Union without unnecessary injury to the known rights of plaintiff, they would have permitted their proselytes to withdraw from plaintiff's employ when and as they became affiliated with the Union,—as their contract of employment required them to do, —and that in this event plaintiff would have been able to secure an adequate supply of nonunion men to take their places. It was with knowledge of this, and because of it, that defendants, through Hughes as their agent, caused the new members to remain at work in plaintiff's mine until a sufficient number of men should be persuaded to join so as to bring about a strike and render it difficult if not practically impossible for plaintiff to continue to exercise its undoubted legal and constitutional right to run its mine "nonunion."

It was one thing for plaintiff to find, from time to time, comparatively small numbers of men to take vacant places in a going mine, another and a much more difficult thing to find a complete gang of new men to start up a mine shut down by a strike, when there might be a reasonable apprehension of violence at the hands of the strikers and their sympathizers. The disordered condition of a mining town in time of strike is matter of common knowledge. It was this kind of intimidation, as well as that resulting from the large organized membership of the Union, that defendants sought to exert upon plaintiff. . . .

Upon all the facts, we are constrained to hold that the purpose entertained by defendants to bring about a strike at plaintiff's mine in order to compel plaintiff, through fear of financial loss, to consent to the unionization of the mine as the lesser evil, was an unlawful purpose, and that the methods resorted to by Hughes—the inducing of employees to unite with the Union in an effort to subvert the system of employment at the mine by concerted breaches of the contracts of employment known to be in force there, not to mention misrepresentation, deceptive statements, and threats of pecuniary loss communicated by Hughes to the men—were unlawful and malicious methods, and not to be justified as a fair exercise of the right to increase the membership of the union.

Therefore, upon the undisputed facts of the case, and the indubitable inferences from them, plaintiff is entitled to relief by injunction. . . . The decree of the Circuit Court of Appeals is reversed . . . for further proceedings in conformity with this opinion.

Justice Brandeis submitted a dissenting opinion in which he stressed the legality of ends and means used by the United Mine Workers of America. His argument is recorded as follows:

. . . The defendants sought to secure the closed *union shop* through a collective agreement with the Union. Since collective bargaining is legal, the fact that the workingmen's agreement is made not by individuals directly with the employer, but by the employees with the Union and by it, on their behalf, with the employer, is of no significance in this connection. The end being lawful, defendant's efforts to unionize the mine can be illegal only if the methods or means pursued were unlawful; unless, indeed, there is some special significance in the expression "unionizing without plaintiff's consent."

. . . It is also urged that defendants are seeking to "coerce" plaintiff to "unionize" its mine. . . . If it is coercion to threaten to strike unless plaintiff consents to a closed shop union, it is coercion also to threaten not to give one employment unless the applicant will consent to a closed nonunion agreement for fear that labor may not be otherwise obtainable; the workman may sign the individual agreement, for fear that employment may not be otherwise obtainable. But such fear does not imply coercion in a legal sense. In other words, an employer, in order to effectuate the closing of his shop to union labor, may exact an agreement to that effect from his employees. The agreement itself being a lawful one, the employer may withhold from the men an economic need—

employment—until they assent to make it. Likewise an agreement closing a shop to nonunion labor being lawful, the Union may withhold from an employer an economic need—labor—until he assents to make it. In a legal sense an agreement entered into, under such circumstances, is voluntarily entered into; and as the agreement is in itself legal, no reason appears why the general rule that a legal end may be pursued by legal means should not be applied. Or, putting it in other words, there is nothing in the character of the agreement which should make unlawful means used to attain it which in other connections are recognized as lawful. . . . There is evidence of an attempt to induce plaintiff's employees to agree to join the Union; but none whatever of any attempt to induce them to violate their contract. Until an employee actually joined the Union he was not, under the contract, called upon to leave plaintiff's employ. There consequently would be no breach of contract until the employee both joined the Union and failed to withdraw from plaintiff's employ. There was no evidence that any employee was persuaded to do that, or that such a course was contemplated. . . .

When this suit was filed no right of the plaintiff had been infringed and there was no reasonable ground to believe that any of its rights would be interfered with. . . .

The *Hitchman* decision made union efforts illegal if they induced a worker to break a contract. In essence, the court added legal substance to what previously was only a worker's moral compunction to live up to an agreement in the form of a yellow-dog contract. The *Hitchman* decision further strengthened the hand of the employer by encouraging the development of company unions. Note, too, that legislative power to regulate labor relations on the basis of the commerce clause was narrowly interpreted to mean a *direct* effect on commerce in the *Adair* decision that voided Section 10 of the Erdman Act. In contrast, the Supreme Court supported its anti-union decision in the *Hitchman* case by observing that the action of the union would be detrimental to goods *destined* for commerce between the states. Because the Supreme Court did not speak out on this application of the Sherman Act to a case involving intrastate commerce *destined* for interstate commerce, existing anti-trust regulation also became a greater hazard for the union movement.

State Regulation of Labor Relations

The *Adair* and *Hitchman* decisions completely upheld the validity of the yellow-dog contract as the courts firmly held to their concept of contractual rights and vacillated on the issue of the direct vs. indirect commerce impact of employee-employer agreements. These decisions had a measurable impact on state laws, some of which made it a criminal offense for an employer to extract a nonunion promise from the worker as a pre-condition of employment. In the *Coppage* v. *Kansas* decision, for example, a Kansas statute prohibiting a yellow-dog contract was declared invalid on grounds found unconstitutional in *Adair* some seven years earlier.[6] The Kansas law was held to be a violation of the due process protection afforded by the Fourteenth Amendment of the Constitution, which limits the power of a state to interfere with freedom of contract. Once again, then, the Supreme Court relied on the concept of "substantive" due process interpretation as they had in the *Adair* decision.[7]

In the *Coppage* decision, Justice Pitney reaffirmed the court's initial 1908 opinion in *Adair* by observing that the right of private property is a right to make contracts. This includes personal employment, through which labor services are exchanged. Arbitrarily interfering with this right

> . . . is a substantial impairment of liberty in the long-established constitutional sense. The right is as essential to the laborer as to the capitalist, to the poor as to the rich; for the vast majority of persons have no other honest way to begin to acquire property, save by working for money. . . .

This does not mean an intent to intimidate the right of individuals to join labor unions, as long as they conform to the law.[8] In short, Justice Pitney clearly noted that asking a man to refrain from union affiliation does not infringe upon his constitutional freedom in that he is free to accept or reject the terms suggested by the employer. The em-

---

[6] 236 U.S. 1 (1915).

[7] "Substantive" due process refers to ruling on the substance or merits of law; that is, denial of union affiliation was not of adequate merit to justify abridgement of the freedom of contract in the eyes of the court.

[8] 236 U.S. 1 (1915).

ployer, however, has the same right to prescribe employment terms as the union has to deny membership so long as coercion and duress are absent. As a consequence of this reasoning, the Supreme Court majority concluded that the 1903 Kansas Act outlawing yellow-dog contracts was void and in violation of the due process clause of the Fourteenth Amendment. Justice Holmes did not agree with the majority opinion: his basic contention was that workingmen quite naturally believe that the only way to secure fair employment terms is by belonging to a union. Therefore, Justice Holmes reasoned, ". . . if that belief, whether right or wrong, may be held by a reasonable man, it seems to me that it may be enforced by law in order to establish the equality of position between the parties in which liberty of contract begins." [9]

A short time later, two other decisions of the Supreme Court denied states the right to more fully develop the legal rights of union members and to develop a more effective system of industrial jurisprudence.[10] The *Truax* decision typifies the court again applying a substantive interpretation to both property rights and due process of law. The *Wolff* case is symptomatic of the colossal failure of the state of Kansas to impose a compulsory arbitration scheme upon disputes in industries essential to the state economy.

Two years after the Arizona territory applied for statehood, the state legislature, in a revision of its code, adopted a provision similar to Section 20 of the Clayton Act. The substance of the Arizona statute was to control the state courts' issuance of injunctions. The statute stipulated that injunctions were forbidden in instances wherein a party peacefully persuaded a person to work or abstain from working. The law was challenged in the case of *Truax* v. *Corrigan,* which reached the Supreme Court in 1921.

The primary issue involved was the legality of state regulation of industrial relations without violating the due process rights of the citizenry. Because of the existence of an Arizona statute limiting injunctive relief sought by employers, the Arizona Supreme Court had earlier refused to enjoin a labor dispute. The dispute was between several members of the Cooks' and Waiters' Union of Bisbee, Arizona, and William Truax, a restaurant owner who had reduced wages and lengthened the work day. This precipitated a strike, as well as significant amounts of publicity that did affect Truax's business. The picketing that was conducted was boisterous but relatively peaceful and, in

[9] *Ibid.*

[10] *Truax* v. *Corrigan,* 257 U.S. 312 (1921) and *Charles Wolff Packing Company* v. *Court of Industrial Relations of Kansas,* 267 U.S. 552 (1925).

the eyes of Chief Justice Cunningham of the Arizona bench, Truax's rights were not violated nor was the Arizona law in conflict with the Fourteenth Amendment of the Constitution. The case was appealed and considered by the Supreme Court of the United States in 1921 on the grounds that upholding the Arizona statute violated the Fourteenth Amendment. Chief Justice Taft, who had locked horns with the founders of the Arizona Constitution in 1911 as President of the United States, delivered the majority opinion in favor of Truax in a split five-to-four decision. The court held that the Arizona law did in fact deprive the business owner of due process of law. Chief Justice Taft argued that the state did not have the right to pass legislation which permitted injurious invasion of property rights, and injunctive relief should have been granted to Truax.

The following reasoning of the Supreme Court invalidated the Arizona Court's decision that plaintiff Truax (a) was not denied due process of law and (b) had no claim to injunctive relief:

WILLIAM TRUAX v. MICHAEL CORRIGAN: 1921
(257 U.S. 312)

Mr. Chief Justice Taft delivering the opinion of the court:

The defendants conspired to injure and destroy plaintiffs' business by inducing their theretofore willing patrons and would-be patrons not to patronize them, and they influence these to withdraw or withhold their patronage. . . . The method of inducing was set out at length, and included picketing, displaying banners, advertising the strike, denouncing plaintiffs as "unfair" to the union, and appealing to customers to stay away from the "English Kitchen," and the circulation of handbills containing abusive and libelous charges against plaintiffs, their employees and their patrons and intimations of injury to future patrons. Copies of the handbills were set forth in exhibits made part of the complaint. . . . The result of this campaign was to reduce the business of the plaintiffs from more than $55,000 a year to one of $12,000. . . . The complaint further averred that the defendants were relying for immunity on the Revised Statutes of Arizona, 1913, which is in part as follows: "No restraining order or injunction shall be granted by any court of this state, or a judge or the judges thereof, in any case between an employer and employees. . . ." The plaintiffs alleged that this paragraph, if it made lawful defendants' acts, contravened the 14th Amendment to the Constitution of the United States by depriving plaintiffs of their property without due process of law, and by denying to plaintiffs the equal protection of the laws, and was, therefore, void and of no effect. Upon the case thus stated the plaintiffs asked a temporary and a permanent injunction.

The defendants filed a demurrer, on two grounds: First, that the complaint did not state facts sufficient to constitute a cause of action, in that the property rights asserted therein were not, under the Revised Statutes of Arizona, 1913, of such character that their irreparable injury might be enjoined, and secondly that upon its face, the complaint showed a want of equity. The Superior Court for Cochise county sustained the demurrer and dismissed the complaint, and this judgment was affirmed by the Supreme Court of Arizona.

A law which operates to make lawful such a wrong as is described in plaintiffs' complaint deprives the owner of the business and the premises of his property without due process, and cannot be held valid under the 14th Amendment. The opinion of the State Supreme Court in this case, if taken alone, seems to show that the statute grants complete immunity from any civil or criminal action to the defendants, for it pronounces their acts lawful. If, however, we are to assume that the criminal laws of Arizona do provide persecution for libels against the plaintiffs, though committed by this particular class of tort-feasors (Truax v. Bisbee Local, C.W.U. 19 Ariz. 379, 171 Pac. 121), still the tort here committed was not a mere libel of plaintiffs. That would not have had any such serious consequences. The libel of the plaintiffs here was not the cause of the injury; it was only one step or link in a conspiracy unlawfully to influence customers. . . .

This brings us to consider the effect in this case of that provision of the 14th Amendment which forbids any state to deny to any person the equal protection of the laws. The clause is associated in the Amendment with the due-process clause, and it is customary to consider them together. It may be that they overlap, that a violation of one may involve at times the violation of the other, but the spheres of the protection they offer are not conterminous. The due process clause brought down from Magna Charta was found in the early State Constitutions and later in the 5th Amendment to the Federal Constitution as a limitation upon the executive, legislative, and judicial powers of the Federal government, while the equality clause does not appear in the 5th Amendment, and so does not apply to congressional legislation. The due process clause requires that every man shall have the protection of

his day in court, and the benefit of the general law,—a law
which hears before it condemns, which proceeds not arbitrarily or
capriciously, but upon inquiry, and renders judgment only after
trial, so that every citizen shall hold his life, liberty, property, and
immunities under the protection of the general rules which govern
society. It, of course, tends to secure equality of law in the sense
that it makes a required minimum of protection for everyone's
right of life, liberty, and property, which the Congress or the legislature may not withhold. Our whole system of law is predicated on
the general fundamental principle of equality of application of the
law. "All men are equal before the law;" "This is a government of
laws, and not of men;" "No man is above the law,"—are all max-
ims showing the spirit in which legislatures, executives, and courts
are expected to make, execute, and apply laws. But the framers
and adopters of this Amendment were not content to depend on a
mere minimum secured by the due process clause, or upon the
spirit of equality which might not be insisted on by local public
opinion. They therefore embodied that spirit in a specific guaranty.

The guaranty was aimed at undue favor and individual or class
privilege, on the one hand, and at hostile discrimination or the oppression of inequality, on the other. It sought an equality of treatment of all persons, even though all enjoyed the protection of due
process. . . . With these views of the meaning of the equality
clause, it does not seem possible to escape the conclusion that, by
the clauses of the Revised Statutes of Arizona, here relied on by
the defendants, as construed by its Supreme Court, the plaintiffs
have been deprived of the equal protection of the law.

. . . If this is not a denial of the equal protection of the laws,
then it is hard to conceive what would be. To hold it not to be,
would be, to use the expression of Mr. Justice Brewer, to make the
guaranty of the equality clause "a rope of sand." We conclude that
the demurrer in this case should have been overruled, the defendants required to answer, and that, if the evidence sustains the
averments of the complaint, an injunction should issue as prayed.

In this decision, the Court expressed annoyance with what it regarded as "abusive" attacks in the form of hurtful picketing activities,
and ruled that the Arizona Court had erred in applying the Arizona
statute. According to the Chief Justice, the unlawful picketing that
occurred should have been enjoined, although the Anti-Injunction Act
itself was not ruled invalid if properly applied by the Arizona Courts

in the future. Nevertheless, this ruling was significant in that it prompted similar decisions on other state statutes modeled after Section 20 of the Clayton Act.

Justice Brandeis' dissenting opinion conflicted markedly with the majority ruling. In his dissent, he noted that the right to do business was a proper one, but it may be interfered with (e.g., a competitor restaurant). Justice Brandeis noted that laws evolved by courts and legislatures as well as permissible means and methods of "interfering" with change must be regarded as government experiments that properly must be discarded if they prove to be a failure. He also argued that change had occurred under the law in England where union members were criminally liable until 1871. Similarly, the laws governing employee-employer struggles in the United States had been modified over the course of more than a century. Courts played a prominent role in this process, because of the absence of legislation. The dissent of Justice Brandeis, which describes trends significant to the evolution of labor law, is recorded as follows:

> Practically every change in the law governing the relation of employer and employee must abridge, in some respect, the liberty or property of one of the parties, if liberty and property be measured by the standard of the law theretofore prevailing. If such changes are made by acts of the legislature, we call the modification an exercise of the police power. And, although the change may involve interference with existing liberty or property of individuals, the statute will not be declared a violation of the due process clause unless the court finds that the interference is arbitrary or unreasonable, or that, considered as a means, the measure has no real or substantial relation of cause to a permissible end. Nor will such changes in the law governing contests between employer and employee be held to be violative of the equal protection clause, merely because the liberty or property of individuals in other relations to each other (for instance, as competitors in trade or as vendor and purchaser) would not, under similar circumstances, be subject to like abridgment. Few laws are of universal application. It is of the nature of our law that it has dealt not with man in general, but with him in relationships. That a peculiar relationship of individuals may furnish legal basis for the classification which satisfies the requirement of the 14th Amendment is clear. That the relation of employer and employee affords a constitutional basis for legislation applicable only to persons standing in that relation has been repeatedly held by this Court. The questions

submitted are whether this statutory prohibition of the remedy by injunction is in itself arbitrary and so unreasonable as to deprive the employer of liberty or property without due process of law; and whether limitation of this prohibition to controversies involving employment denies him equal protection of the laws.

Whether a law enacted in the exercise of the police power is justly subject to the charge of being unreasonable or arbitrary can ordinarily be determined only by a consideration of the contemporary conditions—social, industrial, and political—of the community to be affected thereby. Resort to such facts is necessary, among other things, in order to appreciate the evils sought to be remedied and the possible effects of the remedy proposed. Nearly all legislation involves a weighing of public needs as against private desires; and likewise a way of relative social values. Since government is not an exact science, prevailing public opinion concerning the evils and the remedy is among the important facts deserving consideration; particularly, when the public conviction is both deep-seated and widespread, and has been reached after deliberation. What, at any particular time, is the paramount public need, is, necessarily, largely a matter of judgment. Hence, in passing upon the validity of a law challenged as being unreasonable, aid may be derived from the experience of other counties and of the several states of our Union in which the common law and its conceptions of liberty and of property prevail. . . .

In the United States the rules of the common law governing the struggle between employer and employee have likewise been subjected to modifications. These have been made mainly through judicial decisions. The legal right of workingmen to combine and to strike in order to secure for themselves higher wages, shorter hours, and better working conditions received early general recognition. But there developed great diversity of opinion as to the means by which, and also as to the persons through whom, and upon whom pressure might permissibly be exerted in order to induce the employer to yield to the demands of the workingmen. Courts were required, in the absence of legislation, to determine what the public welfare demanded; whether it would not be best subserved by leaving the contestants free to resort to any means not involving a breach of the peace or injury to tangible property whether it was consistent with the public interest that the contestants should be permitted to invoke the aid of others not directly interested in the matter in controversy; and to what extent inci-

dental injury to persons not parties to the controversy should be
held justifiable. . . .

In England, observance of the rules of the contest has been enforced by the courts almost wholly through the criminal law or
through actions at law for compensation. An injunction was
granted in a labor dispute as early as 1868. But in England resort
to the injunction has not been frequent, and it has played no ap-
preciable part there in the conflict between capital and labor. In
America the injunction did not secure recognition as a possible
remedy until 1888. When, a few years later, its use became extensive and conspicuous, the controversy over the remedy overshadowed in bitterness the question of the relative substantive rights
of the parties. In the storms of protest against this use many
thoughtful lawyers joined. . . . Charges of violating an injunction
were often heard on affidavits merely, without the opportunity of
confronting or cross-examining witnesses. Men found guilty of contempt were committed in the judge's discretion, without either a
statutory limit upon the length of the imprisonment, or the opportunity of effective review on appeal, or the right to release on bail
pending possible revisory proceedings. The effect of the proceeding upon the individual was substantially the same as if he had
been successfully prosecuted for a crime; but he was denied, in the
course of the equity proceedings, those rights which, by the Constitution, are commonly secured to persons charged with a crime.
. . .

It was urged that the real motive in seeking the injunction was
not ordinarily to prevent property from being injured, nor to protect the owner in its use, but to endow property with active, militant power which would make it dominant over men. In other
words, that, under the guise of protecting property rights, the employer was seeking sovereign power. . . .

After the constitutionality and the propriety of the use of the injunction in labor disputes was established judicially, those who opposed the practice sought the aid of Congress and of state legislatures. The bills introduced varied in character and in scope. Many
dealt merely with rights; and, of these, some declared, in effect,
that no act done in furtherance of a labor dispute by a combination of workingmen should be held illegal, unless it would have
been so if done by a single individual; while others purported to
legalize specific practices, like boycotting or picketing. . . .

The Supreme Court of Arizona made a choice between well-established precedents laid down on either side by some of the strongest courts in the country. Can this Court say that thereby it deprived the plaintiff of his property without due process of law? . . . A state, which, despite the 14th Amendment, possesses the power to impose on employers without fault unlimited liability for injuries suffered by employees, and to limit the freedom of contract of some employers, and not of others, surely does not lack the power to select for its citizens that one of conflicting views on boycott by peaceful picketing which its legislature and highest court consider will best meet its conditions and secure the public welfare. The Supreme Court of Arizona, having held as a rule of substantive law that the boycott, as here practiced, was legal at common law; and that the picketing was peaceful, and hence, legal under the statute (whether or not it was legal at common law), necessarily denied the injunction, since, in its opinion, the defendants had committed no legal wrong and were threatening none. . . . The considerations which show that the refusal is not arbitrary or unreasonable show likewise that such refusal does not necessarily constitute a denial of equal protection of the laws merely because some, or even the same, property rights which are excluded by this statute from protection by injunction, receive such protection under other circumstances, or between persons standing in different relations. The acknowledged legislative discretion exerted in classification, so frequently applied in defining rights, extends equally to the grant of remedies. It is for the legislature to say—within the broad limits of the discretion which it possesses —whether or not the remedy for a wrong shall be both criminal and civil, and whether or not it shall be both at law and in equity. A state is free since the adoption of the 14th Amendment, as it was before, not only to determine what system of law shall prevail in it, but, also, by what processes legal rights may be asserted, and in what courts they may be enforced. . . .

For these reasons, as well as for others stated by Mr. Justice Holmes and Mr. Justice Pitney, in which I concur, the judgment of the Supreme Court of Arizona should, in my opinion, be affirmed: first, because, in permitting damage to be inflicted by means of boycott and peaceful picketing, Arizona did not deprive the plaintiff of property without due process of law, or deny him equal protection of the laws; and secondly, because, if Arizona was constitutionally prohibited from adopting this rule of substantive law, it was still free to restrict the extraordinary remedies of equity where it considered their exercise to be detrimental to the public welfare, since such restriction was not a denial to the employer either of due process of law or of equal protection of the laws.

Another incident involving a state attempt to regulate conduct in industrial disputes grew out of a Kansas statute passed in 1920, two years after World War I ended. This was a period when Kansas was experiencing numerous work stoppages, particularly in the coal industry, then very important to the state economy. In spite of joint opposition by both labor and management, the state legislature enacted the Kansas Industrial Relations Act that prohibited strikes and lockouts in the food, fuel, and clothing industries which were deemed essential to the general welfare. Unresolvable disputes in these industries by the parties directly involved had to be submitted to the Kansas Court of Industrial Relations for compulsory arbitration. A test of this unpopular statute was not long in coming. In the *Wolff Packing Company* case, the Industrial Court of Kansas found in favor of the union, and the decision was upheld by the Supreme Court of Kansas. After the Kansas court enforced the wage and hours ruling of the newly created Industrial Court in favor of the worker, the award was appealed to the Supreme Court. Between 1923 and 1925, various issues in this case were brought to the Supreme Court on two different occasions.[11] In these decisions, the Supreme Court ruled that the provisions of the Kansas law conflicted with freedom of contract rights which are protected by the Fourteenth Amendment of the Constitution. Having thus ruled, the compulsory arbitration powers of the Industrial Court were invalid insofar as fixing wages, hours, and other conditions of work.[12]

In summary, attempts to legislate reason into industrial disputes were gradually appearing on the federal and state levels. Unfortunately, the courts of the United States were somewhat reluctant to accept the changes called for by Justice Brandeis in his celebrated *Truax* dissent. The Erdman Act illustrates this problem in that even though Congress had outlawed the yellow-dog contract in the railroad industry, the Supreme Court found the particular anti-yellow-dog provision illegal in the *Erdman* decision. This court's position on yellow-dog contracts was later reaffirmed in the private employer set-

[11] 262 U.S. 522 (1923) and 267 U.S. 522 (1925).

[12] It is interesting to note, however, that the Supreme Court did not invalidate the Industrial Court's imposition of penalties against union leaders who called a strike against the order of the Industrial Court.

ting by the *Hitchman Coal* decision. States that attempted to more effectively control labor strife were also overruled by the Supreme Court, as is demonstrated by repeated validation of the use of injunctions in the *Truax, Coppage,* and *Wolff* decisions. By the early 1900's, the labor union had arrived as an institution with which to be reckoned in a behavioral sense. It was still a long way from being a legally acceptable fabric of American industrial economic life. Injunctive relief and the validity of yellow-dog contracts were two employer weapons of conflict that proved to be most effective in controlling labor organizations until the era of the Great Depression.

The Railway Labor Act: A Prelude to Change

The Railway Labor Act was passed in 1926, nearly four decades after the passage of the first federal labor legislation applying to the railroad industry. Previous federal legislation attempted to provide a framework for collective bargaining and dispute-settlement procedures that were more desirable than outright conflict between the brotherhoods and carriers. Unfortunately, as we have observed, the Arbitration Act of 1888 and the Erdman Act that followed ten years later were not operationally effective in dealing with the serious labor problems in the railway industry. Nevertheless, an attempt to rationalize industrial relations and establish conflict-resolution procedures was embodied in these acts. Although the Newlands Act of 1913 contained provisions for a three-man Board of Mediation designed to improve the voluntary arbitration provisions of the Erdman Act, unrest continued between 1913 and 1916. Passage of the Adamson Act was followed by the Transportation Act returning the railroads to private ownership and operation as World War I ended. Although a nine-man Railway Labor Board was authorized by the Transportation Act and was empowered with publicizing disputes, it lacked enforcement powers of any kind, leaving labor-management relations in a state of turmoil. Furthermore, the yellow-dog contract remained acceptable to the courts. The combination of these forces heightened industry tensions.

In spite of the fact that administrative agencies established by railway legislation prior to 1926 had been less than fully effective in handling disputes in that industry, an official government attitude toward labor-management relations was gradually evolving from these difficult experiences. The culmination of these events came in 1926, when the Railway Labor Act was passed. Not only did the Railway Labor

Act reflect an accumulation of past experience, but it was also significant because of the implications it had for future legislation applying to labor-relations problems throughout the entire economy. Essentially, the 1926 legislation had more detailed and elaborate provisions establishing mediation and conciliation machinery than previous legislation. Each party was encouraged to designate its own bargaining representative free of interference from outsiders; and the rights, duties, and provisions for the protection of these disputants were carefully enunciated. Judicial verification of the 1926 Act occurred as a result of the case of *Texas and New Orleans Railway Company* v. *The Brotherhood of Railway and Steamship Clerks* before the Supreme Court in 1930.[13] The Supreme Court validated the Railway Labor Act as a reasonable exercise of congressional commerce power and approved of labor's right to organize without employer interference. Chief Justice Hughes, speaking for the court, noted that carriers could not complain of the statute on constitutional grounds.

The primary purpose of the Railway Labor Act was to strengthen mediation and voluntary arbitration procedures through three successive routes. First, a nonpartisan Board of Mediation appointed by the President attempted to get disputants to negotiate on their areas of disagreement in a collective bargaining atmosphere. If these mediation efforts failed, the Board would encourage both parties to submit unresolved issues to voluntary arbitration, which would result in a legally enforceable and binding decision to be imposed on the disputants. Finally, if voluntary arbitration was rejected, the Act provided for Presidential appointment of an emergency board when essential transportation services were threatened. These emergency boards were charged with investigating conditions of the dispute and making recommendations to the President within 30 days. Both parties were required to maintain the status quo for an additional 30-day period following Presidential receipt of the report. Although the emergency board recommendations were not binding on either party, it was hoped that the 60-day cooling-off period, as well as the publicity and public opinion dimensions to such proceedings, would influence the outcome of disagreement and help avert conflict. Throughout the investigation proceedings, both parties were prohibited from altering the conditions of the initial dispute. Only after 30 days had elapsed from the time the emergency board filed its final report could the parties to a conflict resume their dispute. The 1926 Act also provided for the establishment of boards of adjustment that were designed to han-

[13] 281 U.S. 548 (1930).

dle disputes related to interpretation of contracts and other grievance matters. This aspect of the Railway Labor Act proved to be relatively unsuccessful in that those few adjustment boards that were established were frequently unable to break existing deadlocks. Nevertheless, a series of interesting conceptual alternatives to undelayed actions were first developed in the Railway Labor Act, and certain of these features found their way into subsequent laws controlling collective bargaining.

By 1934, however, over 2,000 disputes that had not been settled by adjustment boards remained to be adjudicated. Furthermore, the Railway Labor Act of 1926 became increasingly deficient in dealing with the issue of company unions. The Railway Labor Act had no provision for determining or electing representatives; it had not outlawed the yellow-dog contract; and it failed to stipulate the penalties that could be imposed upon carriers in violation of the expressed provision of the Act assuring workers the right to determine union representatives without interference and coercion. As a consequence, the Board of Mediation was less than successful in dealing with numerous issues. Thus, the Railway Labor Act of 1926 was amended in 1934, 1936, and again in 1951.[14] The most important parts of the 1934 amendment consisted of specifically identifying company unions as illegal and outlawing the yellow-dog contract.

Passage of the Railway Labor Act marked the end of a tired era of industrial relations problems leading to more permissive and conciliatory relations for the future. Established dispute-settlement procedures, outlawing the use of yellow-dog contracts and forbidding carrier interference with union formation, were positive statutory law steps towards greater peace on the rails. The major significance of the Railway legislation, and particularly the Railway Labor Act and its subsequent amendments, was the reflection of the changing attitudes that it mirrored. The Act demonstrated that serious attempts to protect and develop conditions for free collective bargaining in a setting of industrial democracy were evolving in the early part of the twentieth century.

The amended Railway Labor Act of 1926 constitutes the primary legislation governing the rail and air transportation industries today. Many of the conceptual and procedural provisions of the Act, such as the emergency board investigatory procedures, are forerunners of

[14] The 1936 amendment placed the air transportation industry under the Railway Labor Act. In 1951 the Act was again amended to allow union security provisions and checkoff agreements.

later labor legislation applicable to other industries. Other attempts to establish equality in labor-management relations throughout all industries appeared not long after the passage of the 1926 legislation —first in the form of the Norris-La Guardia Act.

Summary

An emerging industrial economy in the United States experienced serious labor problems during the early 1900's. The railroad industry presented particularly troublesome industrial relations problems that prompted repeated legislative attempts to regularize collective bargaining relationships. The Erdman Act, the first statutory attempt to outlaw yellow-dog contracts, met with only modest success, and was followed by numerous attempts to democratize labor relations in the railroad industry. The *Adair* and *Hitchman Coal* decisions bear direct testimony on the attitude of the courts towards labor. State attempts to moderate industrial-relations confrontations met with only modest success on all fronts, as is indicated by the Supreme Court's decision to allow injunctive relief in *Truax* v. *Corrigan*. Throughout the first quarter of the century, however, important concepts and administrative systems such as the Railway Labor Board were evolving, as is evidenced by the passage of the Railway Labor Act. With hindsight to our advantage, it is increasingly apparent that sweeping changes were on the horizon, if for no other reason than the vast importance of the railroad industry to a rapidly industrializing economy.

5

LEGALIZATION OF THE LABOR MOVEMENT

The United States' economic vulnerability to railroad labor problems attracted intensified unionization efforts, and therefore forced the development of procedures and laws that could mediate industrial relations conflict. In this chapter we will examine the Norris-La Guardia Act, since it represents a significant lessening of socioeconomic pressure on the labor movement. Declining economic welfare due to the serious depression of the 1930's hastened further change in public policy on many fronts, including labor markets. Although the National Industrial Recovery Act was doomed to judicial failure, it is also examined here because of its significance to labor legislation and court decisions discussed in subsequent chapters.

The Norris-La Guardia Act

One of the most significant milestones promoting trade unionism in the United States was the Norris-La Guardia Act, passed in 1932 and popularly referred to as the Anti-Injunction Act. The basis for congressional passage of this piece of legislation was Article III of the Constitution, which grants Congress the power to establish federal court jurisdiction.[1] The major purpose of this Act, which was readily endorsed by President Hoover, was to sharply restrain the jurisdiction of federal courts to issue injunctive relief in cases arising out of labor disputes. This was accomplished by the precise reasoning and wording of the Act, which was successful in avoiding the vagueness that had made the Clayton Act's injunction provisions ineffective.[2]

LIBERALIZATION OF THE SOCIOECONOMIC PHILOSOPHY

At the time of the depression of the 1930's, the labor movement had been attempting to compete against employer domination for a century and a half. To be effective, it was necessary that combinations of workers and concerted action on the part of employees be regarded as legal and permissible means of achieving an objective. We have seen previously how the courts and statutory laws restricted worker combinations through the application of conspiracy laws and the use of the Sherman Anti-Trust Act as a restraint on organized labor. The first three decades of the twentieth century continued to be difficult ones for the unions because of the application of anti-trust legislation and yellow-dog contracts enforced by injunctions. In addition, legal ambiguities were inherent in court determination of the legality or illegality of means and ends.

Although the historic *Commonwealth* v. *Hunt* case established that employee objectives had to be shown to be illegal if the conspiracy doctrine was to apply, additional difficulties were encountered when the court evaluated the intent in unionizing efforts.[3] Competent jurists could reach contrary decisions in deciding, for example, on the legality of a strike. On the one hand, a jurist might find a peacefully conducted strike to be the lawful attempt to improve economic conditions. In contrast, an equally learned jurist might decide that a strike is illegal and malicious in that its intent is to violate the property rights of employers by bringing economic pressure upon the employer. Determining where coercion begins and persuasion ends was, and is, a major difficulty. As a consequence, conflicting decisions were ren-

[1] Article III stipulates: "The judicial power of the United States shall be vested in one supreme court and in such inferior courts as the congress may . . . establish. . . ."

[2] See Appendix 5.

[3] 4 Metcalf, 111, 45 Mass. (1842).

dered concerning such things as strikes and picketing as means to an end. The problem of distinguishing between persuasive picketing combinations was generally held to be lawful on the one hand, but a combination judged to be conducting picketing under coercion, intimidation, or violence was held unlawful.

The significance of a court injunction was a function of its widespread application in many instances, the speed with which an injunction could be obtained, and the criminal contempt of court charges that it carried if violated. The right of employees to organize could be made meaningless so long as organizing activities, such as strikes, boycotts, or picketing, were held unlawful by the courts and enforced by injunctive relief. The injunction as a legal technique required that the complainant demonstrate that "irreparable damage" would ensue unless injunctive relief was granted by the court. Courts extended the application of injunctions by using them under conditions of only threatened damage to an employer's business. The court's rationale was that the property right was appropriate to injunctive relief. In addition, *ex parte* injunctions were issued under conditions where the union typically did not have an initial opportunity to present its side of the story. By the time a case was brought before a jurist to determine the validity of the request for a permanent injunction, the union strike or picketing action would have been devastated, irrespective of whether or not the injunction was granted on a permanent basis.

The use of the injunction became increasingly popular after the *Debbs* case in 1895. It has been reported that approximately 300 injunctions were issued in connection with the 1922 Railway Strike alone. In one of these instances, the coverage of an injunction was so sweeping that a barber in the community who refused to cut the hair of "scabs" was held in contempt of court for violating the injunction, even though it applied to a dispute in the railroad industry.[4] In addition to lending considerable muscle to anti-trust prosecutions, the injunction was a most effective technique in enforcing yellow-dog contracts, also held to be legal until the 1930's. We have seen previously how the courts held the Erdman Act provision concerning the yellow-dog contract unconstitutional on the grounds that the Constitution guaranteed freedom of contract as a property right to employers. We have also seen how the Clayton Act was misconstrued and its attempts to restrain the use of the injunction were made completely ineffective by the Supreme Court. Supreme Court decisions in the *Du-*

[4] Lieberman, *op. cit.*, p. 241.

plex and *Bedford* cases obliterated the Magna Charta of labor, supposedly embodied in the Clayton Act. It is against this background that organized labor devoted decades of acrimonious campaigning for relief against injunctions and the sweeping jurisdiction allowed the courts. Organized labor continually sought congressional legislative assistance in forcing the judiciary power into a neutral stance on labor disputes. Congress slowly turned sympathetic, especially after the interpretation of the Clayton Act. The Norris-La Guardia Act was finally enacted in 1932, when the American Federation of Labor was at its lowest membership and financial ebb.

THE "NEW" POLICY

The widespread influence of the Norris-La Guardia Act is illustrated by Section 2 of the Act, which declares the policy intent of Congress to be that of giving the worker the right to bargain with full freedom in association, self-organization, and selection of his own representatives free of employer coercion or restraint. This statement of public policy is as follows:

> Whereas under prevailing economic conditions, developed with the aid of governmental authority for owners of property to organize in the corporate and other forms of ownership association, the individual unorganized worker is commonly helpless to exercise actual liberty of contract and to protect his freedom of labor, and thereby to obtain acceptable terms and conditions of employment, wherefore, though he should be free to decline to associate with his fellows, it is necessary that he have full freedom of association, self-organization, and designation of representatives of his own choosing, to negotiate the terms and conditions of his employment, and that he shall be free from the interference, restraint, or coercion of employers of labor, or their agents, in the designation of such representatives or in self-organization or in other concerted activities for the purpose of collective bargaining or other mutual aid or protection; therefore, the following definitions of, and limitations upon, the jurisdiction and authority of the courts of the United States are hereby enacted.[5]

It should also be noted that many of the principles embodied in the Norris-La Guardia Act were quickly duplicated by more than a

[5] See Appendix V for details of the Act.

dozen state legislatures. After the passage of these pieces of legislation at the state level, the courts became a more neutral force in labor-management disputes instead of an extrapolated power base for
the employer.

Sections 1 and 4 of the Norris-La Guardia Act protect nine specific areas of union activity from the injunctive process, indicating
"that no court in the United States, as herein defined, shall have jurisdiction to issue any restraining order . . . in a case involving . . . a
labor dispute, except in strict conformity with provisions of this act;
. . ." The nine areas in which injunctions cannot be issued are court
orders that prohibit persons from doing any of the following:

(1) ceasing to perform work or remain in a previous employment
    relationship,
(2) becoming or remaining a member of a labor union,
(3) giving or withholding financial assistance (e.g., unemployment
    benefits) to persons involved or interested in the labor dispute,
(4) lawfully assisting persons involved in litigation who are inter-
    ested or participating in a labor dispute,
(5) making known the existence of a dispute by methods not in-
    volving violence or fraud,
(6) peaceably assembling to promote the interests of participants in
    a labor dispute,
(7) notifying other persons of an intent to accomplish any acts spec-
    ified in any of the above,
(8) agreeing in common with others to do or refrain from doing
    any of the acts specified above, and
(9) inducing without fraud or violence any of the acts specified
    above.

These provisions of the Norris-La Guardia Act established a protected tactical position for the union. In essence, the union was almost completely unrestrained from using strikes, boycotts, picketing,
and other weapons of conflict free from court intervention so long as
violence or fraud was not involved.

Section 3 of the Norris-La Guardia Act was rather straightforward
and of great importance to the union. Hence, the Congress specifically indicated that agreements or promises not to join, become, or remain a member of a labor organization whether written, implied, or
oral, were contrary to the public policy of the United States and
could not be enforced in any court. In short, the yellow-dog contract

was denied as a basis for granting legal or restraining order relief by any court.

Sections 7 and 8 of the Norris-La Guardia Act further restricted court authority in issuing injunctions by specifying that certain conditions had to be met *prior to* granting a restraining order. Section 7, for example, stated that the court was required to hear testimony in an open hearing that allowed for cross examination prior to granting an injunction. In addition, it stipulated that the court was required to uncover findings of facts that demonstrated to its satisfaction that (a) unlawful acts had been threatened and would be committed if restraint were not allowed; (b) substantial and irreparable injury to complainant's property had to be demonstrated; (c) a complainant would suffer greater injury in the absence of an injunction than would be inflicted upon the defendant if relief were granted; (d) a complainant had no other adequate legal remedy; and (e) the complainant did not have adequate protection of property through public officers. Section 8 simply required as still another condition to granting injunctive relief that the complainant must have attempted to settle the dispute in question through collective negotiation or other conciliatory machinery provided by the government.

The Norris-La Guardia Act repeatedly refers to a "labor dispute" in denying injunctive procedures. In Section 13 of this Act, Congress broadly but rather carefully defined the meaning of a "labor dispute." It was the intent of Congress that a labor dispute would include the following:

> The term "labor dispute" includes any controversy concerning terms or conditions of employment, or concerning the association or representation of persons in negotiating, fixing, maintaining, changing, or seeking to arrange terms or conditions of employment, regardless of whether or not the disputants stand in the approximate relation of employer and employee.[6]

Because of this very clear and rather broad definition of a labor dispute (e.g., inclusion of approximate employer-employee relationships), the organized labor movement received a very clear mandate from Congress to proceed with their organizing activities. It is particularly noteworthy that Congress was cognizant of the interest a labor union might extend beyond direct employee-employer relationships, and these were declared to be within the protective coverage of the Norris-La Guardia Act. The Act was

[6] See Appendix V.

two-edged in that it (a) protected several kinds of activities that might be engaged in by the union from subsequent injunctive coverage by the courts, and (b) required that court hearings prove that certain conditions be met prior to granting an injunction. Even though the conditions under which an injunction might be issued are carefully spelled out and appear to be quite exclusive, the Act did not prohibit issuance of injunctions in every labor dispute. What the Norris-La Guardia Act did accomplish, however, was a restoration of the conventional rules of equity as they existed prior to the court's application of injunctions to labor disputes.

INJUNCTIONS AND "LABOR DISPUTES"

As is true of all congressional legislation, the Norris-La Guardia Act was subjected to the scrutiny of the courts. The legality of portions of the Norris-La Guardia Act was tested on several subsequent occasions. In some of these cases, the court dealt with definitional matters surrounding what constitutes a labor dispute and an employer. In still other instances, the court addressed itself to the Norris-La Guardia Act and injunctive relief in relation to anti-trust legislation. The first of the more important test cases occurred in the 1937 *Senn* v. *Tile Layers' Protective Union* decision.[7]

In the early 1930's, widespread economic problems during the Great Depression in conjunction with the attitude that prompted federal legislation encouraged several states to pass legislation similar to the Norris-La Guardia Act. The State of Wisconsin passed a "baby" Norris-La Guardia Act in 1931, which was modeled after the federal legislation formally passed one year later by Congress. When this portion of the Wisconsin Labor Code [8] was validated by the Supreme Court in the *Senn* case, this afforded comparable judicial approval to the federal statute that so closely resembled the Wisconsin Labor Code on the topic of injunctive relief.

Because of the high incidence of unemployment during the depression, members and ex-members of the Tile Layers' Protective Union contracted for work independently. As a consequence of job underbidding for a short supply of work, the existing union wage scale was under considerable downward pressure. Paul Senn, an ex-plasterer, formed the very small Senn Company in Milwaukee and contracted

[7] 301 U.S. 468 (1937).
[8] Section 103.53.

for tile laying work during the early 1930's. After the passage of the
Wisconsin Labor Code and a modest upsurge in employment, the
local union intensified their organizing efforts. Although Senn was
willing to comply with union terms on wages and hours, the proposed
labor agreement was refused by Senn because it required owners to
refrain from performing labor tasks. By mid-1935, Senn was in the minority of contractor holdouts, and the union initiated peaceful and orderly picketing of Senn's business premises. Senn then requested an
injunction that would restrain the union from picketing his place of
business and otherwise informing his potential customers that his firm
was unfair to labor. The request was denied in the Wisconsin courts
and Senn appealed to the United States Supreme Court, which heard
the case in March and April of 1937. In a very sharply split decision
on the substance of the case and the law, the court denied injunctive
relief to petitioner Senn, thereby upholding Wisconsin's "baby" Norris-La Guardia Act. The decision is recorded as follows:

SENN v. TILE LAYERS' PROTECTIVE UNION: 1937
(301 U.S. 468)

Mr. Justice Brandeis spoke for the majority:

This case presents the question whether the provisions of the
Wisconsin Labor Code which authorize giving publicity to labor
disputes, declare peaceful picketing and patrolling lawful and prohibit granting of an injunction against such conduct, violate, as
here construed and applied, the due process clause or equal protection clause of the Fourteenth Amendment. . . . Senn was engaged at Milwaukee in the tile contracting business under the
name of "Paul Senn & Co., Tile Contracting." His business was a
small one, conducted, in the main, from his residence, with a
showroom elsewhere. He employed one or two journeymen tile
layers and one or two helpers, depending upon the amount of
work he had contracted to do at the time. But, working with his
own hands with tools of the trade, he performed personally on the
jobs much work of a character commonly done by a tile layer or a
helper. Neither Senn, nor any of his employees, was at the time
this suit was begun a member of either union, and neither had any
contractual relations with them. . . .

The trial court denied the injunction and dismissed the bill. On
the findings made, it ruled that the controversy was "a labor dispute" within the meaning of (the Wisconsin Code); that the picket-

ing, done solely in furtherance of the dispute, was "lawful" under (the Code); that it was not unlawful for the defendants "to advise, notify or persuade, without fraud, violence or threat thereof, any person or persons, of the existence of said labor dispute; . . ." Senn appealed to the Supreme Court of the State, which affirmed the judgment of the trial court and denied a motion of rehearing, two judges dissenting. The case is here on appeal. . . . The hearings . . . were concerned mainly with questions of state law. Senn insisted there that the statute was no defense, because the controversy was not a "labor dispute" within the meaning of the law. The courts ruled that the controversy was a "labor dispute;" and that the acts done by the defendant were among those declared "lawful" by Section 103.53. . . . Those issues involved the construction and application of the statute and the Constitution of the State. As to them the judgment of its highest court is conclusive. The question for our decision is whether the statute, as applied to the facts found, took Senn's liberty or property or denied him equal protection of the laws in violation of the Fourteenth Amendment. . . . He (Senn) contends that the right to work in his business with his own hands is a right guaranteed by the Fourteenth Amendment and that the State may not authorize unions to employ publicity and picketing to induce him to refrain from exercising it.

The unions concede that Senn, so long as he conducts a nonunion shop, has the right to work with his hands and tools. He may do so, as freely as he may work his employees longer hours and at lower wages than the union rules permit. He may bid for contracts at a low figure based upon low wages and long hours. But the unions contend that, since Senn's exercise of the right to do so is harmful to the interests of their members, they may seek by legal means to induce him to agree to unionize his shop and to refrain from exercising his right to work with his own hands. The judgment of the highest court of the state establishes that both the means employed and the end sought by the unions are legal under its law. The question for our determination is whether either the means or the end sought is forbidden by the Federal Constitution.

Clearly the means which the statute authorizes—picketing and publicity—are not prohibited by the Fourteenth Amendment. Members of a union might, without special statutory authorization by a State, make known the facts of a labor dispute, for freedom of speech is guaranteed by the Federal Constitution. The State may in the exercise of its police power regulate the methods

and means of publicity as well as the use of public streets. If the
end sought by the unions is not forbidden by the Federal Constitution the State may authorize working men to seek to attain it by
combining as pickets, just as it permits capitalists and employers
to combine in other ways to attain their desired economic ends.
. . . The end sought by the unions is not unconstitutional. Article
III, which the unions seek to have Senn accept, was found by the
state courts to be not arbitrary or capricious, but a reasonable rule
"adopted by the defendants out of the necessities of employment
within the industry and for the protection of themselves as workers
and craftsmen in the industry." That finding is amply supported by
the evidence. There is no basis for a suggestion that the unions' request that Senn refrain from working with his own hands, or their
employment of picketing and publicity, was malicious; or that
there was a desire to injure Senn. The sole purpose of the picketing was to acquaint the public with the facts and, by gaining its
support, to induce Senn to unionize his shop. There was no effort
to induce Senn to do an unlawful thing. There was no violence, no
force was applied, no molestation or interference, no coercion.
There was only the persuasion incident to publicity. . . .

. . . There is nothing in the Federal Constitution which forbids
unions from competing with nonunion concerns for customers by
means of picketing as freely as one merchant competes with another by means of advertisements in the press, by circulars, or by
his window display. Each member of the unions, as well as Senn,
has the right to strive to earn his living. Senn seeks to do so
through exercise of his individual skill and planning. The union
members seek to do so through combination. Earning a living is
dependent upon securing work; and securing work is dependent
upon public favor. To win the patronage of the public each may
strive by legal means.

Exercising its police power, Wisconsin has declared that in a
labor dispute peaceful picketing and truthful publicity are means
legal for unions. . . . It is contended that in prohibiting an injunction the statute denied to Senn equal protection of the laws, and
Truax v. *Corrigan*, 257 U. S. 312, *supra*, is invoked. But the issue
suggested by plaintiff does not arise. For we hold that the provisions of the Wisconsin statute which authorized the conduct of the
unions are constitutional. One has no constitutional right to a
"remedy" against the lawful conduct of another.

Affirmed.

The *Senn Tile* case confirmed the constitutionality of legal principles restricting injunctive relief similar to those embodied in the Norris-La Guardia Act. Furthermore, the Court's recognition of the legality of state regulations of picketing was also important. The Supreme Court had found picketing activities to be an illegal infringement on property rights previous to the *Truax* decision. Now, peaceful picketing was protected the same as free speech (more will be said of this matter in Chapter 7). The following dissent to the *Senn* decision written by Justice Butler indicates a measure of the unpopularity with the five-to-four decision.

Plaintiff is a tile layer and has long been accustomed to work as a helper and mechanic in that trade. The question presented is whether, consistently with the due process and equal protection clauses of the Fourteenth Amendment, the State may by statute authorize or make it lawful for labor unions to adopt and carry into effect measures intended and calculated to prevent him from obtaining or doing that work. The decision just announced answers that question in the affirmative. The facts are not in controversy. Let them disclose the concrete application of the legislation now held valid. The trial court found the picketing peaceful and lawful; it did not pass on other acts constituting pressure put on plaintiff. But the unions themselves deemed unlawful much that they had threatened and done to coerce him. The findings say that "the defendants, by their counsel, have stated in open court that they will not pursue the automobile of the plaintiff from his place of business to his jobs; that they will refrain from sending any further letters to architects or contractors, and will not indulge in any acts or conduct referred to in said letters toward said contractors and architects." The trial court held plaintiff not entitled to relief. The supreme court affirmed. . . .

The clauses of the Fourteenth Amendment invoked by plaintiff are: "No State shall . . . deprive any person of life, liberty, or property without due process of law; nor deny to any person within its jurisdiction the equal protection of the laws." Our decisions have made it everywhere known that these provisions forbid state action which would take from the individual the right to engage in common occupations of life, and that they assure equality of opportunity to all under like circumstances. Lest the importance or wisdom of these great declarations be forgotten or neglected, there should be frequent recurrence to decisions of this court that expound and apply them. While this Court has not attempted to define with exactness the liberty thus guaranteed, the term has received much consideration and some of the included things have been definitely stated. Without doubt, it denotes not merely freedom from bodily restraint but also the right of the individual to contract, to engage in any of the common occupations of life, . . . generally to enjoy those privileges long recognized at common law as essential to the orderly pursuit of happiness by free man. The right to follow any of the common occupations of life is an inalienable right. . . . I hold that the liberty of pursuit—the right to follow any of the ordinary callings of life—is one of the privileges of a citizen of the United States. Included in the right of personal liberty and the right of private property—partaking of the nature of each—is the right to make contracts for the acquisition of property. Chief among such contracts is that of personal employment by which labor and other services are exchanged for money or other forms of property. If this right be struck down or arbitrarily interfered with, there is a substantial impairment of liberty in the long-established constitutional sense. . . .

The legislative power of the State can only be exerted in subordination to the fundamental principles of right and justice which the guarantees of the due process and equal protection clauses of the Fourteenth Amendment are intended to preserve. Arbitrary or capricious exercise of that power whereby a wrongful and highly injurious invasion of rights of liberty and property is sanctioned, stripping one of all remedy, is wholly at variance with those principles. . . . The object that defendants seek to attain is an unlawful one. Admittedly, it is to compel plaintiff to quit work as helper or tile layer. Their purpose is not to establish on his jobs better wages, hours, or conditions. If permitted, plaintiff would employ union men and adhere to union requirements as to pay and hours. But, solely because he works, the unions refuse to allow him to unionize and carry on his business. . . . The principles governing competition between rival individuals seeking contracts or opportunity to work as journeymen cannot reasonably be applied in this case. Neither the union nor its members take tile laying contracts. Their interests are confined to employment of helpers and layers, their wages, hours or service, etc. The contest is not between unionized and other contractors or between one employer and another. The immediate issue is between the unions and plaintiff in respect of his right to work in the performance of his own jobs. If as to that they shall succeed, then will come the enforcement of their rules which make him ineligible to work as a journeyman. It cannot be said that, if he should be prevented from laboring as helper or layer, the work for union men to do would be increased. The unions exclude their members from jobs taken by nonunion employers. . . .

The judgment of the state court, here affirmed, violates a principle of fundamental law: That no man may be compelled to hold his life or the means of living at the mere will of others. *Yick Wo* v. *Hopkins,* 118 U. S. 356. The state statute, construed to make lawful the employment of the means here shown to deprive plaintiff of his rights to work or to make lawful the picketing carried on in this case, is repugnant to the due process and equal protection clauses of the Fourteenth Amendment. . . .

I am of opinion that the judgment should be reversed.

Mr. Justice Van Devanter, Mr. Justice McReynolds and Mr. Justice Sutherland join in this dissent.

The following year the Supreme Court heard two additional cases involving the definition of a labor dispute. In *Lauf* v. *Shinner & Co.,* the Supreme Court affirmed the intent and language of Congress to bar injunctive relief to parties standing in an approximate relation of employer and employee, even though the picketing union represented none of Shinner's employees, all of whom appeared to be disinterested in union membership.[9] As a consequence of the Supreme Court's ruling that a labor dispute did exist, it was obligatory for the company to meet all of the conditions of Sections 7 and 8 of the Norris-La Guardia Act. Even though the union that had picketed for bargaining representation was not successful in persuading Shinner's butchers to join, the Supreme Court overruled the lower court's finding that no labor dispute existed and stayed the injunction. Justice Roberts delivered the opinion for the Court that states, in part, that:

The District Court erred in holding that no labor dispute, as defined by the law of Wisconsin, existed between the parties. . . . The error into which the court fell as to the existence of a labor dispute led it into the further error of issuing an order so sweeping as to enjoin acts made lawful by the State statute. The decree forbade all picketing, all advertising that the respondent was unfair

[9] 303 U.S. 323 (1938).

to organized labor, and all persuasion and solicitation of customers not to trade with respondent. . . . The District Court erred in granting an injunction in the absence of findings which the Norris-La Guardia Act makes prerequisite to the exercise of jurisdiction (and) . . . made none of the required findings save as to irreparable injury and lack of remedy at law. It follows that in issuing an injunction it exceeded its jurisdiction. The judgment is reversed. . . .[10]

During the same year, the Supreme Court ruled similarly in *New Negro Alliance* v. *Sanitary Grocery Co.*, a case in which the employer refused to employ Negroes in a store that was newly opened in a Negro area.[11] The New Negro Alliance, a group seeking socioeconomic justice for the Negro, embarked on peaceful picketing. The company requested and received injunctive relief through the District of Columbia courts on the grounds that a labor dispute did not exist. Justice Roberts delivered the majority opinion for the Supreme Court once again, in which the decree of the lower court was reversed. The Supreme Court majority argued that the dispute was a labor dispute subject to the injunctive restraints set forth in the Norris-La Guardia Act.

GOVERNMENT AND THE ANTI-INJUNCTION LAW

The mine fields had been a hotbed of labor unrest for many years, in part because of the working hazards miners were exposed to. In the 1930's they erupted, in part, because of the anti-yellow-dog contract provision of the Norris-La Guardia Act. John L. Lewis, the colorful and powerful leader of the mine workers, led intensified organizing campaigns that were quite successful. Lewis and the United Mine Workers were also instrumental in the formation and success of the Congress for Industrial Organizations (CIO). The action of the miners in particular embittered the public and the Roosevelt Administration during World War II because of the miners' rebellious contempt for public authority. Even though use of the injunction had been severely restricted through the passage of the Norris-La Guardia Act and similar state statutes, labor was not totally immune from the injunction in labor disputes, as the *United States* v. *United Mine Workers* decision reveals.[12]

[10] *Ibid.*
[11] 303 U.S. 552 (1938).
[12] 330 U.S. 258 (1947).

While the coal mines were still under wartime government control, Lewis and the United Mine Workers were served with a temporary injunction restraining them from breaking the *Krug-Lewis* agreement reached earlier. The United Mine Workers did not heed the injunction, and in November 1946, Attorney General Clark charged Lewis and the Mine Workers with criminal contempt of court. Attorneys for the United Mine Workers contested the charge on the fact that the court was without jurisdiction to issue an injunction under the labor dispute terms of the Norris-La Guardia Act. The lower court decision rendered by Justice Goldsborough ruled that the provisions of this Act were not meant to apply to the government as an employer, and the court therefore did have jurisdiction. A fine of $3,-500,000 was assessed against the United Mine Workers and John L. Lewis was individually assessed $10,000 for criminal contempt of court. The defendants appealed the case, which was then heard by the Supreme Court in January 1947. Three separate opinions were written on behalf of the majority decision, which affirmed the lower court ruling. Justices Vinson, Black, and Douglas agreed that the Norris-La Guardia Act did not apply to the government as an employer under the temporary industry-control conditions that existed; however, their reasoning differed. Justices Black and Douglas felt that the United Mine Workers were guilty of contempt of court because they disobeyed Justice Goldsborough's order, but in their view the punitive fines were excessive. Although four of the nine Justices dissented on the applicability of the Norris-La Guardia Act to this case, the United Mine Workers lost their appeal. This and similar labor problems during the War era demonstrated once again that judicial authority can surmount legislative mandates under circumstances that threaten the public interest. Aside from the spectacular fines levied in this instance, the significance of this decision was the Supreme Court's willingness and ability to reason around existing statutory restraints imposed by the Norris-La Guardia Act in national emergency conditions. The Justices demonstrated their ability to intricately evoke emergency-law in the public interest, especially when public opinion is not in support of the actions of organized labor.

THE NATIONAL INDUSTRIAL RECOVERY ACT AND LABOR RELATIONS

The Great Depression of the 1930's was marked by declining income and employment opportunities, thereby favoring employer dominance of labor relations. With the onset of the depression, employees increasingly were unable to better their own conditions and were reluctant to resign from jobs that were very scarce. A good deal of conflict was generated over the system of handling layoffs, a problem in the early 1930's as unemployment affected one-third of the American labor force. In addition, the labor force changed considerably in the early decades of the twentieth century. Increasing numbers of workers were attending and completing high school and bringing more sophisticated ideas on industrial democracy to the labor market. Employers remained reluctant to accept change and generally tended to advocate the individualism and private enterprise philosophies that had prevailed throughout the nineteenth century.

Official federal government approval of the principle of collective bargaining and support of the union movement gradually emerged prior to the 1930's, as is evidenced by the railway labor legislation and numerous rulings by the War Labor Board. The Norris-La Guardia Act of 1932 gave further evidence of an emerging liberal philosophy. The National Industrial Recovery Act (NIRA) was approved on June 6, 1933, as a reaction to the socioeconomic chaos that prevailed during the early years of the depression. The intent of this Act was to "promote the organization of industry for the purpose of cooperative action among trade groups." Under the Act, industry codes of fair competition were to be developed; and standards for hours, wages, and other labor-relations practices were to be set for individual industries. As such, the Act was a distinct departure from the laissez-faire philosophy that had prevailed in the American economy up to this time. The NIRA provided for the establishment of codes of fair competition applicable to a variety of industries, and appealed to business, agriculture, and labor interests throughout the nation.

Section 7(a) proved to be an important provision in this early piece of New Deal legislation. In an attempt to secure labor support for the NIRA, each approved industry code was required to reflect these conditions:

1. That employees shall have the right to organize and bargain collectively through representatives of their own choosing, and shall be free from the interference, restraint, or coercion of employers or labor, or their agents, and the designation of such representatives or in self-organization or in other concerted activities for the purpose of collective bargaining or other mutual aids or protection;

2. That no employee and no one seeking employment shall be required as a condition of employment to join any company union or

to refrain from joining, organizing, or assisting a labor organization of its own choosing.

While Section 7(a) was the most complete federal government endorsement of collective bargaining existing at that time outside of the railway industry, it neglected to specify penalties for failure to comply with the Act. As a consequence, most employers failed to act in accordance with the law. Even though labor's rights in Section 7(a) were not enforceable, the union movement seized upon the alleged intent of the Act and energetically expanded their organizing efforts. Obviously, specifications of employee rights to organize and bargain freely and collectively through their own representatives compounded the controversial nature of the Act. This was not met with a great deal of employer enthusiasm. The major problems with the NIRA were the compliance and enforcement areas, as well as intrepetative difficulties. For example, the statute was not clear in specifying employer actions that were coercive and illegal or how employees were to select representatives. This, of course, led to subsequent unrest that was heightened by liberal interpretation of Section 7(a) by organized labor, now firmly aware of an encouragement of collective bargaining and free union representation.

The United Mine Workers, for example, sent organizers to the coal mining country of Kentucky and West Virginia, and within a period of a few months after passage of the law they had one-third of a million new enrollees. Unionism began to appear in mass-production industries, and organizing efforts were heightened by the Garment Workers' and Amalgamated Clothing Workers' Unions. The American Federation of Labor gradually began to organize previously nonunion industries such as the rubber and auto industries.

The labor disputes and conflicting interpretations that sprung up under Section 7(a) of the NIRA resulted in the establishment of the National Labor Board (August, 1933) to deal with issues arising under the NIRA codes. The National Labor Board also established twenty regional boards comprised of representatives from industry, labor, and the public who were charged with dealing with disputes arising under Section 7(a) of the Act. The National Labor Board, headed by Senator Robert Wagner of New York, was to deal with disputes requiring mediation and voluntary arbitration. This included such issues as determining employer interference, employer domination of organizational rights, and other union representation issues. In carrying out their function, the National Labor Board was precipitating some of the same policies and procedures that were to be followed later by the National Labor Relations Board under the jurisdiction of the 1935 Wagner Act.

Under the National Labor Board, the so-called "Reading Formula" was established where union representation was determined by the majority vote of workers in a plant. If a majority selected either a company union or the independent union, that union represented all workers. This policy, however, was vigorously opposed by employers as well as by Hugh Johnson—one of the prominent officials administering the NIRA. Johnson ultimately overruled the National Labor Board on their system of union representation and declared a system of proportional representation for the automobile industry. This shattered the effectiveness of the Board. As a consequence of these developments, Joint Congressional Resolution No. 44 was approved by President Roosevelt in 1934. Resolution No. 44 recreated a National Labor Relations Board in place of the National Labor Board that had interpretative authority over Section 7(a) as well as the responsibility of conducting elections and holding hearings on labor disputes. The new Board continued the policies and procedures of its predecessor with modest success, and attempted to enlist the support of business for the National Industrial Recovery Act. One of the great weaknesses of the newly-created National Labor Relations Board remained an inability to penalize employers for unfair labor practices in a meaningful manner.[13]

The National Labor Relations Board was also plagued with administrative problems. It was completely dependent upon the Department of Justice and the constitutionality of the National Industry Recovery Act as well as the administrators of the National Recovery Administration. As it turned out, both the newly created Board and the special labor boards that were established under the National Recovery Administration had common jurisdictional authority over labor disputes in industries covered by NIRA codes. As a consequence, President Roosevelt granted authority over labor disputes to the special labor boards that were created for each industry. The shrinking

[13] National Labor Relations Board sanctions consisted of referring violations under Section 7(a) to the Attorney General's Office, who might then refuse to place the NIRA "Blue Eagle" label on the product of employers charged with unfair labor practices.

jurisdiction of the National Labor Relations Board prompted by this move led to its virtual collapse. As these and related legal events were taking place, Senator Robert Wagner Sr. was working on his bill, the Wagner Act. In 1935, the constitutionality of the National Industrial Recovery Act was challenged and ruled upon by the Supreme Court. The Act was declared unconstitutional in the *Schechter* decision, where the court viewed it as an unconstitutional exercise of power by the federal government. Chief Justice Hughes, speaking for the Supreme Court majority, observed that the NIRA was an attempt to govern wages and hours of employees on intrastate transactions and was therefore an illegal exercise of federal power. The reasoning in this decision is recorded as follows:

SCHECHTER POULTRY v. UNITED STATES: 1935
(*295 U.S. 495*)

Mr. Chief Justice Hughes spoke for the majority of the court:

. . . A.L.A. Schechter Poultry Corporation and Schechter Live Poultry Market are corporations conducting wholesale poultry slaughterhouse markets in Brooklyn, New York City. . . .

The "Live Poultry Code" was promulgated under the National Industrial Recovery Act. That section—the pertinent provisions of which are set forth in the margin—authorizes the President to approve "codes of fair competition." Such a code may be approved for a trade or industry, upon applications by one or more trade or industrial associations or groups, if the President finds (1) that such associations or groups "impose no inequitable restrictions on admission to membership therein and are truly representative," and (2) that such codes are not designed "to promote monopolies or to eliminate or oppress small enterprises and will not operate to discriminate against them, and will tend to effectuate the policy" of title I. of the act. Such codes "shall not permit monopolies or monopolistic practices." As a condition of his approval, the President may "impose such conditions (including requirements for the making of reports and the keeping of accounts) for the protection of consumers, competitors, employees and others, and in furtherance of the public interest, and may provide such exceptions to and exemptions from the provisions of such code as the President in his discretion deems necessary to effectuate the policy herein declared." Where such a code has not been approved, the President may prescribe one, either on his own motion or on complaint.

Violation of any provision of a code (so approved or prescribed) "in any transaction in or affecting interstate or foreign commerce" is made a misdemeanor punishable by a fine of not more than $500 for each offense, and each day the violation continues is to be deemed a separate offense. The "Live Poultry Code" was approved by the President on April 13, 1934. Its divisions indicate its nature and scope. The code has eight articles entitled (1) purposes, (2) definitions, (3) hours, (4) wages, (5) general labor provisions, (6) administration, (7) trade practice provisions, and (8) general."

Of the eighteen counts of the indictment upon which the defendants were convicted, aside from the count for conspiracy, two counts charged violation of the minimum wage and maximum hour provisions of the code, . . . The Constitution established a national government with powers deemed to be adequate, as they have proved to be both in war and peace, but these powers of the national government are limited by the constitutional grants. Those who act under these grants are not at liberty to transcend the imposed limits because they believe that more or different power is necessary. Such assertions of extra-constitutional authority were anticipated and precluded by the explicit terms of the Tenth Amendment. "The powers not delegated to the United States by the Constitution, nor prohibited by it to the States, are reserved to the States respectively or to the people."

Did the defendants' transactions directly "affect" interstate commerce so as to be subject to Federal regulation? The power of Congress extends not only to the regulation of transactions which are part of interstate commerce, but to the protection of that commerce from injury. It matters not that the injury may be due to the conduct of those engaged in intrastate operations. . . . The undisputed facts thus afford no warrant for the argument that the poultry handled by defendants at their slaughterhouse markets was in a "current" or "flow" of interstate commerce and was thus subject to congressional regulation. The mere fact that there may be a constant flow of commodities into a State does not mean that the flow continues after the property has arrived and has become commingled with the mass of property within the State and is there held solely for local disposition and use. So far as the poultry herein questioned is concerned, the flow in interstate commerce had ceased. The poultry had come to a permanent rest within the State. It was not held, used or sold by defendants in relation to any further transactions in interstate commerce and was not destined for transportation to other States. Hence, decisions which deal with a stream of interstate commerce—where goods come to rest within a State temporarily and are later to go forward in interstate commerce—and with the regulations of transactions involved in that practical continuity of movement, are not applicable here. . . .

In determining how far the Federal Government may go in controlling intrastate transactions upon the ground that they "affect" interstate commerce, there is a necessary and well-established distinction between direct and indirect effects. The precise line can be drawn only as individual cases arise, but the distinction is clear in principle. . . . The distinction between direct and indirect effects has been clearly recognized in the application of the Anti-Trust Act. Where a combination or conspiracy is formed, with the intent to restrain interstate commerce or to monopolize any part of it, the violation of the statute is clear. . . . But where the intent is absent, and the objectives are limited to intrastate activities, the fact that there may be an indirect effect upon interstate commerce does not subject the parties to the Federal statute, notwithstanding its broad provisions. This principle has frequently been applied in litigation growing out of labor disputes. . . . While (previous) decisions related to the application of the Federal statute, and not to its constitutional validity, the distinction between direct and indirect effects of intrastate transactions upon interstate commerce must be recognized as a fundamental one, essential to the maintenance of our constitutional system. Otherwise, as we have said, there would be virtually no limit to the Federal power, and for all practical purposes we should have a completely centralized government. We must consider the provisions here in question in the light of this distinction.

The question of chief importance relates to the provisions of the Code as to the hours and wages of those employed in defendants' slaughterhouse markets. It is plain that these requirements are imposed in order to govern the details of defendants' management of their local business. The persons employed in slaughtering and selling in local trade are not employed in interstate commerce. Their hours and wages have no direct relation to interstate commerce. The question of how many hours these employees should work and what they should be paid differs in no essential respect from similar questions in other local businesses which handle commodities brought into a State and there dealt in as a part of its internal commerce. This appears from an examination of the considerations urged by the Government with respect to conditions in the poultry trade. Thus, the Government argues that hours and wages affect prices; that slaughterhouse men sell at a small margin above operating costs; that labor represents 50 to 60 per cent of these costs; that a slaughterhouse operator paying lower wages or reducing his cost by exacting long hours of work translates his saving into lower prices; that this results in demands for a cheaper grade of goods, and that the cutting of prices brings about a demoralization of the price structure. Similar conditions may be adduced in relation to other businesses. The argument of the Government proves too much. If the Federal Government may determine the wages and hours of employees in the internal commerce of a State, because of their relation to cost and prices and their indirect effect upon interstate commerce, it would seem that a similar control might be exerted over other elements of cost, also affecting prices, such as the number of employees, rents, advertising, methods of doing business, etc. All the processes of production and distribution that enter into cost could likewise be controlled. If the cost of doing an intrastate business is in itself the permitted object of Federal control, the extent of the regulation of cost would be a question of discretion and not of power.

The Government also makes the point that efforts to enact State legislation establishing high labor standards have been impeded by the belief that unless similar action is taken generally, commerce will be diverted from the States adopting such standards, and that this fear of diversion has led to demands for Federal legislation on the subject of wages and hours. The apparent implication is that the Federal authority under the commerce clause should be deemed to extend to the establishment of rules to govern wages and hours in intrastate trade and industry generally throughout the country, thus overriding the authority of the States to deal with domestic problems arising from labor conditions in their internal commerce.

It is not the province of the Court to consider the economic advantages or disadvantages of such a centralized system. It is sufficient to say that the Federal Constitution does not provide for it. Our growth and development have called for wide use of the commerce power of the Federal Government in its control over the expanded activities of interstate commerce and in protecting that commerce from burdens, interferences and conspiracies to restrain and monopolize it. But the authority of the Federal Government may not be pushed to such an extreme as to destroy the distinction, which the commerce clause itself establishes, between commerce "among the several States" and the internal concerns of a State. The same answer must be made to the contention that is based upon the serious economic situation which led to the passage of the Recovery Act—the fall in prices, the decline in wages and employment, and the curtailment of the market for commodities. Stress is laid upon the great importance of maintaining wage distributions which would provide the necessary stimulus in starting "the cumulative forces making for expanding commercial activity." Without in any way disparaging this motive, it is enough to say that the recuperative efforts of the Federal Government must be made in a manner consistent with the authority granted by the Constitution.

We are of the opinion that the attempt through the provisions of the Code to fix the hours and wages of employees of defendants in their intrastate business was not a valid exercise of Federal power. . . .

The Schechter decision was important in that it negated union protection furnished by the NIRA, which was of particular significance in the area of free employee associations. These events precipitated passage of the Wagner Act in 1935, the most significant expression of public policy towards labor.

Summary

A most significant break with tradition occurred in 1932 with the passage of the Norris-La Guardia Act. This important piece of legislation sharply restricted use of the injunction and outlawed the yellow-dog contract, two weapons of conflict that were repeatedly used by management for several decades in an attempt to thwart unionization. The legality of the Norris-La Guardia Act was obtained by proxy in the *Senn Tile* decision. The court quickly became even more involved than it had been in the past in difficult but important decisions such as definition of a labor dispute under the new legislation. Further difficulties continued to plague labor relations, including the question of the applicability of Norris-La Guardia to the government as an employer. Moreover, the seriousness of the depression of the

1930's prompted further legislation that changed labor relations. For example, the National Industrial Recovery Act, even though invalidated in the *Schechter Poultry* case, was influential in establishing a new climate between labor and management. As the decade of the 1930's reached a half-way point, the Wagner Act changed employee-employer relationships dramatically, as the following chapter reveals.

APPENDIX 5

The Norris-La Guardia Anti-Injunction Act
(*March 23, 1932, 72d Congress*)

SECTION 1. That no court of the United States, as herein defined, shall have jurisdiction to issue any restraining order or temporary or permanent injunction in a case involving or growing out of a labor dispute, except in a strict conformity with the provisions of this Act; nor shall any such restraining order or temporary or permanent injunction be issued contrary to the public policy declared in this Act.

SEC. 2. In the interpretation of this Act and in determining the jurisdiction and authority of the courts of the United States, as such jurisdiction and authority are herein defined and limited, the public policy of the United States is hereby declared as follows:

Whereas under prevailing economic conditions, developed with the aid of governmental authority for owners of property to organize in the corporate and other forms of ownership association, the individual unorganized worker is commonly helpless to exercise actual liberty of contract and to protect his freedom of labor, and thereby to obtain acceptable terms and conditions of employment, wherefore, though he should be free to decline to associate with his fellows, it is necessary that he have full freedom of association, self-organization, and designation of representatives of his own choosing, to negotiate the terms and conditions of his employment, and that he shall be free from the interference, restraint, or coercion of employers of labor, or their agents, in the designation of such representatives or in self-organization or in other concerted activities for the purpose of collective bargaining or other mutual aid or protection; therefore, the following definitions of, and limitations upon, the jurisdiction and authority of the courts of the United States are hereby enacted.

SEC. 3. Any undertaking or promise, such as is described in this section, or any other undertaking or promise in conflict with the public policy declared in section 2 of this Act, is hereby declared to be contrary to the public policy of the United States, shall not be enforceable in any court of the United States and shall not afford any basis for the granting of legal or equitable relief by any such court, including specifically the following:

Every undertaking or promise hereafter made, whether written or oral; express or implied, constituting or contained in any contract or agreement of hiring or employment between any individual, firm, company, association, or corporation, and any employee or prospective employee of the same, whereby

(a) Either party to such contract or agreement undertakes or promises not to join, become, or remain a member of any labor organization or of any employer organization; or

(b) Either party to such contract or agreement undertakes or promises that he will withdraw from an employment relation in the event that he joins, becomes, or remains a member of any labor organization or of any employer organization.

Sec. 4. No court of the United States shall have jurisdiction to issue any restraining order or temporary or permanent injunction in any case involving or growing out of any labor dispute to prohibit any person or persons participating or interested in such dispute (as these terms are herein defined) from doing, whether singly or in concert, any of the following acts:

(a) Ceasing or refusing to perform any work or to remain in any relation of employment;

(b) Becoming or remaining a member of any labor organization or of any employer organization, regardless of any such undertaking or promise as is described in section 3 of this Act;

(c) Paying or giving to, or withholding from, any person participating or interested in such labor dispute, any strike or unemployment benefits or insurance, or other moneys or things of value;

(d) By all lawful means aiding any person participating or interested in any labor dispute who is being proceeded against in, or is prosecuting, any action or suit in any court of the United States or of any State;

(e) Giving publicity to the existence of, or the facts involved in, any labor dispute, whether by advertising, speaking, patrolling, or by any other method not involving fraud or violence;

(f) Assembling peaceably to act or to organize to act in promotion of their interests in a labor dispute;

(g) Advising or notifying any person of an intention to do any of the acts heretofore specified;

(h) Agreeing with other persons to do or not to do any of the acts heretofore specified; and

(i) Advising, urging, or otherwise causing or inducing without fraud or violence the acts heretofore specified, regardless of any such undertaking or promise as is described in section 3 of this Act.

Sec. 5. No court of the United States shall have jurisdiction to issue a restraining order or temporary or permanent injunction upon the ground

that any of the persons participating or interested in a labor dispute constitute or are engaged in an unlawful combination or conspiracy because of
the doing in concert of the acts enumerated in section 4 of this Act.

SEC. 6. No officer or member of any association or organization, and
no association or organization participating or interested in a labor dispute,
shall be held responsible or liable in any court of the United States for the
unlawful acts of individual officers, members, or agents, except upon clear
proof of actual participation in, or actual authorization of, such acts, or of
ratification of such acts after actual knowledge thereof.

SEC. 7. No court of the United States shall have jurisdiction to issue a
temporary or permanent injunction in any case involving or growing out
of a labor dispute, as herein defined, except after hearing the testimony of
witnesses in open court (with opportunity for cross-examination) in support
of the allegations of a complaint made under oath, and testimony in opposition thereto, if offered, and except after findings of fact by the court, to the
effect

(a) That unlawful acts have been threatened and will be committed unless restrained or have been committed and will be continued unless restrained, but no injunction or temporary restraining order shall be issued on
account of any threat or unlawful act excepting against the person or persons, association, or organization making the threat of committing the unlawful act or actually authorizing or ratifying the same after actual knowledge thereof;

(b) That the substantial and irreparable injury to complainant's property
will follow;

(c) That as to each item of relief granted greater injury will be inflicted
upon complainant by the denial of relief than will be inflicted upon defendants by the granting of relief;

(d) That complainant has no adequate remedy at law; and

(e) That the public officers charged with the duty to protect complainant's property are unable or unwilling to furnish adequate protection.

Such hearing shall be held after due and personal notice thereof has
been given, in such manner as the court shall direct, to all known persons
against whom relief is sought, and also to the chief of those public officials
of the county and city within which the unlawful acts have been threatened
or committed charged with the duty to protect complainant's property: Provided, however, That if a complainant shall also allege that, unless a temporary restraining order shall be issued without notice, a substantial and irreparable injury to complainant's property will be unavoidable, such a temporary restraining order may be issued upon testimony under oath, sufficient,
if sustained, to justify the court in issuing a temporary injunction upon a
hearing after notice. Such a temporary restraining order shall be effective
for no longer than five days and shall become void at the expiration of said
five days. No temporary restraining order or temporary injunction shall be

issued except on condition that complainant shall first file an undertaking with adequate security in an amount to be fixed by the court sufficient to recompense those enjoined for any loss, expense, or damage caused by the improvident or erroneous issuance of such order or injunction, including all reasonable costs (together with a reasonable attorney's fee) and expense of defense against the order or against the granting of any injunctive relief sought in the same proceeding and subsequently denied by the court.

The undertaking herein mentioned shall be understood to signify an agreement entered into by the complainant and the surety upon which a decree may be rendered in the same suit or proceeding against said complainant and surety, upon a hearing to assess damages of which hearing complainant and surety shall have reasonable notice, the said complainant and surety submitting themselves to the jurisdiction of the court for that purpose. But nothing herein contained shall deprive any party having a claim or cause of action under or upon such undertaking from electing to pursue his ordinary remedy by suit at law or in equity.

SEC. 8. No restraining order or injunctive relief shall be granted to any complainant who has failed to comply with any obligation imposed by law which is involved in the labor dispute in question, or who has failed to make every reasonable effort to settle such dispute either by negotiation or with the aid of any available governmental machinery of mediation or voluntary arbitration.

SEC. 9. No restraining order or temporary or permanent injunction shall be granted in a case involving or growing out of a labor dispute, except on the basis of findings of fact made and filed by the court in the record of the case prior to the issuance of such restraining order or injunction; and every restraining order or injunction granted in a case involving or growing out of a labor dispute shall include only a prohibition of such specific act or acts as may be expressly complained of in the bill of complaint or petition filed in such case and as shall be expressly included in said findings of fact made and filed by the court as provided herein.

SEC. 10. Whenever any court of the United States shall issue or deny any temporary injunction in a case involving or growing out of a labor dispute, the court shall, upon the request of any party to the proceedings and on his filing the usual bond for costs, forthwith certify as in ordinary cases the record of the case to the circuit court of appeals for its review. Upon the filing of such record in the circuit court of appeals, the appeal shall be heard and the temporary injunctive order affirmed, modified, or set aside with the greatest possible expedition, giving the proceeding precedence over all other matters except older matters of the same character.

SEC. 11. In all cases of contempt arising under the laws of the United States governing the issuance of injunctions or restraining orders in any case involving or growing out of a labor dispute, the accused shall enjoy the right to a speedy and public trial by an impartial jury of the State and district wherein the contempt shall have been committed.

This section shall not apply to contempts committed in the presence of the court or so near thereto as to interfere directly with the administration of justice nor to the misbehavior, misconduct, or disobedience of any officer of the court in respect to the writs, orders or processes of the court.

SEC. 12. (a) *Summary Disposition.* A criminal contempt may be punished summarily if the judge certifies that he saw or heard the conduct constituting the contempt and that it was committed in the actual presence of the court. The order of contempt shall recite the facts and shall be signed by the judge and entered of record.

(b) *Disposition upon Notice and Hearing.* A criminal contempt except as provided in subdivision (a) of this rule shall be prosecuted on notice. The notice shall state the time and place of hearing, allowing a reasonable time for the preparation of the defense, and shall state the essential facts constituting the criminal contempt charged and describe it as such. The notice shall be given orally by the judge in open court in the presence of the defendant or, on application of the United States Attorney or of an attorney appointed by the court for that purpose, by an order to show cause or an order of arrest. The defendant is entitled to a trial by jury in any case in which an act of Congress so provides. He is entitled to admission to bail as provided in these rules. If the contempt charged involves disrespect to or criticism of a judge, that judge is disqualified from presiding at the trial or hearing except with the defendant's consent. Upon a verdict or finding of guilt the court shall enter an order fixing the punishment.

SEC. 13. When used in this act and for the purposes of this act

(a) A case shall be held to involve or to grow out of a labor dispute when the case involves persons who are engaged in the same industry, trade, craft, or occupation; or have direct or indirect interests therein; or who are employees of the same employer; or who are members of the same or an affiliated organization of employers or employees; whether such dispute is (1) between one or more employers or associations of employers and one or more employees or associations of employees; (2) between one or more employers or associations of employers and one or more employers or associations of employers; (3) between one or more employees or associations of employees and one or more employees or associations of employees; or when the case involves any conflicting or competing interests in a "labor dispute" (as hereinafter defined) of "persons participating or interested" therein (as hereinafter defined).

(b) A person or association shall be held to be a person participating or interested in a labor dispute if relief is sought against him or it, and if he or it is engaged in the same industry, trade, craft, or occupation in which such dispute occurs, or has a direct or indirect interest therein, or is a member, officer, or agent of any association composed in whole or in part of employers or employees engaged in such industry, trade, craft, or occupation.

(c) The term "labor dispute" includes any controversy concerning terms or conditions of employment, or concerning the association or representation of persons in negotiating, fixing, maintaining, changing, or seeking to arrange terms or conditions of employment, regardless of whether or not the disputants stand in the proximate relation of employer and employee.

(d) The term "court of the United States" means any court of the United States whose jurisdiction has been or may be conferred or defined or limited by Act of Congress, including the courts of the District of Columbia.

Sec. 14. If any provision of this Act or the application thereof to any person or circumstance is held unconstitutional or otherwise invalid, the remaining provisions of the Act and the application of such provisions to other persons or circumstances shall not be affected thereby.

Sec. 15. All Acts and parts of Acts in conflict with the provisions of this Act are hereby repealed.

6

THE ERA OF THE
NATIONAL LABOR
RELATIONS ACT

This chapter examines the conditions that nurtured the legislative proposal for the National Labor Relations Act, the Act itself, and the declaration of constitutionality by the Supreme Court in 1937. We first examine the environment that encouraged the passage of the National Labor Relations Act; this is followed by a presentation of some evidence that indicates a change in the federal climate. This change is clearly expressed in the legislation itself as a policy statement as well as in the scope of coverage of the Act. The manner in which the National Labor Relations Board was established and charged with the administration and perpetuation of the declared policy is then discussed. This includes a close look at those activities enumerated in the National Labor Relations Act: representation proceedings; the rights of employees and those practices listed as unfair practices on the part of the employers; and the procedures for filing unfair practice charges. Finally, consideration will be given to pertinent portions of the opinion of the Supreme Court in establishing the constitutionality of the National Labor Relations Act.

The National Labor Relations Act

THE CHANGING ENVIRONMENT FOR ORGANIZED LABOR

As we have seen, for approximately eighteen years preceding the passage of the Norris-La Guardia Act in 1932, the activities of labor unions and their attempts to organize workers were severely hampered by the scurrilous willingness of the courts to issue injunctions to employers. Efforts at organization were also impeded by the applications of the Sherman Anti-Trust Act and the Clayton Act. After the passage of the Norris-La Guardia Act, it was anticipated that labor organizations would achieve a larger degree of freedom and would not be constrained by the provisions of the anti-trust legislation. The impact of the Norris-La Guardia Act had the effect of preventing interference in labor union activities. This included boycotting, picketing, and striking insofar as they remained peaceful and lawful. The interpretation also extended to include secondary activities and the involvement of third parties in labor disputes. Ultimately, this served to release labor from the restrictions that had been placed on those covered by the anti-trust legislation.

With the passage of the National Industrial Recovery Act (NIRA) in the following year (1933), the boundaries within which labor unions could lawfully function were enlarged even further. As noted in the previous chapter, the NIRA removed many of the restrictions set forth in the Sherman Anti-Trust Act and the Clayton Act, and provided in Section 7 (a):

> . . . That employees shall have the right to organize and bargain collectively through representatives of their own choosing, and shall be free from interference, restraint or coercion of employers of labor, or their agents, and in the designation of such representatives or in self-organization or in other concerted activities for the purpose of collective bargaining or other mutual aid and protection.[1]

Economic conditions and congressional attitude were such that in spite of the intensive opposition of employers and systematic pressure by employer organizations, the National Labor Relations Act was en-

[1] Public Law No. 67 (73d Cong.).

acted and a whole new era began for the labor union movement. This historic event occurred just one month after the National Industrial Recovery Act was declared unconstitutional.

The decision handed down by the Supreme Court on May 27, 1935, in the case of *Schechter Poultry Corporation* v. *United States* [2] declared that the National Industrial Recovery Act was unconstitutional. The court's decision was quickly countered by the passage of a bill that had been originally introduced by Senator Robert Wagner in February, 1935. This bill became the National Labor Relations Act, more commonly known as the Wagner Act. After lengthy debate and consideration of numerous proposed amendments, the bill was signed by President Franklin Roosevelt on July 5, 1935.[3] Upon signing this historic legislation sanctioning the labor union as an institution in the American economy, the President made the following comments:

> This Act defines, as part of our substantive law, the right of self-organization of employees in industry for the purpose of collective bargaining, and provides methods by which the government can safeguard that legal right. . . .
>
> A better relationship between labor and management is the high purpose of this Act. . . . It aims to remove one of the chief causes of economic strife. By preventing practices which tend to destroy the independence of labor, it seeks, for every worker within its scope, that freedom of choice and action which is justly his.[4]

In order to arrive at a complete understanding of the content of the National Labor Relations Act and to see more clearly the scope of its coverage, key sections of the legislation need to be examined. (The entire Act may be found in Appendix 6.)

THE NATIONAL LABOR RELATIONS ACT AS A POLICY STATEMENT AND ITS COVERAGE

The National Labor Relations Act, popularly known as the Wagner Act, was designed ". . . to diminish the causes of labor disputes

[2] 295 U.S. 495 (1935).

[3] U.S., *Congressional Record*, 74th Cong., 1st Sess., 1935, Vol. 79. Pt. 10, p. 10719.

[4] *Public Papers and Addresses of Franklin D. Roosevelt* (New York: Random House, 1938, Vol. IV), pp. 294–295.

burdening or obstructing interstate and foreign commerce. . . ." [5] The federal attitude is presented very clearly in Section 1 of the NLRA, identified as the statement of findings and policies:

> . . . It is hereby declared to be the policy of the United States to eliminate the causes of certain substantial obstructions to the free flow of commerce and to mitigate and eliminate these obstructions when they have occurred by encouraging the practice and procedure of collective bargaining and by protecting the exercise by workers of full freedom of association, self-organization, and designation of representatives of their own choosing, for the purpose of negotiating the terms and conditions of their employment or other mutual aid or protection.[6]

Section 2 sets forth definitions of terms as used in the Act. It should be noted that the United States government, the separate states, or any political subdivisions of the United States are not included as an employer. Furthermore, labor organizations not acting in the capacity of an employer are also explicitly excluded from this classification. To qualify as an employee, a person cannot be working individually in agriculture, as a home owner's domestic, or be employed by his parent or spouse. Employees who are not working because of a labor dispute or an unfair labor practice issue which has resulted in their not working are bona fide employees so long as they are not otherwise gainfully employed. This means that qualified striking employees continue to remain in the employ of the employer being struck and may, in most instances, receive back wages after they return to work.

THE NATIONAL LABOR RELATIONS BOARD

The 1935 legislation created a new National Labor Relations Board (NLRB) that was charged with monitoring the Wagner Act. Sections 3 through 12 of the Act (excepting 7 and 8) deal with the organization, functions, and duties of the NLRB. The National Labor Relations Act provided for Presidential appointment of a three-member NLRB. The appointments were designated for a five-year term, except for the initial appointments that were staggered on a one-year, three-year, and five-year basis. In addition, the President was to designate one of these appointees to serve in the capacity of chairman.

[5] U.S., *Statutes at Large*, XLIX, Pt. 1, 449.
[6] *Ibid.*

The salaries for NLRB members were initially established at $10,000 annually, and it was also stipulated that any member was eligible for reappointment. Acceptance of an appointment to serve on the NLRB required that those persons who serve in this capacity relinquish all other employment during their tenure of service.

The NLRB has the power to appoint employees to perform those services that are necessary for it to function properly. These include attorneys, regional directors, examiners, and others. The NLRB may also utilize the services of other regional or local agencies. The only restriction explicitly stated with regard to the employment practices of the NLRB is a statement prohibiting the appointment of persons to be utilized as mediators or conciliators or statisticians. These services are to be obtained from the Department of Labor insofar as it is possible. The legislation further grants the NLRB the power to establish rules and regulations that are necessary for carrying out the objectives of the National Labor Relations Act. The NLRB is required to prepare an annual report to the Congress and the President in which there is a statement of cases heard, decisions handed down, and a list of the persons employed by the NLRB.

The functions of the NLRB can best be understood by identifying them as (1) overseeing the process of worker selection of union representatives and (2) the responsibility for protecting the rights of employees or the prevention of unfair labor practices on the part of the employer as set forth in Sections 7 and 8 of the Act. Basically, the power of the NLRB in these instances is that of issuing an order to cease and desist from the action complained of, as well as recommending whatever affirmative action is necessary to right the wrong that has taken place. It may also, of course, dismiss the complaint if such is warranted in light of their findings of fact. Should a party refuse to take cognizance of an order from the NLRB, the latter may petition any Court of Appeals, or under certain circumstances the U.S. District Court of the Supreme Court for the enforcement of its order. The aggrieved party in an unfair labor practice issue also has the right to court review of the NLRB's order. The court may affirm, disaffirm, or modify the order of the NLRB either in part or in whole.

REPRESENTATION PROCEEDINGS AND ELECTIONS

Section 9(a) of the National Labor Relations Act provides:

. . . Representatives designated or selected for the purpose of collective bargaining by the majority of the employees in a unit

appropriate for such purposes, shall be the exclusive representatives . . . for the purposes of collective bargaining in respect to
rates of pay, wages, hours of employment, or other conditions of
employment. . . .[7]

The National Labor Relations Board is also given the power to decide the unit that will be appropriate for purposes of collective bargaining. This unit may be an employee unit, a craft unit, a plant unit,
or some subdivision of these.

In the event there is a question affecting commerce with respect to
employee representation, Section 9(c) gives the Board the power to
investigate the issue and then certify to all parties concerned ". . . in
writing, the name or names of the representatives that have been designated or selected."[8] The Board is also required to conduct a hearing in the process of the investigation. Furthermore, the Board may
ascertain the representative by taking a secret ballot or some other
suitable method.

These provisions designed to cover the representation and elections process resulted in creating some interesting problems. It is obvious that the legislation is written in rather general terms: as a result, the NLRB resolved certain specific problems by exercising its
own ingenuity within the broad confines of the written legislation.
Some problems arose in the matter of elections: as indicated above,
the legislation states that the representative shall be designated by a
majority. It does not, however, indicate whether this is to mean a majority of the employees who are qualified to vote or a majority of the
votes cast. The NLRB eventually resolved this by ruling that the majority applies only to those votes actually cast.

The legislation is also silent on the matter of an employer filing a
petition for a representation election. The NLRB resolved this problem by deciding that elections would be conducted only when the
employer could show that two or more unions were attempting to act
as his employees' representatives. Because of the tremendous numbers
of petitions for elections filed by unions, the NLRB found it necessary
to adopt the rule that an election could be held only if there was an
indication that the petitioner had the support of no less than thirty
percent of the employees involved. No provisions were included in
the legislation that would prevent a competitive union from continuing an organizing campaign after losing an election. As a result, rival

[7] *Ibid.*, p. 453.
[8] *Ibid.*

unions could interfere with the smooth functioning of the employer-employee relationship. Another problem with regard to the elections section of the National Labor Relations Act should be mentioned, even though it has since been clarified by amending legislation: the issue of employee eligibility to vote when on strike. Prior to an NLRB ruling, an employer of a struck plant might conceivably hire new employees to replace those on strike. If an election were held during this period, the employees on strike would not vote, and their representative could easily be voted out by a majority nonunion vote. It was finally ruled by the NLRB that if the strike issue was economic (a dispute over wages, hours, or working conditions), as opposed to an unfair labor practices issue (a violation of one of the provisions of the National Labor Relations Act), both those workers on strike as well as those hired to replace them were eligible to vote. In the case of an unfair labor practice strike, however, only those employees protesting the issue and on strike were deemed eligible to vote.[9]

RIGHTS OF EMPLOYEES AND UNFAIR LABOR PRACTICES

Perhaps the most significant sections of the National Labor Relations Act to the worker are Sections 7 and 8, which deal with the rights of employees. Section 7 grants employees the right to organize and participate in labor organization activities. It further grants the right to bargain collectively through chosen representatives and to engage in concerted activities to accomplish this purpose. Section 8 then identifies those activities that are to be considered unfair labor practices on the part of the employer. There are five of these set forth in the National Labor Relations Act:

SEC. 8(a). It shall be an unfair labor practice for an employer—
(1). To interfere with, restrain, or coerce employees in the exercise of the rights guaranteed in Section 7.
(2). To dominate or interfere with the formation or administration of any labor organization or contribute financial or other support to it: *Provided,* That subject to rules and regulations made and published by the Board pursuant to Section 6(a), an employer shall not be prohibited from permitting employees to confer with him during working hours without loss of time or pay.
(3). By discrimination in regard to hire or tenure of employment

[9] H. R. Northrup and G. F. Bloom, *Government and Labor* (Homewood: Richard D. Irwin, Inc., 1963), pp. 58–60.

or any term or condition of employment to encourage or discourage membership in any labor organization: *Provided*, That nothing in this Act, or in the National Industrial Recovery Act (U.S.C., Supp. VII, Title 15, Secs. 701–712), as amended from time to time, or in any code or agreement with a labor organization (not established, maintained, or assisted by any action defined in this Act as an unfair labor practice) to require as a condition of employment membership therein, if such labor organization is the representative of the employees as provided in Section 9(a), in the appropriate collective bargaining unit covered by such agreement when made.

(4). To discharge or otherwise discriminate against an employee because he has filed charges or given testimony under this Act.

(5). To refuse to bargain collectively with the representatives of his employees, subject to the provisions of Section 9(a).[10]

Each of these unfair labor practices is examined separately below and illustrated by an affirmed or enforced order on that point that validates each unfair practice.

1. Interference, Restraint, or Coercion

New England Tank Industries, the employer in this complaint, was charged with an unfair labor practice when he indicated to persons applying for jobs that if they were members of the union they would not be employed. This employer also issued warnings that it was his intention to "break" the union.[11]

2. Domination of a Labor Organization

Western Reserve Telephone Company, the employer, was charged with a violation because of "suggestions" he made about the formation of employee committees or inside unions, and thus was interfering or dominating the administration of a union by ". . . allowing foremen to read to employees proposal to establish committee, (2) asking employees to attend a meeting and to explain proposed committee to them, and (3) soliciting and instructing employees to attend meetings or establish committee."[12]

3. Discrimination in Union Security Agreements

At the Airlectro Products Company, a member of Local 5806 of the Steelworkers filed an opposition to an employer claim of a voluntary quit. The National Labor Relations Board ruled in favor of the employee and found that the employer had discriminatorily discharged

[10] U.S., *Statutes at Large*, XLIX, Pt. 1, 452.

[11] 133 NLRB 175 (1961).

[12] 138 NLRB 755 (1962).

her. This was a violation of the agreement between labor and management. In this instance the employee, a vice president of the union, left the employer's plant without permission after expressing dissatisfaction about the employer's administration of the union contract and the extension of this contract by the employer and the union.[13]

4. Discrimination for Giving Testimony or Filing Charges

Gibbs Corporation was charged with an unfair labor practice when it discharged nineteen employees who had filed charges with the National Labor Relations Board. The employees had requested an investigation of a contract that they believed was collusively designed and would deprive them of their rights.[14]

5. Refusal to Bargain

The National Labor Relations Board found a complaint charging refusal to bargain was warranted against the Hurley Company. The Board ruled that the wholly-owned subsidiary of this company must be considered one with the parent organization insofar as collective bargaining was concerned.[15]

PROCEDURE FOR FILING AN UNFAIR LABOR PRACTICE CHARGE

Section 10 of the National Labor Relations Act identifies the power of the NLRB in the prevention of unfair labor practices and the procedure the NLRB will follow when these unfair labor practice charges are made.

When the NLRB receives notice that any person is or has been engaged in an unfair labor practice, the Board (or an agent designated by it) has the power to have a complaint served on the party named. This complaint identifies the charges and contains a notice for a hearing. The time for the hearing must permit at least five days to elapse from the time the complaint is served. Before an order is issued on the complaint, the party or parties conducting the hearing may amend it. The party against whom the complaint has been filed then has the opportunity to appear, answer, and to present testimony. This testimony may be given either in person or by another means. The party who is conducting the hearing may permit others to present testimony as he feels appropriate; rules of evidence do not apply as they do in a court of law or equity. All of the testimony presented at the hearing is preserved in written form and is filed with the NLRB. The NLRB may require additional testimony at the conclusion of the

[13] 131 NLRB 982 (1961).
[14] 131 NLRB 955 (1961).
[15] 136 NLRB 551 (1962).

hearing if the NLRB believes, in light of the record, that the party against whom the complaint was filed is now or has engaged in an unfair labor practice, findings of fact are made, and a cease and desist order is issued. The NLRB may also require affirmative action to be taken, if such is appropriate. The NLRB may also require that reports be made to indicate compliance. Should the NLRB believe that the testimony does not indicate that an unfair labor practice has or does exist, the NLRB issues an order to dismiss the complaint. Moreover, the NLRB may modify, in whole or in part, or set aside any order it has issued prior to the filing of a transcript of the record.

Power is also given to the NLRB to petition the appropriate court under certain circumstances (see Sec. 10 (e) of National Labor Relations Act in the Appendix). It may petition for enforcement of an order, for other temporary relief, or to obtain a restraining order. Records of the entire proceedings and findings are filed with the court that enters a decree to enforce, modify, or set aside the NLRB order. The court considers the issue as it appears in the record unless circumstances are such that the court deems additional evidence is warranted. Should new evidence justify it, the NLRB may recommend modification of a previous order or that a prior order be set aside by the court. The judgment of the court is subject, of course, to higher court review.

Aggrieved parties may also petition for court review to set aside or modify a final order of the NLRB. After proper records have been filed with the court and the NLRB is in receipt of a copy of the petition, the procedure followed is the same as that outlined in (8) above. It should also be noted that the institution of the processes of court review by either the NLRB or the aggrieved party does not stay the original NLRB order, unless the court so decrees.

It can be seen from the foregoing that this legislation is basically simple and its purpose is clear. It grants the employee an opportunity to equalize his bargaining position with the employer, should the employee choose to have union representation. It also provides the employee with an avenue through which he might be relieved of and protected from unfair employer practices. Finally, the Act establishes an administrative unit (NLRB) designed to effectively represent the interests of the employee and prevent unjust activity on the part of the employer.

CONSTITUTIONALITY OF THE NATIONAL LABOR RELATIONS ACT

As with all legislation, the National Labor Relations Act was to be subject to a test of constitutionality before the Supreme Court. It was not until April 12, 1937, some twenty-one months after it had been signed into law by the President, that the constitutionality of the Act was determined in *NLRB* v. *Jones & Laughlin Steel Corporation.*

Before this case reached the Supreme Court the NLRB had found Jones & Laughlin Steel Corporation guilty of an unfair labor practice, and thus in violation of the National Labor Relations Act. The initial proceeding was brought by the Beaver Valley Lodge No. 200, an affiliate of the Amalgamated Association of Iron, Steel, and Tin Workers. The union alleged that Jones & Laughlin had discriminated against workers and had fired thirteen (this was later reduced to ten) men who had been participating in organizational activities at the employer's Aliquippa, Pennsylvania plant. The NLRB found the charges to be valid and issued an order to Jones & Laughlin to cease and desist from this coercive and discriminatory practice. In addition, the corporation was ordered to reinstate ten of the employees with back pay. The corporation was also ordered to post notices for a thirty-day period indicating that it would not discriminate either against present union members or those employees who wished to acquire membership.

When Jones & Laughlin failed to comply as ordered, the NLRB filed a petition for enforcement with the Circuit Court of Appeals. This court did not grant the petition, and held that the order was not within the range of federal power. The Supreme Court granted certiorari (review), and found the facts with respect to the nature and scope of respondent's business to be valid. Summarily, these facts included: (1) the corporation was engaged in the manufacture of steel and pig iron; (2) the corporation had plants in Pittsburgh and Aliquippa, Pennsylvania, with nineteen subsidiaries; (3) the corporation owned and operated ". . . ore, coal and limestone properties, lake and river transportation facilities, and terminal railroads located at its manufacturing plants. It owns or controls mines in Michigan and Minnesota. It operates four ore steamships on the Great Lakes, used in the transportation of ore to factories. . . . Approximately 75 per cent of its product is shipped out of Pennsylvania." [16]

Jones & Laughlin Steel Corporation contested the ruling which was made by the NLRB by stating:

(1) that the Act is in reality a regulation of labor relations and not of interstate commerce;

(2) that the Act can have no application to the respondent's relations with its production employees because they are not subject to regulation by the Federal Government; and

[16] 301 U.S. 1 (1937).

(3) that the provisions of the Act violate Sec. 2 of Article III and the Fifth and Seventh Amendments of the Constitution of the United States.[17]

With this as background, pertinent excerpts of the opinion of the Supreme Court follow:

NATIONAL LABOR RELATIONS BOARD v.
JONES & LAUGHLIN STEEL CORPORATION: 1937
(301 U.S. 1)

The Supreme Court of the United States, Mr. Chief Justice Hughes delivering the opinion:

. . . Practically all the federal evidence in the case, except that which dealt with the nature of respondent's business, concerned its relations with the employees in the Aliquippa plant whose discharge was the subject of the complaint. These employees were active leaders in the labor union. Several were officers and others were leaders of particular groups. Two of the employees were motor inspectors; one was a tractor driver; three were crane operators; one was a washer in the coke plant; and three were laborers. Three other employees were mentioned in the complaint, but it was withdrawn as to one of them and no evidence was heard on the action taken with respect to the other two.

While respondent criticizes the evidence and the attitude of the Board, which is described as being hostile toward employers and particularly toward those who insisted upon their constitutional rights, respondent did not take advantage of its opportunity to present evidence to refute that which was offered to show discrimination and coercion. In this situation, the record presents no ground for setting aside the order of the Board so far as the facts pertaining to the circumstances and purpose of the discharge of the employees are concerned. Upon that point it is sufficient to say that the evidence supports the findings of the Board that respondent discharged these men "because of their union activity and for the purpose of discouraging membership in the union." We turn to the questions of law which respondent urges in contesting the validity and application of the Act.

First. The Scope of the Act.—The Act is challenged in its entirety as an attempt to regulate all industry, thus invading the re-
[17] *Ibid.*

served powers of the States over their local concerns. It is asserted that the references in the Act to interstate and foreign commerce are tolerable at best; that the Act is not a true regulation of such commerce or of matters which directly affect it but on the contrary has the fundamental object of placing under the compulsory supervision of the federal government all industrial labor relations within the nation. The argument seeks support in the broad words of the preamble (section one) and in the sweep of the provisions of the Act, and it is further insisted that its legislative history shows an essential universal purpose in the light of which its scope cannot be limited by either construction or by the application of the separability clause.

If this conception of terms, intent and consequent inseparability were sound, the Act would necessarily fall by reason of the limitation upon the federal power which inheres in the constitutional grant, as well as because of the explicit reservation of the Tenth Amendment. . . .

There can be no question that the commerce thus contemplated by the Act (aside from that within a Territory or the District of Columbia) is interstate and foreign commerce in the constitutional sense. The Act also defines the term "affecting commerce" sec. 2(7):

"The term 'affecting commerce' means in commerce, or burdening or obstructing commerce or the free flow of commerce, or having led or tending to lead to a labor dispute burdening or obstructing commerce or the free flow of commerce."

This definition is one of exclusion as well as inclusion. The grant of authority to the Board does not purport to extend to the relationship between all industrial employees and employers. Its terms do not impose collective bargaining upon all industry regardless of effects upon interstate or foreign commerce. It purports to reach only what may be deemed to burden or obstruct that commerce and, thus qualified, it must be construed as contemplating the exercise of control within constitutional bounds. It is a familiar principle that acts which directly burden or obstruct interstate or foreign commerce, or its free flow, are within the reach of the congressional power. Acts having that effect are not rendered immune because they grow out of labor disputes. . . . It is the effect upon commerce, not the source of the injury, which is the criterion. *Second Employers' Liability Cases*, 223 U.S. 1, 51. Whether

or not particular action does affect commerce in such a close and
intimate fashion as to be subject to federal control, and hence to
lie within the authority conferred upon the Board, is left by the
statute to be determined as individual cases arise. We are thus to
inquire whether in the instant case the constitutional boundary has
been passed.

Second. The unfair labor practices in question.—The unfair
labor practices found by the Board are those defined in Sec. 8, subdivisions (1) and (3). . . . Thus, in its present application, the statute goes no further than to safeguard the right of employees to
self-organization and to select representatives of their own choosing for collective bargaining or other mutual protection without restraining or coercion by their employer. . . .

*Third. The application of the Act to employees engaged in
production.—The principle involved.*—Respondent says that
whatever may be said of employees engaged in interstate commerce, the industrial relations and activities in the manufacturing
department of respondent's enterprise are not subject to federal
regulation. The argument rests upon the proposition that manufacturing in itself is not commerce. . . .

. . . The various parts of respondent's enterprise are described
as interdependent and as thus involving "a great movement of iron
ore, coal and limestone along well-defined paths to the steel mills,
thence through them, and thence in the form of steel products into
the consuming centers of the country—a definite and well-under-
stood course of business." It is urged that these activities constitute
a "stream" or "flow" of commerce, of which the Aliquippa manufacturing plant is the focal point, and that industrial strife at that
point would cripple the entire movement. . . .

. . . Respondent says that the Aliquippa plant is extensive in
size and represents a large investment in buildings, machinery and
equipment. The raw materials which are brought to the plant are
delayed for long periods and, after being subjected to manufacturing processes, "are changed substantially as to character, utility
and value." The finished products which emerge "are to a large extent manufactured without reference to pre-existing orders and
contracts and are entirely different from the raw materials which
enter at the other end." Hence respondent argues that "If importation and exportation in interstate commerce do not singly transfer
purely local activities into the field of congressional regulation, it

should follow that their combination would not alter the local situation." *Arkadelphia Milling Co.* v. *St. Louis Southwestern Railways Co.,* 249 U.S. 134, 151; *Oliver Iron Co.* v. *Lord, supra.*

We do not find it necessary to determine whether these features of defendant's business dispose of the asserted analogy to the "stream of commerce" cases. The instances in which that metaphor has been used are but particular, and not exclusive, illustrations of the protective power which the government invokes in support of the present Act. The congressional authority to protect interstate commerce from burdens and obstructions is not limited to transactions which can be deemed to be an essential part of the "flow" of interstate or foreign commerce. Burdens and obstructions may be due to injurious action, springing from other sources. The fundamental principle is that the power to regulate commerce is the power to enact "all appropriate legislation" for "its protection and advancement" (*The Daniel Ball,* 10 Wall. 557, 564); to adopt measures "to promote its growth and insure its safety" (*County of Mobile* v. *Kimball,* 102 U.S. 691, 696, 697); "to foster, protect, control and restrain." *Second Employers' Liability Cases, supra,* p. 47. See *Texas & N.O.R. Co.* v. *Railway Clerks, supra.* That power is plenary and may be exerted to protect interstate commerce "no matter what the source of the dangers which threaten it." *Second Employers' Liability Cases,* p. 51; *Schechter Corp.* v. *United States, supra.* Although activities may be intrastate in character when separately considered, if they have such a close and substantial relation to interstate commerce that their control is essential or appropriate to protect that commerce from burdens and obstructions, Congress cannot be denied the power to exercise that control. *Schechter Corp.* v. *United States, supra.* Undoubtedly the scope of this power must be considered in the light of our dual system of government and may not be extended so as to embrace effects upon interstate commerce so indirect and remote that to embrace them, in view of our complex society, would effectually obliterate the distinction between what is national and what is local and create a completely centralized government. *Id.* The question is necessarily one of degree. . . .

Fourth. Effects of the unfair labor practice in respondent's enterprise.—Giving full weight to respondent's contention with respect to a break in the complete continuity of the "stream of commerce" by reason of respondent's manufacturing operations, the fact remains that the stoppage of those operations by industrial

strife would have a most serious effect upon interstate commerce.
. . . When industries organize themselves on a national scale, making their relation to interstate commerce the dominant factor in
their activities, how can it be maintained that their industrial
labor relations constitute a forbidden field into which Congress
may not enter when it is necessary to protect interstate commerce
from the paralyzing consequences of industrial war? We have
often said that interstate commerce itself is a practical conception.
It is equally true that interferences with that commerce must be appraised by a judgment that does not ignore actual experience. . . .

The Act does not compel agreements between employers and
employees. It does not compel any agreement whatever. It does
not prevent the employer "from refusing to make a collective contract and hiring individuals on whatever terms" the employer "may
by unilateral action determine." The Act expressly provides in Sec.
9(a) that any individual employee or a group of employees shall
have the right at any time to present grievances to their employer.
The theory of the Act is that free opportunity for negotiation with
accredited representatives of employees is likely to promote industrial peace and may bring about the adjustments and agreements which the Act in itself does not attempt to compel. As we
said in *Texas & N.O.R. Co.* v. *Railway Clerks, supra*, and repeated
in *Virginian Railway Co.* v. *System Federation No. 40*, the cases of
Adair v. *United States*, 208 U.S. 161, and *Coppage* v. *Kansas*, 236
U.S. 1, are inapplicable to legislation of this character. The Act
does not interfere with the normal exercise of the right of the employer to select its employees or to discharge them. The employer
may not, under cover of that right, intimidate or coerce its employees with respect to their self-organization and representation, and,
on the other hand, the Board is not entitled to make its authority a
pretext for interference with the right of discharge when that right
is exercised for other reasons than such intimidation and coercion.
The true purpose is the subject of investigation with full opportunity to show the facts. It would seem that when employers freely
recognize the right of their employees to their own organization
and their unrestricted right of representation there will be much
less occasion for controversy in respect to the free and appropriate
exercise of the right of selection and discharge.

The Act has been criticized as one-sided in its application; that
it subjects the employer to supervision and restraint and leaves untouched the abuses for which employees may be responsible; that

it fails to provide a more comprehensive plan,—with better assurances of fairness to both sides and with increased chances of success in bringing about, if not compelling, equitable solutions of industrial disputes affecting interstate commerce. But we are dealing with the power of Congress, not with a particular policy or with the extent to which policy should go. . . .

The order of the Board required the reinstatement of the employees who were found to have been discharged because of their "union activity" and for the purpose of "discouraging membership in the union." That requirement was authorized by the Act. Section 10(c), 29 U.S.C.A. Sec. 160(c). In *Texas & N.O.R. Co.* v. *Railway & S.S. Clerks, supra,* a similar order for restoration to service was made by the court in contempt proceedings for the violation of an injunction issued by the court to restrain an interference with the right of employees as guaranteed by the Railway Labor Act of 1926. The requirement of restoration to service, of employees discharged in violation of the provisions of that Act, was thus a sanction imposed in the enforcement of a judicial decree. We do not doubt that Congress could impose a like sanction for the enforcement of its valid regulation. The fact that in the one case it was a judicial sanction, and in the other a legislative one, is not an essential difference in determining its propriety.

Respondent complains that the Board not only ordered reinstatement but directed the payment of wages for the time lost by the discharge, less amounts earned by the employee during that period. This part of the order was also authorized by the Act. Sec. 10(c). It is argued that the requirement is equivalent to a money judgment and hence contravenes the Seventh Amendment with respect to trial by jury. The Seventh Amendment provides that "In suits at common law, where the value in controversy shall exceed twenty dollars, the right of trial by jury shall be preserved." The Amendment thus preserves the right which existed under the common law when the Amendment was adopted. . . . Thus it has no application to cases where recovery of money damages is an incident to equitable relief even though damages might have been recovered in an action at law. . . . It does not apply where the proceeding is not in the nature of a suit at common law. . . .

The instant case is not a suit at common law or in the nature of such a suit. The proceeding is one unknown to the common law. It is a statutory proceeding. Reinstatement of the employee and payment for time lost are requirements imposed for violation of the statute and are remedies appropriate to its enforcement. The contention under the Seventh Amendment is without merit.

Our conclusion is that the order of the Board was within its competency and that the Act is valid as here applied. The judgment of the Circuit Court of Appeals is reversed and the case is remanded for further proceedings in conformity with this opinion.

This decision is without question one of the most significant landmarks in the area of employer-employee relations in the United States. The holding of the Supreme Court not only gave federal sanction to organized labor by establishing the constitutionality of the National Labor Relations Act, but also enlarged the definition of commerce to include both those activities that "affect" commerce as well as those that "move" in interstate commerce. Prior to this time, the Supreme Court had expressed the attitude that labor-management issues arising from the manufacture of products were of intrastate character and thus regulation of them rightly belonged to the several states. This decision clearly removes activities affecting commerce from state jurisdiction and brings them within the federal arena. It is of interest to note that the decision in *Jones & Laughlin* was reinforced almost immediately by subsequent decisions handed down by the Supreme Court in several other cases.[18]

Summary

The National Labor Relations Act was one of the most revolutionary pieces of legislation ever to be passed by Congress. It marks the first entry of the government in the field of industrial labor relations. In the years following its passage tremendous growth was seen in union membership, which increased from 3.9 million in 1935 to 15 million in 1947.

The purpose of the National Labor Relations Act was the improvement of the relations between labor and management and the prevention of practices that infringe on the rights of labor. In order to work toward the achievement of these results, the legislation gave employees the right to bargain collectively through chosen representatives.

[18] *NLRB* v. *Fruehauf Trailer Co.*, 301 U.S. 49; *NLRB* v. *Friedman-Marks Clothing Co.*, 301 U.S. 58; *Associated Press* v. *NLRB*, 301 U.S. 103; and *Washington V & M Coach Co.* v. *NLRB*, 301 U.S. 142.

In addition, the National Labor Relations Act provided for the establishment of a National Labor Relations Board so that (1) the democratic process should be preserved in the selection and election of bargaining representatives, and (2) employees would have meaningful protection from unfair labor practices.

If the sole purpose of the Wagner Act was to promote collective bargaining, and this is measured in terms of membership growth, it can be argued that the legislation was an unqualified success. However, the legislation was subject to severe criticism. Probably the bulk of this criticism was directed at the National Labor Relations Board, which was frequently charged with bias. That the legislation itself was biased cannot be doubted; therefore, one might question whether it would be possible to administer such legislation in such a way as to prevent bias. There were also claims that the act was not at fault, but rather the failure of management and union to cooperate was the real obstacle to a peaceful relationship.

In conclusion, it may be said that the legislation did generally accomplish its stated purpose; that this may have been done with attendant and undesirable side effects will be considered in a later chapter.

APPENDIX 6

The National Labor Relations Act
(*July 5, 1935, 75th Congress*)

FINDINGS AND POLICY

SECTION 1. The denial by employers of the right of employees to organize and the refusal by employers to accept the procedure of collective bargaining lead to strikes and other forms of industrial strife or unrest, which have the intent or the necessary effect of burdening or obstructing commerce by (a) impairing the efficiency, safety, or operation of the instrumentalities of commerce; (b) occurring in the current of commerce; (c) materially affecting, restraining, or controlling the flow of raw materials or manufactured or processed goods from or into the channels of commerce, or the prices of such materials or goods in commerce; or (d) causing diminution of employment and wages in such volume as substantially to impair or disrupt the market for goods flowing from or into the channels of commerce.

The inequality of bargaining power between employees who do not possess full freedom of association or actual liberty of contract, and employers who are organized in the corporate or other forms of ownership association substantially burdens and affects the flow of commerce, and tends to aggravate recurrent business depressions, by depressing wage rates and the purchasing power of wage earners in industry and by preventing the stabilization of competitive wage rates and working conditions within and between industries.

Experience has proved that protection by law of the right of employees to organize and bargain collectively safeguards commerce from injury, impairment, or interruption, and promotes the flow of commerce by removing certain recognized sources of industrial strife and unrest, by encouraging practices fundamental to the friendly adjustment of industrial disputes arising out of differences as to wages, hours, or other working conditions, and by restoring equality of bargaining power between employers and employees.

It is hereby declared to be the policy of the United States to eliminate the causes of certain substantial obstructions to the free flow of commerce and to mitigate and eliminate these obstructions when they have occurred by encouraging the practice and procedure of collective bargaining and by protecting the exercise by workers of full freedom of association, self-organization, and designation of representatives of their own choosing, for the purpose of negotiation the terms and conditions of their employment or other mutual aid or protection.

DEFINITIONS

SEC. 2. When used in this Act—

(1) The term "person" includes one or more individuals, partnerships, associations, corporations, legal representatives, trustees, trustees in bankruptcy, or receivers.

(2) The term "employer" includes any person acting in the interest of an employer, directly or indirectly, but shall not include the United States, or any State or political subdivision thereof, or any person subject to the Railway Labor Act, as amended from time to time, or any labor organization (other than when acting as an employer), or anyone acting in the capacity of officer or agent of such labor organization.

(3) The term "employee" shall include any employee, and shall not be limited to the employees of a particular employer, unless the Act explicitly states otherwise, and shall include any individual whose work has ceased as a consequence of, or in connection with, any current labor dispute or because of any unfair labor practice, and who has not obtained any other regular and substantially equivalent employment, but shall not include any individual employed as an agricultural laborer, or in the domestic service of any family or person at his home, or any individual employed by his parent or spouse.

(4) The term "representatives" includes any individual or labor organization.

(5) The term "labor organization" means any organization of any kind,

any agency or employee representation committee or plan, in which em-
participate and which exists for the purpose, in whole or in part, of
with employers concerning grievances, labor disputes, wages, rates
of employment, or conditions of work.

rm "commerce" means trade, traffic, commerce, transporta-
nication among the several States, or between the District of
y Territory of the United States and any State or other Ter-
en any foreign country and any State, Territory, or the Dis-
ia, or within the District of Columbia or any Territory, or
n the same State but through any other State or any Terri-
ct of Columbia or any foreign country.

"affecting commerce" means in commerce, or burdening or
merce or the free flow of commerce, or having led or tend-
a labor dispute burdening or obstructing commerce or the
merce.

rm "unfair labor practice" means any unfair labor practice
listed on 8.

(9) e term "labor dispute" includes any controversy concerning terms,
tenure or conditions of employment, or concerning the association or representation of persons in negotiating, fixing, maintaining, changing, or seeking
to arrange terms or conditions of employment, regardless of whether the
disputants stand in the proximate relation of employer and employee.

(10) The term "National Labor Relations Board" means the National
Labor Relations Board created by section 3 of this Act.

(11) The term "old Board" means the National Labor Relations Board
established by Executive Order Numbered 6763 of the President on June
29, 1934, pursuant to Public Resolution Numbered 44, approved June 19,
1934 (48 Stat. 1183), and reestablished and continued by Executive Order
Numbered 7074 of the President of June 15, 1935, pursuant to Title I of
the National Industrial Recovery Act (48 Stat. 195) as amended and continued by Senate Joint Resolution 133 approved June 14, 1935.

NATIONAL LABOR RELATIONS BOARD

SEC. 3. (a) There is hereby created a board, to be known as the "National Labor Relations Board" (hereinafter referred to as the "Board"),
which shall be composed of three members, who shall be appointed by the
President, by and with the advice and consent of the Senate. One of the
original members shall be appointed for a term of one year, one for a term
of three years, and one for a term of five years, but their successors shall be
appointed for terms of five years each, except that any individual chosen to
fill a vacancy shall be appointed only for the unexpired term of the member
whom he shall succeed. The President shall designate one member to serve
as chairman of the Board. Any member of the Board may be removed by
the President, upon notice and hearing, for neglect of duty or malfeasance
in office, but for no other cause.

(b) A vacancy in the Board shall not impair the right of the remaining members to exercise all the powers of the Board, and two members of the Board shall, at all times, constitute a quorum. The Board shall have an official seal which shall be judicially noticed.

(c) The Board shall at the close of each fiscal year make a report in writing to Congress and to the President stating in detail the cases it has heard, the decisions it has rendered, the names, salaries, and duties of all employees and officers in the employ or under the supervision of the Board, and an account of all moneys it has disbursed.

SEC. 4. (a) Each member of the Board shall receive a salary of $10,000 a year, shall be eligible for reappointment, and shall not engage in any other business, vocation, or employment. The Board shall appoint, without regard for the provisions of the civil-service laws but subject to the Classification Act of 1923, as amended, an executive secretary, and such attorneys, examiners, and regional directors, and shall appoint such other employees with regard to existing laws applicable to the employment and compensation of officers and employees of the United States, as it may from time to time be needed. Attorneys appointed under this section may, at the direction of the Board, appear for and represent the Board in any case in court. Nothing in this Act shall be construed to authorize the Board to appoint individuals for the purpose of conciliation or mediation (or for statistical work), where such service may be obtained from the Department of Labor.

(b) Upon the appointment of the three original members of the Board and the designation of its chairman, the old Board shall cease to exist. All employees of the old Board shall be transferred to and become employees of the Board with salaries under the Classification Act of 1923, as amended, without acquiring by such transfer a permanent or civil service status. All records, papers, and property of the old Board shall become records, papers, and property of the Board, and all unexpended funds and appropriations for the use and maintenance of the old Board shall become funds and appropriations available to be expended by the Board in the exercise of the powers, authority, and duties conferred on it by this Act.

(c) All of the expenses of the Board, including all necessary traveling and subsistence expenses outside the District of Columbia incurred by the members or employees of the Board under its orders, shall be allowed and paid on the presentation of itemized vouchers therefore approved by the Board or by any individual it designates for that purpose.

SEC. 5. The principal office of the Board shall be in the District of Columbia, but it may meet and exercise any or all of its powers at any other place. The Board may, by one or more of its members or by such agents or agencies as it may designate, prosecute any inquiry necessary to its functions in any part of the United States. A member who participates in such an inquiry shall not be disqualified from subsequently participating in a decision of the Board in the same case.

SEC. 6. (a) The Board shall have authority from time to time to make, amend, and rescind such rules and regulations as may be necessary to carry out the provisions of this Act. Such rules and regulations shall be effective upon publication in the manner which the Board shall prescribe.

RIGHTS OF EMPLOYEES

SEC. 7. Employees shall have the right to self-organization, to form, join, or assist labor organizations, to bargain collectively through representatives of their own choosing, and to engage in concerted activities, for the purpose of collective bargaining or other mutual aid or protection.

SEC. 8. It shall be an unfair labor practice for an employer—

(1) To interfere with, restrain, or coerce employees in the exercise of the rights guaranteed in section 7.

(2) To dominate or interfere with the formation or administration of any labor organization or contribute financial or other support to it: *Provided,* That subject to rules and regulations made and published by the Board pursuant to section 6(a), an employer shall not be prohibited from permitting employees to confer with him during working hours without loss of time or pay.

(3) By discrimination in regard to hire or tenure of employment or any term or condition of employment to encourage or discourage membership in any labor organization: *Provided,* That nothing in this Act, or in the National Industrial Recovery Act (U.S.C., Supp. VII, title 15, secs. 701–702), as amended from time to time, or in any code or agreement approved or prescribed thereunder, or in any other statute of the United States, shall preclude an employer from making an agreement with a labor organization (not established, maintained, or assisted by any action defined in this Act as an unfair labor practice) to require as a condition of employment membership therein, if such labor organization is the representative of the employees as provided in section 9(a), in the appropriate collective bargaining unit covered by such agreement when made.

(4) To discharge or otherwise discriminate against an employee because he has filed charges or given testimony under this Act.

(5) To refuse to bargain collectively with the representatives of his employees, subject to the provisions of section 9(a).

REPRESENTATIVES AND ELECTIONS

SEC. 9. (a) Representatives designated or selected for the purposes of collective bargaining by the majority of the employees in a unit appropriate for such purposes, shall be the exclusive representatives of all the employees in such unit for the purposes of collective bargaining in respect to rates of pay, wages, hours of employment, or other conditions of employment: *Provided,* That any individual employee or a group of employees shall have the right at any time to present grievances to their employer.

(b) The Board shall decide in each case whether, in order to insure to employees the full benefit of their right to self-organization and to collective bargaining, and otherwise to effectuate the policies of this Act, the unit appropriate for the purposes of collective bargaining shall be the employer unit, craft unit, plant unit, or subdivision thereof.

(c) Whenever a question affecting commerce arises concerning the representation of employees, the Board may investigate such controversy and certify to the parties, in writing, the name or names of the representatives that have been designated or selected. In any such investigation, the Board shall provide for an appropriate hearing upon due notice, either in conjunction with a proceeding under section 10 or otherwise, and may take a secret ballot of employees, or utilize any other suitable method to ascertain such representatives.

(d) Whenever an order of the Board made pursuant to section 10(c) is based in whole or in part upon facts certified following an investigation pursuant to subsection (c) of this section, and there is a petition for the enforcement or review of such order, such certification and the record of such investigation shall be included in the transcript of the entire record required to be filed under subsections 10(e) or 10(f), and thereupon the decree of the court enforcing, modifying, or setting aside in whole or in part the order of the Board shall be made and entered upon the pleadings, testimony, and proceedings set forth in such transcript.

PREVENTION OF UNFAIR LABOR PRACTICES

SEC. 10 (a) The Board is empowered, as hereinafter provided, to prevent any person from engaging in any unfair labor practice (listed in section 8) affecting commerce. This power shall be exclusive, and shall not be affected by any other means of adjustment or prevention that has been or may be established by agreement, code, law, or otherwise.

(b) Whenever it is charged that any person has engaged in or is engaging in any such unfair labor practice, the Board, or any agent or agency designated by the Board for such purposes, shall have power to issue and cause to be served upon such person a complaint stating the charges in that respect, and containing a notice of hearing before the Board or a member thereof, or before a designated agent or agency, at a place therein fixed, not less than five days after the serving of said complaint. Any such complaint may be amended by the member, agent, or agency conducting the hearing or the Board in its discretion at any time prior to the issuance of an order based thereon. The person so complained of shall have the right to file an answer to the original or amended complaint and to appear in person or otherwise and give testimony at the place and time fixed in the complaint. In the discretion of the member, agent or agency conducting the hearing or the Board, any other person may be allowed to intervene in the said proceeding and to present testimony. In any such proceeding the rules of evidence prevailing in courts of law or equity shall not be controlling.

(c) The testimony taken by such member, agent or agency or the Board shall be reduced to writing and filed with the Board. Thereafter, in its discretion, the Board upon notice may take further testimony or hear argument. If upon all the testimony taken the Board shall be of the opinion that any person named in the complaint has engaged in or is engaging in any such unfair labor practice, then the Board shall state its findings of fact and shall issue and cause to be served on such person an order requiring such person to cease and desist from such unfair labor practice, and to take such affirmative action, including reinstatement of employees with or without back pay, as will effectuate the policies of this Act. Such order may further require such person to make reports from time to time showing the extent to which it has complied with the order. If upon all the testimony taken the Board shall be of the opinion that no person named in the complaint has engaged in or is engaging in any such unfair labor practice, then the Board shall state its findings of fact and shall issue an order dismissing the said complaint.

(d) Until a transcript of the record in a case shall have been filed in a court, as hereinafter provided, the Board may at any time, upon reasonable notice and in such manner as it shall deem proper, modify or set aside, in whole or in part, any finding or order made or issued by it.

(e) The Board shall have power to petition any circuit court of appeals of the United States (including the Court of Appeals of the District of Columbia), or if all the circuit courts of appeals to which application may be made are on vacation, any district court of the United States (including the Supreme Court of the District of Columbia), within any circuit or district, respectively, wherein the unfair labor practice in question occurred or wherein such person resides or transacts business, for the enforcement of such order and for appropriate temporary relief or restraining order, and shall certify and file in the court a transcript of the entire record in the proceeding, including the pleadings and testimony upon which such order was entered and the findings and order of the Board. Upon such filing, the court shall cause notice thereof to be served upon such person, and thereupon shall have jurisdiction of the proceeding and of the question determined therein, and shall have power to grant such temporary relief of restraining order as it deems just and proper, and to make and enter upon the pleadings, testimony, and proceedings set forth in such transcript a decree enforcing, modifying, and enforcing as so modified, or setting aside in whole or in part the order of the Board. No objection that has not been urged before the Board, its member, agent or agency, shall be considered by the court, unless the failure or neglect to urge such objection shall be excused because of extraordinary circumstances. The findings of the Board as to the facts, if supported by evidence and shall show to the satisfaction of the court that such additional evidence is material and that there were reasonable grounds for the failure to adduce such evidence in the hearing before the Board, its member, agent, or agency, the court may order such additional evidence to be taken before the Board, its member, agent, or agency, and to be made a part of the transcript. The Board may modify its findings as to the facts, or make new findings, by reason of additional evidence so taken and filed, and it shall file such modified or new findings, which, if supported by evidence, shall be conclusive, and shall file its recommendations, if any, for the modification or setting aside of its original order. The jurisdiction of the court shall be exclusive and its judgement and decree shall be final, except that the same shall be subject to review by the appropriate circuit court of appeals if application was made to the district court as hereinabove provided, and by the Supreme Court of the United States upon writ of certiorari or certification as provided in sections 239 and 240 of the Judicial Code, as amended (U.S.C., title 28, secs. 346 and 347).

(f) Any person aggrieved by a final order of the Board granting or denying in whole or in part the relief sought may obtain a review of such order in any circuit court of appeals of the United States in the circuit wherein the unfair labor practice in question was alleged to have been engaged in or wherein such person resides or transacts business, or in the Court of Appeals of the District of Columbia, by filing in such court a written petition praying that the order of the Board be modified or set aside. A copy of such petition shall be forthwith served upon the Board, and thereupon the aggrieved party shall file in the court a transcript of the entire record in the proceeding, certified by the Board, including the pleading and testimony upon which the order complained of was entered and the findings and order of the Board. Upon such filing, the court shall proceed in the same manner as in the case of an application by the Board under subsection (e), and shall have the same exclusive jurisdiction to grant to the Board such temporary relief or restraining order as it deems just and proper, and in like manner to make and enter a decree enforcing, modifying, and enforcing as so modified, or setting aside in whole or in part the order of the Board; and the findings of the Board as to the facts, if supported by evidence, shall in like manner be conclusive.

(g) The commencement of proceedings under subsection (e) or (f) of this section shall not, unless specifically ordered by the court, operate as a stay of the Board's order.

(h) When granting appropriate temporary relief or a restraining order, or making and entering a decree enforcing, modifying, and enforcing as so modified or setting aside in whole or in part an order of the Board, as provided in this section, the jurisdiction of courts sitting in equity shall not be limited by the Act entitled "An Act to amend the Judicial Code and to define and limit the jurisdiction of courts sitting in equity, and for other purposes," approved March 23, 1932 (U.S.C., VII, title 29, secs. 101–115).

(i) Petitions filed under this Act shall be heard expeditiously, and if possible within ten days after they have been docketed.

INVESTIGATORY POWERS

SEC. 11. For the purpose of all hearings and investigations, which, in the opinion of the Board, are necessary and proper for the exercise of the powers vested in it by section 9 and section 10—

(1) The Board, or its duly authorized agents or agencies, shall at all reasonable times have access to, for the purpose of examination, and the right

to copy any evidence of any person being investigated or proceeded against that relates to any matter under investigation or in question. Any member of the Board shall have power to issue subpenas requiring the attendance and testimony of witnesses and the production of any evidence that relates to any matter under investigation or in question before the Board, its member, agent, or agency conducting the hearing or investigation. Any member of the Board, or any agent or agency designated by the Board for such purposes, may administer oaths and affirmations, examine witnesses, and receive evidence. Such attendance of witnesses and the production of such evidence may be required from any place in the United States or any Territory or possession thereof, at any designated place of hearing.

(2) In case of contumacy or refusal to obey a subpena issued to any person, any District Court of the United States or the United States courts of any Territory or possession, or the Supreme Court of the District of Columbia, within the jurisdiction of which the inquiry is carried on or within the jurisdiction of which said person guilty of contumacy or refusal to obey is found or resides or transacts business, upon application by the Board shall have jurisdiction to issue to such person an order requiring such person to appear before the Board, its member, agent, or agency, there to produce evidence if so ordered, or there to give testimony touching the matter under investigation or in question; and any failure to obey such order of the court may be punished by said court as a contempt thereof.

(3) No person shall be excused from attending and testifying or from producing books, records, correspondence, documents, or other evidence in obedience to the subpena of the Board, on the ground that the testimony or evidence required of him may tend to incriminate him or subject him to a penalty or forfeiture; but no individual shall be prosecuted or subjected to any penalty or forfeiture for or on account of any transaction, matter, or thing concerning which he is compelled, after having claimed his privilege against self-incrimination, to testify or produce evidence, except that such individual so testifying shall not be exempt from prosecution and punishment for perjury committed in so testifying.

(4) Complaints, orders, and other process and papers of the Board, its member, agent, or agency, may be served either personally or by registered mail or by telegraph or by leaving a copy thereof at the principal office or place of business of the person required to be served. The verified return by the individual so serving the same setting forth the manner of such service shall be proof of the same, and the return post office receipt or telegraph receipt therefor when registered and mailed or telegraphed as aforesaid shall be proof of service of the same. Witnesses summoned before the Board, its member, agent, or agency, shall be paid the same fees and mileage that are paid witnesses in the courts of the United States, and witnesses whose depositions are taken and the persons taking the same shall severally be entitled to the same fees as are paid for like services in the courts of the United States.

(5) All process of any court to which application may be made under

this Act may be served in the judicial district wherein the defendant or other person required to be served resides or may be found.

(6) The several departments and agencies of the Government, when directed by the President, shall furnish the Board, upon its request, all records, papers, and information in their possession relating to any matter before the Board.

SEC. 12. Any person who shall willfully resist, prevent, impede, or interfere with any member of the Board or any of its agents or agencies in the performance of duties pursuant to this Act shall be punished by a fine of not more than $5,000 or by imprisonment for not more than one year, or both.

LIMITATIONS

SEC. 13. Nothing in this Act shall be construed so as to interfere with or impede or diminish in any way the right to strike.

SEC. 14. Wherever the application of the provisions of section 7(a) of the National Industrial Recovery Act (U.S.C., Supp. VII, title 15, sec. 707(a)), as amended from time to time, or of section 77B, paragraphs (l) and (m) of the Act approved June 7, 1934, entitled "An Act to amend an Act entitled 'An Act to establish a uniform system of bankruptcy throughout the United States' approved July 1, 1898, and Acts amendatory thereof and supplementary thereto" (48 Stat. 922, pars. (l) and (m), as amended from time to time, or of Public Resolution Numbered 44, approved June 19, 1934 (48 Stat. 1183), conflicts with the application of the provisions of this Act, this Act shall prevail: *Provided,* That in any situation where the provisions of this Act cannot be validly enforced, the provisions of such other Acts shall remain in full force and effect.

SEC. 15. If any provision of this Act, or the application of such provision to any person or circumstance, shall be held invalid, the remainder of this Act, or the application of such provision to persons or circumstances other than those as to which it is held invalid, shall not be affected thereby.

SEC. 16. This Act may be cited as the "National Labor Relations Act."
Approved, July 5, 1935.

7

LABOR AND THE ANTI-TRUST LAWS

The freedom granted to labor organizations by the passage of the National Labor Relations Act did not immediately mean that all union activities would be assessed only in light of the provisions of this Act. For example, the organizational activity of labor unions was still subject to the previously established anti-trust legislation, primarily the Sherman Anti-Trust Act. It will be recalled that the Norris-La Guardia Act explicitly identified those activities that were to be considered lawful and not actionable. While some of these activities had been identified as those that could result in restraining trade (strikes, picketing, boycotts) the 1932 legislation removed them, to some extent, from this category in the absence of violence.

Labor Freed from Anti-Trust Legislation

The Norris-La Guardia Act marked the beginning of organized labor's legal rights and the National Labor Relations Act lent tremendous strength and support to the growth and expansion of labor or-

167

ganizations. It was not until 1940, however, that the Supreme Court handed down a decision of great significance to the application of anti-trust laws to labor unions in *Apex Hosiery Company* v. *Leader*.[1] In this case the court held that while striking employees may impede an employer's opportunity to compete in the market, this does not by itself justify a Sherman Act violation.

We will consider here three cases of great significance that illustrate the attitude of the Supreme Court as to the appropriateness of using the anti-trust laws to prevent or place limitations on labor activities.

THE APEX CASE

The plaintiff in this case was the Apex Hosiery Company, established in Pennsylvania and engaged in the manufacture of hosiery for interstate distribution. Apex brought action naming William Leader and the American Federation of Full Fashioned Hosiery Workers, Philadelphia Branch No. 1, Local 706, as respondents. The suit claimed a violation of the Sherman Anti-Trust Act.

The circumstances surrounding the issue revealed the following: The Apex Hosiery Company had approximately 2,500 workers in its employ, and at the time of the issue (April, 1937) the shop was non-union. A request was made by the American Federation of Full Fashioned Hosiery Workers to consummate a collective bargaining agreement with Apex, but the latter made no effort to do so. A short time later Apex, having heard that the union had planned to demonstrate at the site, dismissed its workers for half a day. A crowd formed outside the plant with William Leader, President of the local Hosiery Workers Union, among them. The head of the Apex plant declined to meet with the union, whereupon Leader declared a sitdown strike against Apex. Some of the union membership in the crowd took over the plant and occupied it until June 23, 1937. The plant was equipped with new locks by the union and keys were given only to strikers. The union provided essentials and strike benefits to those occupying the plant. During the tenure of their occupancy, damage was done to company property to such an extent that Apex could not resume production for a period of three months after the company reoccupied its property. Apex made repeated requests to be permitted access to finished goods in order to ship orders that had been received. These finished goods amounted to some 130,000 pairs of ho-

[1] 310 U.S. 469 (1940).

siery. The requests were denied by the union. As a result, the petitioner maintained that distribution of his goods into interstate commerce was prevented.

The chronological progress of the case through the courts started on June 5, 1937, when Apex sought a preliminary injunction from the Federal District Court. The action was denied and the court maintained that an injunction could not be issued from that court because it lacked jurisdiction. Moreover, the defendants were not attempting to restrain commerce, but rather were only trying to influence the plaintiff to accept their wish for a closed shop.

On June 21, 1937, Apex appealed the case to the Circuit Court of Appeals. The judge in this court decided the defendants' actions were a restraint of trade and interstate commerce according to the Sherman Anti-Trust Act. Furthermore, the court maintained that because there was a conspiracy to do so, the federal courts did have jurisdiction. Thus, the decision of the District Court was reversed and an injunction was issued. The union took the Circuit Court of Appeals decision to the Supreme Court on December 13, 1937, where the high court reversed the Circuit Court of Appeals decision and granted a writ of certiorari. The case thus was remanded to the Federal District Court, the injunction was vacated, and the complaint dismissed for "moot" [2] cause.

The main issue, however, was not dead. The Apex Hosiery Company filed an action under the anti-trust law violation and was awarded damages in the amount of $237,210.85 by the Federal District Court. Because the Sherman Anti-Trust Act provides for triple damages, the final award amounted to $711,632.55. As might be expected, the union swiftly appealed to the Circuit Court, which handed down a decision on November 29, 1939. The court ruled: (1) the intent of the union was merely to organize production workers at the plant and not to restrain trade; (2) the amount of production Apex contributed to the total industry output was not sufficient to have any real effect on the public; (3) The circuit court used the term "commerce" as it applies in the Wagner Act and not as it applied in the Sherman Anti-Trust Act; and (4) an unlawful act does not constitute conspiracy in restraint of trade. In light of this, the judge ruled the Sherman Anti-Trust Act did not apply and therefore the decision of the lower court was reversed.

The Apex Company then went to the Supreme Court, which handed down an opinion in May, 1940. The majority opinion was based on the issue as to whether or not the evidence showed that

[2] A hypothetical or debatable issue.

there was restraint of trade. In developing its opinion the court made several points which clarified the position of labor under anti-trust legislation. First, the court observed that Congress had given no indication that labor unions should enjoy total exclusion from the Sherman Anti-Trust Act. It was further noted that the Sherman Anti-Trust Act was aimed at trusts and combinations that were established to control the market and encourage monopolies threatening or restraining free competition.

The court had not condemned restraints on competition except when combinations and conspiracies were entered into in order to affect prices or prevent buyers of the benefits of a free market.

In this case, when the activities of the union resulted in the petitioner's goods being kept from the market, the intent in no way was to affect prices or the competitive market, but merely to induce Apex to accept the union demand. The court argued that this cannot be said to have been forbidden by the Sherman Anti-Trust Act.

Even though a restraint on the sale of an employee's services to an employer may curtail competition among employees, the Clayton Act clearly stated that human labor is neither a commodity nor an article of commerce, and cannot be classified as a combination or conspiracy in restraint of trade.

While a strike or work stoppage tries to force an employer to concede to employees' demands and thereby affects the former's ability to compete in the market, the court believed that this did not place the situation within the purview of the Sherman Anti-Trust Act. A basic objective of any labor organization is the removal of price competition when differences in labor standards is the basic consideration. The Sherman Anti-Trust Act, according to the court, does not prohibit this. While secondary boycotts have been considered by the court to have had the effect of restraining trade and affecting the market, the effect was in the marketplace and not within the local plant. The fact that these acts were accompanied by violence in no way qualifies them as violations of the Sherman Anti-Trust Act because this law was not designed to provide a remedy for violations of local laws. With the above as its basis, the Supreme Court affirmed the holding of the Circuit Court of Appeals and reversed the judgment against the union for triple damages.

THE HUTCHESON CASE

The opinion of the Supreme Court in the Apex case was more firmly established in the following year in *United States* v. *Hutche-*

son.[3] This case involved a jurisdictional dispute and whether or not the peaceful activities attendant to it constituted a violation of the Sherman Anti-Trust Act. The judicial interpretation found the activities that took place in this case qualified for protection under Section 20 of the Clayton Act. This case is of particular significance because the decision had the effect of almost excluding from the federal anti-trust laws all union activities. It is also significant in that it incorporates into the opinion the application of more than one statute.

UNITED STATES V. HUTCHESON: 1941
(*312 U.S. 219*)

The Supreme Court of the United States, Mr. Justice Frankfurter delivering the opinion:

Whether the use of conventional, peaceful activities by a union in controversy with a rival union over certain jobs is a violation of the Sherman Law, Act of July 2, 1890, 26 Stat. 209, as amended, 15 U.S.C. Sec. 1, is the question. It is sharply presented in this case because it arises in a criminal prosecution. Concededly an injunction either at the suit of the Government or of the employer could not issue.

Summarizing the long indictment, these are the facts. Anheuser-Busch, Inc., operating a large plant in St. Louis, contracted with Borsari Tank Corporation for the erection of an additional facility. The Gaylord Container Corporation, a lessee of adjacent property from Anheuser-Busch, made a similar contract for a new building with the Stocker Company. Anheuser-Busch obtained the materials for brewing and other operations and sold its finished products largely through interstate shipments. The Gaylord Corporation was equally dependent on interstate commerce for marketing its goods, as were the construction companies for their building materials. Among the employees of Anheuser-Busch were members of the United Brotherhood of Carpenters and Joiners of America and of the International Association of Machinists. The conflicting claims of these two organizations, affiliated with the American Federation of Labor, in regard to the erection and dismantling of machinery had long been a source of controversy between them. Anheuser-Busch had had agreements with both organizations whereby the Machinists were given the disputed jobs and the Carpenters agreed to submit all disputes to arbitration. But in 1939

[3] 312 U.S. 219 (1941).

the president of the Carpenters, their general representative, and two officials of the Carpenters' local organization, the four men under indictment, stood on the claim of the Carpenters for the jobs. Rejection by the employer of the Carpenters' demand and the refusal of the latter to submit to arbitration were followed by a strike of the Carpenters, called by the defendants against Anheuser-Busch and the construction companies, a picketing of Anheuser-Busch and its tenant, and a request through circular letters and the official publication of the Carpenters that union members and their friends refrain from buying Anheuser-Busch beer.

These activities on behalf of the Carpenters formed the charge of the indictment as a criminal combination and conspiracy in violation of the Sherman Law. Demurrers denying that what was charged constituted a violation of the laws of the United States were sustained, and the case came here under the Criminal Appeals Act. . . .

Section 1 of the Sherman Law on which the indictment rested is as follows: "Every contract, combination in the form of trust or otherwise, or conspiracy in restraint of trade or commerce among the several States, or with foreign nations, is hereby declared to be illegal." The controversies engendered by its application to trade union activities and the efforts to secure legislative relief from its consequences are familiar history. The Clayton Act of 1914 was the result. Act of October 15, 1914, 38 Stat. 730. "This statute was the fruit of unceasing agitation, which extended over more than twenty years and was designed to equalize before the law the position of workingmen and employer as industrial combatants." *Duplex Printing Press Co.* v. *Deering,* 254 U.S. 443, 484. Section 20 of that Act, . . . withdrew from the general interdict of the Sherman Law specifically enumerated practices of labor unions by prohibiting injunctions against them—since the use of the injunction has been the major source of dissatisfaction—and also relieved such practices of all illegal taint by the catch-all provision, "nor shall any of the acts specified in this paragraph be considered or held to be violations of any law of the United States." The Clayton Act gave rise to new litigation and to renewed controversy in and out of Congress regarding the status of trade unions. By the generality of its terms the Sherman Law had necessarily compelled the courts to work out its meaning from case to case. It was widely believed that into the Clayton Act courts read the very beliefs which that Act was designed to remove. Specifically the courts restricted the scope of Sec. 20 to trade union activities directed against an employer by his own employees. *Duplex Printing Press Co.* v. *Deering, supra.* Such a view, it was urged, both by powerful judicial dissents and informed lay opinion, misconceived the area of economic conflict that had best be left to economic forces and the pressure of public opinion and not subjected to the judgment of courts. Id. 254 U. S. at page 485, 486. Agitation again led to legislation and in 1932 Congress wrote the Norris-La Guardia Act. Act of March 23, 1932, 47 Stat. 70, 29 U.S.C. Secs. 101–115.

The Norris-La Guardia Act removed the fetters upon trade union activities, which, according to judicial construction, Sec. 20 of the Clayton Act had left untouched, by still further narrowing the circumstances under which the federal courts could grant injunctions in labor disputes. More especially, the Act explicitly formulated the "public policy of the United States" in regard to the industrial conflict, and by its light established that the allowable area of union activity was not to be restricted, as it had been in the *Duplex* case to an immediate employer-employee relation. Therefore, whether trade union conduct constitutes a violation of the Sherman Law is to be determined only by reading the Sherman Law and Sec. 20 of the Clayton Act and the Norris-La Guardia Act as a harmonizing text of outlawry of labor conduct.

Were, then, the acts charged against the defendants prohibited or permitted, by these three interlacing statutes? If the facts laid in the indictment come within the conduct enumerated in Sec. 20 of the Clayton Act they do not constitute a crime within the general terms of the Sherman Law because of the explicit command of that section that such conduct shall not be "considered or held to be violations of any law of the United States." So long as a union acts in its self interest and does not combine with non-labor groups, the licit and the illicit under Sec. 20 are not to be distinguished by any judgment regarding the wisdom or unwisdom, the rightness or wrongness, the selfishness or unselfishness of the end of which the particular union activities are the means. There is nothing remotely within the terms of Sec. 20 that differentiates between trade union conduct directed against an employer because of a controversy arising in the relation between employer and employee, as such, and conduct similarly directed but ultimately due to an internecine struggle between two unions seeking the favor of the same employer. Such strife between competing unions has been an obdurate conflict in the evolution of so-called craft unionism and has undoubtedly been one of the potent forces in the modern development of industrial unions. These conflicts have intensified industrial tension but there is not the slightest warrant for saying that Congress has made Sec. 20 inapplicable to trade union conduct resulting from them.

In so far as the Clayton Act is concerned, we must therefore dispose of this case as though we had before us precisely the same conduct on the part of the defendants in pressing claims against Anheuser-Busch for increased wages, or shorter hours, or other elements of what are called working conditions. The fact that what was done in a competition for jobs against the Machinists rather than against, let us say, a company union is a differentiation which Congress had not put into the federal legislation and which therefore we cannot write into it.

It is at once apparent that the acts with which the defendants are charged are the kinds of acts protected by Sec. 20 of the Clayton Act. The refusal of the Carpenters to work for Anheuser-Busch or on construction work being done for it and its adjoining tenant, and the peaceful attempt to get members of other unions similarly to refuse to work, are plainly within the free scope accorded to workers by Sec. 20 for "terminating any relation of employment," or "ceasing to perform any work or labor," or "recommending, advising, or persuading others by peaceful means so to do." The picketing of Anheuser-Busch premises with signs to indicate that Anheuser-Busch was unfair to organized labor, a familiar practice in these situations, comes with the language "attending at any place where any such person or persons may lawfully be, for the purpose of peacefully obtaining or communicating information, or from peacefully persuading any person to work or to abstain from working." Finally, the recommendation to union members and their friends not to buy or use the product of Anheuser-Busch is explicitly covered by "ceasing to patronize . . . any party to such dispute, or from recommending, advising, or persuading others by peaceful and lawful means so to do."

Clearly, then, the facts here charged constitute lawful conduct under the Clayton Act unless the defendants cannot invoke that Act because outsiders to the immediate dispute also shared in the conduct. But we need not determine whether the conduct is legal within the restrictions which *Duplex Printing Press Co.* v. *Deering* gave to the immunities of Sec. 20 of the Clayton Act. Congress in the Norris-La Guardia Act has expressed the public policy of the United States and defined its conception of a "labor dispute" in terms that no longer leave room for doubt. *Milk Wagon Drivers' Union* v. *Lake Valley Farm Products, Inc.*, 311 U.S. 91. This was done, as we recently said, in order to "obviate the results of the judicial construction" theretofore given the Clayton Act. *New Negro Alliance* v. *Sanitary Grocery Co.*, 303 U.S. 552, 562; see *Apex Hosiery Co.* v. *Leader*, 310 U.S. 469, 507 n. 26. Such a dispute, Sec. 13(c) provides, "includes any controversy concerning terms or conditions of employment, or concerning the association or representation of persons in negotiating, fixing, maintaining, changing, or seeking to arrange terms or conditions of employment, regardless of whether or not the disputants stand in the proximate relation of employer and employee." And under Sec. 13(b) a person is "participating or interested in a labor dispute" if he "is engaged in the same industry, trade, craft, or occupation, in which such dispute occurs, or has a direct or indirect interest therein, or is a member, officer, or agent of any association composed in whole or in part of employers or employees engaged in such industry, trade, craft, or occupation."

To be sure, Congress expressed this national policy and determined the bounds of a labor dispute in an act explicitly dealing with the further withdrawal of injunctions in labor controversies. But to argue, as it was urged before us, that the *Duplex* case still governs for purposes of a criminal prosecution is to say that that which on the equity side of the court is allowable conduct may in a criminal proceeding become the road to prison. It would be strange indeed that although neither the government nor Anheuser-Busch could have sought an injunction against the acts here challenged, the elaborate efforts to permit such conduct failed to prevent criminal liability punishable with imprisonment and heavy fines. That is not the way to read the will of Congress, particularly when expressed by a statute which, as we have already indicated, is practically and historically one of a series of enactments touching one of the most sensitive national problems. Such legislation must not be read in a spirit of mutilating narrowness. . . .

The relation of the Norris-La Guardia Act to the Clayton Act is not that of a tightly drawn amendment to a technically phrased tax provision. The underlying aim of the Norris-La Guardia Act was to restore the broad purpose which Congress thought it had formulated in the Clayton Act but which was frustrated, so Congress believed, by unduly restrictive judicial construction. This was authoritatively stated by the House Committee on the Judiciary. "The purpose of the bill is to protect the rights of labor in the same manner that Congress intended when it enacted the Clayton Act, October 15, 1914 (38 Stat. L. 738), which act, by reason of its construction and application by the federal courts, is ineffectual to accomplish the congressional intent." H. Rep. No. 669, 72d Congress, 1st Session, p. 3. The Norris-La Guardia Act was a disapproval of *Duplex Printing Press Co.* v. *Deering, supra,* and *Bedford Cut Stone Co.* v. *Journeymen Stone Cutters' Association;* 274 U.S. 37, as the authoritative interpretation of Sec. 20 of the Clayton Act, for Congress now placed its own meaning upon that section. The Norris-La Guardia Act reasserted the original purpose of the Clayton Act by infusing into it the immunized trade union activities as redefined by the later Act. In this light Sec. 20 removes all such allowable conduct from the taint of being a "violation of any law of the United States," including the Sherman Law.

There is no profit in discussing those cases under the Clayton Act which were decided before the courts were furnished the light shed by the Norris-La Guardia Act on the nature of the industrial conflict. And since the facts in the indictment are made lawful by the Clayton Act in so far as "any law of the United States" is concerned, it would be idle to consider the Sherman Law apart from the Clayton Act as interpreted by Congress. Cf. *Apex Hosiery Co.* v. *Leader,* 310 U.S. 469. It was precisely in order to minimize the difficulties to which the general language of the Sherman Law in its application to workers had given rise, that Congress cut through all the tangled verbalisms and enumerated concretely the types of activities which had become familiar incidents of union procedure.

The opinion affirming the lower court's decision makes this case significant first because it removes the activities of unions from the restrictions of the anti-trust legislation to a considerable extent; second, it brings in judicial consideration of three items of legislation and the necessity for considering each by itself as to intent and purpose as well as the interdependence of each law. The importance of this tripartite effect is further illustrated in later cases.

THE ALLEN BRADLEY COMPANY

The opinion rendered in the *Apex Hosiery Co.* v. *Leader* and *United States* v. *Hutcheson* cases did not completely settle the issue of the applicability of anti-trust laws to labor unions. The issue was before the Supreme Court again in *Allen Bradley Co., et al.* v. *Local Union No. 3, et al.*[4] In this case the court concerned itself with the secondary boycott activities of the union and whether or not these union activities were restraints of trade as identified by the Sherman Anti-Trust Act.

The situation surrounding the issue involved the Allen Bradley Company, which manufactured electrical equipment products both within the state of New York as well as in other states. However, the company did not have a manufacturing operation within New York City, and the company maintained that it had been prevented from supplying its goods to the New York City market because of the activities of the respondent, the International Brotherhood of Electrical Workers, Local No. 3. The construction market in the city almost exclusively used that electrical equipment which carried a union label. If other than union-made goods were installed, sites were either struck or picketed. Eventually the union was effective in establishing a large number of closed-shop agreements with electrical equipment contractors and manufacturers throughout the city. These agreements meant that the contractors would buy from local manufacturers who operated under closed shop agreements with Local No. 3. Ultimately this situation expanded to such an extent as to involve the entire industry. The three groups involved, manufacturers, contractors, and union, combined to develop a successful agency to deal with unwilling or uncooperative manufacturers and/or contractors. As a result, the records revealed that employment, wages and growth within the industry enjoyed large gains. The opposite was true for those who operated outside the New York City area. Those who manufactured outside the city, feeling the effect of this combined effort, decided to make a legal issue of the situation and filed suit on December 9, 1935. The suit was based on a violation of the anti-trust laws and asked that an injunction be issued to prevent the union from refusing to work on non-union-made goods. Specifically, the plaintiff charged that a conspiracy had been entered into, that the closed-shop agree-

[4] 325 U.S. 797 (1945).

ments compelled contractors to refuse to work on non-union-made materials, that this resulted in a boycott that was unlawful, and finally that enforcement was effected by threats of strikes and violence.

The court appointed a special master to investigate and report his findings to the court. On June 10, 1943, the court held that while the union had a right to enter into closed-shop agreements and select its members, it could do this only by making a reasonable and not an arbitrary decision. The strikes to induce employment of members were thereby unlawful and Allen Bradley, petitioners, were entitled to injunctive relief as well as a judgment for a violation of the Sherman Act by the union.[5]

The union took the case to the Circuit Court of Appeals. This court reversed the decision of the District Court and the case was dismissed. The case was then taken by Allen Bradley Company to the Supreme Court. On June 18, 1945, Justice Black delivered the opinion of the court, with Justice Murphy dissenting. The principle issue was identified by the court as a question of ". . . whether it is a violation of the Sherman Anti-Trust Act for labor unions and their members, prompted by a desire to get and hold jobs for themselves at good wages and under high working standards; to combine with employers and with manufacturers of goods to restrain competition in, and to monopolize the marketing of, such goods." [6]

Using *Apex Hosiery Co.* v. *Leader* as an authority, the court held that the combination of businessmen as described in this case was a violation of the Sherman Anti-Trust Act. This combination served to restrain trade, prevent the shipment of goods from the New York City market, control the price of these goods, and discriminate against potential customers. The only way the violation would not be obtained would be if these activities could not be brought under the Act because the union took an active part in them. The question then to be considered by the court becomes ". . . do labor unions violate the Sherman Act when, in order to further their own interests as wage earners, they aid and abet businessmen to do the precise things which that Act prohibits?" [7]

It is necessary to a good understanding of this decision to briefly look at the reasoning and considerations of the court. It will be recalled that the Sherman Anti-Trust Act did not explicitly exclude

[5] For an excellent review of court proceedings in this case see: Elias Lieberman, *Unions Before the Bar* (New York: Harper and Brothers, 1950), pp. 272–286.

[6] 325 U.S. 797 (1945).

[7] *Ibid.*

labor unions from its coverage. As a result, two attitudes developed toward the meaning of the legislation. The early view was that Congress had intended this legislation to eliminate pressures exerted by combinations and trusts resulting in high prices and market control. The Sherman Anti-Trust Act was thus viewed as a law to regulate trade, the distribution and sale of goods, and not employee-employer relationships. This view also held that labor had the right to act as it felt warranted either individually or as a group to better its economic position. If such activity resulted in working or not working, purchasing or not purchasing, or efforts to induce others to so act, this did not bring it under the coverage of the Sherman Anti-Trust Act. In short, anti-trust laws were designed to regulate trade, and labor, not being a commodity, could not be treated as such.

The alternative attitude argued that if the free flow of trade was disturbed or, if a combination of any group tended to create a monopoly, this was a violation of the Sherman Act. Using this reasoning, employees who combined in an effort to acquire increased wages were a prohibited monopoly. This was the attitude that was adopted by the federal courts and as a result, the injunction was used to prevent organized union activity.

The Sherman Act was amended and strengthened by the passage of the Clayton Act in 1914. While its primary purpose was to eliminate trade practices that served to injure competition, it did this by using language appropriate to commercial activity and not labor union activity. However, the Act contained no explicit language to suggest that businesses utilizing the services of labor could remove themselves from Sherman Act coverage. The Clayton Act did explicitly concern itself with some labor activities by stating ". . . labor of a human being is not a commodity or article of commerce. Nothing contained in the anti-trust laws shall be construed to forbid the existence and operation of labor, agricultural or horticultural organizations, instituted for the purpose of mutual help, . . . from lawfully carrying out the legitimate objects thereof . . ." [8] In addition, the legislation also placed restrictions on the issuance of injunctions when labor disputes were involved. This did not have the widespread effect that was anticipated, as we have seen in our consideration of the *Duplex* and *Bedford* cases. The Norris-La Guardia Act also received judicial consideration in the *Allen-Bradley* case. This legislation provided an even wider arena in which labor activities could take place and added even more restrictions on the use of injunctions.

[8] 26 Stat. 209, Ch. 647, Secs. 1–8, 51st Cong., 1st Sess. (1914).

When reaching a decision here, then, as we saw in *United States* v. *Hutcheson,* the court was required to take cognizance of each of these legislative enactments to determine whether or not the activities of labor unions do violate the anti-trust laws. The court declared:

. . . we have two declared congressional policies which it is our responsibility to reconcile. The one seeks to preserve a competitive business economy; the other to preserve the rights of labor to organize to better its conditions through the agency of collective bargaining. We must determine here how far Congress intended activities under one of these policies to neutralize the results envisioned by the other.[9]

Based on the preceding considerations, the following conclusions were reached by the court: first, the activities in which the union participated were not violations of the law and are contained in Section 20 of the Clayton Act as activities against which neither an injunction nor restraining order can issue; furthermore, while Section 6 of the Clayton Act gives immunity to labor organizations that are instituted for the purpose of mutual help when, as in this case, the union acted in concert with businesses who had the power to eliminate competition, such concerted action removed the activity from the protective umbrella of Section 6; finally, anti-trust legislation was designed to prevent monopolies and protect competition. It is unlikely that Congress would construct legislation intended to accomplish this purpose and at the same time intend that labor unions would be free to act with and for business to impede the achievement of this objective. Because the union did aid manufacturers in activity that violated the anti-trust laws, the decision made by the district court must stand.

The court recognized that its decision created an undesirable situation. By ruling as it did, the court held that the same activities performed by the same labor union may or may not be held as a violation of the Sherman Act. That is, if the labor union performs these acts by itself, the violation does not exist. However, the same acts performed in combination with business groups do result in a violation. The ruling of the United States Supreme Court thus reversed that of the Circuit Court of Appeals, and the case was remanded to the District Court.

In the same year in *Hunt* v. *Crumboch* [10] it was also held that the

[9] 325 U.S. 797 (1945).
[10] 325 U.S. 821 (1945).

anti-trust legislation was not applicable. For purposes of discussion and analysis, pertinent excerpts from the opinion follow:

HUNT v. CRUMBOCH: 1945
(*325 U.S. 821*)

The Supreme Court of the United States, Mr. Justice Black delivering the opinion:

. . . The question here is whether an organization of laboring men violated the Sherman Act, as amended, 26 Stat. 209, 38 Stat. 730, by refusing to admit to membership petitioner's employees, and by refusing to sell their services to petitioner, thereby making it impossible for petitioner profitably to continue in business.

For about fourteen years prior to 1939, the petitioner, a business partnership engaged in motor trucking, carried freight under a contract with the Great Atlantic & Pacific Tea Co. (A & P). Eighty-five percent of the merchandise thus hauled by petitioner was interstate, from and to Philadelphia, Pennsylvania. The respondent union, composed of drivers and helpers, was affiliated with other A. F. of L. unions whose members worked at loading and hauling of freight by motor truck. In 1937, the respondent union called a strike of the truckers and haulers of A & P in Philadelphia for the purpose of enforcing a closed shop. The petitioner, refusing to unionize its business, attempted to operate during the strike. Much violence occurred. One of the union men was killed near union headquarters, and a member of the petitioner partnership was tried for the homicide and acquitted. A & P and the union entered into a closed-shop agreement, whereupon all contract haulers working for A & P, including the petitioner, were notified that their employees must join and become members of the union. All of the other contractor haulers except petitioner either joined the union or made closed-shop agreements with it. The union, however, refused to negotiate with the petitioner, and declined to admit any of its employees to membership. Although petitioner's services had been satisfactory, A & P, at the union's instigation, cancelled its contract with petitioner in accordance with the obligations of its closed-shop agreement with the union. Later, the petitioner obtained a contract with a different company, but again at the union's instigation, and upon the consummation of a closed-shop contract by that company with the union, petitioner lost that contract and business. Because of the union's refusal to negotiate with the petitioner and to accept petitioner's employees as members, the petitioner was unable to obtain any further hauling contracts in Philadelphia. The elimination of the petitioner's service did not in any manner affect the interstate operations of A & P or other companies.

The petitioner then instituted this suit in a federal district court against respondents, the union and its representatives, praying for an injunction and asking for treble damages. Demurrers to the complaint were overruled, the case was tried, findings of fact were made, and the district court rendered a judgment for the respondents on the ground that petitioner had failed to prove a cause of action under the anti-trust laws. 47 F. Supp. 571. The Circuit Court of Appeals affirmed, holding that the fact that respondent's actions had caused petitioner to go out of business was not such a restraint of interstate commerce as would be actionable under the Sherman and Clayton Acts. 143 F 2d 902. We granted certiorari because of the questions involved concerning the responsibility of labor unions under the anti-trust laws.

The "destruction" of petitioner's business resulted from the fact that the union members, acting in concert, refused to accept employment with the petitioner, and refused to admit to their association anyone who worked for petitioner. The petitioner's loss of business is therefore analogous to the case of a manufacturer selling goods in interstate commerce who fails in business because union members refused to work for him. Had a group of petitioner's business competitors conspired and combined to suppress petitioner's business by refusing to sell goods and services to it, such a combination would have violated the Sherman Act. *Binderup* v. *Pathe Exchange;* 263 U.S. 291, 312; *Fashion Originator's Guild* v. *Federal Trade Commission,* 312 U.S. 457. A labor union which aided and abetted such a group would have been equally guilty. *Allen Bradley Co.* v. *Local Union No. 3, ante,* p. 797. The only combination here, however, was one of workers alone and what they refused to sell petitioner was their labor.

It is not a violation of the Sherman Act for laborers in combination to refuse to work. They can sell or not sell their labor as they please, and upon such terms and conditions as they choose, without infringing the anti-trust laws. *Apex Hosiery Co.* v. *Leader,* 310 U.S. 469, 502–503. A worker is privileged under congressional enactments, acting either alone or in concert with his fellow workers, to associate or to decline to associate with other workers, to accept, refuse to accept, or to terminate a relationship of employment, and his labor is not to be treated as "a commodity or article of commerce." . . . *American Steel Foundries* v. *Tri-City Council*, 257 U.S. 184, 209. It was the exercise of these rights that created the situation which caused the petitioner to lose its hauling contracts and its business.

It is argued that their exercise falls within the condemnation of the Sherman Act, because the union members' refusal to accept employment was due to personal antagonism against the petitioner arising out of the killing of a union man. But Congress in the Sherman Act and the legislation which followed it manifested no purpose to make *any* kind of refusal to accept personal employment a violation of the anti-trust laws. Such an application of those laws would be a complete departure from their spirit and purpose. Cf. *Apex Hosiery Co.* v. *Leader, supra*, 512; *Allen Bradley* v. *Local Union No. 3, supra*. Moreover, "So long as a union acts in its self-interest and does not combine with nonlabor groups, the licit and the illicit under Sec. 20 are not to be distinguished by any judgment regarding the wisdom or unwisdom, the rightness or wrongness, the selfishness or unselfishness of the end of which the particular union activities are the means." *United States* v. *Hutcheson*, 312 U.S. 219, 232. . . .

Finally, it is faintly suggested that our decisions in *Steele* v. *L. & N. R. Co.*, 323 U.S. 192; *Tunstall* v. *Brotherhood*, 323 U.S. 210, and *Wallace Corp.* v. *Labor Board*, 323 U.S. 248, require that we hold that respondents' conduct violated the Sherman Act. Those cases stand for the principle that a bargaining agent owes a duty not to discriminate unfairly against any of the group it purports to represent. But if the record showed discrimination against employees here, it would not even tend to show a violation of the Sherman Act. Congress has indicated no purpose to make a union's breach of duty to employees in a collective bargaining group an infraction of the Sherman Act.

The controversy in the instant case, between a union and an employer, involves nothing more than a dispute over employment, and the withholding of labor services. It cannot therefore be said to violate the Sherman Act, as amended. That Act does not purport to afford remedies for all torts committed by or against persons engaged in interstate commerce. "The maintenance in our federal system of a proper distribution between state and national governments of police authority and of remedies private and public for public wrongs is of far-reaching importance. An intention to disturb the balance is not lightly to be imputed to Congress." *Apex Hosiery Co.* v. *Leader*, 310 U.S. 469, 513. Whether the respondents' conduct amounts to an actionable wrong subjecting them to liability for damages under Pennsylvania law is not our concern.

The Laws of Picketing

Picketing may be described as an activity carried on by labor organizations to publicly display disagreements that exist between employer and employee. In its simplest form it usually involves a person or persons patrolling a front of the place of business of the employer with whom there is conflict. Normally, the pickets carry signs or placards that state the reason for the disagreement. Problems arise as to the lawfulness or unlawfulness of picketing activity when, as a result of the picketing, violence erupts, disinterested or secondary parties become involved, there is evidence of coercion, and more recently with the kinds of information that are communicated or publicized by the picketing.

BACKGROUND AND ATTITUDE

The right to picket is of great import to labor. It is through this process that disputing employees may inform other labor union members and the empathetic public of the reason that they believe an employer is unfair. This permits the public to refrain from patronizing the employer and allows other than the picketing union members to refuse to cross the picket lines either to patronize or service the employer, if they so wish. Thus, considerable economic pressure can be exerted on the employer that ultimately may result in his conceding to or compromising with the demands being made. Prior to the passage of the Clayton Act, the attitude of the Supreme Court toward picketing was generally that the activity was not lawful because the activity itself, regardless of its form, was held to be a tortious act. When the Clayton Act was written, a provision was included that permitted the use of peaceful persuasion (e.g., picketing) to either encourage or discourage persons from working or not working. Modifications were made by the Supreme Court in handing down subsequent decisions.

There were two cases brought before the court during 1921 dealing with the issue. These rulings provide an indication of the Supreme Court's view of the lawfulness of picketing activities. The first of these cases, *American Steel Foundries* v. *Tri-City Central Trades Council*,[11] considered picketing in relation to: (1) whether or not Section 20 of the Clayton Act applies; (2) whether or not irreparable injury to property or to property right is intended to extend to a business; and (3) whether or not "dispute" does not include that between an employer and those who are not his employees and are not seeking employment.

This case started in 1914 when the American Steel Foundries reopened its plant. When operations were resumed, only about one-fourth of its former employees were put back on the job, and these with reduced wages. The union attempted to meet with the company to discuss the wage cut but the company refused. The plant was struck and picketed. The company went before the district court and filed charges against the union claiming that because of the strike and violence accompanying the picketing they were unable to hire employees. An injunction was issued ordering all activity to cease. This included any form of threats or persuasion that might be used to influence present or future employees. The case was appealed and the decision reversed in 1916. The court maintained that peaceful picketing should have been allowed and that persuasion could be used. Thus, the injunction should have prohibited only those activities which were not lawful and should not have restricted the parties from persuading or picketing.

The case was presented to the Supreme Court in 1919 and the decision handed down in 1921 after appeal by the company. The high court held that the applicability of Section 20 should be determined according to whether or not the picketing was "peaceful." To be held peaceful there must be free access and egress to and from the premises, the means used to induce participation must be lawful, and the purpose of such activity should in no way lead to intimidation and obstruction. Thus, the decision of the Circuit Court of Appeals was reversed only in part.

The second case heard in this same year was *Truax* v. *Corrigan*.[12] In this case the court found that the owner was deprived of business without due process and therefore the law was operating in violation of the Fourteenth Amendment to the Constitution. The plaintiff here

[11] 257 U.S. 184 (1921).
[12] 257 U.S. 312 (1921).

owned and operated a restaurant. After a disagreement between the owner and the union regarding working conditions, the employees went on strike and the union commenced picketing activities in front of the restaurant. These activities included not only picketing but also displaying banners, appeals to customers to stay away from the restaurant, and the distribution of hand-bills making charges against the owner of the restaurant. The plaintiff presented evidence to the court that as a result of these activities his average daily receipts had dropped from $156 to $75. The plaintiff believed that if these activities were allowed to go on, eventually his business would be totally ruined and the injury inflicted irreparable. Further, because the defendants were not solvent, plaintiff could not hope to recover even if awarded damages. It was contended that because of these circumstances plaintiff had no adequate remedy at law. In addition, the complainant declared that the defendants were claiming immunity for their activities under Paragraph 1464 of the Revised Statutes of Arizona 1913. The pertinent section of the statute states in part:

> . . . No restraining order or injunction shall be granted by any court of this state, . . . in any case between an employer and employees, . . . or between persons employed and persons seeking employment, involving or growing out of a dispute concerning terms or conditions of employment, unless necessary to prevent irreparable injury to property or to a property right of the party making the application, for which injury there is no adequate remedy at law. . . .[13]

The plaintiff maintained that if the statute meant that the activities of the defendants were lawful, the statute violated the Fourteenth Amendment and served to deprive the plaintiff of his property without due process of law and thus did not permit the plaintiff equal protection of the law. It is of interest to note that Truax had been unsuccessful in his attempts to get a judgment in both the Superior Court for Cochise County and the Supreme Court of Arizona. In a very close decision, the United States Supreme Court held for the plaintiff.

The court considered that the plaintiff's business was a property right, and if there is intentional injury to this right by conspiracy this is a tort. Concerted action either with unlawful object or through unlawful means was viewed as a conspiracy. The consideration in this case then had to be based on whether or not the means used by the

[13] *Ibid.*

defendants to reach their intended object were lawful. The court determined that the activities carried out by the defendants

> . . . were an unlawful annoyance and a hurtful nuisance in respect of the free access to the plaintiff's place of business. . . . It was compelling every customer or would-be customer to run the gauntlet of most uncomfortable publicity, aggressive and annoying importunity, libelous attacks and fear of injurious consequences, illegally inflicted, to his reputation and standing in the community. No wonder that a business of $50,000 was reduced to only one-fourth of its former extent. Violence could not have been more effective. It was moral coercion by illegal annoyance and obstruction and it thus was plainly a conspiracy. . . .[14]

In considering the question of due process, the court determined that the state in this case had enacted legislation which intruded on the property rights of its citizens, as we observed in the previous chapter. In so doing, it left the plaintiff without remedy because it denied him the issuance of an injunction and thus denied his equal protection of the law.

The court also maintained that a proper analogy could not be made between Section 20 of the Clayton Act and Paragraph 1464 of the Arizona Statute. The court here made reference to *American Steel Foundries* v. *Tri-City Central Trades Council* and the finding that peaceful picketing was a contradiction of terms but that it was lawful for a single individual at plant entrances to inform and persuade employees to participate in strike activity. However, the construction put upon these words by the Supreme Court of Arizona made Paragraph 1464 of the statute so different in meaning from Section 20 of the Clayton Act that they might as well be in totally different languages. Consequently, an injunction was granted and the controversial section of the Arizona Statute was declared unconstitutional.

There is little, if any, evidence of change in the Supreme Court's attitude toward picketing from the time of the two preceding cases until 1937. During and toward the end of this eleven-year period, several incidents served to affect the national climate for employer-employee relations. Economically the country entered the depression, the political atmosphere changed with the inauguration of a new President, and legislatively three laws were enacted, the Norris-La Guardia Act, the National Industrial Recovery Act, and the National Labor Rela-

[14] *Ibid.*

tions Act. All of these things added to the impetus and acceptance of
the American labor movement. In addition, a modification could be
seen at the state level when several states passed legislation closely
adhering to the federal policy in the form of "little Wagner Acts."
With this change in state and federal philosophy, the *Senn* v. *Tile Layers' Protective Union* case went through the courts.[15] The point at issue
here was the legality of the injunction provisions of the Wisconsin Labor Code against peaceful picketing and if these provisions constituted
a violation of the due process or equal protection clause of the Fourteenth Amendment. Senn argued that because of this prohibition he
was being deprived of his right to work.

Senn's main contention was simply that because of the union's in-
sistence that "Article III" (see above) be included in a union shop
agreement, he was being deprived of his right to work in his own business, a right the Fourteenth Amendment guarantees. Therefore, he
claimed, the State could not authorize the picketing and/or publicity
undertaken by the union which prevented him from exercising his
constitutional right.

The Supreme Court of Wisconsin had held that both the means and
the end sought by the union were legal. The United States Supreme
Court identified its purpose as determining whether or not the means
or the end were forbidden by the federal Constitution. In order to do
so, the Court considered several points. (1) Neither picketing nor publicity, the means used, were prohibited. (2) Freedom of speech permits publicizing facts with regard to a labor dispute; however, through
the exercise of its police power, a state may influence the means used.
(3) As long as the end is legal, the State is able to permit labor to combine as pickets in order to reach this end. (4) Article III, the end the
union was seeking, was not unconstitutional but was necessary for the
protection of the workers in the industry. (5) The annoyance that may
result from publicity was not held to be an intrusion on Senn's constitutional guarantees. (6) There is no constitutional right that guarantees a remedy for the lawful conduct of another. Using these facts as a
basis for its decision, the Supreme Court affirmed the judgment of the
lower courts and held for the defendants.

Three years later, a major case was heard and established new criteria to be used in determining the lawfulness and/or unlawfulness of
picketing. A state statute is again at issue in the case of *Thornhill* v.
State of Alabama. Section 3448 of the Alabama Code of 1923 forbade
loitering or picketing, and again it was claimed by Thornhill that this
violated the Constitution. In delivering the opinion of the court, Jus-

[15] 301 U.S. 468 (1937).

tice Murphy declared: ". . . We think that Section 3448 is invalid on its face. . . . Members of a union might, without special statutory authorization by a state, make known the facts of a labor dispute, for freedom of speech is guaranteed by the Federal Constitution." [16] Thus, we have a ruling for the first time sanctioning peaceful picketing as an expression of opinion, protected by the constitutional provision that assures the right of free speech. In addition, the Thornhill decision contains language that clearly indicates that states do not have the power to enact legislation that prohibits peaceful picketing.

For purposes of analysis and comparison, the opinion of the Supreme Court follows:

THORNHILL v. STATE OF ALABAMA: 1940
(*310 U.S. 88*)

The Supreme Court of the United States, Mr. Justice Murphy delivering the opinion:

Petitioner, Byron Thornhill, was convicted in the Circuit Court of Tuscaloosa County, Alabama, of the violation of Section 3448 of the State Code of 1923. The Code Section reads as follows: "Sec. 3448. Loitering or picketing forbidden.—Any person or persons, who, without a just cause or legal excuse therefore, go near to or loiter about the premises or place of business of any person, firm, corporation, or association of people, engaged in lawful business, for the purpose, or with the intent of influencing, or inducing other persons not to trade with, buy from, sell to, have business dealings with, or be employed by such persons, firm, corporation, or association or who picket the works or place of business of such other persons, firms, corporations, or associations of persons, for the purpose of hindering, delaying, or interfering with or injuring any lawful business or enterprise of another, shall be guilty of a misdemeanor; but nothing herein shall prevent any person from soliciting trade or business for a competitive business."

At the close of the case for the State, petitioner moved to exclude all the testimony taken at the trial on the ground that Section 3448 was violative of the Constitution of the United States. The Circuit Court overruled the motion, found petitioner "guilty of loitering and picketing as charged in the complaint," and entered judgment accordingly. The judgment was affirmed by the Court of Appeals, which considered the constitutional question and sus-

[16] *Thornhill v. State of Alabama*, 310 U.S. 88 (1940).

tained the section on the authority of two previous decisions in the
Alabama courts. . . . A petition for certiorari was denied by the
Supreme Court of the State. The case is here on certiorari granted
because of the importance of the questions presented. . . .

The proofs consist of the testimony of two witnesses for the
prosecution. It appears that petitioner on the morning of his arrest
was seen "in company with six or eight other men" "on the picket
line" at the plant of the Brown Wood Preserving Company. Some
weeks previously a strike order had been issued by a Union, apparently affiliated with the American Federation of Labor, which
had as members all but four of the approximately one hundred employees of the plant. Since that time a picket line with two picket
posts of six to eight men each had been maintained around the
plant twenty-four hours a day. The picket posts appear to have
been on Company property, "on a private entrance for employees,
and not on any public road." One witness explained that practically all the employees live on Company property . . . and that
the Union holds its meetings on Company property. No demand
was ever made upon the men not to come on the property. There
is no testimony indicating the nature of the dispute . . . or the
course of events which led to the issuance of the strike order, or
the nature of the efforts for conciliation.

The Company scheduled a day for the plant to resume operations. One of the witnesses, Clarence Simpson, who was not a
member of the Union, on reporting to the plant on the day indicated, was approached by petitioner who told him that "they were
on strike and did not want anybody to go up there to work." None
of the other employees said anything to Simpson, who testified:
"Neither Mr. Thornhill nor any other employee threatened me on
the occasion testified to. Mr. Thornhill approached me in a peaceful manner, and did not put me in fear; he did not appear to be mad.
I then turned and went back to the house, and did not go to
work." The other witness, J. M. Walden, testified: "At the time Mr.
Thornhill and Clarence Simpson were talking to each other, there
was no one else present and I heard no harsh words and saw nothing threatening in the manner of either man." For engaging in
some or all of these activities, petitioner was arrested, charged,
and convicted as described.

First. The freedom of speech and of the press, which are secured by the First Amendment against abridgment by the United

States, are among the fundamental personal rights and liberties which are secured to all persons by the Fourteenth Amendment against abridgment by a state.

The safeguarding of these rights to the ends that men may speak as they think on matters vital to them and that falsehoods may be exposed through the processes of education and discussion is essential to free government. . . . Abridgment of freedom of speech and of the press, however, impairs those opportunities for public education that are essential to effective exercise of the power of correcting error through the process of popular government. Compare *United States* v. *Carolene Products,* 304 U.S. 144, 152, 153n. More legislative preference for one rather than another means for combating substantive evils, therefore, may well prove an inadequate foundation on which to rest regulations which are aimed at or in their operation diminish the effective exercise of rights so necessary to the maintenance of democratic institutions. It is imperative that, when the effective exercise of these rights is claimed to be abridged, the courts should "weigh the circumstances" and "appraise the substantiality of the reasons advanced" in support of the challenged regulations. *Schneider* v. *State,* 309 U.S. 147, 161, 162.

Second. The section in question must be judged upon its face. The finding against petitioner was a general one. It did not specify the testimony upon which it rested. The charges were framed in the words of the statute and so must be given a like construction. The courts below expressed no intention of narrowing the construction put upon the statute by prior State decisions. In these circumstances, there is no occasion to go behind the face of the statute or of the complaint for the purpose of determining whether the evidence, together with the permissible inferences to be drawn from it, could ever support a conviction founded upon different and more precise charges. "Conviction upon a charge not made would be sheer denial of due process." *De Jonge* v. *Oregon,* 299 U.S. 353, 362; *Stromberg* v. *California,* 283 U.S. 359, 367, 368. The State urges that petitioner may not complain of the deprivation of any rights but his own. It would not follow that on this record petitioner could not complain of the sweeping regulations here challenged. . . .

Third. Section 3448 has been applied by the State courts so as to prohibit a single individual from walking slowly and peacefully back and forth on the public sidewalk in front of the premises of an employer, without speaking to anyone, carrying a sign or placard on a staff above his head stating only the fact that the employer did not employ union men affiliated with the American Federation of Labor; the purpose of the described activity was concededly to advise customers and prospective customers of the relationship existing between the employer and its employees and thereby to induce such customers not to patronize the employer. *O'Rourke* v. *City of Birmingham*, 27 Ala. App. 133, 168 So. 206, cert. denied, 232 Ala. 355, 168 So. 209. The statute as thus authoritatively construed and applied leaves room for no exceptions based upon either the number of persons engaged in the proscribed activity, the peaceful character of their demeanor, the nature of their dispute with an employer, or the restrained character and the accurateness of the terminology used in notifying the public of the facts of the dispute.

The numerous forms of conduct proscribed by Section 3448 are subsumed under two offences: the first embraces the activities of all who "without a just cause or legal excuse" "go near to or loiter about the premises" of any person engaged in a lawful business for the purpose of influencing or inducing others to adopt any of certain enumerated courses of action; the second, all who "picket" the place of business of any such person "for the purpose of hindering, delaying, or interfering with or injuring any lawful business or enterprise of another." It is apparent that one or the other of the offenses comprehends every practicable method whereby the facts of a labor dispute may be publicized in the vicinity of the place of business of an employer. The phrase "without a just cause or legal excuse" does not in any effective manner restrict the breadth of the regulation; the words themselves have no ascertainable meaning either inherent or historical.

Fourth. We think that Section 3448 is invalid on its face.

The freedom of speech and of the press guaranteed by the Constitution embraces at least the liberty to discuss publicly and truthfully all matters of public concern without previous restraint or fear of subsequent punishment. . . . Freedom of discussion, if it would fulfill its historic function in this nation, must embrace all issues about which information is needed or appropriate to enable the members of society to cope with the exigencies of their period.

In the circumstances of our times the dissemination of information concernng the facts of a labor dispute must be regarded as within that area of free discussion that is guaranteed by the Constitution. *Hague* v. *C.I.O.,* 307 U.S. 496; *Schneider* v. *State,* 308 U.S. 147, 155, 162–63; See *Senn* v. *Tile Layers' Union,* 301 U.S. 468, 478. It is recognized now that satisfactory hours and wages and working conditions in industry and a bargaining position which makes these possible have an importance which is no less than the interests of those in the business or industry directly concerned. . . . The merest glance at State and Federal legislation on the subject demonstrates the force of the argument that labor relations are not matters of mere local or private concern. Free discussion concerning the conditions in industry and the causes of labor disputes appears to us indispensable to the effective and intelligent use of the processes of popular government to shape the destiny of modern industrial society. The issues raised by regulations, such as are challenged here, infringing upon the right of employees effectively to inform the public of the facts of a labor dispute are part of this larger problem. We concur in the observation of Mr. Justice Brandeis, speaking for the Court in *Senn's* case (301 U.S. at page 478): "Members of a union might, without special statutory authorization by a State, make known the facts of a labor dispute, for freedom of speech is guaranteed by the Federal Constitution."

It is true that the rights of employers and employees to conduct their economic affairs and to compete with others for a share in the products of industry are subject to modification or qualification in the interests of the society in which they exist. This is but an instance of the power of the State to set the limits of permissible contest open to industrial combatants. See Mr. Justice Brandeis in 254 U.S. 443 at page 488. It does not follow that the State in dealing with the evils arising from industrial disputes may impair the effective exercise of the right to discuss freely industrial relations which are matters of public concern. A contrary conclusion could be used to support abridgment of freedom of speech and of the press concerning almost every matter of importance to society.

The range of activities proscribed by Section 3448, whether characterized as picketing or loitering or otherwise, embraces nearly every practicable, effective means whereby those interested—including the employees directly affected—may enlighten the public on the nature and causes of a labor dispute. The safeguarding of these means is essential to the securing of an informed and educated public opinion with respect to a matter which is of public concern.

The State urges that the purpose of the challenged statute is the protection of the community from the violence and breaches of the peace, which, it asserts, are the concomitants of picketing. The power and the duty of the State to take adequate steps to preserve the peace and to protect the privacy, the lives, and the property of its residents cannot be doubted. But no clear and present danger of destruction of life or property, or invasion of the right of privacy, or breach of the peace can be thought to be inherent in the activities of every person who approaches the premises of an employer and publicizes the facts of a labor dispute involving the latter. We are not now concerned with picketing en masse or otherwise conducted which might occasion such imminent and aggravated danger to these interests as to justify a statute narrowly drawn to cover the precise situation giving rise to the danger. . . . Section 3448 in question here does not aim specifically at serious encroachments on those interests and does not evidence any such care in balancing these interests against the interest of the community and that of the individual in freedom of discussion on matters of public concern.

It is not enough to say that Section 3448 is limited or restricted in its application to such activity as takes place at the scene of the labor dispute. "The streets are natural and proper places for the dissemination of information and opinion; and one is not to have the exercise of his liberty of expression in appropriate places abridged on the plea that it may be exercised in some other place." *Schneider* v. *State*, 308 U.S. 147, 161; *Hague* v. *C.I.O.*, 307 U.S. 496, 515, 516. The danger of breach of the peace or serious invasion of rights of property or privacy at the scene of a labor dispute is not sufficiently imminent in all cases to warrant the legislature in determining that such place is not appropriate for the range of activities outlawed by Section 3448.

As we saw in the *Senn Tile* case, whether or not peaceful picketing was lawful depended upon the laws of the state. The court in *Thornhill* v. *Alabama* clearly established that peaceful picketing was merely a form of free speech and as such was protected as a basic right under the Constitution.

LIMITATIONS ON PICKETING AS FREE SPEECH

The issue of free speech and picketing was considered again in *Bakery and Pastry Drivers & Helpers' Local 802 of the International Brotherhood of Teamsters* v. *Wohl.*[17] Here the court held that (1) the picketing activity was the only avenue available for the parties to communicate their grievances to patrons, and (2) if an injunction was issued to prevent this, it would intrude on the constitutionally protected right of free speech.

The picketing activity began when Wohl, a bakery goods peddler, applied for membership but failed to join the union. The union tried to effect an arrangement with the non-union peddlers where they would work for six days and hire a union member who was not employed on the seventh day. The union also suggested that the relief man need not be paid a full day's pay, if he did not work a full day, but that he be paid the union scale of $6.00 for a part-day rather than the full-day rate of $9.00. Wohl himself earned approximately $32.00 per week and had to keep his truck, which he also had to purchase, in good repair. Wohl complied with union demands for approximately ten weeks. When Wohl refused to continue this practice, the union placed two pickets close to a bakery from which Wohl made purchases. A sign bearing Wohl's name, carried by one of the pickets, stated: "A bakery route driver works seven days a week. We ask employment for a union relief man for one day. Help us spread employment and maintain a union wage, hour, and condition. Bakery & Pastry Drivers & Helpers Local 802, I. B. of T., Affiliated with A.F.L." In the case of another driver, a union member followed the driver to locate some of his customers. The union then informed the customers of the dispute and, in one instance, threatened to picket the vicinity of his shop, if he continued to patronize this driver.

The trial court granted injunctive relief, and the decision was upheld on appeal. When the Supreme Court heard the case, the decision was reversed. In so doing Justice Jackson, speaking to the court, stated in part:

> . . . We ourselves can perceive no substantive evil of such magnitude as to mark a limit to the right of free speech which the petitioners sought to exercise. The record in this case does not contain the slightest suggestion of embarrassment in the task of governance; there are no findings and no circumstances from which we

[17] 315 U.S. 769 (1942).

can draw the inference that the publication was attended or likely to be attended by violence, force or coercion, or conduct otherwise unlawful or oppressive; and it is not indicated that there was an actual or threatened abuse of the right to free speech through the use of excessive picketing. A state is not required to tolerate in all places and all circumstances even peaceful picketing by an individual. But so far as we can tell, respondents' mobility and their insulation from the public as middlemen made it practically impossible for petitioners to make known their legitimate grievances to the public whose patronage was sustaining the peddler system except by the means here employed and contemplated; and those means are such as to have slight, if any, repercussions upon the interest of strangers to the issue.

The decision of the Court of Appeals must accordingly be Reversed.[18]

A violation in the application of the Thornhill Doctrine first emerges in *Milkwagon Drivers' Union of Chicago* v. *Meadowmoor Dairies, Inc.*[19] It will be recalled that as a result of the Thornhill decision, peaceful picketing came under the protection of the freedom of speech guarantee in the federal Constitution. In this case, the Milkwagon Drivers' Union appealed to the United States Supreme Court for a reversal of the Illinois Supreme Court decision which sustained the issuance of an injunction against the activities that had been carried on by the union against Meadowmoor Dairies.

The circumstances surrounding the issue involve the system used for the distribution of milk in Chicago. Milk was sold by dairy companies to the owners and operators of trucks, who in turn sold to retailers. The truck vendors did not maintain the same working standards as those of union members. The union took action against the dairies in an effort to force compliance to their established standards. A suit brought by Meadowmoor Dairies requested that the court issue a preliminary injunction to restrain all union conduct, whether violent or peaceful.

Upon investigation, it was revealed that while there was evidence that there had been peaceful picketing, there was also a great deal of evidence of violence. The issue came before the United States Supreme Court to decide whether the state can give license to its courts to enjoin peaceful picketing when there are separate acts of violence

[18] *Ibid.*
[19] 312 U.S. 287 (1941).

involved. The court stressed that the Thornhill Doctrine allows publicizing the facts of a labor dispute when such is not accompanied by threats because peaceful picketing provides workingmen an avenue of communication in accord with constitutional guarantees. However, when these appeals to reason are made in an atmosphere of violence they become ". . . part of an instrument of force." [20] Justice Frankfurter further declared:

. . . We have already adverted to the generous scope that must be given to the guarantee of free speech. Especially in this attitude to be observed where, as in labor controversies, the feelings of even the most detached minds may become engaged and a show of violence may make still further demands on calm judgment. It is therefore relevant to remind that the power to deny what otherwise would be lawful picketing derives from the power of the states to prevent future coercion. Right to free speech in the future cannot be forfeited because of disassociated acts of past violence. Nor may a state enjoin peaceful picketing merely because it may provoke violence in others. . . . Inasmuch as the injunction was based on findings made in 1937, this decision is no bar to resort to the state court for modification of the terms of the injunction should that court find that the passage of time has deprived the picketing of its coercive influence. In the exceptional cases warranting restraint upon normally free conduct, the restraint ought to be defined by clear and guarded language. According to the best practice, a judge himself should draw the specific terms of such restraint and not rely on drafts submitted by the parties. But we do not have revisory power over state practice, provided such practice is not used to evade constitutional guarantees. . . . We are here concerned with power and not with the wisdom of its exercise. We merely hold that in the circumstances of the record before us the injunction authorized by the Supreme Court of Illinois does not transgress its constitutional power. . . .

We do not qualify the *Thornhill* and *Carlson* decisions. We reaffirm them. They involved statutes baldly forbidding all picketing near an employer's place of business. Entanglement with violence was expressly out of those cases. The statutes had to be dealt with on their face, and therefore we struck them down. . . . We would not strike down a statute which authorized the courts of Illinois to prohibit picketing when they should find that violence had given

[20] *Ibid.*, p. 296.

to the picketing a coercive effect whereby it would operate de-
structively as force and intimidation. Such a situation is presented
by this record. It distorts the meaning of things to generalize the
terms of an injunction derived from and directed towards violent
misconduct as though it were an abstract prohibition of all picketing wholly unrelated to the violence involved.[21]

Thus, the *Milkwagon Drivers* decision declared picketing illegal because it had been accompanied by violence and embodied coercive
effects.

Yet another modification of the Thornhill Doctrine occurred in the
Carpenters and Joiners of America, Local No. 213 v. *Ritter's Cafe*[22]
decision. While the act of picketing in this case was deemed peaceful
and thus, an exercise of free speech, the court also indicated here that
it is within the power of the state to ". . . confine the sphere of communication to that directly related to the dispute."[23]

The respondent, Ritter, had contracted with a man named Plaster
for the construction of a building. The details of the construction
were left entirely to the contractor, Plaster. These details included
the selection of persons who would be employed on the construction.
Plaster chose to engage carpenters and painters who were not members of the union. As soon as construction started, picket lines were
established by members of the union. However, the lines were not established at the construction site but rather in front of Ritter's Cafe, a
restaurant owned and operated by Ritter, located one and one-half
miles from the construction site. The pickets carried signs which originally stated: "This Place is Unfair to Carpenters & Joiners Union of
America, Local No. 213, and Painters Local No. 130, affiliated with
American Federation of Labor." The wording was subsequently modified to read: "The Owner of This Cafe Has Awarded a Contract to
Erect a Building to W. A. Plaster Who is Unfair to the Carpenters
Union 213 and Painters Union 130, Affiliated with the American Federation of Labor."[24]

As a result of this activity, several things happened. The employees of Ritter's Cafe, all of whom were union members, went out on
strike; suppliers' drivers, who were members of a union, would not
cross the picket line; members of trade unions were prevented from
patronizing the restaurant; and Ritter's business was reduced by sixty

[21] *Ibid.*, 296–298.
[22] 315 U.S. 722 (1942).
[23] *Ibid.*
[24] *Ibid.*

percent. The Texas courts held that the purpose of the picketing activity was directed toward Ritter to force him to make Plaster use union members to work on the construction Plaster had under contract. The courts held that the activities of the union were violative of state anti-trust laws and they were enjoined from picketing at the restaurant. No restriction was made with regard to the new building site.

Justice Frankfurter delivered the opinion of the Supreme Court on the union's claim that the decisions of the lower courts constituted an infringement on freedom of speech, guaranteed by the due process clause in the Fourteenth Amendment. The opinion appears in part as follows:

CARPENTERS & JOINERS UNION OF AMERICA, LOCAL NO. 213
v. RITTER'S CAFE: 1942
(315 U.S. 722)

The Supreme Court of the United States, Mr. Justice Frankfurter delivering the opinion:

. . . The economic contest between employer and employee has never concerned merely the immediate disputants. The clash of such conflicting interests inevitably implicates the well-being of the community. Society has therefore been compelled to throw its weight into the contest. The law has undertaken to balance the effort of the employer to carry on his business free from the interference of others against the effort of labor to further its economic self-interest. And every intervention of government in this struggle has in some respect abridged the freedom of action of one or the other or both.

. . . The right of the state to determine whether the common interest is best served by imposing some restrictions upon the use of weapons for inflicting economic injury in the struggle of conflicting industrial forces has not previously been doubted. . . . *Truax* v. *Corrigan, supra,* at 372, . . . and *Senn* v. *Tile Layers Protective Union,* 301 U.S. 468, 481. But the petitioners now claim that there is to be found in the Due Process Clause of the Fourteenth Amendment a constitutional command that peaceful picketing must be wholly immune from regulation by the community in order to protect the general interest, that the states must be powerless to confine the use of this industrial weapon within reasonable bounds.

The constitutional right to communicate peaceably to the public the facts of a legitimate dispute is not lost merely because a labor dispute is involved, *Thornhill* v. *Alabama*, 310 U.S. 88, or because the communication takes the form of picketing, even when the communication does not concern a dispute between an employer and those directly employed by him. *American Federation of Labor* v. *Swing*, 312 U.S. 321. But the circumstance that a labor dispute is the occasion of exercising freedom of expression does not give that freedom any greater constitutional sanction or render it completely inviolable. Where, as here, claims on behalf of free speech are met with claims on behalf of the authority of the state to impose reasonable regulations in behalf of the community as a whole, the duty of this Court is plain. Whenever state action is challenged as a denial of "liberty," the question always is whether the state has violated "the essential attributes of that liberty." Mr. Chief Justice Hughes in *Near* v. *Minnesota*, 283 U.S. 697, 708. While the right of free speech is embodied in the liberty safe-guarded by the Due Process Clause, that Clause postulates the au-thority of the states to translate into law local policies "to promote the health, safety, morals and general welfare of its people . . . The limits of this sovereign power must always be determined with appropriate regard to the particular subject of its exercise." *Ibid.*, at 707.

In the circumstances of the case before us Texas has declared that its general welfare would not be served if, in a controversy between a contractor and building workers' unions, the unions were permitted to bring to bear the full weight of familiar weapons of industrial combat against a restaurant business, which, as a business, has no nexus with the building dispute but which hap-pens to be owned by a person who contracts with the builder. The precise question is, therefore, whether the Fourteenth Amendment prohibits Texas from drawing this line in confining the area of un-restricted industrial warfare.

Texas has undertaken to localize industrial conflict by prohibit-ing the exertion of concerted pressure directed at the business, wholly outside the economic context of the real dispute, of a per-son whose relation to the dispute arises from his business dealings with one of the disputants. The state has not attempted to outlaw whatever psychological pressure may be involved in the mere com-munication by an individual of the facts relating to his differences with another. Nor are we confronted here with a limitation upon speech in circumstances where there exists an "interdependence of economic interest of all engaged in the same industry" . . . The line drawn by Texas in this case is not the line drawn by New York in the Wohl case. The dispute there related to the conditions under which bakery products were sold and delivered to retailers. The business of the retailers was therefore directly involved in the dispute. In picketing the retail establishments, the union members would only be following the subject-matter of their dispute. Here we have a different situation. The dispute concerns the labor conditions surrounding the construction of a building by a contractor. Texas has deemed it desirable to insulate from the dispute an establishment which industrially has no connection with the dispute. Texas has not attempted to protect other business enterprises of the building contractor, Plaster, who is the petitioners' real adversary. We need not therefore consider problems that would arise if Texas had undertaken to draw such a line.

It is true that by peaceful picketing workingmen communicate their grievances. As a means of communicating the facts of a labor dispute peaceful picketing may be a phase of the constitutional right of free utterance. But recognition of peaceful picketing as an exercise of free speech does not imply that the states must be without power to confine the sphere of communication to that directly related to the dispute. Restriction of picketing to the area of the industry within which a labor dispute arises leaves open to the disputants other traditional modes of communication. To deny to the states the power to draw this line is to write into the Constitution the notion that every instance of peaceful picketing—anywhere and under any circumstances—is necessarily a phase of the controversy which provoked the picketing. Such a view of the Due Process Clause would compel the states to allow the disputants in a particular industrial episode to conscript neutrals having no relation to either the dispute or the industry in which it arose.

In forbidding such conscription of neutrals, in the circumstances of the case before us, Texas represents the prevailing, and probably the unanimous, policy of the states. We hold that the Constitution does not forbid Texas to draw the line which has been drawn here. To hold otherwise would be to transmute vital constitutional liberties into doctrinaire dogma. We must be mindful that "the right of employers and employees to conduct their economic affairs and to compete with others for a share in the products of industry are subject to modification or qualification in the interests of the society in which they exist. This is but an instance of the power of the State to set the limits of permissible contest open to industrial combatants." *Thornhill* v. *Alabama*, 310 U.S. 88, 103–104.

It is not for us to assess the wisdom of the policy underlying the law of Texas. Our duty is at an end when we find that the Fourteenth Amendment does not deny her the power to enact that policy into law.

In short, the reasoning of the court in this case implies that the involvement of a neutral party to the dispute gave Texas the right to enjoin the activity.

A final consideration on the controversial question of free speech and picketing can be illustrated by considering the facts brought out in a case involving *International Brotherhood of Teamsters, Local 309* v. *Hanke*.[25] A. E. Hanke, along with three sons, conducted a used automobile and automobile repair business. They also sold gasoline and automobile accessories. Hanke had been a member of Local 309 since entering the business, a period of approximately one and one-half years. At the end of this period, the union asked Hanke to conform to the hours of work stipulated in the union shop agreement, and informed Hanke that failure to conform would mean loss of his union shop card. Hanke, believing that he could not continue his business if he agreed to close on nights, weekends, and holidays, did not comply and his name was removed from the list of Local 309.

A picket appeared in front of the shop and carried a sign showing a drawing of a union shop card and stating "Union People Look for the Union Shop Card." While the picketing activity was peaceful, the picket did make note of people who went into the shop by taking down their license numbers. Because of the picketing, business declined and supplying truck drivers refused to make deliveries. Hanke filed suit, and was granted a permanent injunction as well as $250. On appeal from the decision of the Washington courts, the Supreme Court declared in its opinion:

> . . . It is not for us to pass judgment on cases not now before us. But when one considers that issues not unlike those that are here have been similarly viewed by other States and by the Congress of the United States, we cannot conclude that Washington, in holding the picketing in these cases to be for an unlawful object, has struck a balance so inconsistent with rooted traditions of a free people

[25] 339 U.S. 470 (1950).

that it must be found an unconstitutional choice. Mindful as we are that a phase of picketing is communication, we cannot find that Washington has offended the Constitution. . . .[26]

Once more, then, the high court has held that it was within the power of the state to regulate picketing activity without infringing upon constitutional freedom.

Summary

The National Labor Relations Act served to clear up some of the confusion about the applicability of the anti-trust laws to situations involving labor disputes. As we saw in the *Apex* case, the activity of striking employees, even though it may affect ability to compete in the market, does not by itself justify a Sherman Act violation. Later, in the *Hutcheson* case the activities attendant to the dispute were protected by the Clayton Act; and in the *Allen Bradley* case the attitude of the court was displayed when it was declared that the anti-trust law was designed to regulate trade, not employee-employer relationships. The inapplicability of anti-trust laws was further demonstrated by the decision in the *Hunt* case.

With respect to picketing, several issues come forth. We learned that peaceful picketing was lawful even when accompanied by persuasion. The right to picket was further strengthened in the *Truax* case when the court declared the state statute was unconstitutional and an intrusion on property rights when picketing was prohibited. This was additionally reinforced by the *Thornhill* decision, which not only declared picketing lawful but brought it under the protection of the Constitution.

It would appear that the National Labor Relations Act clarified many issues that intruded upon the collective bargaining process and provided labor with the leverage it needed to compete with the strength and power of management.

[26] *Ibid.*

8

THE TAFT-HARTLEY ACT AND LABOR-MANAGEMENT RELATIONS

In the twelve-year period during which the activities of labor and management were governed by the provisions of the National Labor Relations Act, several things occurred to change public attitudes and ultimately, policy. In 1935, the year when the National Labor Relations Act was enacted, there were approximately four million union members. By 1947 union membership had increased to approximately fifteen million. The American Federation of Labor accounted for over 46 percent, and the remainder represented unaffiliated membership. This chapter examines the social and economic conditions that were significant in influencing the amendments to the National Labor Relations Act as well as the amendments themselves. Specifically included are the modifications of those sections covering unfair practices and bargaining and the reorganization of the National Labor Relations Board. The remaining provisions of the legislation are discussed in the following chapter.

205

Conditions Leading to Amendment
of the Wagner Act

General dissatisfaction with the National Labor Relations Act had been in evidence almost from the time of its passage. A steady growth in union membership combined with increasing amounts of power and pressure exerted on industry by organized labor resulted in the introduction of over one hundred bills before Congress in an effort to amend the legislation during the twelve years spanning 1935 to 1947. Moreover, during one-half of this period the United States was engaged in defense and wartime production. The cooperation, coordination, and efficiency with which American industry converted their productive resources to this effort had considerable effect on public attitudes. At the same time, the activities of elements of the labor movement were conducive to having a negative impact on public opinion. The passage of the War Labor Disputes Act of 1943 (the Smith-Connally Act) over the veto of President Roosevelt illustrates the changing socioeconomic climate. This act was passed as a result of strikes and general disruptions that had occurred previously, including the then-existing coal industry strike. Summarily, this act, which was temporary legislation to be in force only until six months after the war had ended, provided that a thirty-day notice had to be given when labor intended to strike. After this period, a vote would be taken of the workers to decide whether or not the strike would take place. A majority vote was required if the strike was to be considered legal.

It is also of interest to note that the President had established a War Labor Board to settle labor disputes, which became active in 1942 one month after the declaration of war. The composition of the Board included representatives of labor and management as well as public representatives. The means by which the Board undertook to settle labor disputes was mediation or arbitration. The War Labor Disputes Act strengthened the Board by giving it statutory authority.[1]

There were forty instances of government seizure during the war period, of which twenty-one were the result of non-compliance on the part of labor unions. These seizures meant that the government took control of the industry temporarily because there was a threatened stoppage of work that would impair national welfare. While under governmental control neither strikes nor lockouts could take place. At

[1] Boards established by Executive Order legally had advisory power only.

the close of the war, these controls were removed. Industry enhanced its public image by a relatively smooth conversion to peacetime production and contributed to avoidance of a depression that had been anticipated in this conversion period. Labor, on the other hand, in 1945, the year following the war, was involved in 4,750 strikes; this affected 3,325,000 workers and 12.2 percent of the total employed. In 1946 there were 4,985 strikes involving 4,600,000 workers, or 14.5 percent of those employed.[2] Criticism was also leveled against the labor unions' increased wage demands and their impact on inflation, the imbalance of power that had resulted from the Wagner Act provisions, and charges of Communist sympathies within the structure of organized labor. Pressures intensified from proponents of these charges, and a change in the national political scene resulted in concerted post-war efforts to effect amendments to the National Labor Relations Act.

A bill was introduced in the House by Representative Francis Case in 1946. The bill was designed to incorporate changes in the National Relations Act deemed desirable in light of public opinion. Provisions were made for the settlement of disputes by a mediation board composed of labor and management representatives, a cooling-off period prior to going out on strike, outlawing force and violence during disputes, limitations on the use of secondary boycotts, and elimination of supervisory personnel as a part of a bargaining unit that also contained non-supervisory workers. Even though the bill made its way successfully through both the House and the Senate, it was vetoed by President Harry Truman. When the 80th Congress opened in 1947, several bills were introduced to both the Senate and House labor committees. Senator Robert Taft became the chairman of the Labor and Public Welfare Committee, and the House Committee on Education and Labor was chaired by Congressman Fred Hartley, Jr.[3] Hearings were opened by the Senate committee on January 29, 1947, and by the House committee on February 5, 1947. Volumes of testimony were heard and over two hundred witnesses appeared before these committees. The House bill reached the floor on April 10, and when a final vote was taken on April 17, the measure passed this body 308 to 107. On this same date the bill from the Labor and Public Welfare Committee reached the floor of the

[2] *The Economic Almanac* (New York: National Industrial Conference Board, Inc., 1951), pp. 236–237; and *Monthly Labor Review*, Vol. 74, No. 3 (March, 1952), pp. 328–375.

[3] It may be of interest to note that the membership of the latter committee included Representatives Richard Nixon and John Kennedy.

Senate. Debate commenced on April 23. The vote was taken on May 13, and the House bill as amended by the Senate was passed.[4] A joint conference between representatives from the House and the Senate was called in order to effect a compromise bill. The result was The Labor-Management Relations Act, also known as the Taft-Hartley Act, which passed the House on June 3 and the Senate on June 4. The bill was sent to the President on June 9. The President had to sign or veto the act within a ten-day period, otherwise it would become law without Presidential signature. On the final day of this ten-day period President Truman acted by returning the bill with a veto message. The President identified some specific reasons for his action, which include the following:

1. The bill would substantially increase strikes. . . .

2. The bill arbitrarily decides, against the workers, certain issues which are normally the subject of collective bargaining, and thus restricts the area of voluntary agreement. . . .

3. The bill would expose employers to numerous hazards by which they could be annoyed and harassed. . . .

4. The bill would deprive workers of vital protection which they now have under the law. . . .

5. The bill abounds in provisions which would be unduly burdensome or actually unworkable. . . .

6. The bill would establish an ineffective and discriminatory emergency procedure for dealing with major strikes affecting the public health and safety. . . .

7. The bill would discriminate against employees. . . .

8. The bill would disregard in important respects the unanimous convictions of employer and labor representatives at the National Labor-Management Conference in November, 1945. . . .

9. The bill raises serious issues of public policy which transcend labor-management difficulties.[5]

At the end of his message, the President declared ". . . This bill is perhaps the most serious economic and social legislation of the past decade. . . . I have concluded that the bill is a clear threat to the successful working of our democratic society." [6]

[4] The amendment had substituted the Senate bill for the House bill after the enacting clause.

[5] U.S., *Congressional Record*, 80th Cong., 1st Sess., 1947, XCIII, Pt. 6, 7486–7488.

[6] *Ibid.*, 7488.

Shortly thereafter another vote was taken, and the bill passed the House with 331 yeas, 83 nays, and 15 not voting. After twenty-six hours of continuous debate and filibuster, the Senate adjourned, having resolved to vote on the bill by three o'clock during the next session. At the next session the bill passed the Senate with 68 yeas, 25 nays, and 2 not voting, thereby overriding the veto of the President. Those in the Senate who were opposed to the legislation at one time considered bringing Senator Robert Wagner to Washington from New York, where he was confined and seriously ill, that he might cast a nay vote. Senator Wagner, who was responsible for the 1935 National Labor Relations Act, was willing to make the trip to cast his vote even if it jeopardized his life. It was determined, however, that the passage of the act was so well assured it would be of no use to subject the Senator to this possibility.

With the passage of the Labor-Management Relations Act, a whole new era began in union-employer relations. In contrast to the more limited scope and relative straightforwardness of the earlier National Labor Relations Act, the Taft-Hartley Act is a comprehensive and complex piece of legislation. For this reason, the remainder of this chapter will be devoted to a detailed analysis of its various provisions.[7]

The Labor-Management Relations Act, 1947 (The Taft-Hartley Act)

The Taft-Hartley Act contains five titles. Title I amends the National Labor Relations Act, Title II deals with conciliation and mediation in labor disputes and the procedures to be followed in the event of a strike that could result in a national emergency, Title III covers violations of agreements and unlawful payments and contributions. The latter title also deals with boycotts and strikes by employees of the United States. Title IV establishes a Joint Committee on Labor-Management Relations, and Title V qualifies and defines terms used in the legislation. The changes made by the amending legislation in the National Labor Relations Act are examined below.

AMENDMENTS TO THE NATIONAL LABOR RELATIONS ACT

Section 1 of the National Labor Relations Act (Findings and Policy) was enlarged in order to emphasize and declare as a policy of the United States the encouragement of collective bargaining.

[7] The complete Act may be found in Appendix 8.

Changes were also made in some of the definitions contained in Section 2 of the original act. "Person" was enlarged to include labor organizations; "employer" was extended to include their agents; and those excluded as employers was expanded to include ". . . any wholly owned Government corporation, or any Federal Reserve Bank, . . . or any corporation or association operating a hospital, if no part of the net earnings inures to the benefit of any private shareholder or individual . . ."[8] Added to the list of those excluded from the earlier classification of "employee" were independent contractors, supervisors, and any individual subject to the Railway Labor Act. The exclusion of supervisors from the "employee" classification made it necessary to define the supervisor in the 1947 amendment as:

> . . . any individual having authority in the interest of the employer to hire, transfer, suspend, lay off, recall, promote, discharge, assign, reward, or discipline other employees, or responsibly to direct them, or to adjust their grievances, or effectively to recommend such action, if in connection with the foregoing the exercise of such authority is not of a merely routine or clerical nature, but requires the use of independent judgment.[9]

UNFAIR LABOR PRACTICES AND RIGHTS OF EMPLOYEES

Major changes were made in Sections 7 and 8 of the National Labor Relations Act by the Taft-Hartley amendments. Section 7, giving an employee the right to join a union of his own choosing and to participate in activities necessary for the purpose of collective bargaining, was enlarged. As amended, this section also gave the employee the right to refrain from any or all of these activities unless membership in a labor organization was lawful according to the provisions of Section 8(a)(3) of the act (see following). The effect of this modification was to give an employee a choice of joining or not joining a union, even though a collective bargaining agreement might be in existence. This statement in conjunction with Section 8(a)(3) outlawed the closed shop.

Several changes were made in Section 8 of the National Labor Relations Act. It will be recalled that this section contained a list of five unfair labor practices by employers.[10] The one change made to these by the Taft-Hartley amendment involved unfair practices that dealt with union security agreements. This unfair labor practice was amended to read as follows:

[8] U.S., *Statutes at Large*, LXI, Part 1, pp. 137–138.
[9] *Ibid.*, p. 138.
[10] See Appendix VI.

. . . It shall be an unfair labor practice for an employer . . . by discrimination in regard to hire or tenure of employment or any term or condition of employment to encourage or discourage membership in any labor organization: *Provided,* That nothing in this Act, or in any other statute of the United States, shall preclude an employer from making an agreement with a labor organization (not established, maintained, or assisted by any action defined in Section 8(a) of this Act as an unfair labor practice) to require as a condition of employment membership therein on or after the thirtieth day following the beginning of such employment or the effective date of such agreement, whichever is the later, (i) if such labor organization is the representative of the employees as provided in Section 9(a), in the appropriate collective-bargaining unit covered by such agreement when made, and (ii) unless following an election held as provided in Section 9(e) within one year preceding the effective date of such agreement, the Board shall have certified that at least a majority of the employees eligible to vote in such election have noted to rescind the authority of such labor organization to make such an agreement: *Provided further,* That no employer shall justify any discrimination against an employee for nonmembership in a labor organization (A) if he has reasonable grounds for believing that such membership was not available to the employee on the same terms and conditions generally applicable to other members, or (B) if he has reasonable grounds for believing that membership was denied or terminated for reasons other than the failure of the employee to tender the periodic dues and the initiation fees uniformly required as a condition of acquiring or retaining membership. . . .[11]

Although the amendments do outlaw the closed shop, it can be readily seen that they do allow a union shop.

One of the major intentions of the Taft-Hartley Act was to equalize the bargaining power of the employer and employee. In order to do this, Section 8(b) was added to the National Labor Relations Act. This section stipulated six activities that will be considered unfair labor practices on the part of unions. These are set forth in full in the Appendix to permit complete study and analysis. Briefly, the Taft-Hartley Act makes it an unfair practice for a labor organization to: coerce employees to join a union against their wishes, exert pressure on employers to discriminate against an employee who has not been admitted to union membership, refuse to bargain collectively, encour-

[11] *Ibid.,* pp. 140–141.

age employees to participate in certain secondary boycott activities, charge excessive or discriminatory membership fees, and cause an employer to pay for services not performed or not to be performed.

Each of these unfair labor practices is examined separately below and illustrated by a description of a charge filed on that point:

1. *Restraint or Coercion.* Fiore Brothers Oil Co., Inc. (Seafarers, Local 355). The National Labor Relations Board held that there was a violation of Section 8(b)(1) when the union accepted the unlawful assistance of an employer to have authorization cards signed in order to be recognized and to execute and enforce a union security agreement.[12]

2. *Discrimination.* St. Joe Paper Co. (Local 118, Teamsters). In this case the union was charged with a violation when it was determined that the agent of the union had told the employer, who had to make a decision as to which of two employees should be laid off, to retain a union man and discharge a non-union man.[13]

3. *Refusal to Bargain.* Standard Oil Co. (Oil, Chemical, and Atomic Workers, Local 11-395). The union in this instance had refused to sign a contract that had already been negotiated until an agreement was reached at another plant of the employer. The second plant was represented by a different local union and had had no connection with the unsigned contract. This constituted a refusal to bargain.[14]

4. *Strikes and Boycotts.* Local 484, Bakery Wagon Drivers and Salesmen (Sunrise Transportation). An unfair labor-practice charge was affirmed here when the union induced the employees of two separate bakeries to participate in strike activity and also made efforts to coerce these bakeries to force them to cease doing business with a common carrier with whom the union had a dispute.[15]

5. *Excessive Fees.* Local 804, Television & Radio Broadcasting Studio Employees (Triangle Publications, Inc.) Employees in this issue were required to join the union as a condition of employment. The union charged an initiation fee of $500. This was found to be excessive for the following reasons: (1) in order to prevent the employer from hiring non-member part-time help, the fee had been increased from $50 to $500; (2) such a fee was not needed by the union to preserve its solvency in that newly organized units charged a fee of $25;

[12] 137 NLRB 191 (1962).
[13] 135 NLRB 1340 (1962).
[14] 137 NLRB 690 (1962).
[15] 137 NLRB 987 (1962).

and (3) no other union was charging a comparable fee for similar kinds of employees.[16]

6. *Featherbedding. American Newspaper Publishers Association* v. *National Labor Relations Board.*[17] The Supreme Court held in this case that paying printers for setting "bogus" type on advertising copy is not an unfair labor practice under Section 8(b)(6). In the opinion, delivered by Justice Burton, it was declared that the ". . . provision condemned only the exactment by a union of pay from an employer in return for services not performed and not to be performed, but not the exactment of pay for work done by an employee with the employer's consent." [18]

Protection from unfair labor practices committed by unions provides, to some degree, protection to both the employer and the employee. Further modifications will be considered as later amendments are discussed. In considering Section 8 of the National Labor Relations Act, it is necessary to note item 8(c), which was added by the Taft-Hartley amendment. This added section is referred to as the "free speech" inclusion and stipulates that making a public expression of opinions, arguments, or views so long as these do not contain promises of benefits or threats of force or reprisal will not be considered an unfair labor practice. The addition of these unfair labor practices on the part of labor organizations resulted in severe criticism of the Taft-Hartley amendments. The Taft-Hartley Act was referred to as an "anti-labor" and a "slave labor" act. It cannot be argued that the identification of these practices did impose restrictions on labor organizations, but it must be recalled that one of the major purposes of the legislation was to effect a balance between management and labor. In this respect the enumeration of these unfair practices does no more to the union organization than did those in the Wagner Act to management.

COLLECTIVE BARGAINING

The National Labor Relations Act was also amended by the addition of Section 8(d) of the Taft-Hartley Act. This section deals with the duties and obligations of the parties in the collective bargaining process and applies to both employer and employee representatives. The purpose of the amendment is to assure that the employer and the employee representatives are aware of their mutual obligation to

[16] 137 NLRB 632 (1962).
[17] 345 U.S. 100 (1953).
[18] *Ibid.*

meet in good faith to discuss the terms and conditions of employment. While Section 8(d) does state that the purpose of the meeting is
to reach agreement and incorporate the terms of the agreement into a
contract between the parties, it does not compel either party to do so
nor does it compel either party to concede to a compromise. This section also provides a procedure that must be followed if one of the
parties to an existing collective bargaining agreement wishes to modify or terminate the agreement. The party who wishes to take such
action must follow four basic procedural steps. First, it is necessary to
give written notice to the other party, no later than sixty days prior
to the contract expiration date. If no such date is contained in the
contract, the notice must be served no less than sixty days prior to
the intention to instigate such action. Second, the notice must include
an offer to meet with the other party to negotiate the proposed
changes or termination of the existing agreement. Third, the party desirous of modifications must also notify the Federal Mediation and
Conciliation Service as well as any state or territorial agencies set up
for the same purposes that a labor dispute does exist before thirty
days has elapsed and agreement has not been reached. Finally, the
existing contract will remain in effect for sixty days after notice has
been given or until the expiration date contained in the contract is
reached, whichever is later. During this time, strikes or lockouts may
not take place. The statute further stipulates that the last three procedural steps enumerated above will not apply should the National
Labor Relations Board declare that the employee representative
named in the contract is no longer certified as such. A judicial interpretation of this provision was given in the case of *NLRB* v.
American National Insurance Company.[19]

During the initial negotiations of a collective bargaining agreement, the union had submitted a contract proposal that contained
provisions for unlimited arbitration. The employer objected to this inclusion and countered it with his own proposal that contained a management functions clause. This clause enumerated a list of activities
that would be considered outside the realm of the arbitration process,
including discipline, promotion, and work scheduling. No agreement
could be reached between the parties on this particular issue, but negotiations continued on other matters. A short time later the employer gave a written statement to the union indicating those provisions with which he was in accord and presented counter proposals
for those with which he could not agree. One of these was labeled

[19] 343 U.S. 395 (1952).

"Functions and Prerogatives of Management" and contained the following provision:

> The right to select and hire, to promote to a better position, to discharge, demote or discipline for cause, and to maintain discipline and efficiency of employees and to determine the schedules of work is recognized by both union and company as the proper responsibility and prerogative of management to be held and exercised by the company, and while it is agreed that an employee feeling himself to have been aggrieved by any decision of the company in respect to such matters, or the union in his behalf, shall have the right to have such decision reviewed by top management officials of the company under the grievances machinery hereinafter set forth, it is further agreed that the final decision of the company made by such top management officials shall not be further reviewable by arbitration.[20]

The union objected to this and complained to the National Labor Relations Board charging an unfair labor practice of refusal to bargain on the part of the employer. Ultimately, agreement was reached and the management functions clause was modified. The modifications excluded promotions and demotions from the clause and made them subjects for consideration by a union-management committee. It was agreed that all other matters in the clause would remain as non-arbitrable.

During this period of negotiation, hearings had started on the complaint the union had filed with the National Labor Relations Board. The Trial Examiner held that while bargaining for the management functions clause did not constitute a failure to bargain in good faith, the fact that the employer had taken unilateral actions based on this clause during the negotiations did constitute such a failure to bargain in good faith. The National Labor Relations Board did not entirely agree with the Trial Examiner and maintained that not only had the employer evidenced bad faith by bargaining on the management functions clause, but in addition had violated Sections 8(a)(5) and (1) of the National Labor Relations Act. As a result, an order was issued to respondent to bargain in good faith in general terms, and an order was also issued that prohibited bargaining on the management functions clause. The Court of Appeals concurred with the view of the Trial Examiner. The United States Supreme Court granted review.

[20] *Ibid.*, p. 398.

NLRB v. American National Insurance Company: 1952
(343 U.S. 395)

The Supreme Court of the United States, Mr. Justice Vinson delivering the opinion:

. . . *First.* The National Labor Relations Act is designed to promote industrial peace by encouraging the making of voluntary agreements governing relations between unions and employers. The Act does not compel any agreement whatsoever between employees and employers. Nor does the Act regulate the substantive terms governing wages, hours and working conditions which are incorporated in an agreement. The theory of the Act is that the making of voluntary labor agreements is encouraged by protecting employees' rights to organize for collective bargaining and by imposing on labor and management the mutual obligation to bargain collectively.

Enforcement of the obligation to bargain collectively is crucial to the statutory scheme. And, as has long been recognized, performance of the duty to bargain requires more than a willingness to enter upon a sterile discussion of union-management differences. Before the enactment of the National Labor Relations Act, it was held that the duty of an employer to bargain collectively required the employer "to negotiate in good faith with his employees' representatives; to match their proposals, if unacceptable, with counterproposals; and to make every reasonable effort to reach an agreement." The duty to bargain collectively, implicit in the Wagner Act as introduced in Congress, was made express by the insertion of the fifth employer unfair labor practice accompanied by an explanation of the purpose and meaning of the phrase "bargain collectively in a good faith effort to reach an agreement." This understanding of the duty to bargain collectively has been accepted and applied throughout the administration of the Wagner Act by the National Labor Relations Board and the Courts of Appeals.

In 1947, the fear was expressed in Congress that the Board "has gone very far, in the guise of determining whether or not employers had bargained in good faith, in setting itself up as the judge of what concessions an employer must make and of the proposals and counterproposals that he may or may not make." Accordingly, the Hartley Bill, passed by the House, eliminated the good faith test and expressly provided that the duty to bargain collectively did not require submission of counterproposals. As amended in the Senate and passed, as the Taft-Hartley Act, the good faith test of bargaining was retained and written into Section 8(d) of the National Labor Relations Act. That section contains the express provision that the obligation to bargain collectively does not compel either party to agree to a proposal or require the making of a concession.

Thus it is now apparent from the statute itself that the Act does not encourage a party to engage in fruitless marathon discussions at the expense of frank statement and support of his position. And it is equally clear that the Board may not, either directly or indirectly, compel concessions or otherwise sit in judgment upon the substantive terms of collective bargaining agreements.

Second. The Board offers in support of the portion of its order before this Court a theory quite apart from the test of good faith bargaining prescribed in Section 8(d) of the Act, a theory that respondent's bargaining for a management functions clause as a counterproposal to the Union's demand for unlimited arbitration was, "per se," a violation of the Act.

Counsel for the Board do not contend that a management functions clause covering some conditions of employment is an illegal contract term. As a matter of fact, a review of typical contract clauses collected for convenience in drafting labor agreements shows that management functions clauses similar in essential detail to the clause proposed by respondent have been included in contracts negotiated by national unions with many employers. The National War Labor Board, empowered during the last war "[t]o decide the dispute, and provide by order the wages and hours and all other terms and conditions (customarily included in collective bargaining agreements), ordered management functions clauses included in a number of agreements." Several such clauses ordered by the War Labor Board provided for arbitration in case of union dissatisfaction with the exercise of management functions, while others, as in the clause proposed by respondent in this case, provided that management decisions would be final. Without intimating any opinion as to the form of management functions clause proposed by respondent in this case or the desirability of including any such clause in a labor agreement, it is manifest that bargaining for management functions clauses is common collective bargaining practice.

If the Board is correct, an employer violates the Act by bargaining for a management functions clause touching any condition of employment without regard to the traditions of bargaining in the particular industry or such other evidence of good faith as the fact in this case that respondent's clause was offered as a counterproposal to the Union's demand for unlimited arbitration. The Board's argument is a technical one for it is conceded that respondent would not be guilty of an unfair labor practice if, instead of proposing a clause that removed some matters from arbitration, it simply refused in good faith to agree to the Union proposal for unlimited arbitration. The argument starts with a finding, not challenged by the court below or by respondent, that at least some of the matters covered by the management functions clause proposed by respondent are "conditions of employment" which are appropriate subjects of collective bargaining under Sections 8(a)(5), 8(d) and 9(a) of the Act. The Board considers the employer bargaining for a clause under which management retains initial responsibility for work scheduling, a "condition of employment," for the duration of the contract is an unfair labor practice because it is "in derogation of" employees' statutory rights to bargain collectively as to conditions of employment.

Conceding that there is nothing unlawful in including a management functions clause in a labor agreement, the Board would permit an employer to "propose" such a clause. But the Board would forbid bargaining for any such clause when the Union declines to accept the proposal, even where the clause is offered as a counterproposal to a Union demand for unlimited arbitration. Ignoring the nature of the Union's demand in this case, the Board takes the position that employers subject to the Act must agree to include in any labor agreement provisions establishing fixed standards for work schedules or any other condition of employment. An employer would be permitted to bargain as to the content of the standard so long as he agrees to freeze a standard into a contract. Bargaining for more flexible treatment of such matters would be denied employers even though the result may be contrary to common collective bargaining practice in the industry. The Board was not empowered so to disrupt collective bargaining practices. On the contrary, the term "bargain collectively" as used in the Act "has been considered to absorb and give statutory approval to the philosophy of bargaining as worked out in the labor movement in the United States." *Telegraphers* v. *Railway Express Agency,* 321 U.S. 342 (1944).

Congress provided expressly that the Board should not pass upon the desirability of the substantive terms of labor agreements. Whether a contract should contain a clause fixing standards for such matters as work scheduling or should provide for more flexible treatment of such matters is an issue for determination across the bargaining table, not by the Board. If the latter approach is agreed upon, the extent of union and management participation in the administration of such matters is itself a condition of employment to be settled by bargaining.

Accordingly, we reject the Board's holding that bargaining for the management functions clause proposed by respondent was, *per se,* an unfair labor practice. Any fears the Board may entertain that use of management functions clauses will lead to evasion of an employer's duty to bargain collectively as to "rates of pay, wages, hours and conditions of employment" do not justify condemning all bargaining for management functions clauses covering any "condition of employment" as *per se* violations of the Act. The duty to bargain collectively is to be enforced by application of the good faith bargaining standards of Section 8(d) to the facts of each case rather than by prohibiting all employers in every industry from bargaining for management functions clauses altogether.

Third. The court below correctly applied the statutory standard of good faith bargaining to the facts of this case. It held that the evidence, viewed as a whole does not show that respondent refused to bargain in good faith by reason of the bargaining for a management functions clause as a counterproposal to the Union's demand for unlimited arbitration. Respondent's unilateral action in changing working conditions during bargaining, now admitted to be a departure from good faith bargaining, is the subject of an enforcement order issued by the court below and not challenged in this Court.

Last term we made it plain that Congress charged the Courts of Appeals, not this Court, with the normal and primary responsibility for reviewing the conclusions of the Board. We stated that this Court "is not the place to review a conflict of evidence nor to reverse a Court of Appeals because were we in its place we would find the record tilting one way rather than the other, though fair-minded judges could find it tilting either way." *National Labor Relations Board* v. *Pittsburgh* S. S. *Co.* 340 U.S. 498, 503 (1951). We repeat and reaffirm this rule, noting its special applicability to cases where, as here, a statutory standard such as "good faith" can have meaning only in its application to the particular facts of a particular case.

Accepting as we do the finding of the court below that respondent bargained in good faith for the management functions clause proposed by it, we hold that respondent was not in that respect guilty of refusing to bargain collectively as required by the National Labor Relations Act. Accordingly, enforcement of paragraph 1(a) of the Board's order was properly denied.

The opinion of the court in this case clearly establishes that the management functions clause was offered by the employer in the form of a counter proposal and as such was not a refusal to bargain collectively.

BARGAINING UNITS

The modifications resulting from the Taft-Hartley amendments also had considerable effect on Section 9 of the National Labor Relations Act that contained provisions relative to the election of representatives. The standards that the National Labor Relations Board would use to rule on appropriate bargaining units were also part of Section 9. Although only the major changes are discussed below, the reader may wish to review the entire section (see Appendix VIII) in order to determine those changes of a less significant but still important nature.

The Wagner Act gave the National Labor Relations Board the power to decide the appropriate bargaining unit. The Taft-Hartley amendment to Section 9(b) added three clarifying provisions. First, the National Labor Relations Board could not make such a decision if the unit was made up of professional and non-professional employees, except when those employees who were classified as professional voted themselves to be included as a part of the unit. In addition, the National Labor Relations Board could not decide that one craft unit was not appropriate simply because a previous Board had determined that another craft unit was the appropriate unit unless the members of the proposed unit voted in opposition to being represented separately. Finally, the National Labor Relations Board was also prohibited from designating a unit as appropriate if it included plant guards, and it could not certify a union as the employees' representative if the membership was mixed (i.e., contained employees other than plant guards).

Major changes were made in the remainder of Section 9 of the Taft-Hartley amendment. Not only were there considerable modifications in established procedures for representatives and elections, but additional subsections were appended.

The terms describing who could file representation petitions and the procedure the Board would follow were much more specifically identified. The amended Act states that a petition may be filed by an individual, an employee, a group of employees, or a labor organization. The petition is to show that ". . . a substantial number of employees (i) wish to be represented for collective bargaining and that their employer declines to recognize their representative . . . or (ii) assert that the individual or labor organization . . . currently recognized . . . is no longer a representative. . . ." [21] An employer may also petition the Board when he has been presented with a claim by a potential representative. After investigation, should the Board feel that a representation question is present, it must conduct a hearing. The hearing typically is conducted in a regional office, and the record of the hearing is transmitted to the Board without recommendation. If the Board determines that a representation question is present, it directs an election by secret ballot.

The legislation further stipulates that a representation election cannot take place if a valid election has occurred during the last twelve months. Also, those employees who are out on strike and who are not entitled to reinstatement are not eligible to vote. If the results of the election do not show a majority vote for one of the choices, the law requires that the two choices that have received the largest numbers of votes will be slated for a run-off election. This section also provided that investigations and hearings may be waived by stipulation and by so doing the parties agree voluntarily to an election under the conduct of the National Labor Relations Board. Finally, Section 9(c) also declares that the Board should not base its decision entirely on the numbers of employees that have been previously organized.

Provisions were also made in this legislation for holding elections to rescind union security authorization. In order to do this, thirty percent of the employees must file a petition with the National Labor Relations Board indicating that this is their wish. Having secured

[21] U.S., *Statutes at Large*, LXI, Part 1, p. 144.

such assurance, the Board will then conduct an election and certify the results, provided no valid election has been held for the preceding twelve-month period.

The Taft-Hartley amendments also added three subsections to Section 9. Each of these was repealed by later legislation, but should be mentioned briefly here in order that the total congressional attitude can be appraised. The first of these set forth several requirements that had to be met by unions before they could exercise their statutory rights. These included filing copies of the organization by-laws and constitution with the Secretary of Labor; the name and principal place of business of the labor organization; the names, titles, and compensation of the principal officers and all who received a salary of more than $5,000 a year; a report indicating the way in which these officers were chosen; the amount required of members as dues and/or initiation fees; statements indicating the procedures followed in elections; the assessment of fines; disbursement of funds; and expulsion of members, among other things. In addition, fiscal year-end financial reports (e.g., income statements and balance sheets) had to be filed with the Secretary of Labor and furnished to the union membership. Still another subsection set forth the obligations of labor organizations to comply with the wishes of the Secretary of Labor as to the manner and form of filing the required financial reports. The final consideration in this section dealt with restrictions on the protection of the legislation to the union unless each of its officers and those of affiliate or constituent organizations had filed a non-Communist affidavit.

It can readily be seen that the Taft-Hartley amendments did indeed place many and extensive new regulations on union activity. Consequently, the Taft-Hartley Act had a very considerable impact on the overall employer-employee relationship.

THE NATIONAL LABOR RELATIONS BOARD

Several changes were made by the Taft-Hartley Act in the composition and functions of the National Labor Relations Board. The size of the Board was increased from three to five members and provision was made for Presidential appointment of a general counsel. The general counsel was given final authority for the investigation of charges, the issuance of complaints, and the prosecution of matters before the Board.

The functions of the Board were also modified somewhat in the area of prevention of unfair labor practices. The Board was given the power to give a state jurisdiction in cases involving labor disputes affecting interstate commerce when state statute did not prohibit it. Limitations were established with regard to the length of time that could elapse between an alleged unfair labor practice charge and the filing of a complaint. The amendment stipulated that a complaint could not be issued if the action had taken place more than six months previously.

The Wagner Act had declared that during the conduct of a hearing rules of evidence as practiced in a court of law or equity would not be controlling. The Taft-Hartley Act struck this statement and specifically added that ". . . any such proceeding shall, so far as practicable, be conducted in accordance with the rules of evidence applicable in the district courts of the United States . . ." [22] In stipulating that back pay may be awarded to an employee who wins reinstatement after filing an unfair labor practice charge, the new statute states that this payment may be required of the employer or the labor organization, whichever is responsible for the discriminatory activity. Still other modifications give the National Labor Relations Board the power to seek temporary injunctions from the courts and to dismiss unfair labor practice charges without hearings when there has been a voluntary adjustment or compliance by the parties involved. The final addition to National Labor Relations Board procedures dealing with prevention of unfair labor practices instructs the Board to seek injunctive relief when it believes a complaint should be issued for jurisdictional disputes and certain kinds of strikes and boycotts, under Section 8(b)(4).

The last amendment of major importance in Title I of the Labor-Management Relations Act is the controversial Section 14. The relatively innocuous Section 14 simply states that while supervisory personnel may join and participate in union activity, they are excluded from the protection of the Act. In other words, employers are not required by this legislation to recognize labor organizations that are representing supervisory personnel. In addition, in Subsection (b) it is declared that:

. . . nothing in this act shall be construed as authorizing the execution or application of agreements requiring membership in a labor organization as a condition of employment in any State or Territory in which such execution or application is prohibited by State or Territorial Law.[23]

[22] *Ibid.*, p. 151.
[23] *Ibid.*, p. 151.

This simple statement giving states the right to prohibit various forms of union security agreements in spite of federal regulations and the attitude of the parties concerned became one of the most significant provisions of the Labor-Management Relations Act. The controversy surrounding 14(b) will be discussed at length in a later portion of the text.

JURISDICTION OF THE NATIONAL LABOR RELATIONS BOARD

The National Labor Relations Act gives the National Labor Relations Board the power to prevent unfair labor practices affecting commerce. The Board also is given the power to cede to any state or territory its jurisdiction over cases that it considers local in character. As we saw in the *Jones and Laughlin* case [24] the Supreme Court held that the legislation was not applicable when disputes occurred in industries whose effect on commerce was slight or not substantial. This is not to say that the employer has to be engaged in interstate commerce for the Board to have jurisdiction. If the Board determines that the flow of interstate commerce is interrupted because of a dispute that prevented the employer's product from entering the market, it may exercise its power.

The Board is not always required to exercise its jurisdiction even though the employer is clearly involved in interstate activity. The Board developed various tests that were used to determine whether or not it would act in certain cases. Frequently these tests were made in terms of gross revenue or volume of business for certain kinds of operations. The use of these tests to determine whether or not the Board would hear an issue created a problem that was not resolved until later legislation was enacted. When the Board refused to take jurisdiction, state courts could not hear the matter because the Board had been given the exclusive authority to do so. This created a situation commonly referred to as "no man's land." There are two cases that illustrate this issue. In the case of *P. S. Guss, Doing Business as Photo Sound Products Manufacturing Company* v. *Utah Labor Relations Board*,[25] the union had filed an unfair labor practice charge with the National Labor Relations Board, who subsequently declined to hear the issue because the employer was engaged in activities that were "predominately local in character." The union then filed the same charges with the Utah Labor Relations Board, which granted relief. The employer appealed the decision to the Supreme Court and the ruling of the lower court was reversed. The Supreme Court ruling

[24] 301 U.S. 1 (1937).
[25] 353 U.S. 1 (1957).

stated that a state could not deal with matters that came under the jurisdiction of the National Labor Relations Board if the Board has not ceded jurisdiction as required by the National Labor Relations Act.

In *Joseph Garner and A. Joseph Garner, Trading as Central Storage and Transfer Company* v. *Teamsters, Chauffeurs and Helpers Local Union No. 776 (A.F.L.) et al.*,[26] the Supreme Court held that the state court could not enjoin union activity when an employer's complaint involved an unfair labor practice and came under the jurisdiction of the National Labor Relations Board.

Summary

As this chapter has illustrated, the Taft-Hartley Act is a lengthy and complex legislative declaration. The purpose of this law is purported to be threefold: to provide some equalization of legal protection to employers and employees because of the enormous increases in power that had come to the unions through the provisions of the National Labor Relations Act; to improve the original act by modifying it through amendment and thereby correct those insufficiencies that had appeared through its application; and to preserve the collective bargaining process and eliminate or mitigate causes of labor disputes.

To fulfill the purposes for which it was designed, the major provisions of the Taft-Hartley Act resulted in identifying practices on the part of unions that were to be considered unfair. The Act also enlarged the National Labor Relations Board and made key modifications in its functions in an effort to increase the efficiency of the operation. The legislation also attempted to clarify issues with respect to picketing and free speech and representation and election proceedings. In addition, this Act put restrictions on the inclusion of supervisory personnel in the bargaining unit, outlawed the use of the closed shop, and gave employees the right to participate or refrain from participating in organizational and collective-bargaining activities. Finally, two provisions of the law that later created a great deal of consternation were the now famous Section 14(b) and the "no man's land" problem. The former, dealing with right-to-work laws, is so written as to permit individual states to pass laws that would deny unions from effecting membership requirements in collective bargaining agreements.

[26] 346 U.S. 485 (1953).

APPENDIX 8

The Labor-Management Relations Act: 1947

To amend the National Labor Relations Act, to provide additional facilities for the mediation of labor disputes affecting commerce, to equalize legal responsibilities of labor organizations and employers, and for other purposes.

Be it enacted by the Senate and House of Representatives of the United States of America in Congress assembled.

SHORT TITLE AND DECLARATION OF POLICY

SECTION 1. (a) This Act may be cited as the "Labor-Management Relations Act, 1947."

(b) Industrial strife which interferes with the normal flow of commerce and with the full production of articles and commodities for commerce, can be avoided or substantially minimized if employers, employees, and labor organizations each recognize under law one another's legitimate rights in their relations with each other, and above all recognize under law that neither party has any right in its relations with any other to engage in acts or practices which jeoparadize the public health, safety, or interest.

It is the purpose and policy of this Act, in order to promote the full flow of commerce, to prescribe the legitimate rights of both employees and employers in their relations affecting commerce, to provide orderly and peaceful procedures for preventing the interference by either with the legitimate rights of the other, to protect the rights of individual employees in their relations with labor organizations whose activities affect commerce and are inimical to the general welfare, and to protect the rights of the public in connection with labor disputes affecting commerce.

TITLE I
AMENDMENT OF NATIONAL LABOR RELATIONS ACT

SECTION 101. The National Labor Relations Act is hereby amended to read as follows:

"FINDINGS AND POLICIES

"SECTION 1. The denial by some employers of the right of employees to organize and the refusal by some employers to accept the procedure of collective bargaining lead to strikes and other forms of industrial strife or unrest, which have the intent or the necessary effect of burdening or obstructing commerce by (a) impairing the efficiency, safety, or operation of the instrumentalities of commerce; (b) occurring in the current of commerce; (c) materially affecting, restraining, or controlling the flow of raw materials or manufactured or processed goods from or into the channels of commerce, or the prices of such materials or goods in commerce; or (d) causing diminution of employment and wages in such volume as substantially to impair or disrupt the market for goods flowing from or into the channels of commerce.

"The inequality of bargaining power between employees who do not possess full freedom of association or actual liberty of contract, and employers who are organized in the corporate or other forms of ownership association substantially burdens and affects the flow of commerce, and tends to aggravate recurrent business depressions, by depressing wage rates and the purchasing power of wage earners in industry and by preventing the stabilization of competitive wage rates and working conditions within and between industries.

"Experience has proved that protection by law of the right of employees to organize and bargain collectively safeguards commerce from injury, impairment, or interruption, and promotes the flow of commerce by removing certain recognized sources of industrial strife and unrest, by encouraging practices fundamental to the friendly adjustment of industrial disputes arising out of differences as to wages, hours, or other working conditions, and by restoring equality of bargaining power between employers and employees.

"Experience has further demonstrated that certain practices by some labor organizations, their officers, and members have the intent or the necessary effect of burdening or obstructing commerce by preventing the free flow of goods in such commerce through strikes and other forms of industrial unrest or through concerted activities which impair the interest of the public in the free flow of such commerce. The elimination of such practices is a necessary condition to the assurance of the rights herein guaranteed.

"It is hereby declared to be the policy of the United States to eliminate the causes of certain substantial obstructions to the free flow of commerce and to mitigate and eliminate these obstructions when they have occurred by encouraging the practice and procedure of collective bargaining and by protecting the exercise by workers of full freedom of association, self-organization, and designation of representatives of their own choosing, for the purpose of negotiating the terms and conditions of their employment or other mutual aid or protection.

"DEFINITIONS

"SEC. 2. When used in this Act—

"(1) The term 'person' includes one or more individuals, labor organizations, partnerships, associations, corporations, legal representatives, trustees, trustees in bankruptcy, or receivers.

"(2) The term 'employer' includes any person acting as an agent of an employer, directly or indirectly, but shall not include the United States or any wholly owned Government corporation, or any Federal Reserve Bank, or any State or political subdivision thereof, or any corporation or association operating a hospital, if no part of the net earnings inures to the benefit of any private shareholder or individual, or any person subject to the Railway Labor Act, as amended from time to time, or any labor organization (other than when acting as an employer), or anyone acting in the capacity of officer or agent of such labor organization.

"(3) The term 'employee' shall include any employee, and shall not be limited to the employees of a particular employer, unless the Act explicitly states otherwise, and shall include any individual whose work has ceased as a consequence of, or in connection with, any current labor dispute or because of any unfair labor practice, and who has not obtained any other regular and substantially equivalent employment, but shall not include any individual employed as an agricultural laborer, or in the domestic service of any family or person at his home, or any individual employed by his parent or spouse, or any individual having the status of an independent contractor, or any individual employed as a supervisor or any individual employed by an employer subject to the Railway Labor Act, as amended from time to time, or by any other person who is not an employer as herein defined.

"(4) The term 'representatives' includes any individual or labor organization.

"(5) The term 'labor organization' means any organization of any kind, or any agency or employee representation committee or plan, in which employees participate and which exists for the purpose, in whole or in part, of dealing with employers concerning grievances, labor disputes, wages, rates of pay, hours of employment, or conditions of work.

"(6) The term 'commerce' means trade, traffic, commerce, transportation, or communication among the several States, or between the District of Columbia or any Territory of the United States and any State or other Territory, or between any foreign country and any State, Territory, or the District of Columbia, or within the District of Columbia or any territory, or between points in the same State but through any other State or any Territory or the District of Columbia or any foreign country.

"(7) The term 'affecting commerce' means in commerce, or burdening or obstructing commerce or the free flow of commerce, or having led or tending to lead to a labor dispute burdening or obstructing commerce or the free flow of commerce.

"(8) The term 'unfair labor practice' means any unfair labor practice listed in section 8.

"(9) The term 'labor dispute' includes any controversy concerning terms, tenure or conditions of employment, or concerning the association or representation of persons in negotiating, fixing, maintaining, changing, or seeking to arrange terms or conditions of employment, regardless of whether the disputants stand in the proximate relation of employer and employee.

"(10) The term 'National Labor Relations Board' means the National Labor Relations Board provided for in section 3 of this Act.

"(11) The term 'supervisor' means any individual having authority, in the interest of the employer, to hire, transfer, suspend, lay off, recall, promote, discharge, assign, reward, or discipline other employees, or responsibly to direct them, or to adjust their grievances, or effectively to recommend such action, if in connection with the foregoing the exercise of such authority is not of a merely routine or clerical nature, but requires the use of independent judgment.

"(12) The term 'professional employee' means—

"(a) any employee engaged in work (i) predominantly intellectual and varied in character as opposed to routine mental, manual, mechanical, or physical work; (ii) involving the consistent exercise of discretion and judgment in its performance; (iii) of such a character that the output produced or the result accomplished cannot be standardized in relation to a given period of time; (iv) requiring knowledge of an advanced type in a field of science or learning customarily acquired by a prolonged course of specialized intellectual instruction and study in an institution of higher learning or a hospital, as distinguished from a general academic education or from an apprenticeship or from training in the performance of routine mental, manual, or physical processes; or

"(b) any employee, who (i) has completed the courses of specialized intellectual instruction and study described in clause (iv) of paragraph (a), and (ii) is performing related work under the supervision of a professional person to qualify himself to become a professional employee as defined in paragraph (a).

"(13) In determining whether any person so as to make such other person responsible for his acts, the question of whether the specific acts performed were actually authorized or subsequently ratified shall not be controlling.

"NATIONAL LABOR RELATIONS BOARD

"SEC. 3. (a) The National Labor Relations Board (hereinafter called the 'Board') created by this Act prior to its amendment by the Labor Management Relations Act, 1947, is hereby continued as an agency of the United States, except that the Board shall consist of five instead of three members, appointed by the President by and with the advice and consent of the Senate. Of the two additional members so provided for, one shall be appointed for a term of five years and the other for a term of two years. Their successors, and the successors of the other members, shall be appointed for terms of five years each, excepting that any individual chosen to fill a vacancy shall be appointed only for the unexpired term of the member whom he shall succeed. The President shall designate one member to serve as Chairman of the Board. Any member of the Board may be removed by the President, upon notice and hearing, for neglect of duty or malfeasance in office, but for no other cause.

"(b) The Board is authorized to delegate to any group of three or more members any or all of the powers which it may itself exercise. A vacancy in the Board shall not impair the right of the remaining members to exercise all of the powers of the Board, and three members of the Board shall, at all times, constitute a quorum of the Board, except that two members shall constitute a quorum of any group designated pursuant to the first sentence hereof. The Board shall have an official seal which shall be judicially noticed.

"(c) The Board shall at the close of each fiscal year make a report in writing to Congress and to the President stating in detail the cases it has heard, the decisions it has rendered, the names, salaries, and duties of all employees and officers in the employ or under the supervision of the Board, and an account of all moneys it has disbursed.

"(d) There shall be a General Counsel of the Board who shall be appointed by the President, by and with the advice and consent of the Senate, for a term of four years. The General Counsel of the Board shall exercise general supervision over all attorneys employed by the Board (other than trial examiners and legal assistants to Board members) and over the officers and employees in the regional offices. He shall have final authority, on behalf of the Board, in respect of the investigation of charges and issuance of complaints under section 10, and in respect of the prosecution of such complaints before the Board, and shall have such other duties as the Board may prescribe or as may be provided by law.

"SEC. 4. (a) Each member of the board and the General Counsel of the Board shall receive a salary of $12,000 a year, shall be eligible for reappointment, and shall not engage in any other business, vocation, or employment. The Board shall appoint an executive secretary, and such attorneys, examiners, and regional directors, and such other employees as it may from time to time find necessary for the proper performance of its duties. The Board may not employ any attorneys for the purpose of reviewing transcripts of hearings or preparing drafts of opinions except that any attorney employed for assignment as a legal assistant to any Board member may for such Board member review such transcripts and prepare such drafts. No trial examiner's report shall be reviewed, either before or after its publication, by any person other than a member of the Board or his legal assistant, and no trial examiner shall advise or consult with the Board with respect to exceptions taken to his findings, rulings, or recommendations. The Board may establish or utilize such regional, local, or other agencies, and utilize such voluntary and uncompensated services, as may from time to time be needed. Attorneys appointed under this section may, at the direction of the Board, appear for and represent the Board in any case in court. Nothing in this Act shall be construed to authorize the Board to appoint individuals for the purpose of conciliation or mediation, or for economic analysis.

"(b) All of the expenses of the Board, including all necessary traveling and subsistence expenses outside the District of Columbia incurred by the members or employees of the Board under its orders, shall be allowed and paid on the presentation of itemized vouchers therefore approved by the Board or by any individual it designates for that purpose.

"Sec. 5. The principal office of the Board shall be in the District of Columbia, but it may meet and exercise any or all of its powers at any other place. The Board may, by one or more of its members or by such agents or agencies as it may designate, prosecute any inquiry necessary to its functions in any part of the United States. A member who participates in such an inquiry shall not be disqualified from subsequently participating in a decision of the Board in the same case.

"Sec. 6. The Board shall have authority from time to time to make, amend, and rescind, in the manner prescribed by the Administrative Procedure Act, such rules and regulations as may be necessary to carry out the provisions of this Act.

"RIGHTS OF EMPLOYEES

"Sec. 7. Employees shall have the right to self-organization, to form, join, or assist labor organizations, to bargain collectively through representatives of their own choosing, and to engage in other concerted activities for the purpose of collective bargaining or other mutual aid or protection, and shall also have the right to refrain from any or all of such activities except to the extent that such right may be affected by an agreement requiring membership in a labor organization as a condition of employment as authorized in section 8(a)(3).

"UNFAIR LABOR PRACTICES

"Sec. 8. (a) It shall be an unfair labor practice for an employer—

"(1) to interfere with, restrain, or coerce employees in the exercise of the rights guaranteed in section 7;

"(2) to dominate or interfere with the formation or administration of any labor organization or contribute financial or other support to it: *Provided,* That subject to rules and regulations made and published by the Board pursuant to section 6, an employer shall not be prohibited from permitting employees to confer with him during working hours without loss of time or pay;

"(3) by discrimination in regard to hire or tenure of employment or any term or condition of employment to encourage or discourage membership in any labor organization: *Provided,* That nothing in this Act, or in any other statute of the United States, shall preclude an employer from making an agreement with a labor organization (not established, maintained, or assisted by any action defined in section 8(a) of this Act as an unfair labor practice) to require as a condition of employment membership therein on or after the thirtieth day following the beginning of such employment or the effective date of such agreement, whichever is the later, (i) if such labor organization is the representative of the employees as provided in section 9(a), in the appropriate collective-bargaining unit covered by such agreement when made; and (ii) if, following the most recent election held as provided in section 9(e) the Board shall have certified that at least a majority of the employees eligible to vote in such election have voted to authorize such labor organization to make such an agreement: *Provided further,* That no employer shall justify any discrimination against an employee for non-membership in a labor organization (A) if he has reasonable grounds for believing that such membership was not available to the employee on the same terms and conditions generally applicable to other members, or (B) if he has reasonable grounds for believing that membership was denied or terminated for reasons other than the failure of the employee to tender the periodic dues and the initiation fees uniformly required as a condition of acquiring or retaining membership;

"(4) to discharge or otherwise discriminate against an employee because he has filed charges or given testimony under this Act;

"(5) to refuse to bargain collectively with the representatives of his employees, subject to the provisions of section 9(a).

"(b) It shall be an unfair labor practice for a labor organization or its agents—

"(1) to restrain or coerce (A) employees in the exercise of the rights guaranteed in section 7: *Provided,* That this paragraph shall not impair the right of a labor organization to prescribe its own rules with respect to the acquisition or retention of membership therein; or (B) an employer in the selection of his representatives for the purposes of collective bargaining or the adjustment of grievances;

"(2) to cause or attempt to cause an employer to discriminate against an employee in violation of subsection (a)(3) or to discriminate against an employee with respect to whom membership in such organization has been denied or terminated on some ground other than his failure to tender the periodic dues and the initiation fees uniformly required as a condition of acquiring or retaining membership;

"(3) to refuse to bargain collectively with an employer, provided it is the representative of his employees subject to the provisions of section 9(a);

"(4) to engage in, or to induce or encourage the employees of any employer to engage in, a strike or a concerted refusal in the course of their employment to use, manufacture, process, transport, or otherwise handle or work on any goods, articles, material, or commodities or to perform any services, where an object thereof is: (A) forcing or requiring any employer or self-employed person to join any labor or employer organization or any employer or other person to cease using, selling, handling, transporting, or otherwise dealing in the products of any other producer, processor, or manufacturer, or to cease doing business with any other person; (B) forcing or requiring any other employer to recognize or bargain with a labor organization as the representative of his employees unless such labor organization has been certified as the representative of such employees under the provisions of section 9; (C) forcing or requiring any employer to recognize or bargain with a particular labor organization as the representative of his employees if another labor organization has been certified as the representative of such employees under the provisions of section 9; (D) forcing or requiring any employer to assign particular work to employees in a particular labor organization or in a particular trade, craft, or class rather than to employees in another labor organization or in another trade, craft, or class, unless such employer is failing to conform to an order or certification of the Board determining the bargaining representative for employees performing such work: *Provided,* That nothing contained in this subsection (b) shall be construed to make unlawful a refusal by any person to enter upon the premises of any employer (other than his own employer), if the employees of such employer are engaged in a strike ratified or approved by a representative of such employees whom such employer is required to recognize under this Act;

"(5) to require of employees covered by an agreement authorized under subsection (a)(3) the payment, as a condition precedent to becoming a member of such organization, of a fee in an amount which the Board finds excessive or discriminatory under all the circumstances. In making such a finding, the Board shall consider, among other relevant factors, the practices and customs of labor organizations in the particular industry, and the wages currently paid to the employees affected; and

"(6) to cause or attempt to cause an employer to pay or deliver or agree to pay or deliver any money or other thing of value, in the nature of an exaction, for services which are not performed or not to be performed.

"(c) The expressing of any views, argument, or opinion or the dissemination thereof, whether in written, printed, graphic, or visual form, shall not constitute or be evidence of an unfair labor practice under any of the provisions of this Act, if such expression contains no threat of reprisal or force or promise of benefit.

"(d) For the purposes of this section, to bargain collectively is the performance of the mutual obligation of the employer and the representative of the employees to meet at reasonable times and confer in good faith with respect to wages, hours, and other terms and conditions of employment, or the negotiation of an agreement, or any question arising thereunder, and the execution of a written contract incorporating any agreement reached if requested by either party, but such obligation does not compel either party to agree to a proposal or require the making of a concession: *Provided,* That where there is in effect a collective-bargaining contract covering employees in an industry affecting commerce, the duty to bargain collectively shall also mean that no party to such contract shall terminate or modify such contract, unless the party desiring such termination or modification—

"(1) serves a written notice upon the other party to the contract of the proposed termination or modification sixty days prior to the expiration date thereof, or in the event such contract contains no expiration date, sixty days prior to the time it is proposed to make such termination or modification;

"(2) offers to meet and confer with the other party for the purpose of negotiating a new contract or a contract containing the proposed modifications;

"(3) notifies the Federal Mediation and Conciliation Service within thirty days after such notice of the existence of a dispute, and simultaneously therewith notifies any State or Territorial agency established to mediate and conciliate disputes within the State or Territory where the dispute occurred, provided no agreement has been reached by that time; and

"(4) continues in full force and effect, without resorting to strike or lock-out, all the terms and conditions of the existing contract for a period of sixty days after such notice is given or until the expiration date of such contract, whichever occurs later:

The duties imposed upon employers, employees, and labor organizations by paragraphs (2), (3), and (4) shall become inapplicable upon an intervening certification of the Board, under which the labor organization or individual, which is a party to the contract, has been superseded as or ceased to be the representative of the employees subject to the provisions of section 9(a), and the duties so imposed shall not be construed as requiring either party to discuss or agree to any modification of the terms and conditions contained in a contract for a fixed period, if such modification is to become effective before such terms and conditions can be reopened under the provisions of the contract. Any employee who engages in a strike within the sixty-day period specified in this subsection shall lose his status as an employee of the employer engaged in the particular labor dispute, for the purposes of sections 8, 9, and 10 of this Act, as amended, but such loss of status for such employee shall terminate if and when he is reemployed by such employer.

"REPRESENTATIVES AND ELECTIONS

"SEC. 9. (a) Representatives designated or selected for the purposes of collective bargaining by the majority of the employees in a unit appropriate for such purposes, shall be the exclusive representatives of all the employees in such unit for the purposes of collective bargaining in respect to rates of pay, wages, hours of employment, or other conditions of employment: *Provided*, That any individual employee or a group of employees shall have the right at any time to present grievances to their employer and to have such grievances adjusted, without the intervention of the bargaining representative, as long as the adjustment is not inconsistent with the terms of a collective-bargaining contract or agreement then in effect: *Provided further*, That the bargaining representative has been given opportunity to be present at such adjustment.

"(b) The Board shall decide in each case whether, in order to assure to employees the fullest freedom in exercising the rights guaranteed by this Act, the unit appropriate for the purposes of collective bargaining shall be the employer unit, craft unit, plant unit, or subdivision thereof: *Provided,* That the Board shall not (1) decide that any unit is appropriate for such purposes if such unit includes both professional employees and employees who are not professional employees unless a majority of such professional employees vote for inclusion in such unit; or (2) decide that any craft unit is inappropriate for such purposes on the ground that a different unit has been established by a prior Board determination, unless a majority of the employees in the proposed craft unit vote against separate representation or (3) decide that any unit is appropriate for such purposes if it includes, together with other employees, any individual employed as a guard to enforce against employees and other persons rules to protect property of the employer or to protect the safety of persons on the employer's premises; but no labor organization shall be certified as the representative of employees in a bargaining unit of guards if such organization admits to membership, or is affiliated directly or indirectly with an organization which admits to membership, employees other than guards.

"(c) (1) Whenever a petition shall have been filed, in accordance with such regulations as may be prescribed by the Board—

"(A) by an employee or group of employees of any individual or labor organization acting in their behalf alleging that a substantial number of employees (i) wish to be represented for collective bargaining and that their employer declines to recognize their representative as the representative defined in section 9(a), or (ii) assert that the individual or labor organization, which has been certified or is being currently recognized by their employer as the bargaining representative, is no longer a representative as defined in section 9(a); or

"(B) by an employer, alleging that one or more individuals or labor organizations have presented to him a claim to be recognized as the representative defined in section 9(a); the Board shall investigate such petition and if it has reasonable cause to believe that a question of representation affecting commerce exists shall provide for an appropriate hearing upon due notice. Such hearing may be conducted by an officer or employee of the regional office, who shall not make any recommendations with respect thereto. If the Board finds upon the record of such hearing that such a question of representation exists, it shall direct an election by secret ballot and shall certify the results thereof.

"(2) In determining whether or not a question of representation affecting commerce exists, the same regulations and rules of decision shall apply irrespective of the identity of the persons filing the petition or the kind of relief sought and in no case shall the Board deny a labor organization a place on the ballot by reason of an order with respect to such labor organization or its predecessor not issued in conformity with section 10(c).

"(3) No election shall be directed in any bargaining unit or any subdivision within which, in the preceding twelve-month period, a valid election shall have been held. Employees on strike who are not entitled to reinstatement shall not be eligible to vote. In any election where none of the choices on the ballot receives a majority, a run-off shall be conducted, the ballot providing for a selection between the two choices receiving the largest and second largest number of valid votes cast in the election.

"(4) Nothing in this section shall be construed to prohibit the waiving of hearings by stipulation for the purpose of a consent election in conformity with regulations and rules of decision of the Board.

"(5) In determining whether a unit is appropriate for the purposes specified in subsection (b) the extent to which the employees have organized shall not be controlling.

"(d) Whenever an order of the Board made pursuant to section 10(c) is based in whole or in part upon facts certified following an investigation pursuant to subsection (c) of this section and there is a petition for the enforcement or review of such order, such certification and the record of such investigation shall be included in the transcript of the entire record required to be filed under section 10(e) or 10(f), and thereupon the decree of the court enforcing, modifying, or setting aside in whole or in part the order of the Board shall be made and entered upon the pleadings, testimony, and proceedings set forth in such transcript.

"(e) (1) Upon the filing with the Board by a labor organization, which is the representative of employees as provided in section 9(a), of a petition alleging that 30 per centum or more of the employees within a unit claimed to be appropriate for such purposes desire to authorize such labor organization to make an agreement with the employer of such employees requiring membership in such labor organization as a condition of employment in such unit, upon an appropriate showing thereof the Board shall, if no question of representation exists, take a secret ballot of such employees, and shall certify the results thereof to such labor organization and to the employer.

"(2) Upon the filing with the Board, by 30 per centum or more of the employees in a bargaining unit covered by an agreement between their employer and a labor organization made pursuant to section 8(a)(3)(ii), of a petition alleging they desire that such authority be rescinded, the Board shall take a secret ballot of the employees in such unit, and shall certify the results thereof to such labor organization and to the employer.

"(3) No election shall be conducted pursuant to this subsection in any bargaining unit or any subdivision within which, in the preceding twelve-month period, a valid election shall have been held.

"(f) No investigation shall be made by the Board of any question affecting commerce concerning the representation of employees, raised by a labor organization under subsection (c) of this section, no petition under section 9(e)(1) shall be entertained, and no complaint shall be issued pursuant to a charge made by a labor organization under subsection (b) of section 10, unless such labor organization and any national or international labor organization of which such labor organization is an affiliate or constituent unit (A) shall have prior thereto filed with the Secretary of Labor copies of its constitution and bylaws and a report, in such form as the Secretary may prescribe, showing—

"(1) the name of such labor organization and the address of its principal place of business;

"(2) the names, titles, and compensation and allowances of its three principal officers and of any of its other officers or agents whose aggregate compensation and allowances for the preceding year exceeded $5,000, and the amount of the compensation and allowances paid to each such officer or agent during such year;

"(3) the manner in which the officers and agents referred to in clause (2) were elected, appointed, or otherwise selected;

"(4) the initiation fee or fees which new members are required to pay on becoming members of such labor organization;

"(5) the regular dues or fees which members are required to pay in order to remain members in good standing of such labor organization;

"(6) a detailed statement of, or reference to provisions of its constitution and bylaws showing the procedure followed with respect to, (a) qualification for or restrictions on membership, (b) election of officers and stewards, (c) calling of regular and special meetings, (d) levying of assessments, (e) imposition of fines, (f) authorization for bargaining demands, (g) ratification of contract terms, (h) authorization for strikes, (i) authorization for disbursement of union funds, (j) audit of union financial transactions, (k) participation in insurance or other benefit plans, and (1) expulsion of members and the grounds therefore; and (B) can show that prior thereto it has—

"(1) filed with the Secretary of Labor, in such form as the Secretary may prescribe, a report showing all of (a) its receipts of any kind and the sources of such receipts, (b) its total assets and liabilities as of the end of its last fiscal year, (c) the disbursements made by it during such fiscal year, including the purposes for which made; and

"(2) furnished to all of the members of such labor organization copies of the financial report required by paragraph (1) hereof to be filed with the Secretary of Labor.

"(g) It shall be the obligation of all labor organizations to file annually with the Secretary of Labor, in such form as the Secretary of Labor may prescribe, reports bringing up to date the information required to be supplied in the initial filing by subsection (f)(A) of this section, and to file with the Secretary of Labor and furnish to its members annually financial reports in the form and manner prescribed in subsection (f)(B). No labor organization shall be eligible for certification under this section as the representative of any employees, no petition under section 9(e)(1) shall be entertained, and no complaint shall issue under section 10 with respect to a charge filed by a labor organization unless it can show that it and any national or international labor organization of which it is an affiliate or constituent unit has complied with its obligation under this subsection.

"(h) No investigation shall be made by the Board of any question affecting commerce concerning the representation of employees, raised by a labor organization under subsection (c) of this section, no petition under section 9(e)(1) shall be entertained, and no complaint shall be issued pursuant to a charge made by a labor organization under subsection (b) of section 10, unless there is on file with the Board an affidavit executed contemporaneously or within the preceding twelve-month period by each officer of such labor organization and the officers of any national or international labor organization of which it is an affiliate or constituent unit that he is not a member of the Communist Party or affiliated with such party, and that he does not believe in, and is not a member of or supports any organization that believes in or teaches, the overthrow of the United States Government by force or by any illegal or unconstitutional methods. The provisions of section 35A of the Criminal Code shall be applicable in respect to such affidavits.

"PREVENTION OF UNFAIR LABOR PRACTICES

"SEC. 10. (a) The Board is empowered, as hereinafter provided, to prevent any person from engaging in any unfair labor practice (listed in section 8) affecting commerce. This power shall not be affected by any other means of adjustment or prevention that has been or may be established by agreement, law, or otherwise: *Provided,* That the Board is empowered by agreement with any agency of any State or Territory to cede to such agency jurisdiction over any cases in any industry (other than mining, manufacturing, communications, and transportation except where predominantly local in character) even though such cases may involve labor disputes affecting commerce, unless the provision of the State or Territorial statute applicable to the determination of such cases by such agency is inconsistent with the corresponding provision of this Act or has received a construction inconsistent therewith.

"(b) Whenever it is charged that any person has engaged in or is engaging in any such unfair labor practice, the Board, or any agent or agency designated by the Board for such purposes, shall have power to issue and cause to be served upon such person a complaint stating the charges in that respect, and containing a notice of hearing before the Board or a member thereof, or before a designated agent or agency, at a place therein fixed, not less than five days after the serving of said complaint: *Provided,* That no complaint shall issue based upon any unfair labor practice occurring more than six months prior to the filing of the charge with the Board and the service of a copy thereof upon the person against whom such charge is made, unless the person aggrieved thereby was prevented from filing such charge by reason of service in the armed forces, in which event the six-month period shall be computed from the day of his discharge. Any such complaint may be amended by the member, agent, or agency conducting the hearing or the Board in its discretion at any time prior to the issuance of an order based thereon. The person so complained of shall have the right to file an answer to the original or amended complaint and to appear in person or otherwise and give testimony at the place and time fixed in the complaint. In the discretion of the member, agent, or agency conducting the hearing or the Board, any other person may be allowed to intervene in the said proceeding and to present testimony. Any such proceeding shall, so far as practicable, be conducted in accordance with the rules of evidence applicable in the district courts of the United States under the rules of civil procedure for the district courts of the United States, adopted by the Supreme Court of the United States pursuant to the Act of June 19, 1934 (U.S.C., title 28, secs. 723-B, 723-C).

"(c) The testimony taken by such member, agent, or agency or the Board shall be reduced to writing and filed with the Board. Thereafter, in its discretion, the Board upon notice may take further testimony or hear argument. If upon the preponderance of the testimony taken the Board shall be of the opinion that any person named in the complaint has engaged in or is engaging in any such unfair labor practice, then the Board shall state its findings of fact and shall issue and cause to be served on such person an order requiring such person to cease and desist from such unfair labor practice, and to take such affirmative action including reinstatement of employees with or without back pay, as will effectuate the policies of this Act: *Provided,* That where an order directs reinstatement of an employee, back pay may be required of the employer or labor organization, as the case may be, responsible for the discrimination suffered by him: *And provided further,* That in determining whether a complaint shall issue alleging a violation of section 8(a)(1) or section 8(a)(2), and in deciding such cases, the same regulations and rules of decision shall apply irrespective of whether or not the labor organization affected is affiliated with a labor organization national or international in scope. Such order may further require such person to make reports from time to time showing the extent to which it has complied with the order. If upon the preponderance of the testimony taken the Board shall not be of the opinion that the person named in the complaint has engaged in or is engaging in any such unfair labor practice, then the Board shall state its findings of fact and shall issue an order dismissing the said complaint. No order of the Board shall require the reinstatement of any individual as an employee who has been suspended or discharged, or the payment to him of any back pay, if such individual was suspended or discharged for cause. In case the evidence is presented before a member of the Board, or before an examiner or examiners thereof, such member, or such examiner or examiners, as the case may be, shall issue and cause to be served on the parties to the proceeding a proposed report, together with a recommended order, which shall be filed with the Board, and if no exceptions are filed within twenty days after service thereof upon such parties, or within such further period as the Board may authorize, such recommended order shall become the order of the Board and become effective as therein prescribed.

"(d) Until a transcript of the record in a case shall have been filed in a court, as hereinafter provided, the Board may at any time, upon reasonable notice and in such manner as it shall deem proper, modify or set aside, in whole or in part, any finding or order made or issued by it.

"(e) The Board shall have power to petition any circuit court of appeals of the United States (including the United States Court of Appeals for the District of Columbia), or if all the circuit courts of appeals to which application may be made are in vacation, any district court of the United States (including the District Court of the United States for the District of Columbia), within any circuit or district, respectively, wherein the unfair labor practice in question occurred or wherein such person resides or transacts business, for the enforcement of such order and for appropriate temporary relief or restraining order, and shall certify and file in the court a transcript of the entire record in the proceedings, including the pleadings and testimony upon which such order was entered and the findings and order of the Board. Upon such filing, the court shall cause notice thereof to be served upon such person, and thereupon shall have jurisdiction of the proceeding and of the question determined therein, and shall have power to grant such temporary relief or restraining order as it deems just and proper, and to make and enter upon the pleadings, testimony, and proceedings set forth in such transcript a decree enforcing, modifying, and enforcing as so modified, or setting aside in whole or in part the order of the Board. No objection that has not been urged before the Board, its member, agent, or agency shall be considered by the court, unless the failure or neglect to urge such objection shall be excused because of extraordinary circumstances. The findings of the Board with respect to questions of fact if supported by substantial evidence on the record considered as a whole shall be conclusive. If either party shall apply to the court for leave to adduce additional evidence and shall show to the satisfaction of the court that such additional evidence is material and that there were reasonable grounds for the failure to adduce such evidence in the hearing before the Board, its member, agent, or agency, the court may order such additional evidence to be taken before the Board, its members, agent, or agency, and to be made a part of the transcript. The Board may modify its findings as to the facts, or make new findings, by reason of additional evidence so taken and filed, and it shall file such modified or new findings, which findings with respect to questions of fact if supported by substantial evidence on the record considered as a whole shall be conclusive, and shall file its recommendations, if any, for the modification or setting aside of its original order. The jurisdiction of the court shall be exclusive and its judgment and decree shall be final, except that the same shall be subject to review by the appropriate circuit court of appeals if application was made to the district court as hereinabove provided, and by the Supreme Court of the United States upon writ of certiorari or certification as provided in sections 239 and 240 of the Judicial Code, as amended (U.S.C., title 28, secs. 346 and 347).

"(f) Any person aggrieved by a final order of the Board granting or denying in whole or in part the relief sought may obtain a review of such order in any circuit court of appeals of the United States in the circuit wherein the unfair labor practice in question was alleged to have been engaged in or wherein such person resides or transacts business, or in the United States Court of Appeals for the District of Columbia, by filing in such court a written petition praying that the order of the Board be modified or set aside. A copy of such petition shall be forthwith served upon the Board, and thereupon the aggrieved party shall file in the court a transcript of the entire record in the proceeding, certified by the Board, including the pleading and testimony upon which the order complained of was entered, and the findings and order of the Board. Upon such filing, the court shall proceed in the same manner as in the case of an application by the Board under subsection (e), and shall have the same exclusive jurisdiction to grant to the Board such temporary relief or restraining order as it deems just and proper, and in like manner to make and enter a decree enforcing, modifying, and enforcing as so modified, or setting aside in whole or in part the order of the Board; the findings of the Board with respect to questions of fact if supported by substantial evidence on the record considered as a whole shall in like manner be conclusive.

"(g) The commencement of proceedings under subsection (e) or (f) of this section shall not, unless specifically ordered by the court, operate as a stay of the Board's order.

"(h) When granting appropriate temporary relief or a restraining order, or making and entering a decree enforcing, modifying, and enforcing as so modified, or setting aside in whole or in part an order on the Board, as provided in this section, the jurisdiction of courts sitting in equity shall not be limited by the Act entitled 'An Act to amend the Judicial Code and to define and limit the jurisdiction of courts sitting in equity, and for other purposes,' approved March 23, 1932 (U.S.C., Supp. VII, title 29, secs. 101–115).

"(i) Petitions filed under this Act shall be heard expeditiously, and if possible within ten days after they have been docketed.

"(j) The Board shall have power, upon issuance of a complaint as provided in subsection (b) charging that any person has engaged in or is engaging in an unfair labor practice, to petition any district court of the United States (including the District Court of the United States for the District of Columbia), within any district wherein the unfair labor practice in question is alleged to have occurred or wherein such person resides or transacts business, for appropriate temporary relief or restraining order. Upon the filing of any such petition the court shall cause notice thereof to be served upon such person, and thereupon shall have jurisdiction to grant to the Board such temporary relief or restraining order as it deems just and proper.

"(k) Whenever it is charged that any person has engaged in an unfair labor practice within the meaning of paragraph (4)(D) of section 8(b), the Board is empowered and directed to hear and determine the dispute out of which such unfair labor practice shall have arisen, unless, within ten days after notice that such charge has been filed, the parties to such dispute submit to the Board satisfactory evidence that they have adjusted, or agreed upon methods for the voluntary adjustment of, the dispute. Upon compliance by the parties to the dispute with the decision of the Board or upon such voluntary adjustment of the dispute, such charge shall be dismissed.

"(1) Whenever it is charged that any person has engaged in an unfair labor practice within the meaning of paragraph (4)(A), (B), or (C) of sec-

tion 8(b), the preliminary investigation of such charge shall be made forthwith and given priority over all other cases except cases of like character in
the office where it is filed or to which it is referred. If, after such investigation, the officer or regional attorney to whom the matter may be referred
has reasonable cause to believe such charge is true and that a complaint
should issue, he shall, on behalf of the Board, petition any district court of
the United States (including the District Court of the United States for the
District of Columbia) within any district where the unfair labor practice in
question has occurred, is alleged to have occurred, or wherein such person
resided or transacts business, for appropriate injunctive relief pending the
final adjudication of the Board with respect to such matter. Upon the filing
of any such petition the district court shall have jurisdiction to grant such
injunctive relief or temporary restraining order as it deems just and proper,
notwithstanding any other provision of law: *Provided further,* That no temporary restraining order shall be issued without notice unless a petition alleges that substantial and irreparable injury to the charging party will be
unavoidable and such temporary restraining order shall be effective for no
longer than five days and will become void at the expiration of such period.
Upon filing of any such petition the courts shall cause notice thereof to be
served upon any person involved in the charge and such person, including
the charging party, shall be given an opportunity to appear by counsel and
present any relevant testimony: *Provided further,* That for the purposes of
this subsection district courts shall be deemed to have jurisdiction of a labor
organization (1) in the district in which such organization maintains its
principal office, or (2) in any district in which its duly authorized officers or
agents are engaged in promoting or protecting the interests of employee
members. The service of legal process upon such officer or agent shall constitute service upon the labor organization and make such organization a
party to the suit. In situations where such relief is appropriate the procedure specified herein shall apply to charges with respect to section
8(b)(4)(D).

"INVESTIGATORY POWERS

"SEC. 11. For the purpose of all hearings and investigations, which, in
the opinion of the Board, are necessary and proper for the exercise of the
powers vested in it by section 9 and section 10—

"(1) The Board, or its duly authorized agents or agencies, shall at all
reasonable times have access to, for the purpose of examination, and the
right to copy any evidence of any person being investigated or proceeded
against that relates to any matter under investigation or in question. The
Board, or any member thereof, shall upon application of any party to such
proceedings, forthwith issue to such party subpenas requiring the attendance and testimony of witnesses or the production of any evidence in such
proceeding or investigation requested in such application. Within five days
after the service of a subpena on any person requiring the production of

any evidence in his possession or under his control, such person may petition the Board to revoke, and the Board shall revoke, such subpena if in its opinion the evidence whose production is required does not relate to any matter under investigation, or any matter in question in such proceedings, or if in its opinion such subpena does not describe with sufficient particularity the evidence whose production is required. Any member of the Board, or any agent or agency designated by the Board for such purposes, may administer oaths and affirmations, examine witnesses, and receive evidence. Such attendance of witnesses and the production of such evidence may be required from any place in the United States or any Territory or possession thereof, at any designated place of hearing.

"(2) In case of contumacy or refusal to obey a subpena issued to any person, any district court of the United States or the United States courts of any Territory or possession, or the District Court of the United States for the District of Columbia, within the jurisdiction of which the inquiry is carried on or within the jurisdiction of which said person guilty of contumacy or refusal to obey is found or resides or transacts business, upon application by the Board shall have jurisdiction to issue to such person an order requiring such person to appear before the Board, its member, agent, or agency, there to produce evidence if so ordered, or there to give testimony touching the matter under investigation or in question; and any failure to obey such order of the court may be punished by said court as a contempt thereof.

"(3) No person shall be excused from attending and testifying or from producing books, records, correspondence, documents, or other evidence in obedience to the subpena of the Board, on the ground that the testimony or evidence required of him may tend to incriminate him or subject him to a penalty of forfeiture; but no individual shall be prosecuted or subjected to any penalty or forfeiture for or on account of any transaction, matter, or thing concerning which he is compelled, after having claimed his privilege against self-incrimination, to testify or produce evidence, except that such individual so testifying shall not be exempt from prosecution and punishment for perjury committed in so testifying.

"(4) Complaints, orders, and other process and papers of the Board, its member, agent, or agency, may be served either personally or by registered mail or by telegraph or by leaving a copy thereof at the principal office or place of business of the person required to be served. The verified return by the individual so serving the same setting forth the manner of such service shall be proof of the same, and the return post office receipt or telegraph receipt therefore when registered and mailed or telegraphed as aforesaid shall be proof of service of the same. Witnesses summoned before the Board, its member, agent, or agency, shall be paid the same fees and mileage that are paid witnesses in the courts of the United States, and witnesses whose depositions are taken and the persons taking the same shall severally be entitled to the same fees as are paid for like services in the courts of the United States.

"(5) All process of any court to which application may be made under this Act may be served in the judicial district wherein the defendant or other person required to be served resides or may be found.

"(6) The several departments and agencies of the Government, when directed by the President, shall furnish the Board, upon its request, all records, papers, and information in their possession relating to any matter before the Board.

"Sec. 12. Any person who shall willfully resist, prevent, impede, or interfere with any member of the Board or any of its agents or agencies in the performance of duties pursuant to this Act shall be punished by a fine of not more than $5,000 or by imprisonment for not more than one year, or both.

"LIMITATIONS

"Sec. 13. Nothing in this Act, except as specifically provided for herein, shall be construed so as either to interfere with or impede or diminish in any way the right to strike, or to affect the limitations or qualifications on that right.

"Sec. 14. (a) Nothing herein shall prohibit any individual employed as a supervisor from becoming or remaining a member of a labor organization, but no employer subject to this Act shall be compelled to deem individuals defined herein as employees for the purpose of any law, either national or local, relating to collective bargaining.

"(b) Nothing in this Act shall be construed as authorizing the execution or application of agreements requiring membership in a labor organization as a condition of employment in any State or Territory in which such execution or application is prohibited by State or Territorial law.

"Sec. 15. Wherever the application of the provisions of section 272 of chapter 10 of the Act entitled 'An Act to establish a uniform system of bankruptcy throughout the United States,' approved July 1, 1898, and Acts amendatory thereof and supplementary thereto (U.S.C., title 11, sec. 672), conflicts with the application of the provisions of this Act, this Act shall prevail: *Provided,* That in any situation where the provisions of this Act cannot be validly enforced, the provisions of such other Acts shall remain in full force and effect.

"Sec. 16. If any provision of this Act, or the application of such provision to any person or circumstances, shall be held invalid, the remainder of this Act, or the application of such provision to persons or circumstances other than those as to which it is held invalid, shall not be affected thereby.

"Sec. 17. This Act may be cited as the 'National Labor Relations Act.'"

EFFECTIVE DATE OF CERTAIN CHANGES

Sec. 102. No provision of this title shall be deemed to make an unfair labor practice any act which was performed prior to the date of the enactment of this Act which did not constitute an unfair labor practice prior thereto, and the provisions of section 8(a)(3) and section (b)(2) of the National Labor Relations Act as amended by this title shall not make an unfair labor practice the performance of any obligation under a collective-bargaining agreement entered into prior to the date of the enactment of this Act, or (in the case of an agreement for a period of not more than one year) entered into on or after such date of enactment, but prior to the effective date of this title, if the performance of such obligation would not have constituted an unfair labor practice under section 8(3) of the National Labor Relations Act prior to the effective date of this title, unless such agreement was renewed or extended subsequent thereto.

Sec. 103. No provisions of this title shall affect any certification of representatives or any determination as to the appropriate collective-bargaining unit, which was made under section 9 of the National Labor Relations Act prior to the effective date of this title until one year after the date of such certification or if, in respect of any such certification, a collective-bargaining contract was entered into prior to the effective date of this title, until the end of the contract period or until one year after such date, whichever first occurs.

Sec. 104. The amendments made by this title shall take effect sixty days after the date of the enactment of this Act, except that the authority of the President to appoint certain officers conferred upon him be section 3 of the National Labor Relations Act as amended by this title may be exercised forthwith.

Title II
Conciliation of Labor Disputes in Industries Affecting Commerce; National Emergencies

Sec. 201. That it is the policy of the United States that—

(a) sound and stable industrial peace and the advancement of the general welfare, health, and safety of the Nation and of the best interests of employers and employees can most satisfactorily be secured by the settlement of issues between employers and employees through the processes of conference and collective bargaining between employers and the representatives of their employees;

(b) the settlement of issues between employers and employees through collective bargaining may be advanced by making available full and adequate governmental facilities for conciliation, mediation, and voluntary arbitration to aid and encourage employers and the representatives of their employees to reach and maintain agreements concerning rates of pay, hours, and working conditions, and to make all reasonable efforts to settle their differences by mutual agreement reached through conferences and collective bargaining or by such methods as may be provided for in any applicable agreement for the settlement of disputes; and

(c) certain controversies which arise between parties to collective-bargaining agreements may be avoided or minimized by making available full and adequate governmental facilities for furnishing assistance to employers and the representatives of their employees in formulating for inclusion within such agreements provision for adequate notice of any proposed changes in the terms of such agreements, for the final adjustment of grievances or questions regarding the application or interpretation of such agreements, and other provisions designed to prevent the subsequent arising of such controversies.

SEC. 202(a) There is hereby created an independent agency to be known as the Federal Mediation and Conciliation Service (herein referred to as the "Service," except that for sixty days after the date of the enactment of this Act such term shall refer to the Conciliation Service of the Department of Labor). The Service shall be under the direction of a Federal Mediation and Conciliation Director (hereinafter referred to as the "Director"), who shall be appointed by the President by and with the advice and consent of the Senate. The Director shall receive compensation at the rate of $12,000 per annum. The Director shall not engage in any other business, vocation, or employment.

(b) The Director is authorized, subject to the civil-service laws, to appoint such clerical and other personnel as may be necessary for the execution of the functions of the Service, and shall fix their compensation in accordance with the Classification Act of 1923, as amended, and may, without regard to the provisions of the civil-service laws and the Classification Act of 1923, as amended, appoint and fix the compensation of such conciliators and mediators as may be necessary to carry out the functions of the Service. The Director is authorized to make such expenditures for supplies, facilities, and services as he deems necessary. Such expenditures shall be allowed and paid upon presentation of itemized vouchers therefore approved by the Director or by any employee designated by him for that purpose.

(c) The principal office of the Service shall be in the District of Columbia, but the Director may establish regional offices convenient to localities in which labor controversies are likely to arise. The Director may by order, subject to revocation at any time, delegate any authority and discretion conferred upon him by this Act to any regional director, or other officer or employee of the Service. The Director may establish suitable procedures for cooperation with the State and local mediation agencies. The Director shall make an annual report in writing to Congress at the end of the fiscal year.

(d) All mediation and conciliation functions of the Secretary of Labor or the United States Conciliation Service under section 8 of the Act entitled "An Act to create a Department of Labor," approved March 4, 1913 (U. S. C., title 29, sec. 51), and all functions of the United States Conciliation Service under any other law are hereby transferred to the Federal Mediation and Conciliation Service, together with the personnel and records of the United States Conciliation Service. Such transfer shall take effect upon the sixtieth day after the date of enactment of this Act. Such transfer shall not affect any proceedings pending before the United States Conciliation Service or any certification, order, rule, or regulation theretofore made by it or by the Secretary of Labor. The Director and the Service shall not be subject in any way to the jurisdiction or authority of the Secretary of Labor or any official or division of the Department of Labor.

FUNCTIONS OF THE SERVICE

SEC. 203. (a) It shall be the duty of the Service, in order to prevent or minimize interruptions of the free flow of commerce growing out of labor disputes, to assist parties to labor disputes in industries affecting commerce to settle such disputes through conciliation and mediation.

(b) The Service may proffer its services in any labor dispute in any industry affecting commerce, either upon its own motion or upon the request of one or more of the parties to the dispute, whenever in its judgment such dispute threatens to cause a substantial interruption of commerce. The Director and the Service are directed to avoid attempting to mediate disputes which would have only a minor effect on interstate commerce if State or other conciliation services are available to the parties. Whenever the Service does proffer its services in any dispute, it shall be the duty of the Service promptly to put itself in communication with the parties and to use its best efforts, by mediation and conciliation, to bring them to agreement.

(c) If the Director is not able to bring the parties to agreement by conciliation within a reasonable time, he shall seek to induce the parties voluntarily to seek other means of settling the dispute without resort to strike, lock-out, or other coercion, including submission to the employees in the bargaining unit of the employer's last offer of settlement for approval or rejection in a secret ballot. The failure or refusal of either party to agree to any procedure suggested by the Director shall not be deemed a violation of any duty or obligation imposed by this Act.

(d) Final adjustment by a method agreed upon by the parties is hereby declared to be the desirable method for settlement of grievance disputes arising over the application or interpretation of an existing collective-bargaining agreement. The Service is directed to make its conciliation and mediation services available in the settlement of such grievance disputes only as a last resort and in exceptional cases.

SEC. 204. (a) In order to prevent or minimize interruptions of the free flow of commerce growing out of labor disputes, employers and employees and their representatives, in any industry affecting commerce, shall—

(1) exert every reasonable effort to make and maintain agreements concerning rates of pay, hours, and working conditions, including provision for adequate notice of any proposed change in the terms of such agreements;

(2) whenever a dispute arises over the terms of application of a collective-bargaining agreement and a conference is requested by a party or pro-

spective party thereto, arrange promptly for such a conference to be held and endeavor in such conference to settle such dispute expeditiously; and

(3) in case such dispute is not settled by conference, participate fully and promptly in such meetings as may be undertaken by the Service under this Act for the purpose of aiding in a settlement of the dispute.

SEC. 205. (a) There is hereby created a National Labor-Management Panel which shall be composed of twelve members appointed by the President, six of whom shall be selected from among persons outstanding in the field of management and six of whom shall be selected from among persons outstanding in the field of labor. Each member shall hold office for a term of three years, except that any member appointed to fill a vacancy occurring prior to the expiration of the term for which his predecessor was appointed shall be appointed for the remainder of such term, and the terms of office of the members first taking office shall expire, as designated by the President at the time of appointment, four at the end of the first year, four at the end of the second year, and four at the end of the third year after the date of appointment. Members of the panel, when serving on business of the panel, shall be paid compensation at the rate of $25 per day, and shall also be entitled to receive an allowance for actual and necessary travel and subsistence expenses while so serving away from their places of residence.

(b) It shall be the duty of the panel, at the request of the Director, to advise in the avoidance of industrial controversies and the manner in which mediation and voluntary adjustment shall be administered, particularly with reference to controversies affecting the general welfare of the country.

NATIONAL EMERGENCIES

SEC. 206. Whenever in the opinion of the President of the United States, a threatened or actual strike or lock-out affecting an entire industry or a substantial part thereof engaged in trade, commerce, transportation, transmission, or communication among the several States or with foreign nations, or engaged in the production of goods for commerce, will, if permitted to occur or to continue, imperil the national health or safety, he may appoint a board of inquiry to inquire into the issues involved in the dispute and to make a written report to him within such time as he shall prescribe. Such report shall include a statement of the facts with respect to the dispute, including each party's statement of its position but shall not contain any recommendations. The President shall file a copy of such report with the Service and shall make its contents available to the public.

SEC. 207. (a) A board of inquiry shall be composed of a chairman and such other members as the President shall determine, and shall have power to sit and act in any place within the United States and to conduct such hearings either in public or in private, as it may deem necessary or proper, to ascertain the facts with respect to the causes and circumstances of the dispute.

(b) Members of a board of inquiry shall receive compensation at the rate of $50 for each day actually spent by them in the work of the board, together with necessary travel and subsistence expenses.

(c) For the purpose of any hearing or inquiry conducted by any board appointed under this title, the provisions of sections 9 and 10 (relating to the attendance of witnesses and the production of books, papers, and documents) of the Federal Trade Commission Act of September 16, 1914, as amended (U.S.C. 19, title 15, secs. 49 and 50, as amended), are hereby made applicable to the powers and duties of such board.

SEC. 208. (a) Upon receiving a report from a board of inquiry the President may direct the Attorney General to petition any district court of the United States having jurisdiction of the parties to enjoin such strike or lock-out or the continuing thereof, and if the court finds that such threatened or actual strike or lock-out—

(i) affects an entire industry or a substantial part thereof engaged in trade, commerce, transportation, transmission, or communication among the several States or with foreign nations, or engaged in the production of goods for commerce; and

(ii) if permitted to occur or to continue, will imperil the national health or safety, it shall have jurisdiction to enjoin any such strike or lock-out, or the continuing thereof, and to make such other orders as may be appropriate.

(b) In any case, the provisions of the Act of March 23, 1932, entitled "An Act to amend the Judicial Code and to define and limit the jurisdiction of courts sitting in equity, and for other purposes," shall not be applicable.

(c) The order or orders of the court shall be subject to review by the appropriate circuit court of appeals and by the Supreme Court upon writ of certiorari or certification as provided in sections 239 and 240 of the Judicial Code, as amended (U.S.C., title 29, secs. 346 and 347).

SEC. 209. (a) Whenever a district court has issued an order under section 208 enjoining acts or practices which imperil or threaten to imperil the national health or safety, it shall be the duty of the parties to the labor dispute giving rise to such order to make every effort to adjust and settle their differences, with the assistance of the Service created by this Act. Neither party shall be under any duty to accept, in whole or in part, any proposal of settlement made by the Service.

(b) Upon the issuance of such order, the President shall reconvene the board of inquiry which has previously reported with respect to the dispute. At the end of a sixty-day period (unless the dispute has been settled by that time), the board of inquiry shall report to the President the current position of the parties and the efforts which have been made for settlement, and shall include a statement by each party of its position and a statement of the employer's last offer of settlement. The President shall make such report available to the public. The National Labor Relations Board, within the succeeding fifteen days, shall take a secret ballot of the employees of each employer involved in the dispute on the question of whether they wish to accept the final offer of settlement made by their employer as stated by him and shall certify the results thereof to the Attorney General within five days thereafter.

SEC. 210. Upon the certification of the results of such ballot or upon a settlement being reached, whichever happens sooner, the Attorney General shall move the court to discharge the injunction, which motion shall then be granted, the President shall submit to the Congress a full and comprehensive report of the proceedings, including the findings of the Board, together with such recommendations as he may see fit to make for consideration and appropriate action.

COMPILATION OF COLLECTIVE BARGAINING AGREEMENTS, ETC.

SEC. 211. (a) For the guidance and information of interested representatives of employers, employees, and the general public, the Bureau of Labor Statistics of the Department of Labor shall maintain a file of copies of all available agreements and actions thereunder settling or adjusting labor disputes. Such file shall be open to inspection under appropriate conditions prescribed by the Secretary of Labor, except that no specific information submitted in confidence shall be disclosed.

(b) The Bureau of Labor Statistics in the Department of Labor is authorized to furnish upon request of the Service, or employers, employees, or their representatives, all available data and factual information which may aid in the settlement of any labor dispute, except that no specific information submitted in confidence shall be disclosed.

EXEMPTION OF RAILWAY LABOR ACT

SEC. 212. The provisions of this title shall not be applicable with respect to any matter which is subject to the provisions of the Railway Labor Act, as amended from time to time.

TITLE III
SUITS BY AND AGAINST LABOR ORGANIZATIONS

SEC. 301. (a) Suits for violation of contracts between an employer and a labor organization representing employees in an industry affecting commerce as defined in this Act, or between any such labor organizations, may be brought in any district court of the United States having jurisdiction of the parties, without respect to the amount in controversy or without regard to the citizenship of the parties.

(b) Any labor organization which represents employees in an industry affecting commerce as defined in this Act and any employer whose activities affect commerce as defined in this Act shall be bound by the acts of its agents. Any such labor organization may sue or be sued as an entity and in behalf of the employees whom it represents in the courts of the United States. Any money judgment against a labor organization in a district court of the United States shall be enforceable only against the organization as an entity and against its assets, and shall not be enforceable against any individual member of his assets.

(c) For the purposes of actions and proceedings by or against labor organizations in the district courts of the United States, district courts shall be deemed to have jurisdiction of a labor organization (1) in the district in which such organization maintains its principal office, or (2) in any district in which its duly authorized officers or agents are engaged in representing or acting for employee members.

(d) The service of summons, subpena, or other legal process of any court of the United States upon an officer or agent of a labor organization, in his capacity as such, shall constitute service upon the labor organization.

(e) For the purpose of this section, in determining whether any person is acting as an "agent" of another person so as to make such other person responsible for his acts, the question of whether the specific acts performed were actually authorized or subsequently ratified shall not be controlling.

RESTRICTIONS ON PAYMENTS TO EMPLOYEE REPRESENTATIVES

SEC. 302. (a) It shall be unlawful for any employer to pay or deliver, or to agree to pay or deliver, any money or other thing of value to any representative of any of his employees who are employed in an industry affecting commerce.

(b) It shall be unlawful for any representative of any employees who are employed in an industry affecting commerce to receive or accept, or to agree to receive or accept, from the employer of such employees any money or other thing of value.

(c) The provisions of this section shall not be applicable (1) with respect to any money or other thing of value payable by an employer to any representative who is an employee or former employee of such employer, as compensation for, or by reason of, his services as an employee of such employer; (2) with respect to the payment or delivery of any money or other thing of value in satisfaction of a judgment of any court or a decision or award of an arbitrator or impartial chairman or in compromise, adjustment, settlement or release of any claim, complaint, grievance, or dispute in the absence of fraud or duress; (3) with respect to the sale or purchase of an article or commodity at the prevailing market price in the regular course of business; (4) with respect to money deducted from the wages of employees in payment of membership dues in a labor organization: *Provided,* That the employer has received from each employee, on whose account such deductions are made, a written assignment which shall not be irrevocable for a period of more than one year, or beyond the termination date of the applicable collective agreement, whichever occurs sooner; or (5) with respect to money or other thing of value paid to a trust fund established by such representative, for the sole and exclusive benefit of the employees of such employer, and their families and dependents, (or of such employees, families, and dependents jointly with the employees of other employers making similar payments, and their families and dependents): *Provided,* That (A) such payments are held in trust for the purpose of paying, either from principal or income or both, for the benefit of employees, their families and dependents, for medical or hospital care, pensions on retirement or death of employees, compensation for injuries or illness resulting from occupational activity or insurance to provide any of the foregoing, or unemployment benefits or life insurance, disability and sickness insurance, or accident insurance; (B) the detailed basis on which such payments are to be made is specified in a written agreement with the employer, and employees and employers are equally represented in the administration of such fund, together with such neutral persons as the representatives of the employers and the representatives of the employees may agree upon and in the event the employer and employee groups deadlock on the administration of such fund and there are no neutral persons empowered to break such deadlock, such agreement provides that the two groups shall agree on an impartial umpire to decide such dispute, or in event of their failure to agree within a reasonable length of time, an impartial umpire to decide such dispute shall, on petition of either group, be appointed by the district court of the United States for the district where the trust fund has its principal office, and shall also contain provisions for an annual audit of the trust fund, a statement of the results of which shall be available for inspection by interested persons at the principal office of the trust fund and at such other places as may be designated in such written agreement; and (C) such payments as are intended to be used for the purpose of providing pensions or annuities for employees are made to a separate trust which provides that the funds held therein cannot be used for any purpose other than paying such pensions or annuities.

(d) Any person who willfully violates any of the provisions of this section shall, upon conviction thereof, be guilty of a misdemeanor and be subject to a fine of not more than $10,000 or to imprisonment for not more than one year, or both.

(e) The district courts of the United States and the United States courts of the Territories and possessions shall have jurisdiction, for cause shown, and subject to the provisions of section 17 (relating to notice to opposite party) of the Act entitled "An Act to supplement existing laws against unlawful restraints and monopolies, and for other purposes," approved October 15, 1914, as amended (U.S.C., title 28, sec. 381), to restrain violations of this section, without regard to the provisions of sections 6 and 20 of such Act of October 15, 1914, as amended (U.S.C., title 15, sec. 17, and title 29, sec. 52), and the provisions of the Act entitled "An Act to amend the Judicial Code and to define and limit the jurisdiction of courts sitting in equity, and for other purposes," approved March 23, 1932 (U.S.C., title 29, secs. 101–115).

(f) This section shall not apply to any contract in force on the date of enactment of this Act, until the expiration of such contract, or until July 1, 1948, whichever first occurs.

(g) Compliance with the restrictions contained in subsection (c)(5)(B) upon contributions to trust funds, otherwise lawful, shall not be applicable to contributions to such trust funds established by collective agreement prior to January 1, 1946, nor shall subsection (c)(5)(A) be construed as prohibiting contributions to such trust funds if prior to January 1, 1947, such funds contained provisions for pooled vacation benefits.

BOYCOTTS AND OTHER UNLAWFUL COMBINATIONS

SEC. 303. (a) It shall be unlawful, for the purposes of this section only, in an industry or activity affecting commerce, for any labor organization to engage in, or to induce or encourage the employees of any employer to engage in, a strike or a concerted refusal in the course of their employment to use, manufacture, process, transport, or otherwise handle or work on any goods, articles, materials, or commodities or to perform any services, where an object thereof is—

(1) forcing or requiring any employer or self-employed person to join any labor or employer organization or any employer or other person to cease using, selling, handling, transporting, or otherwise dealing in the products of any other producer, processor, or manufacturer, or to cease doing business with any other person;

(2) forcing or requiring any other employer to recognize or bargain with a labor organization as the representative of his employees unless such labor organization has been certified as the representative of such employees under the provisions of section 9 of the National Labor Relations Act;

(3) forcing or requiring any employer to recognize or bargain with a particular labor organization as the representative of his employees if another labor organization has been certified as the representative of such employees under the provisions of section 9 of the National Labor Relations Act;

(4) forcing or requiring any employer to assign particular work to employees in a particular labor organization or in a particular trade, craft, or class rather than to employees in another labor organization or in another trade, craft, or class unless such employer is failing to conform to an order or certification of the National Labor Relations Board determining the bargaining representative for employees performing such work.

Nothing contained in this subsection shall be construed to make unlawful a refusal by any person to enter upon the premises of any employer (other than his own employer), if the employees of such employer are engaged in a strike ratified or approved by a representative of such employees whom such employer is required to recognize under the National Labor Relations Act.

(b) Whoever shall be injured in his business or property by reason of any violation of subsection (a) may sue therefore in any district court of the United States subject to the limitations and provisions of section 301 hereof without respect to the amount in controversy, or in any other court having jurisdiction of the parties, and shall recover the damages by him sustained and the cost of the suit.

RESTRICTION ON POLITICAL CONTRIBUTIONS

SEC. 304. Section 313 of the Federal Corrupt Practices Act, 1925 (U.S.C., 1940 edition, title 2, sec. 251; Supp. V title 50, App., sec. 1509), as amended, is amended to read as follows:

"SEC. 313. It is unlawful for any national bank, or any corporation organized by authority of any law of Congress, to make a contribution or expenditure in connection with any election to any political office, or in connection with any primary election or political convention or caucus held to select candidates for any political office, or for any corporation whatever, or any labor organization to make a contribution or expenditure in connection with any election at which Presidential and Vice Presidential electors or a Senator or Representative in, or a Delegate or Resident Commissioner to Congress are to be voted for, or in connection with any primary election or political convention or caucus held to select candidates for any of the foregoing offices, or for any candidate, political committee, or other person to accept or receive any contribution prohibited by this section. Every corporation or labor organization which makes any contribution or expenditure in violation of this section shall be fined not more than $5,000; and every officer or director of any corporation, or officer of any labor organization, who consents to any contribution or expenditure by the corporation or labor organization, as the case may be, in violation of this section shall be fined not more than $1,000 or imprisoned for not more than one year, or both. For the purposes of this section 'labor organization' means any organization of any kind, or any agency or employee representation committee or plan, in which employees participate and which exists for the purpose, in whole or in part, of dealing with employers concerning grievances, labor disputes, wages, rates of pay, hours of employment, or conditions of work."

STRIKES BY GOVERNMENT EMPLOYEES

SEC. 305. It shall be unlawful for any individual employed by the United States or any agency thereof including wholly owned Government corporations to participate in any strike. Any individual employed by the United States or by any such agency who strikes shall be discharged immediately from his employment, and shall forfeit his civil service status, if any, and shall not be eligible for reemployment for three years by the United States or any such agency.

TITLE IV
CREATION OF JOINT COMMITTEE TO STUDY AND REPORT ON BASIC PROBLEMS AFFECTING FRIENDLY LABOR RELATIONS AND PRODUCTIVITY

SEC. 401. There is hereby established a joint congressional committee to be known as the Joint Committee on Labor-Management Relations (hereafter referred to as the committee), and to be composed of seven Members of the Senate Committee of Labor and Public Welfare, to be appointed by the President pro tempore of the Senate, and seven Members of the House of Representatives Committee on Education and Labor, to be appointed by the Speaker of the House of Representatives. A vacancy in membership of the committee shall not affect the powers of the remaining members to execute the functions of the committee, and shall be filled in the same manner as the original selection. The committee shall select a chairman and a vice chairman from among its members.

Sec. 402. The committee, acting as a whole or by subcommittee, shall conduct a thorough study and investigation of the entire field of labor-management relations, including but not limited to—

(1) the means by which permanent friendly cooperation between employers and employees and stability of labor relation may be secured throughout the United States;

(2) the means by which the individual employee may achieve a greater productivity and higher wages, including plans for guaranteed annual wages, incentive profit-sharing and bonus systems;

(3) the internal organization and administration of labor unions, with special attention to the impact on individuals of collective agreements requiring membership in unions as a condition of employment;

(4) the labor relations policies and practices of employers and associations of employers;

(5) the desirability of welfare funds for the benefit of employees and their relation to the social-security system;

(6) the methods and procedures for best carrying out the collective-bargaining processes, with special attention to the effects of industry-wide or regional bargaining upon the national economy;

(7) the administration and operation of existing Federal laws relating to labor relations; and

(8) such other problems and subjects in the field of labor-management relations as the committee deems appropriate.

Sec. 403. The committee shall report to the Senate and the House of Representatives not later than March 15, 1948, the results of its study and investigation, together with such recommendations as to necessary legislation and such other recommendations as it may deem advisable, and shall make its final report not later than January 2, 1949.

Sec. 404. The committee shall have the power, without regard to the civil-service laws and the Classification Act of 1923, as amended, to employ and fix the compensation of such officers, experts, and employees as it deems necessary for the performance of its duties, including consultants who shall receive compensation at a rate not to exceed $35 for each day actually spent by them in the work of the committee, together with their necessary travel and subsistence expenses. The committee is further authorized, with the consent of the head of the department or agency concerned, to utilize the services, information, facilities, and personnel of all agencies in the executive branch of the Government and may request the governments of the several States, representatives of business, industry, finance, and labor, and such other persons, agencies, organizations, and instrumentalities as it deems appropriate to attend its hearings and to give and present information, advice, and recommendations.

SEC. 405. The committee, or any subcommittee thereof, is authorized to hold such hearings; to sit and act at such times and places during the sessions, recesses, and adjourned periods of the Eightieth Congress; to require by subpena or otherwise the attendance of such witnesses and the production of such books, papers, and documents; to administer oaths; to take such testimony; to have such printing and binding done; and to make such expenditures within the amount appropriated therefor; as it deems advisable. The cost of stenographic services in reporting such hearings shall not be in excess of 25 cents per one hundred words. Subpenas shall be issued under the signature of the chairman or vice chairman of the committee and shall be served by any person designated by them.

SEC. 406. The members of the committee shall be reimbursed for travel, subsistence, and other necessary expenses incurred by them in the performance of the duties vested in the committee, other than expenses in connection with meetings of the committee held in the District of Columbia during such times as the Congress is in session.

SEC. 407. There is hereby authorized to be appropriated the sum of $150,000, or so much thereof as may be necessary, to carry out the provisions of this title, to be disbursed by the Secretary of the Senate on vouchers signed by the chairman.

TITLE V
DEFINITIONS

SEC. 501. When used in this Act—

(1) the term "industry affecting commerce" means any industry or activity in commerce or in which a labor dispute would burden or obstruct commerce or tend to burden or obstruct commerce or the free flow of commerce.

(2) The term "strike" includes any strike or other concerted stoppage of work by employees (including a stoppage by reason of the expiration of a collective-bargaining agreement) and any concerted slow-down or other concerted interruption of operations by employees.

(3) The terms "commerce," "labor disputes," "employer," "employee," "labor organization," "representative," "person," and "supervisor" shall have the same meaning as when used in the National Labor Relations Act as amended by this Act.

SAVING PROVISION

SEC. 502. Nothing in this Act shall be construed to require an individual employee to render labor or service without his consent, nor shall anything in this Act be construed to make the quitting of his labor by an individual employee an illegal act; nor shall any court issue any process to compel the performance by an individual employee of such labor or service, without his consent; nor shall the quitting of labor by an employee or employees in good faith because of abnormally dangerous conditions for work at the place of employment of such employee or employees be deemed a strike under this Act.

SEPARABILITY

SEC. 503. If any provision of this Act, or the application of such provision to any person or circumstance, shall be held invalid, the remainder of this Act, or the application of such provision to persons or circumstances other than those as to which it is held invalid, shall not be affected thereby.

JOSEPH W. MARTIN JR.
Speaker of the House of Representatives.
A. H. VANDENBERG
President of the Senate pro tempore.
IN THE HOUSE OF REPRESENTATIVES, U. S.,
June 20, 1947.

The House of Representatives having proceeded to reconsider the bill (H.R. 3020) entitled "An Act to amend the National Labor Relations Act, to provide additional facilities for the mediation of labor disputes affecting commerce, to equalize legal responsibilities of labor organizations and employers, and for other purposes," returned by the President of the United States with his objections, to the House of Representatives, in which it originated, it was

Resolved, That the said bill pass, two-thirds of the House of Representatives agreeing to pass the same.

ATTEST:

JOHN ANDREWS
Clerk.

I certify that this Act originated in the House of Representatives.

JOHN ANDREWS
Clerk.

IN THE SENATE OF THE UNITED STATES,
June 23 (legislative day, April 21), 1947.

The Senate having proceeded to reconsider the bill (H.R. 3020) "An Act to amend the National Labor Relations Act, to provide additional facilities for the mediation of labor disputes affecting commerce, to equalize legal responsibilities of labor organizations and employers, and for other purposes," returned by the President of the United States with his objections, to the House of Representatives, in which it originated, and passed by the House of Representatives on reconsideration of the same, it was

Resolved, That the said bill pass, two-thirds of the Senate having voted in the affirmative.

ATTEST:

CARL A. LOEFFLER
Secretary.

9

NATIONAL
EMERGENCY STRIKES
AND OTHER LABOR-
MANAGEMENT ISSUES

In an effort to encourage peaceful settlement of industrial disputes and assist in the maintenance of stable industrial relations through the process of collective bargaining, the framers of Title II of the Labor Management Relations Act created the Federal Mediation and Conciliation Service. This service was set up as an independent agency responsible for the conduct of all federal mediation and conciliation, including that which was formerly performed by the Department of Labor.

The Federal Mediation and Conciliation Service was designed to prevent or minimize those activities resulting from labor disputes that would interrupt the flow of commerce. The services of this agency may be offered by the agency itself or solicited by the parties involved in the dispute. The legislation cautions the agency against becoming involved with disputes of a local character or those that might better be handled by a state agency. In those instances where the Federal Mediation and Conciliation Service does become involved, the Director is instructed to encourage the disputants to seek other means for settling the issue if the agency has been unsuccessful in effecting a compromise. The legislation also urges that the most desirable method for settling grievance disputes arising from terms of the collective bargaining agreement is that method agreed upon by the parties. The services of the federal agency are to be offered only as a last resort. The parties to a dispute are not legally obliged to follow any suggestion made by the Federal Mediation and Conciliation Service, and refusal to do so does not constitute a violation of the Taft-Hartley Act. The legislation also sets forth the duties of the employer and the employee with respect to maintaining a relationship as free as possible of labor disputes. In essence, the Act urges cooperation in the development, execution, and maintenance of the collective bargaining agreement. However, should issue be taken by either party, contact and conference with the Federal Mediation and Conciliation Service is recommended and encouraged. To assist the Service in the performance of its duties, this legislation also establishes a National Labor-Management Panel composed of twelve persons. The panel membership would be selected because of their expertise in the field of management or labor, each having six representatives. This panel acts at the request of the director of the Federal Mediation and Conciliation Service, offering advice for avoiding or reconciling industrial controversies.

The Pre-Legislation Climate

The year preceding the passage of the Taft-Hartley Act was riddled with strikes and industrial unrest. The automobile industry, hampered by strikes in 1945, had not reached effective settlements by early 1946. A steel strike affecting the entire nation started in January of 1946, and in April bituminous coal mines all over the country were struck. The effect on the nation was so extensive President Truman labeled it a "national disaster." The end result of the last in a long series of coal strikes was government seizure of the coal mines. By May, the government also seized the railroads after the strike preventive machinery of the Railway Labor Act failed and resulted in threatened nationwide transportation stoppages. In this case, however, even the seizure did not prevent the strike. August was further marked with strikes that had drastic effects on shipping operations within the Great Lakes region. In the following month there was a work stoppage of some two weeks by unlicensed maritime personnel on both the East and West coasts as well as the Gulf coastlines. Settlement of this strike was followed by a strike of licensed maritime personnel just eight days later. The latter strike resulted in almost a complete cessation of activity in ports engaged in deep-sea fishing. By late November, strikes again hit the bituminous coal industry which, incidentally, was still held by the government. This resulted in a contempt of court decree against John L. Lewis, which was later appealed.

These incidents represent only a very few examples of the labor unrest that was taking place throughout the United States in the year following World War II. The total national effect was such that President Truman appeared before Congress to urge the passage of emergency legislation that would permit him to take action to prevent future strikes from having the same effects on the national economy.[1] In addition to these events, a decision handed down by the Supreme Court in *United States* v. *United Mine Workers of America*[2] also influenced the legislative climate just prior to the passage of the Taft-Hartley Act. The circumstances of this case are of more than historic interest because the entire conflict area of national emergency disputes versus private rights and freedom is highlighted here. As we indicated earlier, the government had taken over the bituminous coal industry in May of 1946. Shortly thereafter an agreement on the terms and conditions of employment was executed between Secretary of the Interior Julius Krug, who was acting as the Coal Mines' Administrator, and John L. Lewis, then President of the United Mine Workers of America. This agreement, to be honored while the government was in possession of the mines, was in accord with the agreement previously executed by the mineworkers in 1945. Under the terms of the 1945 agreement, Mr. Lewis requested that a meeting be held in October, 1946, for the purposes of discussing wages, hours, and working conditions once again. The government maintained that the agreement between Krug and Lewis was binding during the period the government had possession of the mines, and therefore the reopening clause of the original agreement did not apply. Lewis firmly maintained that such was not the case and that he would consider the Krug-Lewis agreement void if a conference was not held. This threat resulted in Krug's establishing a November conference. No further agreement

[1] *Federal Legislation to End Strikes: A Documentary History*, prepared by the Legislative Reference Service of the Library of Congress, Part I (Washington: U.S. Government Printing Office, 1967), pp. 612–613.

[2] 330 U.S. 258 (1947).

was obtained during these conferences and Lewis announced that as of midnight, November 20, the union would terminate the Krug-Lewis agreement. On November 18 both the Mineworkers' union and Lewis were served with a temporary injunction to prevent their breaking the Krug-Lewis agreement. On the day stated, however (November 20), the miners did not report for work.

A petition was filed by the Attorney General charging the union and Lewis with contempt. A motion to have the complaint and injunction dismissed was filed by the mineworkers, the motion being based on the claim that the court did not have jurisdiction and that the provisions of the Norris-La Guardia Act prevented the issuance of an injunction in a labor dispute. The motion to dismiss was not granted, and the parties were ordered to stand trial. The trial was held and the court concluded that the defendants were guilty as charged. Lewis was assessed a $10,000 fine and the union a fine of $3,500,000. The case was appealed by the defendants to the Supreme Court. In filing the brief for the United States, attorneys made the following points: injunctive relief could have been granted by the district court according to traditional equitable principles; the provisions of the Norris-La Guardia Act and the Clayton Act do not allow the defendants to act outside the jurisdiction of the court; there was proof beyond a reasonable doubt that the defendants were guilty of contempt; and "clear and present danger" to the community was proven present when the defendants failed to withdraw the notice to strike.[3]

UNITED STATES v. UNITED MINE WORKERS OF AMERICA: 1947
(330 U.S. 258)

The Supreme Court of the United States, Mr. Chief Justice Vinson delivering the opinion:

. . . Defendants' first and principal contention is that the restraining order and preliminary injunction were issued in violation of the Clayton and Norris-La Guardia Acts. We have come to a contrary decision.

It is true that Congress decreed in Section 20 of the Clayton Act that "no such restraining order or injunction shall prohibit any person or persons . . . from recommending, advising, or persuading others . . ." to strike. But by the Act itself this provision was made applicable only to cases "between an employer and employ-

[3] *Ibid.*, p. 259.

ees, or between employers and employees, or between employees, or between persons employed and persons seeking employment. . . ." For reasons which will be explained at greater length in discussing the applicability of the Norris-La Guardia Act, we cannot construe the general term "employer" to include the United States, where there is no express reference to the United States and no evident affirmative grounds for believing that Congress intended to withhold an otherwise available remedy from the Government as well as from a specified class of private persons.

Moreover, it seems never to have been suggested that the proscription on injunctions found in the Clayton Act is in any respect broader than that in the Norris-La Guardia Act. Defendants do not suggest in their argument that it is. This Court, on the contrary, has stated that the Norris-La Guardia Act "still further . . . [narrowed] the circumstances under which the federal courts could grant injunctions in labor disputes." Consequently, we would feel justified in this case to consider the application of the Norris-La Guardia Act alone. If it does not apply, neither does the less comprehensive proscription of the Clayton Act; if it does, defendants' reliance on the Clayton Act is unnecessary.

. . . The purpose of the Act is said to be to contribute to the worker's "full freedom of association, self-organization, and designation of representatives of his own choosing, to negotiate the terms and conditions of his employment, and that he shall be free from the interference, restraint, or coercion of employers of labor, or their agents, in the designation of such representatives . . . for the purpose of collective bargaining. . . ." These considerations, on their face, obviously do not apply to the Government as an employer or to relations between the Government and its employees.

. . . The Act does not define "persons." In common usage that term does not include the sovereign, and statutes employing it will ordinarily not be construed to do so. Congress made express provision, Rev Stat Section 1, 1 USCA Section 1, R.S. Section 1, 1 U.S.C. Section 1, for the term to extend to partnerships and corporations, and in Section 13 of the Act itself for it to extend to associations. The absence of any comparable provision extending the term to sovereign governments implies that Congress did not desire the term to extend to them.

Those clauses in Section 13(a) and (b) spelling out the position of "persons" relative to the employer-employee relationship affirmatively suggest that the United States, as an employer, was not meant to be included. Those clauses require that the case involve persons "who are engaged in the same industry, trade, craft or occupation," who "have direct or indirect interests therein," who are "employees of the same employer," who are "members of the same or an affiliated organization of employers or employees," or who stand in some one of other specified positions relative to a dispute over the employer-employee relationship. Every one of these qualifications in Section 13(a) and (b) we think relates to an economic role ordinarily filled by a private individual or corporation, and not by a sovereign government. None of them is at all suggestive of any part played by the United States in its relations with its own employees. We think that Congress' failure to refer to the United States or to specify any role which it might commonly be thought to fill is strong indication that it did not intend that the Act should apply to situations in which the United States appears as employer.

. . . The defendants contend, however, that workers in mines seized by the Government are not employees of the Federal Government; that in operating the mines thus seized, the Government is not engaged in a sovereign function; and that, consequently, the situation in this case does not fall within the area which we have indicated as lying outside the scope of the Norris-La Guardia Act. It is clear, however, that workers in the mines seized by the Government under the authority of the War Labor Disputes Act stand in an entirely different relationship to the Federal Government with respect to their employment from that which existed before the seizure was effected. That Congress intended such to be the case is apparent both from the terms of the statute and from the legislative deliberations preceding its enactment. Section 3 of the War Labor Disputes Act calls for the seizure of any plant, mine, or facility when the President finds that the operation thereof is threatened by strike or other labor disturbance and that an interruption in production will unduly impede the war effort. Congress intended that by virtue of Government seizure, a mine should become, for purposes of production and operation, a Government facility in as complete a sense as if the Government held full title and ownership. Consistently with that view, criminal penalties were provided for interference with the operation of such facilities. Also included were procedures for adjusting wages and conditions of employment of the workers in such a manner as to avoid interruptions in production. The question with which we are confronted is not whether the workers in mines under Government seizure are "employees" of the Federal Government for every purpose which might be conceived, but whether for the purposes of this case, the incidents of the relationship existing between the Government and the workers are those of governmental employer and employee.

. . . It should be observed that the Krug-Lewis agreement was one solely between the Government and the union. The private mine operators were not parties to the contract nor were they made parties to any of its subsequent modifications. It should also be observed that the provisions relate to matters which normally constitute the subject matter of collective bargaining between employer and employee. Many of the provisions incorporated into the agreement for the period of Government operation had theretofore been vigorously opposed by the private operators and have not subsequently received their approval.

It is descriptive of the situation to state that the Government, in order to maintain production and to accomplish the purposes of the seizure, has substituted itself for the private employer in dealing with those matters which formerly were the subject of collective bargaining between the union and the operators. The defendants by their conduct have given practical recognition to this fact. The union negotiated a collective agreement with the Government and has made use of the procedures provided by the War Labor Disputes Act to modify its terms and conditions. The union has apparently regarded the Krug-Lewis agreement as a sufficient contract of employment to satisfy the mine workers' traditional demand of a contract as a condition precedent to their work. The defendant Lewis, in responding to a suggestion of the Secretary of the Interior that certain union demands should be taken to the private operators with the view of making possible the termination of Government possession, stated in a letter dated November 15, 1946: "The Government of the United States seized the mines and entered into a contract. The mine workers do not propose to deal with parties who have no status under that contract." The defendant Lewis in the same letter referred to the operators as "strangers to the Krug-Lewis Agreement" and to the miners as the "400,-000 men who now serve the Government of the United States in the bituminous coal mines."

. . . In the case before us, the District Court had the power to preserve existing conditions while it was determining its own authority to grant injunctive relief. The defendants, in making their private determination of the law, acted at their peril. Their disobedience is punishable as criminal contempt.

Although a different result would follow were the question of jurisdiction frivolous and not substantial, such contention would be idle here. The applicability of the Norris-La Guardia Act to the United States in a case such as this had not previously received judicial consideration, and both the language of the Act and its legislative history indicated the substantial nature of the problem with which the District Court was faced.

Proceeding further, we find impressive authority for the proposition that an order issued by a court with jurisdiction over the subject matter and person must be obeyed by the parties until it is reversed by orderly and proper proceedings. This is true without regard even for the constitutionality of the Act under which the order is issued . . .

Violations of an order are punishable as criminal contempt even though the order is set aside on appeal, *Worden* v. *Searls*, 121 U.S. 14 (1887), or though the basic action has become moot, *Gompers* v. *Bucks Stove & Range Co.*, 221 U.S. 418 (1911).

We insist upon the same duty of obedience where, as here, the subject matter of the suit, as well as the parties, was properly before the court; where the elements of federal jurisdiction were clearly shown; and where the authority of the court of first instance to issue an order ancillary to the main suit depended upon a statute, the scope and applicability of which were subject to substantial doubt. The District Court on November 29, affirmatively decided that the Norris-La Guardia Act was of no force in this case and that injunctive relief was therefore authorized. Orders outstanding or issued after that date were to be obeyed until they expired or were set aside by appropriate proceedings, appellate or otherwise. Convictions for criminal contempt intervening before that time may stand.

. . . The trial court properly found the defendants guilty of criminal contempt. Such contempt had continued for 15 days from the issuance of the restraining order until the finding of guilty. Its willfulness had not been qualified by any concurrent attempt on defendants' part to challenge the order by motion to vacate or other appropriate procedures. Immediately following the finding of guilty, defendant Lewis stated openly in court that defendants would adhere to their policy of defiance. This policy, as the evidence showed, was the germ center of an economic paralysis which was rapidly extending itself from the bituminous coal mines into practically every other major industry of the United States. It was an attempt to repudiate and override the instrument of lawful government in the very situation in which governmental action was indispensable.

The trial court also properly found the defendants guilty of civil contempt. Judicial sanctions in civil contempt proceedings may, in a proper case, be employed for either or both of two purposes: to coerce the defendant into compliance with the court's order, and to compensate the complainant for losses sustained. . . . Where compensation is intended, a fine is imposed, payable to the complainant. Such fine must of course be based upon evidence of complainant's actual loss, and his right, as a civil litigant, to the compensatory fine is dependent upon the outcome of the basic controversy.

But where the purpose is to make the defendant comply, the court's discretion is otherwise exercised. It must then consider the character and magnitude of the harm threatened by the continued contumacy, and the probable effectiveness of any suggested sanction in bringing about the result desired.

It is a corollary of the above principles that a court which has returned a conviction for contempt must, in fixing the amount of a fine to be imposed as a punishment or as a means of securing future compliance, consider the amount of defendant's financial resources and the consequent seriousness of the burden to that particular defendant.

In the light of these principles, we think the record clearly warrants a fine of $10,000 against defendant Lewis for criminal contempt. A majority of the Court, however, does not think that it warrants the unconditional imposition of a fine of $3,500,000 against the defendant union. A majority feels that, if the court below had assessed a fine of $700,000 against the defendant union, this, under the circumstances would not be excessive as punishment for the criminal contempt theretofore committed; and feels that, in order to coerce the defendant union into a future compliance with the court's order, it would have been effective to make the other $2,800,000 of the fine conditional on the defendant's failure to purge itself within a reasonable time. Accordingly, the judgment against the defendant union is held to be excessive. It will be modified so as to require the defendant union to pay a fine of $700,000, and further, to pay an additional fine of $2,800,000 unless the defendant union, within five days after the issuance of the mandate herein, shows that it has fully complied with the temporary restraining order issued November 18, 1946, and the preliminary injunction issued December 4, 1946. The defendant union can effect full compliance only by withdrawing unconditionally the notice given by it, signed John L. Lewis, President, on November 15, 1946, to J. A. Krug, Secretary of the Interior, terminating the Krug-Lewis agreement as of twelve o'clock midnight, Wednesday, November 20, 1946, and by notifying, at the same time, its members of such withdrawal in substantially the same manner as the members of the defendant union were notified of the notice to the Secretary of the Interior above-mentioned; and by withdrawing and similarly instructing the members of the defendant union of the withdrawal of any other notice to the effect that the Krug-Lewis agreement is not in full force and effect until the final determination of the basic issues arising under the said agreement.

We well realize the serious proportions of the fines here imposed upon the defendant union. But a majority feels that the course taken by the union carried with it such a serious threat to orderly constitutional government, and to the economic and social welfare of the nation, that a fine of substantial size is required in order to emphasize the gravity of the offense of which the union was found guilty. The defendant Lewis, it is true, was the aggressive leader in the studied and deliberate noncompliance with the order of the District Court; but, as the record shows, he stated in open court prior to imposition of the fines that "the representatives of the United Mine Workers determined that the so-called Krug-Lewis agreement was breached," and that it was the union's "representatives" who "notified the Secretary of the Interior that the contract was terminated as of November 20th." And certainly it was the members of the defendant union who executed the nationwide strike. Loyalty in responding to the orders of their leader may, in some minds, minimize the gravity of the miners' conduct; but we cannot ignore the effect of their action upon the rights of other citizens, or the effect of their action upon our system of government. The gains, social and economic, which the miners and other citizens have realized in the past are ultimately due to the fact that they enjoy the rights of free men under our system of government. Upon the maintenance of that system depends all future progress to which they may justly aspire. In our complex society, there is a great variety of limited loyalties, but the overriding loyalty of all is to our country and to the institutions under which a particular interest may be pursued.

We are aware that the defendants may have sincerely believed that the restraining order was ineffective and would finally be vacated. However, the Government had sought a declaration of its contractual rights under the Krug-Lewis agreement, effective since May 29, 1946, and solemnly subscribed by the Government and the defendant union. The restraining order sought to preserve conditions until the cause could be determined, and obedience by the defendants would have secured this result. They had full opportunity to comply with the order of the District Court, but they deliberately refused obedience and determined for themselves the validity of the order. When the rule to show cause was issued, provision was made for a hearing as to whether or not the alleged contempt was sufficiently purged. At that hearing the defendants stated to the court that their position remained then in the status which existed at the time of the issuance of the restraining order. Their conduct showed a total lack of respect for the judicial process. Punishment in this case is for that which the defendants had done prior to imposition of the judgment in the District Court, coupled with a coercive imposition upon the defendant union to compel obedience with the court's outstanding order.

We have examined the other contentions advanced by the defendants but have found them to be without merit. The temporary restraining order and the preliminary injunction were properly issued, and the actions of the District Court in these respects are affirmed. The judgment against the defendant Lewis is affirmed. The judgment against the defendant union is modified in accordance with this opinion, and, as modified, that judgment is affirmed.

In addition to the opinion handed down by Chief Justice Vinson, there were five other opinions presented in the record. Justice Jackson concurred except that he believed the courts did not have jurisdiction to issue an injunction in this case because of the Norris-La Guardia Act. Justice Frankfurter agreed with the adjudication but not with

the reasoning that was used in order to reach that decision. Justices
Black and Douglas concurred in part but also dissented in part, and
stated in their opinion:

> . . . our judgment should provide that the defendants pay their re-
> spective fines only in the event that full and unconditional obedi-
> ence to the temporary injunction, including withdrawal of the no-
> tice which purported to terminate the contract, is not had on or
> before a day certain.[4]

Both Justice Murphy and Justice Rutledge filed dissenting opinions.
Thus while the high court was split five-to-four as to the applicability
of the Norris-La Guardia Act, all but two of the justices did agree that
the refusal by Lewis and the United Mine Workers to follow the
order of the lower court was unlawful.

The foregoing incident illustrates the problem facing the framers of
the 1947 legislation. To protect the national economic health and
safety, two legislative courses of action were available. Legislation
could be passed that would authorize government seizure of struck
properties or those threatened with strike so that the activity could
be enjoined. Alternatively, Congress could amend the Norris-La Guardia Act to provide for the issuance of injunctions in certain circumstances.[5] The national emergency strike procedures set forth in Title
II of the 1947 Labor Management Relations Act are the result of Congress opting for the latter alternative.

National Emergency Strike Procedures

Until this time there had been literally no legislative restrictions
on strike activity other than those deemed necessary during World
War II. The Taft-Hartley Act initiated major procedural changes to
be followed for instituting and carrying on these kinds of activities.
While Section 13 of the original Wagner Act established the legitimacy of utilizing the strike tactic, the Taft-Hartley amendment added
a qualifying phrase:

> Nothing in this Act, except as specifically provided for herein,
> shall be construed so as either to interfere with or impede or dim-

[4] *Ibid.*, p. 335.

[5] *Op. cit.*, *Federal Legislation to End Strikes: A Documentary History,*
p. 618.

inish in any way the right to strike, or to affect the limitations or qualifications on that right.[6]

Congress then proceeded to establish certain ground rules for the handling of national emergency strikes. The inclusion of these provisions appears to have been an attempt to effectuate some control that would result in minimizing the numbers and extent of strike activities and, at the same time, make an effort to preserve the basic right to strike. National emergency strike procedures can be summarized as follows:

First, when the President is of the opinion that a strike, lockout, or the threat of such in an industry engaged in interstate commerce will imperil the health or safety of the nation, he is empowered to appoint a board of inquiry. In naming the chairman of the board and all other members, the President is not restricted by the legislation as to how large or from what sources the members of the board shall be selected. The board is not restricted as to where it will conduct its inquiry, including the determination of hearings on a public or private basis. This board is charged with completing a full investigation of the issues surrounding the dispute and must forward a full report containing factual statements regarding the dispute and the position taken by the parties involved. Upon receipt of the report, the President sends a copy to the Federal Mediation and Conciliation Service and makes the contents of the report available to the public. After the President receives a report from the board of inquiry, he may direct the attorney general to petition a U.S. District Court to enjoin the offending activity. The court may find that the strike or lockout, or the threat of a strike or lockout, imperils the general national health and safety and has a detrimental effect on an industry or a substantial part of an industry. Should this be the case the court is empowered to enjoin the activity.

When the parties to the dispute are enjoined by court order the act requires them to make every effort possible to settle the dispute, assisted by the Federal Mediation and Conciliation Service. However, neither party is required to accept any proposal made by the Service. At the time the injunction is issued, the President is to recall the board of inquiry that he dismissed after submission of the initial report. The board of inquiry makes another report to the President sixty days after the activity is enjoined if no settlement has been reached. This report contains a statement of the position of each

[6] See Appendix VIII for complete text.

party. In the report there typically are statements describing the efforts that have been made by the parties in an attempt to settle the dispute, and also a statement indicating the employer's last offer. During the fifteen-day period following the receipt of the report by the President, the National Labor Relations Board conducts a secret ballot of the employees involved in the dispute in an effort to determine whether or not they will accept the final offer of the employer. Within five days of the balloting the results must be certified to the attorney general. Upon this certification the attorney general makes a motion to have the court dismiss the injunction. After the motion is granted and the injunction is dismissed, the President makes a full report of the entire proceedings to Congress. Included in this report are any further recommendations he may wish to make. It should also be noted that the parties to the dispute may arrive at a settlement at any point in this eighty-day procedure. Should this occur, a motion to the court to discharge the injunction would be made.

In the first ten years of its existence, the emergency strike provisions contained in the National Labor Relations Act were utilized twenty-six times and Executive Orders from the President established boards of inquiry. The first of these was in March of 1948. The parties involved were the Union Carbide and Carbon Chemicals Corporation and the Atomic Trades and Labor Council. This was a unit of 900 employees engaged at the Oak Ridge, Tennessee, atomic energy installation. The board was convened because of a threatened strike scheduled for March 5, 1948. The board reported to the President on March 15 and an injunction was issued on March 19. The board was reconvened on March 24 and in the final report, submitted on May 18, the position of the parties was described as unchanged. The last-offer ballot was taken on June 1 and 2 and the final offer of the employer was rejected by a vote of 771-26. The injunction was dissolved on June 11. Even though the injunction was no longer in effect, a strike did not ensue and a settlement was reached on June 15. The President reported to Congress on June 18 and made a recommendation that a study should be made to look into special methods for the handling of future atomic energy disputes. The Federal Mediation and Conciliation Service became involved in this case in February of 1948 and actively conferred with the parties involved. The Service made various efforts to effect a settlement both prior to and during the injunction period. After the dissolution of the injunction, the Service brought the parties together and ultimately an agreement was reached.[7]

[7] *Op. cit.*, *Federal Legislation to End Strikes: A Documentary History*, p. 576.

The merits and effectiveness of the national emergency strike procedure have been argued repeatedly since the passage of the Taft-Hartley Act. The overall effect of these provisions as the direct means of reaching a settlement is not apparent in the record. Only by conjecture could one say that settlements would have occurred sooner or later without this machinery. The kinds of changes that have been suggested range from modest modifications in the present provisions advocating techniques of a less restrictive nature to much more stringent methods of dealing with national emergencies by enacting legislation that would require compulsory arbitration. The success that has been achieved through the national emergency strike procedures may be explained as indirect in that the threat of use may have prevented a resurgence of strikes.

CONSTITUTIONALITY

The constitutionality of the national emergency strike procedures of the Labor-Management Relations Act was established in 1959 in the case of *United Steelworkers* v. *United States*.[8] In this case the constitutionality of the legislation was challenged when an injunction was issued to prevent a strike that was claimed to imperil the national safety. The Supreme Court determined that the provisions in the legislation did not violate the constitutional restrictions on the courts that disallow the exercise of legislative or executive power by the judiciary.

UNITED STEELWORKERS v. UNITED STATES: 1959
(*361 U.S. 39*)

The Supreme Court of the United States, Mr. Justice Douglas delivering the opinion:

The Attorney General sought and obtained in the District Court for the Western District of Pennsylvania an injunction against the continuation of an industry-wide strike of workers in the basic steel industry pursuant to Section 208 of the Labor Management Relations Act, 1947, 61 Stat 155, 29 USC Section 178. We granted certiorari, *post,* p. 878, to review the judgment of the Court of Appeals for the Third Circuit, 271 F2d 676, affirming the District Court. In pertinent part, Section 208 provides that if the District Court—

[8] 361 U.S. 39 (1959).

"finds that . . . [a] threatened or actual strike or lock-out—
(i) affects an entire industry or a substantial part thereof engaged in trade, commerce, transportation, transmission, or communication among the several States or with foreign nations, or
engaged in the production of goods for commerce; and

"(ii) if permitted to occur or to continue, will imperil the national health or safety, it shall have jurisdiction to enjoin any
such strike or lock-out, or the continuing thereof, and to make
such other orders as may be appropriate."

The arguments of the parties here and in the lower courts have
addressed themselves in considerable part to the propriety of the
District Court's exercising its equitable jurisdiction to enjoin the
strike in question once the findings set forth above had been
made. These arguments have ranged widely into broad issues of
national labor policy, the availability of other remedies to the Executive, the effect of a labor injunction on the collective bargaining process, consideration of the conduct of the parties to the labor
dispute in their negotiations, and conjecture as to the course of
those negotiations in the future. We do not believe that Congress
in passing the statute intended that the issuance of injunctions
should depend upon judicial inquiries of this nature. Congress was
not concerned with the merits of the parties' positions or the conduct of their negotiations. Its basic purpose seems to have been to
see that vital production should be resumed or continued for a
time while further efforts were made to settle the dispute. To carry
out its purposes, Congress carefully surrounded the injunction proceedings with detailed procedural devices and limitations. The
public report of a board of inquiry, the exercise of political and executive responsibility personally by the President in directing the
commencement of injunction proceedings, the statutory provisions
looking toward an adjustment of the dispute during the injunction's pendency, and the limited duration of the injunction, represent a congressional determination of policy factors involved in the
difficult problem of national emergency strikes. This congressional
determination of the policy factors is of course binding on the
courts.

The statute imposes upon the courts the duty of finding, upon
the evidence adduced, whether a strike or lock-out meets with the
statutory conditions of breadth of involvement and peril to the national health or safety. We have accordingly reviewed the concurrent findings of the two lower courts. Petitioner here contests the

findings that the continuation of the strike would imperil the national health and safety. The parties dispute the meaning of the statutory term "national health;" the Government insists that the term comprehends the country's general well-being, its economic health; petitioner urges that simply the physical health of the citizenry is meant. We need not resolve this question, for we think the judgment below is amply supported on the ground that the strike imperils the national safety. Here we rely upon the evidence of the strike's effect on specific defense projects; we need not pass on the Government's contention that "national safety" in this context should be given a broader construction and application.

The petitioner suggests that a selective reopening of some of the steel mills would suffice to fulfill specific defense needs. The statute was designed to provide a public remedy in times of emergency; we cannot construe it to require that the United States either formulate a reorganization of the affected industry to satisfy its defense needs without the complete reopening of closed facilities, or demonstrate in court the unfeasibility of such a reorganization. There is no room in the statute for this requirement which the petitioner seeks to impose on the Government.

We are of opinion that the provision in question as applied here is not violative of the constitutional limitation prohibiting courts from exercising powers of a legislative or executive nature, powers not capable of being conferred upon a court exercising solely "the judicial power of the United States." . . . Petitioner contends that the statute is constitutionally invalid because it does not set up any standard of lawful or unlawful conduct on the part of labor or management. But the statute does recognize certain rights in the public to have unimpeded for a time production in industries vital to the national health or safety. It makes the United States the guardian of these rights in litigation. . . . The availability of relief, in the common judicial form of an injunction, depends on findings of fact, to be judicially made. Of the matters decided judicially, there is no review by other agencies of the Government. . . . We conclude that the statute entrusts the courts only with the determination of a "case or controversy," on which the judicial power can operate, not containing any element capable of only legislative or executive determination. We do not find that the termination of the injunction after a specified time, or the machinery established in an attempt to obtain a peaceful settlement of the underlying dispute during the injunction's pendency, detracts from this conclusion.

The result is that the judgment of the Court of Appeals for the Third Circuit, affirming that of the District Court, is affirmed. Our mandate shall issue forthwith.

A discussion of strike activity and the Taft-Hartley provisions for intervention in those strikes that affect the national health and safety would not be complete without consideration of the case of *Youngstown Sheet and Tube Company* v. *Sawyer.*[9] While this case is not an issue under the Taft-Hartley provisions, it is of particular import when considered in terms of the Supreme Court attitude in cases we examined previously concerning government seizure of the bituminous coal industry, *United States* v. *United Mineworkers of America*[10] as well as *United Steelworkers* v. *United States.*[11]

The case we are concerned with here came before the Supreme Court in 1952 after the Taft-Hartley Act was passed. At this time the United States was involved in the Korean conflict. Wages as well as prices were under government control. However, in negotiations with the steel industry the United Steel Workers had presented demands for wage increases that surpassed the levels established by the Wage Stabilization Board. This Board had made a recommendation for a wage level in the steel industry that appeared generous in light of the formulas it had used to establish wages in other industries. In addition, the increase which the Board had recommended was greater than that which the steel industry had indicated it was willing to pay even though less than the union was demanding.

Dissatisfaction with the offers by the industry was such that the union announced on April 4, 1952, a nationwide strike was to be called on April 9. At that time the national emergency strike provisions could have been invoked. However, rather than do this the President issued Executive Order 10340 directing seizure of the steel mills by the Secretary of Commerce. The President did this to prevent the crippling strike, apparently assuming that seizure of private property came within the purview and the authority of the Presidential office and the Commander in Chief of the Armed Forces.

A preliminary order was issued from the Federal District Court against the seizure and the Supreme Court reviewed the issues on

[9] 343 U.S. 579 (1952).
[10] 330 U.S. 258 (1952).
[11] 361 U.S. 39 (1959).

May 3, 1952. Significant portions of the majority opinion of the Supreme Court are summarily presented for purposes of reader analysis.

YOUNGSTOWN SHEET AND TUBE COMPANY v. SAWYER: 1952
(343 U.S. 579)

The Supreme Court of the United States, Mr. Justice Black delivering the opinion:

We are asked to decide whether the President was acting within his constitutional power when he issued an order directing the Secretary of Commerce to take possession of and operate most of the Nation's steel mills. The mill owners argue that the President's order amounts to lawmaking, a legislative function which the Constitution has expressly confided to the Congress and not to the President. The Government's position is that the order was made on findings of the President that his action was necessary to avert a national catastrophe which would inevitably result from a stoppage of steel production, and that in meeting this grave emergency the President was acting within the aggregate of his constitutional powers as the Nation's Chief Executive and the Commander in Chief of the Armed Forces of the United States. . . .

Two crucial issues have developed: *First.* Should final determination of the constitutional validity of the President's order be made in this case which has proceeded no further than the preliminary injunction stage? *Second.* If so, is the seizure order within the constitutional power of the President?

It is urged that there were non-constitutional grounds upon which the District Court could have denied the preliminary injunction and thus have followed the customary judicial practice of declining to reach and decide constitutional questions until compelled to do so. On this basis it is argued that equity's extraordinary injunctive relief should have been denied because (a) seizure of the companies' properties did not inflict irreparable damages, and (b) there were available legal remedies adequate to afford compensation for any possible damages which they might suffer. While separately argued by the Government, these two contentions are here closely related, if not identical. Arguments as to both rest in large part on the Government's claim that should the seizure ultimately be held unlawful, the companies could recover full compensation in the Court of Claims for the unlawful taking. Prior cases in this

Court have cast doubt on the right to recover in the Court of Claims on account of properties unlawfully taken by Government officials for public use as these properties were alleged to have been. . . . Moreover, seizure and governmental operation of these going businesses were bound to result in many present and future damages of such nature as to be difficult, if not incapable, of measurement. Viewing the case this way, and in the light of the facts presented, the District Court saw no reason for delaying decision of the constitutional validity of the orders. We agree with the District Court and can see no reason why that question was not ripe for determination on the record presented. We shall therefore consider and determine that question now.

The President's power, if any, to issue the order must stem either from an act of Congress or from the Constitution itself. There is no statute that expressly authorizes the President to take possession of property as he did here. Nor is there any act of Congress to which our attention has been directed from which such a power can fairly be implied. Indeed, we do not understand the Government to rely on statutory authorization for this seizure. There are two statutes which do authorize the President to take both personal and real property under certain conditions. However, the Government admits that these conditions were not met and that the President's order was not rooted in either of the statutes. The Government refers to the seizure provisions of one of these statutes (Sec. 201(b) of the Defense Production Act) as "much too cumbersome, involved, and time-consuming for the crisis which was at hand."

Moreover, the use of the seizure technique to solve labor disputes in order to prevent work stoppages was not only unauthorized by any congressional enactment; prior to this controversy, Congress had refused to adopt that method of settling labor disputes. When the Taft-Hartley Act was under consideration in 1947, Congress rejected an amendment which would have authorized such governmental seizures in cases of emergency. Apparently it was thought that the technique of seizure, like that of compulsory arbitration, would interfere with the process of collective bargaining. Consequently, the plan Congress adopted in that Act did not provide for seizure under any circumstances. Instead, the plan sought to bring about settlements by use of the customary devices of mediation, conciliation, investigation by boards of inquiry, and public reports. In some instances temporary injunctions were authorized to provide cooling-off periods. All this failing, the unions were left free to strike after a secret vote by employees as to whether they wished to accept their employer's final settlement offer.

It is clear that if the President had authority to issue the order he did, it must be found in some provision of the Constitution. And it is not claimed that the express constitutional language grants this power to the President. The contention is that Presidential power should be implied from the aggregate of his powers under the Constitution. Particular reliance is placed on the provisions in Article II which say that "The executive Power shall be vested in a President. . . ;" that "he shall take care that the Laws be faithfully executed;" and that he "shall be Commander in Chief of the Army and Navy of the United States."

The order cannot properly be sustained as an exercise of the President's military power as Commander in Chief of the Armed Forces. The Government attempts to do so by citing a number of cases upholding broad powers in military commanders engaged in day-to-day fighting in a theater of war. Such cases need not concern us here. Even though "theater of war" be an expanding concept, we cannot with faithfulness to our constitutional system hold that the Commander in Chief of the Armed Forces has the ultimate power as such to take possession of private property in order to keep labor disputes from stopping production. This is a job for the Nation's lawmakers, not for its military authorities.

Nor can the seizure order be sustained because of the several constitutional provisions that grant executive power to the President. In the framework of our Constitution, the President's power to see that the laws are faithfully executed refutes the idea that he is to be a lawmaker. The Constitution limits his functions in the lawmaking process to the recommending of laws he thinks wise and the vetoing of laws he thinks bad. And the Constitution is neither silent nor equivocal about who shall make laws which the President is to execute. The first section of the first Article says that "All legislative powers herein granted shall be vested in a Congress of the United States . . ." After granting many powers to the Congress, Article I goes on to provide that Congress may "make all Laws which shall be necessary and proper for carrying into Execution the foregoing Powers and all other Powers vested by this Constitution in the Government of the United States, or in any Department or Officer thereof."

The President's order does not direct that a congressional policy be executed in a manner prescribed by Congress—it directs that a Presidential policy be executed in a manner prescribed by the President. The preamble of the order itself, like that of many statutes, sets out reasons why the President believes certain policies should be adopted, proclaims these policies as rules of conduct to be followed, and again, like a statute, authorizes a government official to promulgate additional rules and regulations consistent with the policy proclaimed and needed to carry that policy into execution. The power of Congress to adopt such public policies as those proclaimed by the order is beyond question. It can authorize the taking of private property for public use. It can make laws regulating the relationships between employers and employees, prescribing rules designed to settle labor disputes, and fixing wages and working conditions in certain fields of our economy. The Constitution does not subject this lawmaking power of the Congress to Presidential or military supervision or control.

It is said that other Presidents without congressional authority have taken possession of private business enterprises in order to settle labor disputes. But even if this be true, Congress has not thereby lost its exclusive constitutional authority to make laws necessary and proper to carry out the powers vested by the Constitution "in the Government of the United States, or any Department or Officer thereof."

The Founders of this Nation entrusted the lawmaking power to the Congress alone in both good and bad times. It would do no good to recall the historical events, the fears of power and the hopes for freedom that lay behind their choice. Such a review would but confirm our holding that this seizure order cannot stand.

Other Labor-Management Issues

In addition to establishing the procedures for national emergency strikes, Title II of the Taft-Hartley Act also stipulates that copies of all collective bargaining agreements will be retained in a file maintained by the Bureau of Labor Statistics. The Bureau may disseminate factual information about these agreements to the Federal Mediation and Conciliation Service, employers, employees, or their representatives to provide assistance in settling labor disputes. However, if information is submitted to the Bureau that is of a confidential nature, disclosure is not required. The remainder of the Taft-Hartley Act that will be discussed in this chapter is addressed to provisions which affect labor-management relations as a result of violations of agreements, unlawful payments and receipts, restrictions on contributions, unlawful strike and boycott activity, and the creation of a committee to study labor-management problems.

RESTRICTIONS ON PAYMENTS

A labor organization may sue or be sued, not necessarily in terms of the individuals that constitute it but as an entity; and further, a judgment involving money is enforceable against the organization and its assets, not against an individual member. Restrictions are also made regarding those payments that will be considered as unlawful when made by employers. This includes the promise to pay, or the payment of money or other items of value, to any representatives of a firm's employees. Restrictions were also placed on employee representatives to the same degree. Certain exemptions to these provisions were also identified: (1) if a union representative has actually performed a service for the employer he may be paid for these services as an employee; (2) payment may be made to satisfy a judgment or other bona fide award, if such does not result from fraud or duress; and (3) payment may be received by employers from a union representative for the purchase of a commodity as long as the payment is in conformity to the regular market price.

Restrictions are also made on the conduct of the voluntary checkoff, the process by which the employer deducts an amount stipulated for union dues before distributing wages. This obviously helps the union and relieves it of the problem of contacting each of its members to collect dues. While the Taft-Hartley Act does sanction the checkoff procedure, it must be a voluntary relationship, with each employee signing an authorization card before such a deduction can be made.

The final exemption is concerned with payments to trust or welfare funds and holds that an employer may make a payment of money, or other thing of value, if the fund qualifies.[12]

[12] See Appendix VIII for detail.

BOYCOTTS AND OTHER UNLAWFUL COMBINATIONS

The Taft-Hartley Act made strikes and boycotts unlawful when they are carried on for certain specified purposes. While this section was affected by a 1959 amendment, it is significant to look at the restrictions it imposed. It was considered unlawful under the terms of this section:

> . . . for any labor organization to engage in, or to induce or encourage the employees of any employer to engage in, a strike or a concerted refusal in the course of their employment to use, manufacture, process, transport, or otherwise handle or work on any goods, articles, materials, or commodities or to perform any services, where an object thereof is . . .[13]

to force an employer or a self-employed person to join a union or to cease doing business with or handling the products of another; to force an employer to bargain with a labor organization unless it has been certified as the bargaining representative of his employees; or to force the employer to assign work to employees who are members of a particular labor organization, craft, or trade.

While the language of this section does not explicitly state that secondary boycotts are unlawful,[14] it is clear that they are made unlawful by definition. Later legislation extended the prohibitions by adding restrictions on "hot-cargo" agreements making such contracts an unfair labor practice. However, until this was done unions were allowed to use "hot-cargo" clauses to justify secondary boycotts. Provision is also made in this section for filing a suit for damages that may result from violations of these strike provisions.

There are two remaining sections in Title III. The first of these, while it does not prohibit political activity on the part of labor organizations or corporations, does prohibit them from making contributions and expenditures to support elections. It is also illegal to accept such contributions. Penalties are imposed for this activity by fines or imprisonment or both.

The final section is concerned with strikes by government employees. It is declared unlawful for anyone who is in the employ of the

---

[13] U.S., *Statutes at Large*, LXI, Part 1, pp. 158–159.

[14] A secondary boycott is a union refusal to deal with parties neutral to a primary labor dispute designed to bring greater pressure on the primary employer.

United States Government, including government-owned corporations and agencies, to participate in a strike. The penalty for doing this is immediate discharge, forfeiture of civil service status, and ineligibility for reemployment by the government for three years.

THE JOINT COMMITTEE ON LABOR-MANAGEMENT RELATIONS

To complete our study and analysis of the Taft-Hartley Act, consideration must be given to its two remaining titles. Title IV creates a joint committee to study and report on problems that affect amenable labor relations and Title V serves simply to qualify some definitions as well as standard savings and separability clauses.

The joint congressional committee is to be made up of seven members from the Senate Committee on Labor and Public Welfare and an equal number from the House Committee on Education and Welfare. Appointments are to be made by the President pro tem of the Senate and the Speaker of the House respectively. This committee was to investigate and study the labor-management relations field and adjacent areas of activity. This included investigation into the means for obtaining an attitude of cooperation and stability between employers and employees, and methods that would result in increased productivity as well as increased wages. This was to include examination of guaranteed annual-wage plans, incentive and bonus systems, profit-sharing plans, a study of union activity with respect to administration, and the effect of required membership on employees. In addition, a study of employer policy with respect to labor relations and the administration of federal labor relations laws was suggested. The committee was also instructed to look at the matter of industry-wide and regional bargaining procedures, particularly with respect to the effect of this process on the national economy. Welfare funds and social security benefits were also to be studied and compared in an effort to determine their effect on each other as well as on the employee. Finally, a general charge was set forth to investigate and study any other problem the committee believed to be appropriate. The committee was also given the power to employ the necessary persons to carry out its functions, to hold hearings, and to issue subpenas.

Summary

This chapter has shown the considerable extent to which the original National Labor Relations Act was expanded by the inclusion of explicit procedures to be followed to minimize the economic effect of strikes that might result in national emergencies, the additional provisions for the filing of suits by or against labor organizations, and the establishment of a Federal Mediation and Conciliation Service as well as a Joint Committee on Labor-Management Relations.

WEAKNESSES IN THE TAFT-HARTLEY ACT

Probably no legislation is without fault and the Taft-Hartley Act is no exception. During the twelve-year period of operation preceding additional major amendments in 1959, several problem areas emerged in the application and interpretation of this law. These problem areas include activities with respect to "hot-cargo" clauses, secondary boycotts, recognition or organizational picketing, and the "no man's land" jurisdictional issue that arises when the National Labor Relations Board determines disputes to be of local concern. It appears too that while the intent of the legislation was to temper the imbalance of power between unions and employer, in the long run the greatest effect seems to have been to restrict the smaller or less powerful union organizations. Those unions whose organizations were strongly and firmly established were not hampered, to any large degree, by the Taft-Hartley provisions. This is supported by the additional restrictions that were added by the passage of the 1959 legislation, the subject of the following chapter.

PUBLIC POLICY

In conclusion, the Taft-Hartley Act both extended and to some extent contradicted the public policy that the Wagner Act had established. The earlier act brought the federal government and the law quite clearly into the labor-management arena. Stated simply, this was an effort to insure employees and unions that their constitutional rights were protected. Seemingly, this was not possible without reinforcement in the form of specific legislative enactment. The Taft-Hartley Act in essence recognizes that labor-management relations and the process of collective bargaining is a three-way street involving labor, management, and government or public interests. While the original National Labor Relations Act provided the labor movement with the tools it needed to bring industrial relations into a new balance, the amending legislation recognized that a balance could not exist unless similar protections were provided to management. The object of the Taft-Hartley amendments appears to be an indication of a legislative attempt to restore and maintain an equitable and peaceful equilibrium between the labor-management forces while involving government and social interests more directly.

10

THE LABOR-MANAGEMENT REPORTING AND DISCLOSURE ACT (THE LANDRUM-GRIFFIN ACT)

In this chapter we will first briefly examine the events leading to the passage of the Labor-Management Reporting and Disclosure Act (The Landrum-Griffin Act), followed by an analysis of the legislation and the way it amended the Taft-Hartley Act.

Union Democracy and Management

The American Labor Movement has suffered a severe setback in this session of the Congress. A measure designed solely to meet the problem of corruption was transformed by a reactionary coalition in Congress into a law which actually imposes severe, unnecessary, iniquitous, and inequitable restrictions upon the legitimate functions of legitimate unions. . . .[1]

[1] AFL-CIO, *Proceedings of Third Constitutional Convention* (San Francisco, California, 1959), Vol. I, p. 613.

These are the opening words of Resolution No. 169 presented at the 1959 convention of the AFL-CIO. It is our purpose here to examine the events that preceded the passage of legislation that could, in the eyes of union leaders, have such an effect on union activity.

THE MERGER

During the twelve-year period between the passage of the Taft-Hartley Act and the passage of the Landrum-Griffin Act several things happened that undoubtedly affected the content of the 1959 legislation. Almost immediately after enactment, union leaders made unsuccessful efforts to have the Taft-Hartley Act repealed or amended. While there was some consideration of amending legislation in Congress, none of any real consequence was formalized into law.

During this period there was a continuance of activity toward establishing a greater unity between the American Federation of Labor (AFL) and the Congress of Industrial Organizations (CIO). Two events are of significance in the year 1949: the International Confederation of Free Trade Unions was formed and the AFL and the CIO joined the confederation and expressed a desire to work together. It was also in 1949 that a long-standing conflict between the AFL and CIO was somewhat resolved when the CIO expelled those affiliate unions that had been identified as Communist-dominated. Three years later the leadership of both organizations changed as a result of the death of Philip Murray, then president of the CIO, and the death of William Green, then president of the AFL. George Meany succeeded Green and Walter Reuther replaced Murray. These men both proclaimed peace and unity in the labor movement as a primary objective. This objective was partially met in February, 1955, when the merger of these two organizations was consummated. The terms of the merger required concessions on both sides and contained the following provisions: a single trade union center would be created; each chartered or certified affiliate of either the AFL or CIO would become an affiliate of the merged federation; a no-raiding agreement [2] would be incorporated into the Constitution; jurisdictions would not be changed by the merger, and if conflicts occurred every effort would be made to resolve them through mutual agreement; the merged federation would recognize the need for both industrial and craft unions; the federation would adhere to a non-discrimination pol-

[2] This is an agreement between unions that prevents one union from attempting to organize workers who are in the jurisdiction of another union.

icy; and the federation would establish the internal machinery necessary to protect the membership against corruption or Communism.

The government and structure of the merged federation contains a Council of Industrial Organizations, open to all industrial unions in the federation and the current departments of the AFL Executive officers are to be elected in the regular convention and initially the offices of President and Secretary-Treasurer were to be filled from the AFL. The President appoints a Director of Organization who was to come from the CIO initially. The function of this department is to perform organizational activities in cooperation with the various affiliates. The Convention is the governing body and is to meet every two years; officers of the Executive Council are to meet three times a year and are empowered to make decisions to safeguard and promote the best interests of the federation and its affiliated unions. Provisions are also made for an Executive Committee to be made up of the executive officers and six of the federation's twenty-seven Vice Presidents, three from the AFL and three from the CIO. Finally, there is a General Board comprised of the Executive Council and the Presidents of affiliated nationals and internationals. This body is to meet once a year to decide on policy matters that have been deferred to it.

The agreement for the merger also provided for the disposition and absorption of the assets and liabilities of the AFL and the CIO. Stipulations were also set for a per capita tax of four cents per member per month payable to the merged federation by international and national unions and organizing committees. As federal labor unions and local industrial unions were to pay a per capita tax of not less than eighty cents per member per month, departments within the merged federation and the Council were to establish their own per capita tax. It was also agreed to preserve those agreements then in existence; e.g., the No-Raiding Agreement between the AFL-CIO, the Organizational Disputes Agreement in the CIO, and the Internal Disputes Plan within the AFL.[3]

THE MCCLELLAN COMMITTEE

The merger of these two organizations did not quell public criticism of labor union activities that had been building since the end of World War II. Congressional investigations had begun even prior to the merger and, in an effort to discourage additional legislation and improve their public image, the AFL-CIO adopted a Code of Ethical

[3] Arthur J. Goldberg, *AFL-CIO Labor United* (New York: McGraw-Hill Book Company, 1964), pp. 266–271.

Practices in 1956 and 1957. Also in 1957 the Teamsters Union was expelled from the newly-merged AFL-CIO. There were six separate
items considered in the Code of Ethical Practices. The first of these
established guidelines for the issuance of local union charters to prevent the development of "paper locals." This was the name given to
those organizations whose charters had been secured by groups
whose purpose was personal gain rather than the promotion of the
welfare of workers. The second item of the Code dealt with health
and welfare funds and recommended the following policies: (1) no
union official paid a full salary by the union will receive any additional pay if his duties involve the administration of the health and
welfare fund, nor may he receive payment from the fund established
to provide for health, welfare, and retirement; (2) persons with administrative responsibility or influence over these funds may not have
personal ties that result in personal gain from outside agencies who
serve the fund; (3) fund records should be subject to at least an annual audit and kept according to accepted accounting practice; (4)
audit reports should be made available to the membership; (5) the
beneficiaries should receive an annual report from fund administrators; (6) if the benefits from the fund are received through a commercial insurance carrier, the selection of the carrier should be done by
competitive bids; (7) when the union participates in the administration of the investment of fund reserves, every effort should be made
to avoid investment that results in personal gain; (8) if anyone connected with the welfare program receives an unethical payment, he
should be removed from his position and appropriate legal steps taken;
(9) the program should provide some redress against the unjust denial of claims and a complete record of claims experience; (10) the
duty to police the activities surrounding these funds could best be accomplished by the local membership and other union officials; and
(11) if pursuing these policies results in the need for a constitutional
amendment, this should be accomplished as soon as possible. Item
Three of the Code deals with racketeers, crooks, Communists, and
fascists, stating that unions should undertake to prevent persons from
taking office who participate in corrupt practices or support Communist or fascist agencies. Also, a person convicted of any crime involving moral turpitude, or known as a crook or racketeer, or who actively participates in Communist Party or fascist activities should not
act in an official capacity. Investments and business interests of union
officials is the subject of Code Four, where it is recommended that
union officials should have no conflict of interest between their personal business and performance of their duties as employee represen-

tatives. Union officials also must not have a substantial interest or ownership in the business and must not accept kickbacks from a business firm with whom they are bargaining collectively. The fifth Ethical Practices Code is concerned with further procedures that should be adopted for financial practices and proprietary activities of unions. In general, this involves the adoption of minimum accounting and financial controls and acceptable purchasing practices. Restrictions are also made that would prevent loans, investments, and purchases or sales that would result in personal gain to any officer, representative, or employee of the union. This Code also prevents personal loans to officers and members of the union as well as to the businesses with whom it bargains collectively. The last item in the Code of Ethical Practices is concerned with union democratic processes. In making its recommendation the Committee on Ethical Practices declared that the Taft-Hartley Act interfered with what had been successful efforts on the part of unions to have good attendance and participation in union activities. It was further noted that it would be necessary to establish new principles, but only to restate the democratic principles already accepted by the labor movement.[4]

Neither Congress nor the public was dissuaded by these activities. In this same year, in January of 1957, the Select Committee on Improper Activities in the Labor or Management Field was established. This committee was made up of eight senators, led by Senator John McClellan. The membership originally included Karl Mundt, John Kennedy, Barry Goldwater, Sam Ervin, Jr., Joseph McCarthy, Pat McNamara, and Irving Ives. Robert Kennedy was appointed as Chief Council and served in that capacity until September 6, 1959. The charge to this committee directed it:

> . . . to conduct an investigation and study of the extent to which criminal and other improper practices or activities are, or have been, engaged in in the field of labor-management relations or in groups or organizations of employees or employers, to the detriment of the interests of the public, employers, or employees, and to determine whether any charges are required in the laws . . . in order to protect such interests against the occurrence of such practices or activities.[5]

[4] AFL-CIO, *Proceedings of Second Constitutional Convention* (Atlantic City, New Jersey, 1957), Vol. II, pp. 73–94.

[5] U.S. Senate, Select Committee on Improper Activities in the Labor or Management Field, *Final Report*, 86th Cong., 2d Sess., 1960, Report No. 1139, p. 868.

Hearings started on February 26, 1957. The interim report filed in March of 1958 made several recommendations on which it was hoped that Congress would take action, including recommendations for legislation that would regulate and control pensions, health and welfare funds, insure union democracy, curb activities of middlemen in labor-management disputes, and clarification of the "no man's land" problem. These recommendations were made after 104 days of hearings, examining 486 witnesses, and taking 17,489 pages of testimony.[6]

LEGISLATIVE ACTION

On June 2, 1958, the Kennedy-Ives Bill was introduced in the Senate. This bill contained six titles, five of which dealt with the practices uncovered by the McClellan Committee investigations and the sixth with modifications of some of the Taft-Hartley provisions. The bill passed the Senate 88-1 but House reaction to the bill was not favorable. Six bills were introduced to the 86th Congress during its first session in 1959. The last of these, S. 1555, was reported back from committee on April 14, 1959.. After lengthy debate and with various amendments this bill passed the Senate 90-1 on April 25, 1959. Action on labor-reform legislation was also taking place in the House. Nine bills had been introduced to this body as well as the bill that had been passed by the Senate. On August 14, 1959, the Landrum-Griffin bill was passed by the House 303-125. The bill went to the Conference Committee and on September 3, 1959, the report of the committee was agreed to in the Senate 95-2 and the following day in the House 352-52. The Act was signed by the President on September 14, 1959.

The Landrum-Griffin Act

The Landrum-Griffin Act was designed

. . . to provide for the reporting and disclosure of certain financial transactions and administrative practices of labor organizations and employers, to prevent abuses in the administration of trusteeships by labor organizations, and to provide standards with respect to the election of officers of labor organizations, and for other purposes.[7]

[6] *Ibid.*
[7] U.S., *Statutes at Large,* LXXIII, 519.

In the declaration of findings, purposes, and policy the act reaffirms the belief that the federal government has a responsibility to protect the rights of employees and their relationships with employers and organizations that represent them. This section also decrees that the Congress, because of evidence placed before it, believed additional legislation was necessary to provide protection against breaches of trust, corruption, low standards of responsibility, and unethical conduct. Finally, this legislation was alleged to be necessary to strengthen the policies declared in the National Labor Relations Act and to avoid further obstructions of commerce. The Act consists of seven titles: the first presents a Bill of Rights for members of labor organizations; Titles II through VI deal with reporting requirements, trusteeships, and safeguards for labor organizations; and Title VII presents amendments to the National Labor Relations Act.

THE BILL OF RIGHTS FOR UNION MEMBERS

The Bill of Rights in the Landrum-Griffin Act is an attempt to control internal union practices and to set forth for union members those same guarantees that are contained in the federal Constitution for all citizens. The first of these declares that members of labor organizations shall have the right to nominate and vote for candidates to office in the organization and to participate in the conduct of the organization's business. This right is, of course, subject to the rules and regulations contained in the bylaws and constitution of the organization. In making this qualification the legislation uses the term "reasonable" when making reference to the organization rules. In addition, the membership is assured of the rights of freedom of speech and assembly and the opportunity to speak freely with respect to matters of organization business. The Bill of Rights also prevents increases in dues and fees except when the local membership votes by secret ballot to do so or a majority of delegates at a convention vote to do so. Further guarantees include prohibiting a labor organization from interfering with an individual member instituting court action or acting as a witness whether or not the labor organization is involved in the suit. Safeguards are also included to protect a member against fines, suspension, or expulsion unless he had been properly notified of the charges, given time to prepare his defense, and granted a full hearing. This title also stipulates that civil action may be brought for violation of these provisions and that the provisions do not affect rights already assured prior to the passage of the legislation. Labor organizations are also required to give each member a copy of the

collective bargaining agreement to which the union has committed itself and to inform each member of the provisions of the Landrum-
Griffin Act.

REPORTING BY LABOR ORGANIZATIONS

While it is generally believed that the Landrum-Griffin Act put
further restrictions on labor organizations, it should be pointed out
that it also placed additional requirements on the employer. This is
clearly demonstrated in Title II, which deals with reports that are to
be filed by labor organizations, their officers, and employees, and also
reports by employers. Labor organizations are required to adopt and
submit to the Secretary of Labor a copy of their constitution and bylaws that contains the name and address of the organization, the
name and title of the officers, the fees required from new or transferred members as well as any other payments that are necessary to
retain membership. There are also numerous miscellaneous requirements for detailed statements describing union-member relationships.[8]

Labor organizations are further required to file annual financial reports that describe in detail their financial operations for the year.
These are to include the identification of assets and liabilities at the
beginning and end of the year, a record of receipts and their source,
a report of disbursements, including salaries paid of more than
$10,000, a record of loans of over $250 to any union connected personnel indicating the purpose for which the loan was secured, the
security presented and the method by which it would be repaid.
Reports of any loans to any business and the details involved must be
reported as well as any other disbursements should the Secretary of
Labor require. The information in these reports is to be made available
to the membership of the reporting organization, as are the books or
records from which the information was taken. Because of the expanded
reporting requirements in the Landrum-Griffin Act, subsections (f),
(g), and (h) of Section 9 of the National Labor Relations Act were
repealed.

Officers and employees are also required to file reports with the
Secretary of Labor with regard to some of their individual activities.
The only people excluded from this requirement are clerical and custodial personnel. This report is to contain a list that describes any financial transactions that could in some way conflict with trust relationships. This includes activities undertaken by the person's spouse or
minor children.[9] Securities that are exempt from these provisions are:

[8] For a breakdown of these see Appendix 10.

[9] The details of this provision may be found in Appendix 10.

. . . bona fide investments in securities traded on a securities exchange registered as a national securities exchange under the Securities Exchange Act of 1934, in shares registered under the Investment Company Act of 1940, or in securities of a public utility holding company registered under the Public Utility Holding Company Act of 1935, or to report any income derived therefrom.[10]

Employers are required to file reports with the Secretary of Labor when payments or other things of value have been made or promised to a labor organization or its officers or employees unless these payments were made by a credit institution or are specifically exempted by Section 302(c) of the Labor-Management Relations Act of 1947, as amended. Employers are also obligated to report payments to any employees or groups of employees who attempted to persuade others to either exercise or not exercise the right to organize and bargain collectively unless these employers are aware of the payment. Further, if expenditures are made in order to interfere with, restrain, or coerce employees from exercising that right or to obtain information with respect to activities attendant to a labor dispute between that employer and the union (unless the purpose is to use such information for an ". . . administrative or arbitral proceeding or a criminal or civil judicial proceeding"), a report must also be filed as prescribed by the legislation. Finally, agreements with consultants or contractors whose purpose is either to influence decisions or to gather information with respect to collective bargaining or activities surrounding a labor dispute, unless as excepted above, must also be reported in detail to the Secretary of Labor within thirty days after such an agreement is consummated. The reports become public information and may be examined on request. Willful violation of these provisions carries criminal penalties and the Secretary of Labor may bring civil action for injunctive relief for a suspected violation.

TRUSTEESHIPS

Title III is devoted to the matter of trusteeships. The trusteeship is designed to be used when the national union determines that a local body is either involved in corrupt practices or is not being operated efficiently. Abuses in the use of this device were brought out during the McClellan Committee investigation. As stated in the Interim Report of this committee:

. . . the trusteeship principle itself was thoroughly abused in practice. Designed to safeguard union members' interests, trustee-

[10] *Ibid.*

ships as applied by international officers of the bakers not only depredated the funds but despoiled all democratic rights of the rank and file. Voting on matters of local interest ended, local officers, board members, and shop stewards ceased to function, and in their place were installed aides in every way subservient to the trustee. Even when trusteeships were removed, locals lived under the threat of their reimposition. The simple act of filing new charges against the local by someone in the international office or by only one local member would do the trick, an easy one among people riddled with fear of their superior officers.[11]

As a result of these findings, controls for trusteeships were incorporated into the Landrum-Griffin Act. The Act requires that whenever a labor organization assumes a trusteeship it must file a report with the Secretary of Labor within thirty days and every six months thereafter. The report must be signed by the principal officers of each of the organizations involved and must contain the name and address of the body under trusteeship, the date on which the trusteeship was established, and the reasons for it as well as the manner by which delegates to conventions are selected from the subordinate organization and the degree to which the subordinate body participates in the election of the officers of the organization which has assumed the trusteeship. In addition, a detailed report must be made as to the financial condition of the organization when it was put under trusteeship and annually thereafter. The appropriate reasons for placing a union under trusteeship include: correcting corruption or financial malpractice, assuring proper performance of the terms of the bargaining agreements and the bargaining representative, restoring the democratic process in the organization, and to see that the legitimate objects of a labor organization are carried out.

The Secretary of Labor may bring action against a labor organization for violating the terms of Title III after he has investigated a complaint and has found probable cause. Penalty for violation may result in a fine up to $10,000, twelve months imprisonment, or both.

ELECTIONS

Elections and election procedures were also the subject of intensive inquiry by the McClellan Committee, and Title IV of the Lan-

[11] U.S. Senate, Select Committee on Improper Activities in the Labor or Management Field, *Interim Report*, 85th Cong., 2d Sess., 1958, Report No. 1417, p. 130.

drum-Griffin Act is the result. In an effort to strengthen and insure democratic processes in the internal affairs of unions, this Title provides a detailed procedure for the election of officers in labor organizations. National and international bodies are required to elect officers at least every five years and local labor organizations every three years. In the local organization the election shall be by a secret ballot of the membership in good standing and for the national or international either in the same way or by a convention of delegates, selected by the membership in good standing by secret ballot.

Labor organizations are required to assist any candidates in the mailing of campaign literature to members in good standing and may not discriminate against a candidate in this respect. The candidate is responsible for paying for this service. All candidates are given the right of access to the membership list of the labor organization in which he is seeking election, at least once within thirty days prior to the election. The officers of intermediate bodies are not included in the process outlined above and must be elected at least every four years. The election of these persons, too, is to be by secret ballot of the membership in good standing or representatives who have been selected by secret ballot.

The legislation also stipulates that every member in good standing will have a reasonable opportunity to nominate candidates for election, is eligible himself for nomination, and has a right to vote without threat of penalty, discipline, or improper interference by the organization. Notice must be given to all of the membership at least fifteen days before an election is to take place. The results of the election are to be published for each local union and the ballots, as well as all other records, are to be preserved for one year. The voting procedure for delegates at a convention is to be in accord with the constitution and bylaws as long as they are not inconsistent with the federal legislation. A labor organization is prohibited from using money from dues or assessments and an employer is prohibited from giving any financial support to promote the candidacy of any individual. The labor organization may use money from these sources to prepare notices and informational statements of facts surrounding the issues but not the candidates. Provision is also made to allow for removing someone from office if the constitution and bylaws do not have an adequate provision for this.

Before the Secretary of Labor takes any action on a complaint by a union member that charges a violation of the election procedures, all of the internal remedies available to the complainant must have been exhausted, or, if he has not received a final decision within three months after invoking these remedies, he may also file a complaint. The Secretary of Labor then conducts an investigation and if he finds probable cause he may bring civil action against the labor organization to have the election declared invalid and to either direct the conduct of another election or to conduct a hearing to remove the officers. The court may also exercise its judgment as to what action may be necessary to preserve the assets of the labor organization.

SAFEGUARDS FOR UNION MEMBERS

Several safeguards were established for unions in Title V. The first of these is concerned with fiduciary responsibilities of officers in labor organizations. The language of the provision sets forth the trust relationship between the administrative element of the organization and the membership. When a member of the organization suspects that there has been a misappropriation of assets he can bring suit in a federal district court if, after a reasonable time, no action has been taken by the organization to rectify the situation or provide appropriate relief. Criminal penalties for violation are established that permit the imposition of a maximum fine of $10,000, a maximum prison sentence of five years, or both.

Title V makes it mandatory for all employees of a labor organization, or a trust in which the labor organization has an interest and who handle funds or other property, to be bonded if annual financial receipts are more than $5,000. The bond must be individual or schedule in form, will be fixed at the beginning of the fiscal year, and will be for an amount of no less than ten per cent of the amounts handled either by the individual or his predecessor for the preceding fiscal year but never for more than $500,000. If there was no predecessor the bond is to be no less than $1,000 in the case of a local union and $10,000 for all others. Again, criminal penalties can be imposed for violation not to exceed one year imprisonment and/or a $5,000 fine. Specific prohibitions are made against certain persons holding office or acting as a labor-relations consultant in this Title. Persons banned from acting in these capacities are those who are members of the Communist Party or those who have been convicted of certain kinds of crimes.[12] These persons are prohibited from serving in these positions for five years after leaving the membership of the Communist Party or for five years after conviction of a crime or release from prison. The prohibition can be lifted before the five-year period if citizenship rights are restored or the Federal Parole Board determines

[12] See Appendix X for a list of these crimes.

that the individual wishing to serve in either capacity would not be contrary to the intent of the Act.

The final inclusion in Title V amends a section of the Labor-Management Relations Act that has to do with employer payments to the representatives of their employees. The added language serves to tighten the kinds and methods of payments that are lawful and closes some of the loopholes in the earlier legislation.

MISCELLANEOUS PROVISIONS

Title VI contains several miscellaneous provisions, one of which gives the Secretary of Labor the power to conduct an investigation when he believes there has been, or it appears there will be, a violation of any of the provisions of the Act (except Title I, the Bill of Rights for union members), or amendments to other legislative enactments. In making his investigation he may inspect records and accounts, as well as question persons involved, in an effort to collect factual information.

This Title also declares extortionate picketing unlawful. Extortionate picketing is picketing to obtain payment from an employer against his wishes and which results in personal gain. There is a criminal penalty for violation of this provision up to a maximum of twenty years in prison, a $10,000 fine, or both. Prohibitions are also placed on labor organizations with respect to taking disciplinary action against members that would in any way violate the member's rights under the provisions of the Act. Threats of violence or violence to prevent or dissuade members from exercising their rights under the Act are also prohibited.

Amendments to the Labor-Management Relations Act

The legislation discussed in the preceding paragraphs represents new requirements of the Landrum-Griffin Act. The final Title of this statute is devoted to amendments to the Taft-Hartley Act and those portions of it that are amended portions of the Wagner Act.

THE NATIONAL LABOR RELATIONS BOARD

Modifications were made in the functions performed by the National Labor Relations Board. The authority of the Board was extended to permit the delegation of its power to regional directors, thereby permitting them to determine appropriate bargaining units and to rule on matters of representation. A provision was also included for filling a vacancy in the office of the general counsel. The President is authorized to appoint a person to act in that capacity for no more than forty days unless a nomination to fill the vacancy is before the Senate or the session of the Senate to which the nomination was submitted has adjourned.

"NO MAN'S LAND"

The Landrum-Griffin Act added a new subsection to Section 14 of the National Labor Relations Act. The purpose of this amendment was to clear up the problem that existed with respect to federal versus state jurisdiction when the National Labor Relations Board declined hearing a complaint. As we saw in *Joseph Garner* v. *Teamsters, Chauffeurs and Helpers Local 776* [13] and in *P. S. Guss* v. *Utah Labor Relations Board* [14] (Chapter Five), states could not assume jurisdiction when the National Labor Relations Board refused a case. This created the situation referred to as "no man's land." Section 14(c), in an effort to close this loophole, affirms the authority of the Board to decline jurisdiction when the effect of the dispute on commerce is not substantial enough to justify action by the Board. In October of 1958, the National Labor Relations Board established jurisdictional standards and the Landrum-Griffin Act states that these are to be retained as guidelines for declining jurisdiction. The standards are as follows:

1. Non-retail; $50,000 outflow or inflow, direct or indirect.
2. Office buildings; Gross revenue of $100,000 of which $25,000 is derived from organizations which meet any of the new standards.
3. Retail Concerns; $500,000 gross volume of business.
4. Instrumentalities, links, and channels of Interstate Commerce; $50,000 from interstate (or linkage) part of enterprise or from services performed for employers in commerce.
5. Public Utilities; $250,000 gross volume, or meet Standard 1 (non-retail).
6. Transit Systems; $250,000 gross volume. (Except taxicabs, as

[13] 346 U.S. 485 (1953).
[14] 353 U.S. 1 (1957).

to which the retail test, $500,000 gross volume of business, shall apply.)

    7. Newspapers and Communications Systems; Radio, television, telegraph, and telephone; $100,000 gross volume. Newspapers; $200,000 gross volume.

    8. National Defense; Substantial impact on national defense.

    9. Business in the Territories and District of Columbia; D. C. —Plenary Territories—standards apply.

    10. Associations; Regarded as a single employer.[15]

    11. Hotels and Motels; $500,000 gross revenue. (Excluded are permanent or residential hotels or motels, i.e., those as to which 75 percent of their guests remain one month or more.) [16]

In addition, the Landrum-Griffin Act declares that nothing shall prevent a state from then assuming the jurisdiction the Board has declined.

BOYCOTTS AND PICKETING

    Section 8 of the National Labor Relations Act as amended was subject to four additional amendments in the Landrum-Griffin Act. The first of these deals with strikes and boycotts. The Taft-Hartley Act had attempted to make secondary boycotts an unfair labor practice; however, the language of the legislation was such that when it was put to test in the courts several loopholes developed. These were identified by the Supreme Court in this way:

> . . . Since only inducement of "employees" was proscribed, direct inducement of a supervisor as the secondary employer by threats of labor trouble was not prohibited. Since only a "strike or a concerted refusal" was prohibited, pressure upon a single employee was not forbidden. Finally, railroads, airlines, and municipalities were not "employers" under the act and therefore inducement or encouragement of their employees was not unlawful. . . .[17]

[15] 23rd Annual Report of the National Labor Relations Board for the Fiscal Year ended June 30, 1959 (Washington: U.S. Government Printing Office, 1959), p. 8.

[16] This guideline was approved at a later date.

[17] *National Labor Relations Board* v. *Fruit and Vegetable Packers and Warehousemen,* Local 760, 377 U.S. 48 (1964).

The amendment changed the language in order to bring these elements under the coverage of the legislation and added additional qualifications by including a new subsection.

The second important amendment to Section 8(b) was the addition of Subsection 7 dealing with picketing. As we have seen in our discussion of *Thornhill* v. *State of Alabama,* picketing that is conducted peaceably is protected by the constitutional guarantee of freedom of speech.[18] The Landrum-Griffin amendment places statutory restrictions on peaceful picketing by explicitly stating that certain forms of recognition or organizational picketing are considered to be an unfair labor practice. The legislative language prohibits this form of picketing when the activity is threatened or takes place to force or require an employer to either recognize or bargain with a labor organization or to force or require employees to accept the union doing the picketing as their bargaining representative. The circumstances that must surround the picketing for it to be an unlawful activity are: when another labor organization has been lawfully recognized and the question of representation cannot be raised according to Section 9(c); when a period of twelve months has not elapsed since a valid election has been held; and when a petition for an election has not been filed within a thirty-day period after the picketing has started. The third provision is qualified in two respects—if a petition is filed the National Labor Relations Board will expedite the election and secondly, that these restrictions in no way prohibit picketing if the object is to truthfully advise the public:

> . . . that an employer does not employ members of, or have a contract with, a labor organization, unless an effect of such picketing is to induce any individual employed by any other person in the course of his employment, not to pick up, deliver or transport any goods or not to perform any services.[19]

The language of this amendment serves to strengthen restrictions on activities that produce a secondary effect even though the picketing itself is primary in nature.

"HOT CARGO"

"Hot-cargo" agreements receive special attention in the Landrum-Griffin amendments where it is made an unfair labor practice for both

[18] 310 U.S. 88 (1940).
[19] U.S., *Statutes at Large,* LXXIII, 523.

the employer and the union to be parties to an agreement in which the employer agrees to refuse to handle goods or do business with another employer. A proviso is added to this, however, that exempts the construction industry and the agreements made between an employer and a labor union with respect to subcontracting work done at the construction site. Furthermore, certain persons in the garment industry who are involved with parts of an integrated process of production are also exempt from this provision.

The building and construction industry is again singled out in the final amendment to Section 8 with respect to pre-hire contracts. It is explicitly stated here that it will not be considered an unfair labor practice for such an employer to make an agreement with a labor organization that represents workers he may or does employ which requires membership seven days after employment. Also, the agreement between the employer and the labor organization may require the employer to notify the labor organization of jobs that are available so that the latter may supply applicants. The agreement may also list job qualifications and priority provisions.

ECONOMIC STRIKERS

The final amendment in the Landrum-Griffin Act with which we are concerned deals with the voting eligibility of strikers. Prior to this amendment, those employees who were out on an economic strike and not eligible for reinstatement were not eligible to vote in representation elections. In amending this section the restriction is lifted and employees in this category are now permitted to vote if an election occurs within a period of twelve months from the beginning of the strike. This amendment was designed to prevent what had become known as "union busting." Prior to the enactment of this provision, employees who were on strike and had been replaced by the employer could not participate in an election for a representative. If such an election was held, it was then possible for the non-striking workers to vote "no union" and remove it as the worker representative.

Summary

This chapter, in presenting an analysis of the events related to the Labor-Management Reporting and Disclosure Act, pointed out several incidents that are of major import to labor-management relations in the United States. It was during this period that a degree of unity was attained within the labor movement itself when the AFL and CIO were successful in accomplishing a merger. This merger provided an organizational structure that would permit a more solidly coordinated effort and an atmosphere of singleness of purpose for the working men and women whose membership the federation represents. The investigations and hearings conducted by the Select Committee on Improper Activities in the Labor or Management Field not only revealed extensive evidence of corruption and improper practices on the part of some union officials, but the publicity these hearings enjoyed through the then relatively new mass medium of television undoubtedly had a large effect on public attitude and the pressures exerted for legislative action. The result was the Landrum-Griffin Act, of significance primarily because it marks the first successful effort by the government into the conduct of the internal affairs of unions.

EVALUATION OF THE LANDRUM-GRIFFIN ACT

In order to evaluate the Landrum-Griffin Act it is necessary to consider it in terms of its intended purpose. The declaration of purpose in the legislation itself was identified as protecting the rights of employees with respect to employers and labor organizations; providing protection against breaches of trust, corruption, low standards of responsibility and unethical conduct; and strengthening and perpetuating the policies set forth in the National Labor Relations Act. The Landrum-Griffin Act has attempted to do this by requiring reports from labor organizations and employers that disclose factual information about certain financial transactions and administrative practices and by establishing standards for instituting trusteeships and the conduct of elections for officers in labor organizations. In addition, the legislation explicitly identifies and states employee rights with respect to the employment relationship. It would be totally unrealistic to maintain that the legislation has been entirely effective in accomplishing the declared objectives. Nevertheless, it must be recognized that the law has gone a long way in effecting corrective action in many instances and the act also provides the necessary thrust to permit action to be taken in other instances. It should be recognized that no legislation is totally self-imposing or self-enforcing, but is ready to serve those it is designed to protect, if apathy and lethargy are overcome by positive action.

APPENDIX 10

The Labor-Management Reporting and Disclosure Act

PUBLIC LAW 86-257
86TH CONGRESS, S. 1555
SEPTEMBER 14, 1959

AN ACT

To provide for the reporting and disclosure of certain financial transactions and administrative practices of labor organizations and employers, to prevent abuses in the administration of trusteeships by labor organizations, to provide standards with respect to the election of officers of labor organizations, and for other purposes.

Be it enacted by the Senate and House of Representatives of the United States of America in Congress assembled,

SHORT TITLE

SECTION 1. This Act may be cited as the "Labor-Management Reporting and Disclosure Act of 1959".

DECLARATION OF FINDINGS, PURPOSES, AND POLICY

SEC. 2. (a) The Congress finds that, in the public interest, it continues to be the responsibility of the Federal Government to protect employees' rights to organize, choose their own representatives, bargain collectively, and otherwise engage in concerted activities for their mutual aid or protection; that the relations between employers and labor organizations and the millions of workers they represent have a substantial impact on the commerce of the Nation; and that in order to accomplish the objective of a free flow of commerce it is essential that labor organizations, employers, and their officials adhere to the highest standards of responsibility and ethical conduct in administering the affairs of their organizations, particularly as they affect labor-management relations.

(b) The Congress further finds, from recent investigations in the labor and management fields, that there have been a number of instances of breach of trust, corruption, disregard of the rights of individual employees, and other failures to observe high standards of responsibility and ethical conduct which require further and supplementary legislation that will afford necessary protection of the rights and interests of employees and the public generally as they relate to the activities of labor organizations, employers, labor relations consultants, and their officers and representatives.

(c) The Congress, therefore, further finds and declares that the enactment of this Act is necessary to eliminate or prevent improper practices on the part of labor organizations, employers, labor-relations consultants, and their officers and representatives which distort and defeat the policies of the Labor-Management Relations Act, 1947, as amended, and the Railway Labor Act, as amended, and have the tendency or necessary effect of burdening or obstructing commerce by (1) impairing the efficiency, safety, or operation of the instrumentalities of commerce; (2) occurring in the current of commerce; (3) materially affecting, restraining, or controlling the flow of raw materials or manufactured or processed goods into or from the channels of commerce, or the prices of such materials or goods in commerce; or (4) causing diminution of employment and wages in such volume as substantially to impair or disrupt the market for goods flowing into or from the channels of commerce.

DEFINITIONS

SEC. 3. For the purposes of titles I, II, III, IV, V (except section 505), and VI of this Act—

(a) "Commerce" means trade, traffic, commerce, transportation, transmission, or communication among the several States or between any State and any place outside thereof.

(b) "State" includes any State of the United States, the District of Columbia, Puerto Rico, the Virgin Islands, American Samoa, Guam, Wake Island, the Canal Zone, and Outer Continental Shelf lands defined in the Outer Continental Shelf Lands Act (43 U.S.C. 1331–1343).

(c) "Industry affecting commerce" means any activity, business, or industry in commerce or in which a labor dispute would hinder or obstruct commerce or the free flow of commerce and includes any activity or industry "affecting commerce" within the meaning of the Labor-Management Relations Act, 1947, as amended, or the Railway Labor Act, as amended.

(d) "Person" includes one or more individuals, labor organizations, partnerships, associations, corporations, legal representatives, mutual companies, joint-stock companies, trusts, unincorporated organizations, trustees, trustees in bankruptcy, or receivers.

(e) "Employer" means any employer or any group or association of employers engaged in an industry affecting commerce (1) which is, with respect to employees engaged in an industry affecting commerce, an employer within the meaning of any law of the United States relating to the employment of any employees or (2) which may deal with any labor organization concerning grievances, labor disputes, wages, rates of pay, hours of employment, or conditions of work, and includes any person acting directly or indirectly as an employer or as an agent of an employer in relation to an employee but does not include the United States or any corporation wholly owned by the Government of the United States or any State or political subdivision thereof.

(f) "Employee" means any individual employed by an employer, and includes any individual whose work has ceased as a consequence of, or in connection with, any current labor dispute or because of any unfair labor practice or because of exclusion or expulsion from a labor organization in any manner or for any reason inconsistent with the requirements of this Act.

(g) "Labor dispute" includes any controversy concerning terms, tenure, or conditions of employment, or concerning the association or representation of persons in negotiating, fixing, maintaining, changing, or seeking to arrange terms or conditions of employment, regardless of whether the disputants stand in the proximate relation of employer and employee.

(h) "Trusteeship" means any receivership, trusteeship, or other method of supervision or control whereby a labor organization suspends the autonomy otherwise available to a subordinate body under its constitution or by-laws.

(i) "Labor organization" means a labor organization engaged in an industry affecting commerce and includes any organization of any kind, any agency, or employee representation committee, group, association, or plan so engaged in which employees participate and which exists for the purpose, in whole or in part, of dealing with employers concerning grievances, labor disputes, wages, rates of pay, hours, or other terms or conditions of employment, and any conference, general committee, joint or system board, or joint council so engaged which is subordinate to a national or international labor organization, other than a State or local central body.

(j) A labor organization shall be deemed to be engaged in an industry affecting commerce if it—

(1) is the certified representative of employees under the provisions of the National Labor Relations Act, as amended, or the Railway Labor Act, as amended; or

(2) although not certified, is a national or international labor organization or a local labor organization recognized or acting as the representative of employees of an employer or employers engaged in an industry affecting commerce; or

(3) has chartered a local labor organization or subsidiary body which is representing or actively seeking to represent employees of employers within the meaning of paragraph (1) or (2); or

(4) has been chartered by a labor organization representing or actively seeking to represent employees within the meaning of paragraph (1) or (2) as the local or subordinate body through which such employees may enjoy membership or become affiliated with such labor organization; or

(5) is a conference, general committee, joint or system board, or joint council, subordinate to a national or international labor organization, which includes a labor organization engaged in an industry affecting commerce within the meaning of any of the preceding paragraphs of this subsection, other than a State or local central body.

(k) "Secret ballot" means the expression by ballot, voting machine, or otherwise, but in no event by proxy, of a choice with respect to any election or vote taken upon any matter, which is cast in such a manner that the person expressing such choice cannot be identified with the choice expressed.

(l) "Trust in which a labor organization is interested" means a trust or other fund or organization (1) which was created or established by a labor organization, or one or more of the trustees or one or more members of the governing body of which is selected or appointed by a labor organization, and (2) a primary purpose of which is to provide benefits for the members of such labor organization or their beneficiaries.

(m) "Labor relations consultant" means any person who, for compensation, advises or represents an employer, employer organization, or labor organization concerning employee organizing, concerted activities, or collective-bargaining activities.

(n) "Officer" means any constitutional officer, any person authorized to perform the functions of president, vice president, secretary, treasurer, or other executive functions of a labor organization, and any member of its executive board or similar governing body.

(o) "Member" or "member in good standing," when used in reference to a labor organization, includes any person who has fulfilled the requirements for membership in such organization, and who neither has voluntarily withdrawn from membership nor has been expelled or suspended from membership after appropriate proceedings consistent with lawful provisions of the constitution and bylaws of such organization.

(p) "Secretary" means the Secretary of Labor.

(q) "Officer, agent, shop steward, or other representative," when used with respect to a labor organization, includes elected officials and key administrative personnel, whether elected or appointed (such as business agents, heads of departments or major units, and organizers who exercise substantial independent authority), but does not include salaried nonsupervisory professional staff, stenographic, and service personnel.

(r) "District court of the United States" means a United States district court and a United States court of any place subject to the jurisdiction of the United States.

Title I
Bill of Rights of Members of Labor Organizations

BILL OF RIGHTS

SEC. 101. (a)(1) EQUAL RIGHTS.—Every member of a labor organization shall have equal rights and privileges within such organization to nominate candidates, to vote in elections or referendums of the labor organization, to attend membership meetings, and to participate in the deliberations and voting upon the business of such meetings, subject to reasonable rules and regulations in such organization's constitution and bylaws.

(2) FREEDOM OF SPEECH AND ASSEMBLY.—Every member of any labor organization shall have the right to meet and assemble freely with other members; and to express any views, arguments, or opinions; and to

express at meetings of the labor organization his views, upon candidates in an election of the labor organization or upon any business properly before the meeting, subject to the organization's established and reasonable rules pertaining to the conduct of meetings: *Provided,* That nothing herein shall be construed to impair the right of a labor organization to adopt and enforce reasonable rules as to the responsibility of every member toward the organization as an institution and to his refraining from conduct that would interfere with its performance of its legal or contractual obligations.

(3) DUES, INITIATION FEES, AND ASSESSMENTS.—Except in the case of a federation of national or international labor organizations, the rates of dues and initiation fees payable by members of any labor organization in effect on the date of enactment of this Act shall not be increased, and no general or special assessment shall be levied upon such members, except—

(A) in the case of a local labor organization, (i) by majority vote by secret ballot of the members in good standing voting at a general or special membership meeting, after reasonable notice of the intention to vote upon such question, or (ii) by majority vote of the members in good standing voting in a membership referendum conducted by secret ballot; or

(B) in the case of a labor organization, other than a local labor organization or a federation of national or international labor organizations, (i) by majority vote of the delegates voting at a regular convention, or at a special convention of such labor organization held upon not less than thirty days' written notice to the principal office of each local or constituent labor organization entitled to such notice, or (ii) by majority vote of the members in good standing of such labor organization voting in a membership referendum conducted by secret ballot, or (iii) by majority vote of the members of the executive board or similar governing body of such labor organization, pursuant to express authority contained in the constitution and bylaws of such labor organization: *Provided,* That such action on the part of the executive board or similar governing body shall be effective only until the next regular convention of such labor organization.

(4) PROTECTION OF THE RIGHT TO SUE.—No labor organization shall limit the right of any member thereof to institute an action in any court, or in a proceeding before any administrative agency, irrespective of whether or not the labor organization or its officers are named as defendants or respondents in such action or proceeding, or the right of any member of a labor organization to appear as a witness in any judicial, administrative, or legislative proceeding, or to petition any legislature or to communicate with any legislator: *Provided,* That any such member may be required to exhaust reasonable hearing procedures (but not to exceed a four-month lapse of time) within such organization, before instituting legal or administrative proceedings against such organizations or any officer thereof: *And provided further,* That no interested employer or employer association shall directly or indirectly finance, encourage, or participate in, except as a party, any such action, proceeding, appearance, or petition.

(5) SAFEGUARDS AGAINST IMPROPER DISCIPLINARY ACTION.
—No member of any labor organization may be fined, suspended, expelled,
or otherwise disciplined except for nonpayment of dues by such organization or by any officer thereof unless such member has been (A) served with
written specific charges; (B) given a reasonable time to prepare his defense;
(C) afforded a full and fair hearing.

(b) Any provision of the constitution and bylaws of any labor organization which is inconsistent with the provisions of this section shall be of no
force or effect.

CIVIL ENFORCEMENT

SEC. 102. Any person whose rights secured by the provisions of this title
have been infringed by any violation of this title may bring a civil action in
a district court of the United States for the district where the alleged violation occurred, or where the principal office of such labor organization is located.

RETENTION OF EXISTING RIGHTS

SEC. 103. Nothing contained in this title shall limit the rights and remedies of any member of a labor organization under any State or Federal law
or before any court or other tribunal, or under the constitution and bylaws
of any labor organization.

RIGHT TO COPIES OF COLLECTIVE-BARGAINING AGREEMENTS

SEC. 104. It shall be the duty of the secretary or corresponding principal
officer of each labor organization, in the case of a local labor organization,
to forward a copy of each collective-bargaining agreement made by such
labor organization with any employer to any employee who requests such a
copy and whose rights as such employee are directly affected by such
agreement, and in the case of a labor organization other than a local labor
organization, to forward a copy of any such agreement to each constituent
unit which has members directly affected by such agreement; and such officer shall maintain at the principal office of the labor organization of which
he is an officer copies of any such agreement made or received by such
labor organization, which copies shall be available for inspection by any
member or by any employee whose rights are affected by such agreement.
The provisions of section 210 shall be applicable in the enforcement of this
section.

INFORMATION AS TO ACT

SEC. 105. Every labor organization shall inform its members concerning
the provisions of this Act.

Title II
Reporting by Labor Organizations, Officers and Employees of Labor Organizations, and Employers

REPORT OF LABOR ORGANIZATIONS

Sec. 201. (a) Every labor organization shall adopt a constitution and bylaws and shall file a copy thereof with the Secretary, together with a report, signed by its president and secretary or corresponding principal officers, containing the following information—

(1) the name of the labor organization, its mailing address, and any other address at which it maintains its principal office or at which it keeps the records referred to in this title;

(2) the name and title of each of its officers;

(3) the initiation fee or fees required from a new or transferred member and fees for work permits required by the reporting labor organization;

(4) the regular dues or fees or other periodic payments required to remain a member of the reporting labor organization; and

(5) detailed statements, or references to specific provisions of documents filed under this subsection which contain such statements, showing the provision made and procedures followed with respect to each of the following: (A) qualifications for or restrictions on membership, (B) levying of assessments, (C) participation in insurance or other benefit plans, (D) authorization for disbursement of funds of the labor organization, (E) audit of financial transactions of the labor organization, (F) the calling of regular and special meetings, (G) the selection of officers and stewards and of any representatives to other bodies composed of labor organizations' representatives, with a specific statement of the manner in which each officer was elected, appointed, or otherwise selected, (H) discipline or removal of officers or agents for breaches of their trust, (I) imposition of fines, suspensions, and expulsions of members, including the grounds for such action and any provision made for notice, hearing, judgment on the evidence, and appeal procedures, (J) authorization for bargaining demands, (K) ratification of contract terms, (L) authorization for strikes, and (M) issuance of work permits. Any change in the information required by this subsection shall be reported to the Secretary at the time the reporting labor organization files with the Secretary the annual financial report required by subsection (b).

(b) Every labor organization shall file annually with the Secretary a financial report signed by its president and treasurer or corresponding principal officers containing the following information in such detail as may be necessary accurately to disclose its financial condition and operations for its preceding fiscal year—

(1) assets and liabilities at the beginning and end of the fiscal year;

(2) receipts of any kind and the sources thereof;

(3) salary, allowances, and other direct or indirect disbursements, (in-

cluding reimbursed expenses) to each officer and also to each employee who, during such fiscal year, received more than $10,000 in the aggregate from such labor organization and any other labor organization affiliated with it or with which it is affiliated, or which is affiliated with the same national or international labor organization;

(4) direct and indirect loans made to any officer, employee, or member, which aggregated more than $250 during the fiscal year, together with a statement of the purpose, security, if any, and arrangements for repayment;

(5) direct and indirect loans to any business enterprise, together with a statement of the purpose, security, if any, and arrangements for repayment; and

(6) other disbursements made by it including the purposes thereof; all in such categories as the Secretary may prescribe.

(c) Every labor organization required to submit a report under this title shall make available the information required to be contained in such report to all of its members, and every such labor organization and its officers shall be under a duty enforceable at the suit of any member of such organization in any State court of competent jurisdiction or in the district court of the United States for the district in which such labor organization maintains its principal office, to permit such member for just cause to examine any books, records, and accounts necessary to verify such report. The court in such action may, in its discretion, in addition to any judgment awarded to the plaintiff or plaintiffs, allow a reasonable attorney's fee to be paid by the defendant, and costs of the action.

(d) Subsections (f), (g), and (h) of section 9 of the National Labor Relations Act, as amended, are hereby repealed.

(e) Clause (i) of section 8(a)(3) of the National Labor Relations Act, as amended, is amended by striking out the following: "and has at the time the agreement was made or within the preceding twelve months received from the Board a notice of compliance with sections 9(f), (g), (h)."

REPORT OF OFFICERS AND EMPLOYEES OF LABOR ORGANIZATIONS

SEC. 202. (a) Every officer of a labor organization and every employee of a labor organization (other than an employee performing exclusively clerical or custodial services) shall file with the Secretary a signed report listing and describing for his preceding fiscal year—

(1) any stock, bond, security, or other interest, legal or equitable, which he or his spouse or minor child directly or indirectly held in, and any income or any other benefit with monetary value (including reimbursed expenses) which he or his spouse or minor child derived directly or indirectly from, an employer whose employees such labor organization represents or is actively seeking to represent, except payments and other benefits received as a bona fide employee or such employer;

(2) any transaction in which he or his spouse or minor child engaged, directly or indirectly, involving any stock, bond, security, or loan to or from, or other legal or equitable interest in the business of an employer

whose employees such labor organization represents or is actively seeking to represent;

(3) any stock, bond, security, or other interest, legal or equitable, which he or his spouse or minor child directly or indirectly held in, and any income or any other benefit with monetary value (including reimbursed expenses) which he or his spouse or minor child directly or indirectly derived from, selling or leasing to, or otherwise dealing with, the business of an employer whose employees such labor organization represents or is actively seeking to represent;

(4) any stock, bond, security, or other interest, legal or equitable, which he or his spouse or minor child directly or indirectly held in, and any income or any other benefit with monetary value (including reimbursed expenses) which he or his spouse or minor child directly or indirectly derived from, a business any part of which consists of buying from, or selling or leasing directly or indirectly to, or otherwise dealing with such labor organization;

(5) any direct or indirect business transaction or arrangement between him or his spouse or minor child and any employer whose employees his organization represents or is actively seeking to represent, except work performed and payments and benefits received as bona fide employee of such employer and except purchases and sales of goods or services in the regular course of business at prices generally available to any employee of such employer; and

(6) any payment of money or other thing of value (including reimbursed expenses) which he or his spouse or minor child received directly or indirectly from any employer or any person who acts as a labor relations consultant to an employer, except payments of the kinds referred to in section 302(c) of the Labor-Management Relations Act, 1947, as amended.

(b) The provisions of paragraphs (1), (2), (3), (4), and (5) of subsection (a) shall not be construed to require any such officer or employee to report his bona fide investments in securities traded on a securities exchange registered as a national securities exchange under the Securities Exchange Act of 1934, in shares in an investment company registered under the Investment Company Act of 1940, or in securities of a public utility holding company registered under the Public Utility Holding Company Act of 1935, or to report any income derived therefrom.

(c) Nothing contained in this section shall be construed to require any officer or employee of a labor organization to file a report under subsection (a) unless he or his spouse or minor child holds or has held an interest, has received income or any other benefit with monetary value or a loan, or has engaged in a transaction described therein.

REPORT OF EMPLOYERS

SEC. 203. (a) Every employer who in any fiscal year made—

(1) any payment or loan, direct or indirect, of money or other thing of value (including reimbursed expenses), or any promise or agreement there-

for, to any labor organization or officer, agent, shop steward, or other representative of a labor organization, or employee of any labor organization, except (A) payments or loans made by any national or State bank, credit union, insurance company, savings and loan association or other credit institution and (B) payments of the kind referred to in section 302(c) of the Labor-Management Relations Act, 1947, as amended;

(2) any payment (including reimbursed expenses) to any of his employees, or any group or committee of such employees, for the purpose of causing such employee or group or committee of employees to persuade other employees to exercise or not to exercise, or as the manner of exercising, the right to organize and bargain collectively through representatives of their own choosing unless such payments were contemporaneously or previously disclosed to such other employees;

(3) any expenditure, during the fiscal year, where an object thereof, directly or indirectly, is to interfere with, restrain, or coerce employees in the exercise of the right to organize and bargain collectively through representatives of their own choosing, or is to obtain information concerning the activities of employees or a labor organization in connection with a labor dispute involving such employer, except for use solely in conjunction with an administrative or arbitral proceeding or a criminal or civil judicial proceeding;

(4) any agreement or arrangement with a labor relations consultant or other independent contractor or organization pursuant to which such person undertakes activities where an object thereof, directly or indirectly, is to persuade employees to exercise or not to exercise, or persuade employees as to the manner of exercising, the right to organize and bargain collectively through representatives of their own choosing, or undertakes to supply such employer with information concerning the activities of employees or a labor organization in connection with a labor dispute involving such employer, except information for use solely in conjunction with an administrative or arbitral proceeding or a criminal or civil judicial proceeding; or

(5) any payment (including reimbursed expenses) pursuant to an agreement or arrangement described in subdivision (4);
shall file with the Secretary a report, in a form prescribed by him, signed by its president and treasurer or corresponding principal officers showing in detail the date and amount of each such payment, loan, promise, agreement, or arrangement and the name, address, and position, if any, in any firm or labor organization of the person to whom it was made and a full explanation of the circumstances of all such payments, including the terms of any agreement or understanding pursuant to which they were made.

(b) Every person who pursuant to any agreement or arrangement with an employer undertakes activities where an object thereof is, directly or indirectly—

(1) to persuade employees to exercise or not to exercise, or persuade employees as to the manner of exercising, the right to organize and bargain collectively through representatives of their own choosing; or

(2) to supply an employer with information concerning the activities of

employees of a labor organization in connection with a labor dispute involving such employer, except information for use solely in conjunction with an administrative or arbitral proceeding or a criminal or civil judicial proceeding;

shall file within thirty days after entering into such agreement or arrangement a report with the Secretary, signed by its president and treasurer or corresponding principal officers, containing the name under which such person is engaged in doing business and the address of its principal office, and a detailed statement of the terms and conditions of such agreement or arrangement. Every such person shall file annually, with respect to each fiscal year during which payments were made as a result of such an agreement or arrangement, a report with the Secretary, signed by its president and treasurer or corresponding principal officers, containing a statement (A) of its receipts of any kind from employers on account of labor relations advice or services, designating the sources thereof, and (B) of its disbursements of any kind, in connection with such services and the purposes thereof. In each such case such information shall be set forth in such categories as the Secretary may prescribe.

(c) Nothing in this section shall be construed to require any employer or other person to file a report covering the services of such person by reason of his giving or agreeing to give advice to such employer or representing or agreeing to represent such employer before any court, administrative agency, or tribunal of arbitration or engaging or agreeing to engage in collective bargaining on behalf of such employer with respect to wages, hours, or other terms or conditions of employment or the negotiation of an agreement or any question arising thereunder.

(d) Nothing contained in this section shall be construed to require an employer to file a report under subsection (a) unless he has made an expenditure, payment, loan, agreement, or arrangement of the kind described therein. Nothing contained in this section shall be construed to require any other person to file a report under subsection (b) unless he was a party to an agreement or arrangement of the kind described therein.

(e) Nothing contained in this section shall be construed to require any regular officer, supervisor, or employee of an employer to file a report in connection with services rendered to such employer nor shall any employer be required to file a report covering expenditures made to any regular officer, supervisor, or employee of an employer as compensation for service as a regular officer, supervisor, or employee of such employer.

(f) Nothing contained in this section shall be construed as an amendment to, or modification of the rights protected by, section 8(c) of the National Labor Relations Act, as amended.

(g) The term "interfere with, restrain, or coerce" as used in this section means interference, restraint, and coercion which, if done with respect to the exercise of rights guaranteed in section 7 of the National Labor Relations Act, as amended, would, under section 8(a) of such Act, constitute an unfair labor practice.

ATTORNEY-CLIENT COMMUNICATIONS EXEMPTED

SEC. 204. Nothing contained in this Act shall be construed to require an attorney who is a member in good standing of the bar of any State, to include in any report required to be filed pursuant to the provisions of this Act any information which was lawfully communicated to such attorney by any of his clients in the course of a legitmate attorney-client relationship.

REPORTS MADE PUBLIC INFORMATION

Sec. 205.(a) The contents of the reports and documents filed with the Secretary pursuant to sections 201, 202, and 203 shall be public information, and the Secretary may publish any information and data which he obtains pursuant to the provisions of this title. The Secretary may use the information and data for statistical and research purposes, and compile and publish such studies, analyses, reports, and surveys based thereon as he may deem appropriate.

(b) The Secretary shall by regulation make reasonable provision for the inspection and examination, on the request of any person, of the information and data contained in any report or other document filed with him pursuant to section 201, 202, or 203.

(c) The Secretary shall by regulation provide for the furnishing by the Department of Labor of copies of reports or other documents filed with the Secretary pursuant to this title, upon payment of a charge based upon the cost of service. The Secretary shall make available without payment of a charge, or require any person to furnish, to such State agency as is designated by law or by the Governor of the State, copies of any reports and documents filed by such person with the Secretary pursuant to section 201, 202, or 203, or of information and data contained therein. No person shall be required by reason of any law of any State to furnish to any officer or agency of such State any information included in a report filed by such person with the Secretary pursuant to the provisions of this title, if a copy of such report, or of the portion thereof containing such information, is furnished to such officer or agency. All moneys received in payment of such charges fixed by the Secretary pursuant to this subsection shall be deposited in the general fund of the Treasury.

RETENTION OF RECORDS

SEC. 207. (a) Each labor organization shall file the initial report required under section 201(a) within ninety days after the date on which it first becomes subject to this Act.

(b) Each person required to file a report under section 201(b), 202, 203(a), or the second sentence of 203(b) shall file such report within ninety days after the end of each of its fiscal years; except that where such person is subject to section 201(b), 202, 203(a), or the second sentence of 203(b), as the case may be, for only a portion of such a fiscal year (because the date of enactment of this Act occurs during such person's fiscal year or such person becomes subject to this Act during its fiscal year) such person may consider that portion as the entire fiscal year in making such report.

RULES AND REGULATIONS

Sec. 208. The Secretary shall have authority to issue, amend, and rescind rules and regulations prescribing the form and publication of reports required to be filed under this title and such other reasonable rules and regulations (including rules prescribing reports concerning trusts in which a labor organization is interested) as he may find necessary to prevent the circumvention or evasion of such reporting requirements. In exercising his power under this section the Secretary shall prescribe by general rule simplified reports for labor organizations or employers for whom he finds that by virtue of their size a detailed report would be unduly burdensome, but the Secretary may revoke such provision for simplified forms of any labor organization or employer if he determines, after such investigation as he deems proper and due notice and opportunity for a hearing, that the purposes of this section would be served thereby.

CRIMINAL PROVISIONS

SEC. 209. (a) Any person who willfully violates this title shall be fined not more than $10,000 or imprisoned for not more than one year, or both.

(b) Any person who makes a false statement or representation of a material fact, knowing it to be false, or who knowingly fails to disclose a material fact, in any document, report, or other information required under the provisions of this title shall be fined not more than $10,000 or imprisoned for not more than one year, or both.

(c) Any person who willfully makes a false entry in or willfully conceals, withholds, or destroys any books, records, reports, of statements required to be kept by any provision of this title shall be fined not more than $10,000 or imprisoned for not more than one year, or both.

(d) Each individual required to sign reports under sections 201 and 203 shall be personally responsible for the filing of such reports and for any statement contained therein which he knows to be false.

CIVIL ENFORCEMENT

SEC. 210. Whenever it shall appear that any person has violated or is about to violate any of the provisions of this title, the Secretary may bring a civil action for such relief (including injunctions) as may be appropriate. Any such action may be brought in the district court of the United States where the violation occurred or, at the option of the parties, in the United States District Court for the District of Columbia.

TITLE III
TRUSTEESHIPS

REPORTS

SEC. 301. (a) Every labor organization which has or assumes trusteeship over any subordinate labor organization shall file with the Secretary within thirty days after the date of the enactment of this Act or the imposition of any such trusteeship, and semiannually thereafter, a report, signed by its president and treasurer or corresponding principal officers, as well as by the trustees of such subordinate labor organization, containing the following information: (1) the name and address of the subordinate organization; (2) the date of establishing the trusteeship; (3) a detailed statement of the reason or reasons for establishing or continuing the trusteeship; and (4) the nature and extent of participation by the membership of the subordinate organization in the selection of delegates to represent such organization in regular or special conventions or other policy-determining bodies and in the election of officers of the labor organization which has assumed trusteeship over such subordinate organization. The initial report shall also include a full and complete account of the financial condition of such subordinate organization as of the time trusteeship was assumed over it. During the continuance of a trusteeship the labor organization which has assumed trusteeship over a subordinate labor organization shall file on behalf of the subordinate labor organization the annual financial report required by section 201(b) signed by the president and treasurer or corresponding principal officers of the labor organization which has assumed such trusteeship and the trustees of the subordinate labor organization.

(b) The provisions of section 201(c), 205, 206, 208, and 210 shall be applicable to reports filed under this title.

(c) Any person who willfully violates this section shall be fined not more than $10,000 or imprisoned for not more than one year, or both.

(d) Any person who makes a false statement or representation of a material fact, knowing it to be false, or who knowingly fails to disclose a material fact, in any report required under the provisions of this section or willfully makes any false entry in or willfully withholds, conceals, or destroys any documents, books, records, reports, or statements upon which such report is based, shall be fined not more than $10,000 or imprisoned for not more than one year, or both.

(e) Each individual required to sign a report under this section shall be personally responsible for the filing of such report and for any statement contained therein which he knows to be false.

PURPOSES FOR WHICH A TRUSTEESHIP MAY BE ESTABLISHED

SEC. 302. Trusteeships shall be established and administered by a labor organization over a subordinate body only in accordance with the constitution and bylaws of the organization which has assumed trusteeship over the subordinate body and for the purpose of correcting corruption or financial malpractice, assuring the performance of collective-bargaining agreements or other duties of a bargaining representative, restoring democratic procedures, or otherwise carrying out the legitimate objects of such labor organization.

UNLAWFUL ACTS RELATING TO LABOR ORGANIZATION UNDER TRUSTEESHIP

SEC. 303. (a) During any period when a subordinate body of a labor organization is in trusteeship, it shall be unlawful (1) to count the vote of delegates from such body in any convention or election of officers of the labor organization unless the delegates have been chosen by secret ballot in an election in which all the members in good standing of such subordinate body were eligible to participate, or (2) to transfer to such organization any current receipts or other funds of the subordinate body except the normal per capita tax and assessments payable by subordinate bodies not in trusteeship: *Provided,* That nothing herein contained shall prevent the distribution of the assets of a labor organization in accordance with its constitution and bylaws upon the bona fide dissolution thereof.

(b) Any person who willfully violates this section shall be fined not more than $10,000 or imprisoned for not more than one year, or both.

ENFORCEMENT

SEC. 304. (a) Upon the written complaint of any member or subordinate body of a labor organization alleging that such organization has violated the provisions of this title (except section 301) the Secretary shall investigate the complaint and if the Secretary finds probable cause to believe that such violation has occurred and has not been remedied he shall, without disclosing the identity of the complainant, bring a civil action in any district court of the United States having jurisdiction of the labor organization for such relief (including injunctions) as may be appropriate. Any member of subordinate body of a labor organization affected by any violation of this title (except section 301) may bring a civil action in any district court of the United States having jurisdiction of the labor organization for such relief (including injunctions) as may be appropriate.

(b) For the purpose of actions under this section, district courts of the United States shall be deemed to have jurisdiction of a labor organization (1) in the district in which the principal office of such labor organization is located, or (2) in any district in which its duly authorized officers or agents are engaged in conducting the affairs of the trusteeship.

(c) In any proceeding pursuant to this section a trusteeship established by a labor organization in conformity with the procedural requirements of its constitution and bylaws and authorized or ratified after a fair hearing either before the executive board or before such other body as may be provided in accordance with its constitution or bylaws shall be presumed valid for a period of eighteen months from the date of its establishment and shall not be subject to attack during such period except upon clear and convincing proof that the trusteeship was not established or maintained in good faith for a purpose allowable under section 302. After the expiration of eighteen months the trusteeship shall be presumed invalid in any such proceeding and its discontinuance shall be decreed unless the labor organization shall show by clear and convincing proof that the continuation of the trusteeship is necessary for a purpose allowable under section 302. In the latter event the court may dismiss the complaint or retain jurisdiction of the cause on such conditions and for such period as it deems appropriate.

REPORT TO CONGRESS

SEC. 305. The Secretary shall submit to the Congress at the expiration of three years from the date of enactment of this Act a report upon the operation of this title.

COMPLAINT BY SECRETARY

SEC. 306. The rights and remedies provided by this title shall be in addition to any and all other rights and remedies at law or in equity: *Provided,* That upon the filing of a complaint by the Secretary the jurisdiction of the district court over such trusteeship shall be exclusive and the final judgment shall be res judicata.

TITLE IV
ELECTIONS

TERMS OF OFFICE; ELECTION PROCEDURES

SEC. 401. (a) Every national or international labor organization, except a federation of national or international labor organizations, shall elect its officers not less often than once every five years either by secret ballot among the members in good standing or at a convention of delegates chosen by secret ballot.

(b) Every local labor organization shall elect its officers not less often than once every three years by secret ballot among the members in good standing.

(c) Every national or international labor organization, except a federation of national or international labor organizations, and every local labor organization, and its officers, shall be under a duty, enforceable at the suit of any bona fide candidate for office in such labor organization in the district court of the United States in which such labor organization maintains its principal office, to comply with all reasonable requests of any candidate to distribute by mail or otherwise at the candidate's expense campaign literature in aid of such person's candidacy to all members in good standing of such labor organization and to refrain from discrimination in favor of or against any candidate with respect to the use of lists of members, and whenever such labor organizations or its officers authorize the distribution by mail or otherwise to members of campaign literature on behalf of any candidate or of the labor organization itself with reference to such election, similar distribution at the request of any other bona fide candidate shall be made by such labor organization and its officers, with equal treatment as to the expense of such distribution. Every bona fide candidate shall have the right, once within 30 days prior to an election of a labor organization in which he is a candidate, to inspect a list containing the names and last known addresses of all members of the labor organization who are subject to a collective-bargaining agreement requiring membership therein as a condition of employment, which list shall be maintained and kept at the principal office of such labor organization by a designated official thereof. Adequate safeguards to insure a fair election shall be provided, including the right of any candidate to have an observer at the polls and at the counting of the ballots.

(d) Officers of intermediate bodies, such as general committees, system boards, joint boards, or joint councils, shall be elected not less often than once every four years by secret ballot among the members in good standing or by labor organization officers representative of such members who have been elected by secret ballot.

(e) In any election required by this section which is to be held by secret ballot a reasonable opportunity shall be given for the nomination of candidates and every member in good standing shall be eligible to be a candidate and to hold office (subject to section 504 and to reasonable qualifications uniformly imposed) and shall have the right to vote for or otherwise support the candidate or candidates of his choice, without being subject to penalty, discipline, or improper interference or reprisal of any kind by such organization or any member thereof. Not less than fifteen days prior to the election notice thereof shall be mailed to each member at his last known home address. Each member in good standing shall be entitled to one vote. No member whose dues have been withheld by his employer for payment to such organization pursuant to his voluntary authorization provided for in a collective-bargaining agreement shall be declared ineligible to vote or be a candidate for office in such organization by reason of alleged delay or default in the payment of dues. The votes cast by members of each local labor organization shall be counted, and the results published, separately. The election shall be conducted in accordance with the constitution and bylaws of such organization insofar as they are not inconsistent with the provisions of this title.

(f) When officers are chosen by a convention of delegates elected by secret ballot, the convention shall be conducted in accordance with the constitution and bylaws of the labor organization insofar as they are not inconsistent with the provisions of this title. The officials designated in the constitution and bylaws or the secretary, if no other is designated, shall preserve for one year the credentials of the delegates and all minutes and other records of the convention pertaining to the election of officers.

(g) No moneys received by any labor organization by way of dues, assessment, or similar levy, and no moneys of an employer shall be contributed or applied to promote the candidacy of any person in an election subject to the provisions of this title. Such moneys of a labor organization may be utilized for notices, factual statements of issues not involving candidates, and other expenses necessary for the holding of an election.

(h) If the Secretary, upon application of any member of a local labor organization, finds after hearing in accordance with the Administrative Procedure Act that the constitution and bylaws of such labor organization do not provide an adequate procedure for the removal of an elected officer guilty of serious misconduct, such officer may be removed, for cause shown and after notice and hearing, by the members in good standing voting in a secret ballot conducted by the officers of such labor organization in accordance with its constitution and bylaws insofar as they are not inconsistent with the provisions of this title.

(i) The Secretary shall promulgate rules and regulations prescribing minimum standards and procedures for determining the adequacy of the removal procedures to which reference is made in subsection (h).

ENFORCEMENT

Sec. 402. (a) A member of a labor organization—

(1) who has exhausted the remedies available under the constitution and bylaws of such organization and of any parent body, or

(2) who has invoked such available remedies without obtaining a final decision within three calendar months after their invocation, may file a complaint with the Secretary within one calendar month thereafter alleging the violation of any provision of section 401 (including violation of the constitution and bylaws of the labor organization pertaining to the election and removal of officers). The challenged election shall be presumed valid pending a final decision thereon (as hereinafter provided) and in the interim the affairs of the organization shall be conducted by the officers elected or in such other manner as its constitution and bylaws may provide.

(b) The Secretary shall investigate such complaint and, if he finds probable cause to believe that a violation of this title has occurred and has not been remedied, he shall, within sixty days after the filing of such complaint, bring a civil action against the labor organization as an entity in the district court of the United States in which such labor organization maintains its principal office to set aside the invalid election, if any, and to direct the conduct of an election or hearing and vote upon the removal of officers under the supervision of the Secretary and in accordance with the provisions of this title and such rules and regulations as the Secretary may prescribe. The court shall have power to take such action as it deems proper to preserve the assets of the labor organization.

(c) If, upon a preponderance of the evidence after a trial upon the merits, the court finds—

(1) that an election has not been held within the time prescribed by section 401, or

(2) that the violation of section 401 may have affected the outcome of an election, the court shall declare the election, if any, to be void and direct the conduct of a new election under supervision of the Secretary and, so far as lawful and practicable, in conformity with the constitution and by-laws of the labor organization. The Secretary shall promptly certify to the court the names of the persons elected, and the court shall thereupon enter a decree declaring such persons to be the officers of the labor organization. If the proceeding is for the removal of officers pursuant to subsection (h) of section 401, the Secretary shall certify the results of the vote and the court shall enter a decree declaring whether such persons have been removed as officers of the labor organization.

(d) An order directing an election, dismissing a complaint, or designating elected officers of a labor organization shall be appealable in the same manner as the final judgment in a civil action, but an order directing an election shall not be stayed pending appeal.

APPLICATION OF OTHER LAWS

SEC. 403. No labor organization shall be required by law to conduct elections of officers with greater frequency or in a different form or manner than is required by its own constitution or bylaws, except as otherwise provided by this title. Existing rights and remedies to enforce the constitution and bylaws of a labor organization with respect to elections prior to the conduct thereof shall not be affected by the provisions of this title. The remedy provided by this title for challenging an election already conducted shall be exclusive.

EFFECTIVE DATE

SEC. 404. The provisions of this title shall become applicable—

(1) ninety days after the date of enactment of this Act in the case of a labor organization whose constitution and bylaws can lawfully be modified or amended by action of its constitutional officers or governing body, or

(2) where such modification can only be made by a constitutional convention of the labor organization, not later than the next constitutional convention of such labor organization after the date of enactment of this Act, or one year after such date, whichever is sooner. If no such convention is held within such one-year period, the executive board or similar governing body empowered to act for such labor organization between conventions is empowered to make such interim constitutional changes as are necessary to carry out the provisions of this title.

TITLE V
SAFEGUARDS FOR LABOR ORGANIZATIONS

FIDUCIARY RESPONSIBILITY OF OFFICERS OF LABOR ORGANIZATIONS

SEC. 501. (a) The officers, agents, shop stewards, and other representatives of a labor organization occupy positions of trust in relation to such organization and its members as a group. It is, therefore, the duty of each such person, taking into account the special problems and functions of a labor organization, to hold its money and property solely for the benefit of the organization and its members and to manage, invest, and expend the same in accordance with its constitution and bylaws and any resolutions of the governing bodies adopted thereunder, to refrain from dealing with such organization as an adverse party or in behalf of an adverse party in any matter connected with his duties and from holding or acquiring any pecuniary or personal interest which conflicts with the interests of such organization, and to account to the organization for any profit received by him in whatever capacity in connection with transactions conducted by him or under his direction on behalf of the organization. A general exculpatory provision in the constitution and bylaws of such a labor organization or a general exculpatory resolution of a governing body purporting to relieve any such person of liability for breach of the duties declared by this section shall be void as against public policy.

(b) When any officer, agent, shop steward, or representative of any labor organization is alleged to have violated the duties declared in subsection (a) and the labor organization or its governing board or officers refuse or fail to sue or recover damages or secure an accounting or other appropriate relief within a reasonable time after being requested to do so by any member of the labor organization, such member may sue such officer, agent, shop steward, or representative in any district court of the United States or in any State court of competent jurisdiction to recover damages or secure an accounting or other appropriate relief for the benefit of the labor organization. No such proceeding shall be brought except upon leave of the court obtained upon verified application and for good cause shown, which application may be made ex parte. The trial judge may allot a reasonable part of the recovery in any action under this subsection to pay the fees of counsel prosecuting the suit at the instance of the member of the labor organization and to compensate such member for any expenses necessarily paid or incurred by him in connection with the litigation.

(c) Any person who embezzles, steals, or unlawfully and willfully abstracts or converts to his own use, or the use of another, any of the moneys, funds, securities, property, or other assets of a labor organization of which he is an officer, or by which he is employed, directly or indirectly, shall be fined not more than $10,000 or imprisoned for not more than five years, or both.

BONDING

Sec. 502. (a) Every officer, agent, shop steward, or other representative or employee of any labor organization (other than a labor organization whose property and annual financial receipts do not exceed $5,000 in value), or of a trust in which a labor organization is interested, who handles funds or other property thereof shall be bonded for the faithful discharge of his duties. The bond of each such person shall be fixed at the beginning of the organization's fiscal year and shall be in an amount not less than 10 per centum of the funds handled by him and his predecessor or predecessors, if any, during the preceding fiscal year, but in no case more than $500,000. If the labor organization or the trust in which a labor organization is interested does not have a preceding fiscal year, the amount of the bond shall be, in the case of a local labor organization, not less than $1,000, and in the case of any other labor organization or of a trust in which a labor organization is interested, not less than $10,000. Such bonds shall be individual or schedule in form, and shall have a corporate surety company as surety thereon. Any person who is not covered by such bonds shall not be permitted to receive, handle, disburse, or otherwise exercise custody or control of the funds or other property of a labor organization or of a trust in which a labor organization is interested. No such bond shall be placed through an agent or broker or with a surety company in which any labor organization or any officer, agent, shop steward, or other representative of a labor organization has any direct or indirect interest. Such surety company shall be a corporate surety which holds a grant of authority from the Secretary of the Treasury under the Act of July 30, 1947 (6 U.S.C. 6-13), as an acceptable surety on Federal bonds.

(b) Any person who willfully violates this section shall be fined not more than $10,000 or imprisoned for not more than one year, or both.

MAKING OF LOANS; PAYMENT OF FINES

SEC. 503. (a) No labor organization shall make directly or indirectly any loan or loans to any officer or employee of such organization which results in a total indebtedness on the part of such officer or employee to the labor organization in excess of $2,000.

(b) No labor organization or employer shall directly or indirectly pay the fine of any officer or employee convicted of any willful violation of this Act.

(c) Any person who willfully violates this section shall be fined not more than $5,000 or imprisoned for not more than one year, or both.

PROHIBITION AGAINST CERTAIN PERSONS HOLDING OFFICE

SEC. 504. (a) No person who is or has been a member of the Communist Party or who has been convicted of, or served any part of a prison term resulting from his conviction of, robbery, bribery, extortion, embezzlement, grand larceny, burglary, arson, violation of narcotics laws, murder, rape, assault with intent to kill, assault which inflicts grievous bodily injury, or a violation of title II or III of this Act, or conspiracy to commit any such crimes, shall serve—

(1) as an officer, director, trustee, member of any executive board or similar governing body, business agent, manager, organizer, or other employee (other than as an employee performing exclusively clerical or custodial duties) of any labor organization, or

(2) as a labor relations consultant to a person engaged in an industry or

activity affecting commerce, or as an officer, director, agent, or employee (other than as an employee performing exclusively clerical or custodial duties) of any group or association of employers dealing with any labor organization, during or for five years after the termination of his membership in the Communist Party, or for five years after such conviction or after the end of such imprisonment, unless prior to the end of such five-year period, in the case of a person so convicted or imprisoned, (A) his citizenship rights, having been revoked as a result of such conviction, have been fully restored, or (B) the Board of Parole of the United States Department of Justice determines that such person's service in any capacity referred to in clause (1) or (2) would not be contrary to the purposes of this Act. Prior to making any such determination the Board shall hold an administrative hearing and shall give notice of such proceeding by certified mail to the State, county, and Federal prosecuting officials in the jurisdiction or jurisdictions in which such person was convicted. The Board's determination in any such proceeding shall be final. No labor organization or officer thereof shall knowingly permit any person to assume or hold any office or paid position in violation of this subsection.

(b) Any person who willfully violates this section shall be fined not more than $10,000 or imprisoned for not more than one year, or both.

(c) For the purposes of this section, any person shall be deemed to have been "convicted" and under the disability of "conviction" from the date of the judgment of the trial court or the date of the final sustaining of such judgment on appeal, whichever is the later event, regardless of whether such conviction occurred before or after the date of enactment of this Act.

AMENDMENT TO SECTION 302, LABOR-MANAGEMENT
RELATIONS ACT, 1947

SEC. 505. Subsections (a), (b), and (c) of section 302 of the Labor-Management Relations Act, 1947, as amended, are amended to read as follows:

"SEC. 302. (a) It shall be unlawful for any employer or association of employers or any person who acts as a labor-relations expert, adviser, or consultant to an employer or who acts in the interest of an employer to pay, lend, or deliver, or agree to pay, lend, or deliver, any money or other thing of value—

"(1) to any representative of any of his employees who are employed in an industry affecting commerce; or

"(2) to any labor organization, or any officer or employee thereof, which represents, seeks to represent, or would admit to membership, any of the employees of such employer who are employed in an industry affecting commerce; or

"(3) to any employee or group or committee of employees of such employer employed in an industry affecting commerce in excess of their normal compensation for the purpose of causing such employee or group or committee directly or indirectly to influence any other employees in the exercise of the right to organize and bargain collectively through representatives of their own choosing; or

"(4) to any officer or employee of a labor organization engaged in an industry affecting commerce with intent to influence him in respect to any of his actions, decision, or duties as a representative of employees or as such officer or employee of such labor organization.

"(b) (1) It shall be unlawful for any person to request, demand, receive, or accept, or agree to receive or accept, any payment, loan, or delivery of any money or other thing of value prohibited by subsection (a).

"(2) It shall be unlawful for any labor organization, or for any person acting as an officer, agent, representative, or employee of such labor organization, to demand or accept from the operator of any motor vehicle (as defined in part II of the Interstate Commerce Act) employed in the transportation of property in commerce, or the employer of any such operator, any money or other thing of value payable to such organization or to an officer, agent, representative or employee thereof as a fee or charge for the unloading, or in connection with the unloading, of the cargo of such vehicle: *Provided,* That nothing in this paragraph shall be construed to make unlawful any payment by an employer to any of his employees as compensation for their services as employees.

"(c) The provisions of this section shall not be applicable (1) in respect to any money or other thing of value payable by an employer to any of his employees whose established duties include acting openly for such employer in matters of labor relations or personnel administration or to any representative of his employees, or to any officer or employee of a labor organization, who is also an employee or former employee of such employer, as compensation for, or by reason of, his service as an employee of such employer; (2) with respect to the payment or delivery of any money or other thing of value in satisfaction of a judgment of any court or a decision or award of an arbitrator or impartial chairman or in compromise, adjustment, settlement, or release of any claim, complaint, grievance, or dispute in the absence of fraud or duress; (3) with respect to the sale or purchase of an article or commodity at the prevailing market price in the regular course of business; (4) with respect to money deducted from the wages of employees in payment of membership dues in a labor organization: *Provided,* That the employer has received from each employee, on whose account such deductions are made, a written assignment which shall not be irrevocable for a period of more than one year, or beyond the termination date of the applicable collective agreement, which ever occurs sooner; (5) with respect to money or other thing of value paid to a trust fund established by such representative, for the sole and exclusive benefit of the employees of such employer, and their families and dependents (or of such employees, families, and dependents jointly with the employees of other employers making similar payments, and their families and dependents): *Provided,* That (A) such payments are held in trust for the purpose of paying, either from principal or income or both, for the benefit of employees, their families and dependents, for medical or hospital care, pensions on retirement or death of employees, compensation for injuries or illness resulting from occupational activity or insurance to provide any of the foregoing, or unemployment benefits or life insurance, disability and sickness insurance, or accident insurance; (B) the detailed basis on which such payments are to be made is specified in a written agreement with the employer, and employees and employers are equally represented in the administration of such fund, together with such neutral persons as the representatives of the employers and the representatives of employees may agree upon and in the event the employer and employee groups deadlock on the administration of such fund and there are no neutral persons empowered to break such deadlock, such agreement provides that the two groups shall agree on an impartial umpire to decide such dispute, or in event of their failure to agree within a reasonable length of time, an impartial umpire to decide such dispute shall, on petition of either group, be appointed by the district court of the United States for the district where the trust fund has its principal office, and shall also contain provisions for an annual audit of the trust fund, a statement of the results of which shall be available for inspection by interested persons at the principal office of the trust fund and at such other places as may be designated in such written agreement; and (C) such payments as are intended to be used for the purpose of providing pensions or annuities for employees are made to separate trust which provides that the funds held therein cannot be used for any purpose other than paying such pensions or annuities; or (6) with respect to money or other thing of value paid by any employer to a trust fund established by such representative for the purpose of pooled vacation, holiday, severance or similar benefits, or defraying costs of apprenticeship or other training programs: *Provided,* That the requirements of clause (B) of the proviso to clause (5) of this subsection shall apply to such trust funds."

Title VI
Miscellaneous Provisions

INVESTIGATIONS

Sec. 601. (a) The Secretary shall have power when he believes it necessary in order to determine whether any person has violated or is about to violate any provision of this Act (except title I or amendments made by this Act to other statutes) to make an investigation and in connection therewith he may enter such places and inspect such records and accounts and question such persons as he may deem necessary to enable him to determine the facts relative thereto. The Secretary may report to interested persons or officials concerning the facts required to be shown in any report required by this Act and concerning the reasons for failure or refusal to file such a report or any other matter which he deems to be appropriate as a result of such an investigation.

(b) For the purpose of any investigation provided for in this Act, the provisions of sections 9 and 10 (relating to the attendance of witnesses and the production of books, papers, and documents) of the Federal Trade Commission Act of September 16, 1914, as amended (15 U.S.C.49, 50), are hereby made applicable to the jurisdiction, powers, and duties of the Secretary or any officers designated by him.

EXTORTIONATE PICKETING

SEC. 602. (a) It shall be unlawful to carry on picketing on or about the premises of any employer for the purpose of, or as part of any conspiracy or in furtherance of any plan or purpose for, the personal profit or enrichment of any individual (except a bona fide increase in wages or other employee benefits) by taking or obtaining any money or other thing of value from such employer against his will or with his consent.

(b) Any person who willfully violates this section shall be fined not more than $10,000 or imprisoned not more than twenty years, or both.

RETENTION OF RIGHTS UNDER OTHER FEDERAL AND STATE LAWS

SEC. 603. (a) Except as explicitly provided to the contrary, nothing in this Act shall reduce or limit the responsibilities of any labor organization or any officer, agent, shop steward, or other representative of a labor organization, or of any trust in which a labor organization is interested, under any other Federal law or under the laws of any State, and, except as explicitly provided to the contrary, nothing in this Act shall take away any right or bar any remedy to which members of a labor organization are entitled under such other Federal law or law of any State.

(b) Nothing contained in titles I, II, III, IV, V, or VI of this Act shall be construed to supersede or impair or otherwise affect the provisions of the Railway Labor Act, as amended, or any of the obligations, rights, benefits, privileges, or immunities of any carrier, employee, organization, representative, or person subject thereto; nor shall anything contained in said titles (except section 505) of this Act be construed to confer any rights, privileges, immunities, or defenses upon employers, or to impair or otherwise affect the rights of any person under the National Labor Relations Act, as amended.

EFFECT ON STATE LAWS

SEC. 604. Nothing in this Act shall be construed to impair or diminish the authority of any State to enact and enforce general criminal laws with respect to robbery, bribery, extortion, embezzlement, grand larceny, burglary, arson, violation of narcotics laws, murder, rape, assault with intent to kill, or assault which inflicts grievous bodily injury, or conspiracy to commit any of such crimes.

SERVICE OF PROCESS

SEC. 605. For the purposes of this Act, service of summons, subpena, or other legal process of a court of the United States upon an officer or agent of a labor organization in his capacity as such shall constitute service upon the labor organization.

ADMINISTRATIVE PROCEDURE ACT

Sec. 606. The provisions of the Administrative Procedure Act shall be applicable to the issuance, amendment, or rescission of any rules or regulations, or any adjudication, authorized or required pursuant to the provisions of this Act.

OTHER AGENCIES AND DEPARTMENTS

Sec. 607. In order to avoid unnecessary expense and duplication of functions among Government agencies, the Secretary may make such arrangements or agreements for cooperation or mutual assistance in the performance of his functions under this Act and the functions of any such agency as he may find to be practicable and consistent with law. The secretary may utilize the facilities or services of any department, agency, or establishment of the United States or of any State or political subdivision of a State, including the services of any of its employees, with the lawful consent of such department, agency, or establishment; and each department, agency, or establishment of the United States is authorized and directed to cooperate with the Secretary and, to the extent permitted by law, to provide such information and facilities as he may request for his assistance in the performance of his functions under this Act. The Attorney General or his representative shall receive from the Secretary for appropriate action such evidence developed in the performance of his functions under this Act as may be found to warrant consideration for criminal prosecution under the provisions of this Act or other Federal law.

CRIMINAL CONTEMPT

Sec. 608. No person shall be punished for any criminal contempt allegedly committed outside the immediate presence of the court in connection with any civil action prosecuted by the Secretary or any other person in any court of the United States under the provisions of this Act unless the facts constituting such criminal contempt are established by the verdict of the jury in a proceeding in the district court of the United States, which jury shall be chosen and empaneled in the manner prescribed by the law governing trial juries in criminal prosecutions in the district courts of the United States.

PROHIBITION ON CERTAIN DISCIPLINE BY LABOR ORGANIZATION

Sec. 609. It shall be unlawful for any labor organization, or any officer, agent, shop steward, or other representative of a labor organization, or any employee thereof to fine, suspend, expel, or otherwise discipline any of its members for exercising any right to which he is entitled under the provisions of this Act. The provisions of section 102 shall be applicable in the enforcement of this section.

DEPRIVATION OF RIGHTS UNDER ACT BY VIOLENCE

SEC. 610. It shall be unlawful for any person through the use of force or violence, or threat of the use of force or violence, to restrain, coerce, or intimidate, or attempt to restrain, coerce, or intimidate any member of a labor organization for the purpose of interfering with or preventing the exercise of any right to which he is entitled under the provisions of this Act. Any person who willfully violates this section shall be fined not more than $1,000 or imprisoned for not more than one year, or both.

SEPARABILITY PROVISIONS

SEC. 611. If any provision of this Act, or the application of such provision to any person or circumstances, shall be held invalid, the remainder of this Act or the application of such provision to persons or circumstances other than those as to which it is held invalid, shall not be affected thereby.

TITLE VII
AMENDMENTS TO THE LABOR-MANAGEMENT RELATIONS ACT, 1947, AS AMENDED

FEDERAL-STATE JURISDICTION

SEC. 701. (a) Section 14 of the National Labor Relations Act, as amended, is amended by adding at the end thereof the following new subsection:

"(c) (1) The Board, in its discretion, may, by rule of decision or by published rules adopted pursuant to the Administrative Procedure Act, decline to assert jurisdiction over any labor dispute involving any class or category of employers, where, in the opinion of the Board, the effect of such labor dispute on commerce is not sufficiently substantial to warrant the exercise of its jurisdiction: *Provided,* That the Board shall not decline to assert jurisdiction over any labor dispute over which it would assert jurisdiction under the standards prevailing upon August 1, 1959.

"(2) Nothing in this Act shall be deemed to prevent or bar any agency or the courts of any State or Territory (including the Commonwealth of Puerto Rico, Guam, and the Virgin Islands), from assuming and asserting jurisdiction over labor disputes over which the Board declines, pursuant to paragraph (1) of this subsection, to assert jurisdiction."

(b) Section 3(b) of such Act is amended to read as follows:

"(b) The Board is authorized to delegate to any group of three or more members any or all of the powers which it may itself exercise. The Board is also authorized to delegate to its regional directors its powers under section 9 to determine the unit appropriate for the purpose of collective bargaining, to investigate and provide for hearings, and determine whether a question of representation exists, and to direct an election or take a secret ballot under subsection (c) or (e) of section 9 and certify the results thereof, except that upon the filing of a request therefore with the Board by any interested person, the Board may review any action of a regional director delegated to him under this paragraph, but such a review shall not, unless specifically ordered by the Board, operate as a stay of any action taken by the regional director. A vacancy in the Board shall not impair the right of the remaining members to exercise all of the powers of the Board, and three members of the Board shall, at all times, constitute a quorum of the Board, except that two members shall constitute a quorum of any group designated pursuant to the first sentence hereof. The Board shall have an official seal which shall be judicially noticed."

ECONOMIC STRIKERS

SEC. 702. Section 9(c)(3) of the National Labor Relations Act, as amended, is amended by amending the second sentence thereof to read as follows: "Employees engaged in an economic strike who are not entitled to reinstatement shall be eligible to vote under such regulations as the Board shall find are consistent with the purposes and provisions of this Act in any election conducted within twelve months after the commencement of the strike."

VACANCY IN OFFICE OF GENERAL COUNSEL

SEC. 703. Section 3(d) of the National Labor Relations Act, as amended, is amended by adding after the period at the end thereof the following: "In case of a vacancy in the office of the General Counsel the President is authorized to designate the officer or employee who shall act as General Counsel during such vacancy, but no person or persons so designated shall so act (1) for more than forty days when the Congress is in session unless a nomination to fill such vacancy shall have been submitted to the Senate, or (2) after the adjournment sine die of the session of the Senate in which such nomination was submitted."

BOYCOTTS AND RECOGNITION PICKETING

SEC. 704. (a) Section 8(b)(4) of the National Labor Relations Act, as amended, is amended to read as follows:

"(4)(i) to engage in, or to induce or encourage any individual employed by any person engaged in commerce or in an industry affecting commerce to engage in, a strike or a refusal in the course of his employment to use, manufacture, process, transport, or otherwise handle or work on any goods, articles, materials, or commodities or to perform any services; or (ii) to threaten, coerce, or restrain any person engaged in commerce or in an industry, affecting commerce, where in either case an object thereof is—

"(A) forcing or requiring any employer or self-employed person to join any labor or employer organization or to enter into any agreement which is prohibited by section 8(e);

'(B) forcing or requiring any person to cease using, selling, handling, transporting, or otherwise dealing in the products of any other producer, processor, or manufacturer, or to cease doing business with any other person, or forcing or requiring any other employer to recognize or bargain with a labor organization as the representative of his employees unless such labor organization has been certified as the representative of such employees under the provisions of section 9: *Provided,* That nothing contained in this clause (B) shall be construed to make unlawful, where not otherwise unlawful, any primary strike or primary picketing;

"(C) forcing or requiring any employer to recognize or bargain with a particular labor organization as the representative of his employees if another labor organization has been certified as the representative of such employees under the provisions of section 9;

"(D) forcing or requiring any employer to assign particular work to employees in a particular labor organization or in a particular trade, craft, or class rather than to employees in another labor organization or in another trade, craft, or class, unless such employer is failing to conform to an order or certification of the Board determining the bargaining representative for employees performing such work: *Provided,* That nothing contained in this subsection (b) shall be construed to make unlawful a refusal by any person to enter upon the premises of any employer (other than his own employer), if the employees of such employer are engaged in a strike ratified or approved by a representative of such employees whom such employer is required to recognize under this Act: *Provided further,* That for the purposes of this paragraph (4) only, nothing contained in such paragraph shall be construed to prohibit publicity, other than picketing, for the purpose of truthfully advising the public, including consumers and members of a labor organization, that a product or products are produced by an employer with whom the labor organization has a primary dispute and are distributed by another employer, as long as such publicity does not have an effect of inducing any individual employed by any person other than the primary employer in the course of his employment to refuse to pick up, deliver, or transport any goods, or not to perform any services, at the establishment of the employer engaged in such distribution;"

(b) Section 8 of the National Labor Relations Act, as amended, is amended by adding at the end thereof the following new subsection:

"(e) It shall be an unfair labor practice for any labor organization and any employer to enter into any contract or agreement, express or implied, whereby such employer ceases or refrains or agrees to cease or refrain from handling, using, selling, transporting or otherwise dealing in any of the products of any other employer, or to cease doing business with any other person, and any contract or agreement entered into heretofore or hereafter containing such an agreement shall be to such extent unenforceable and void: *Provided,* That nothing in this subsection (e) shall apply to an agreement between a labor organization and an employer in the construction industry relating to the contracting or subcontracting of work to be done at the site of the construction, alteration, painting, or repair of a building, structure, or other work: *Provided further,* That for the purposes of this subsection (e) and section 8(b)(4)(B) the terms 'any employer,' 'any person engaged in commerce or an industry affecting commerce,' and 'any person' when used in relation to the terms 'any other producer, processor, or manufacturer,' 'any other employer,' or 'any other person' shall not include persons in the relation of a jobber, manufacturer, contractor, or subcontractor working on the goods or premises of the jobber or manufacturer or performing parts of an integrated process of production in the apparel and clothing industry: *Provided further*, That nothing in this Act shall prohibit the enforcement of any agreement which is within the foregoing exception."

(c) Section 8(b) of the National Labor Relations Act, as amended, is amended by striking out the word "and" at the end of paragraph (5), striking out the period at the end of paragraph (6), and inserting in lieu thereof a semicolon and the word "and," and adding a new paragraph as follows:

"(7) to picket or cause to be picketed, or threaten to picket, or cause to be picketed, any employer where an object thereof is forcing or requiring an employer to recognize or bargain with a labor organization as the representative of his employees, or forcing or requiring the employees of an employer to accept or select such labor organization as their collective-bargaining representative, unless such labor organization is currently certified as the representative of such employees:

"(A) where the employer has lawfully recognized in accordance with this Act any other labor organization and a question concerning representation may not appropriately be raised under section 9(c) of this Act,

"(B) where within the preceding twelve months a valid election under section 9(c) of this Act has been conducted, or

"(C) where such picketing has been conducted without a petition under section 9(c) being filed within a reasonable period of time not to exceed thirty days from the commencement of such picketing: *Provided*, That when such a petition has been filed the Board shall forthwith, without regard to the provisions of section 9(c)(1) or the absence of a showing of a substantial interest on the part of the labor organization, direct an election in such unit as the Board finds to be appropriate and shall certify the results thereof: *Provided further*, That nothing in this subparagraph (C) shall be construed to prohibit any picketing or other publicity for the purpose of truthfully advising the public (including consumers) that an employer does not employ members of, or have a contract with, a labor organization, unless an effect of such picketing is to induce any individual employed by any other person in the course of his employment, not to pick up, deliver or transport any goods or not to perform any services.

"Nothing in this paragraph (7) shall be construed to permit any act which would otherwise be an unfair labor practice under this section 8(b)."

(d) Section 10(1) of the National Labor Relations Act, as amended, is amended by adding after the words "section 8(b)," the words "or section 8(e) or section 8(b)(7)," and by striking out the period at the end of the third sentence and inserting in lieu thereof a colon and the following: "*Provided further*, That such officer or regional attorney shall not apply for any restraining order under section 8(b)(7) if a charge against the employer under section 8(a)(2) has been filed and after the preliminary investigation, he has reasonable cause to believe that such charge is true and that a complaint should issue."

(e) Section 303(a) of the Labor-Management Relations Act, 1947, is amended to read as follows:

"(a) It shall be unlawful, for the purpose of this section only, in an industry or activity affecting commerce, for any labor organization to engage in any activity or conduct defined as an unfair labor practice in section 8(b)(4) of the National Labor Relations Act, as amended."

BUILDING AND CONSTRUCTION INDUSTRY

SEC. 705. (a) Section 8 of the National Labor Relations Act, as amended by section 704(b) of this Act, is amended by adding at the end thereof the following new subsection:

"(f) It shall not be an unfair labor practice under subsections (a) and (b) of this section for an employer engaged primarily in the building and construction industry to make an agreement covering employees engaged (or who, upon their employment, will be engaged) in the building and construction industry with a labor organization of which building and construction employees are members (not established, maintained, or assisted by any action defined in section 8(a) of this Act as an unfair labor practice) because (1) the majority status of such labor organization has not been established under the provisions of section 9 of this Act prior to the making of such agreement, or (2) such agreement requires as a condition of employment, membership in such labor organization after the seventh day following the beginning of such employment or the effective date of the agreement, whichever is later, or (3) such agreement requires the employer to notify such labor organization of opportunities for employment with such employer, or gives such labor organization an opportunity to refer qualified applicants for such employment, or (4) such agreement specifies minimum training or experience qualifications for employment or provides for priority in opportunities for employment based upon length of service with such employer, in the industry or in the particular geographical area: *Provided,* That nothing in this subsection shall set aside the final proviso to section 8(a)(3) of this Act: *Provided further,* That any agreement which would be invalid, but for clause (1) of this subsection, shall not be a bar to a petition filed pursuant to section 9(c) or 9(e)."

(b) Nothing contained in the amendment made by subsection (a) shall be construed as authorizing the execution or application of agreements requiring membership in a labor organization as a condition of employment in any State or Territory in which such execution or application is prohibited by State or Territorial law.

PRIORITY IN CASE HANDLING

SEC. 706. Section 10 of the National Labor Relations Act, as amended, is amended by adding at the end thereof a new subsection as follows:

"(m) Whenever it is charged that any person has engaged in an unfair labor practice within the meaning of subsection (a)(3) or (b)(2) of section 8, such charge shall be given priority over all other cases except cases of like character in the office where it is filed or to which it is referred and cases given priority under subsection (1)."

EFFECTIVE DATE OF AMENDMENTS

SEC. 707. The amendments made by this title shall take effect sixty days after the date of the enactment of this Act and no provision of this title shall be deemed to make an unfair labor practice, any act which is performed prior to such effective date which did not constitute an unfair labor practice prior thereto.

Approved September 14, 1959.

11

UNION ACTIVITIES
AND COLLECTIVE
BARGAINING

The Landrum-Griffin Act and its amendments to the Taft-Hartley Act had a significant effect on the lawfulness of certain kinds of union activities and the climate in which collective bargaining takes place. In this chapter consideration will be given to the weapons of conflict that are used by unions and the scope of the collective bargaining process, including a look at the parties involved, bargaining units and strategies, and some typical contract considerations. Finally, we will consider the alternatives that exist for the parties when agreement cannot be reached.

Unions and Weapons of Conflict

The amendments in the Landrum-Griffin Act had a substantial effect on the weapons of conflict available to labor organizations. As we have seen, the basic techniques used to exert pressure on employers by labor organizations were picketing, strikes, boycotts, and, to a lesser degree, "hot-cargo" agreements. Let us look at each of these activities individually and ascertain the legality or illegality of each by an illustrative case.

STRIKES AND BOYCOTTING

In *National Labor Relations Board* v. *Servette, Inc.*,[1] a strike had been called by Local 848 of the Wholesale Delivery Drivers and Salesmen's Union against Servette, a wholesale distributor of specialty foods. The managers of food chains that handled merchandise supplied by Servette were approached by union representatives who asked that they cooperate by discontinuing to handle the products distributed by Servette. While making this request, the union representatives also indicated that handbills would be passed out in front of those stores that refused to cooperate. A complaint was filed which charged a violation of Section 8(b) i and ii of the National Labor Relations Act prohibiting certain kinds of strike and picketing activity. The complaint was dismissed by the National Labor Relations Board. The Court of Appeals set aside the order of the Board and the case came to the Supreme Court.

NATIONAL LABOR RELATIONS BOARD v. SERVETTE, INC.: 1964
(*377 U.S. 46*)

The Supreme Court of the United States, Mr. Justice Brennan delivering the opinion:
. . . The Court of Appeals correctly read the term "individual" in subsection (i) as including the supermarket managers, but it erred in holding that the Local's attempts to enlist the aid of the managers constituted inducement of the managers in violation of the subsection. The 1959 statute amended § 8(b)(4)(A) of the National Labor Relations Act, which made it unlawful to induce or encourage "the employees of any employer" to strike or engage in a "concerted" refusal to work. We defined the central thrust of that statute to be to forbid "a union to induce employees to strike against their employer when an object is to force him or another person to cease doing business with some third party." *Local 1976, Carpenters' Union* v. *Labor Board*, 357 US 93, 98. In the instant case, how-

[1] 377 U.S. 46 (1964).

ever, the Local, in asking the managers not to handle Servette items, was not attempting to induce or encourage them to cease performing their managerial duties in order to force their employers to cease doing business with Servette. Rather, the managers were asked to make a managerial decision which the Board found was within their authority to make. Such an appeal would not have been a violation of § 8(b)(4)(A) before 1959, and we think the legislative history of the 1959 amendments makes it clear that the amendments were not meant to render such an appeal an unfair labor practice.

The 1959 amendments were designed to close certain loopholes in the application of § 8(b)(4)(A) which had been exposed in Board and court decisions. Thus, it had been held that the term "the employees of any employer" limited the application of the statute to those within the statutory definition of "employees" and "employer." Section 2(2) of the National Labor Relations Act defines "employer" to exclude the federal and state governments and their agencies or subdivisions, nonprofit hospitals, and employers subject to the Railway Labor Act. 29 U.S.C. § 152(2). The definition of "employee" in § 2(3) excludes agricultural laborers, supervisors, and employees of an employer subject to the Railway Labor Act. 29 U.S.C. § 152(3). Furthermore, since the section proscribed only inducement to engage in a strike or "concerted" refusal to perform services, it had been held that it was violated only if the inducement was directed at two or more employees. To close these loopholes, subsection (i) substituted the phrase "any individual employed by any person" for "the employees of any employer," and deleted the word "concerted." The first change was designed to make the provision applicable to refusals by employees who were not technically "employees" within the statutory definitions, and the second change was intended to make clear that inducement directed to only one individual was proscribed. But these changes did not expand the type of conduct which § 8(b)(4)(A) condemned, that is, union pressures calculated to induce the employees of a secondary employer to withhold their services in order to force their employer to cease dealing with the primary employer.

Moreover, the division of § 8(b)(4) into subsections (i) and (ii) by the 1959 amendments has directed relevance to the issue presented by this case. It had been held that § 8(b)(4)(A) did not reach threats of labor trouble made to the secondary employer himself. Congress decided that such conduct should be made unlawful, but only when it amounted to conduct which "threaten[s],

coerce [s] or restrain [s] any person"; hence the addition of subsection (ii). The careful creation of separate standards differentiating
the treatment of appeals to the employees of the secondary employer not to perform their employment services, from appeals for
other ends which are attended by threats, coercion or restraint, argues conclusively against the interpretation of subsection (i) as
reaching the Local's appeals to the supermarket managers in this
case. If subsection (i), in addition to prohibiting inducement of employees to withhold employment services, also reaches an appeal
that the managers exercise their delegated authority by making a
business judgment to cease dealing with the primary employer,
subsection (ii) would be almost superfluous. Harmony between (i)
and (ii) is best achieved by construing subsection (i) to prohibit
inducement of the managers to withhold their services from their
employer, and subsection (ii) to condemn an attempt to induce
the exercise of discretion only if the inducement would "threaten,
coerce, or restrain" that exercise.

We turn finally to the question whether the proviso to amended
§ 8(b)(4) protected the Local's handbilling. The Court of Appeals,
following its decision in *Great Western Broadcasting Corp.* v.
Labor Board, 310 F2d 591 (C.A. 9th Cir), held that the proviso did
not protect the Local's conduct because, as a distributor, Servette
was not directly involved in the physical process of creating the
products, and thus "does not produce any products." The Board on
the other hand followed its ruling in *Lohman Sales Co.* 132 NLRB
901, that products "produced by an employer" included products
distributed, as here, by a wholesaler with whom the primary dispute exists. We agree with the Board. The proviso was the outgrowth of a profound Senate concern that the unions' freedom to
appeal to the public for support of their case be adequately safe-
guarded. We elaborated the history of the proviso in *Labor Board*
v. *Fruit & Vegetable Packers, Local 760,* post, p. 58, decided today.
It would fall far short of achieving this basic purpose if the proviso
applied only in situations where the union's labor dispute is with
the manufacturer or processor. Moreover, a primary target of the
1959 amendments was the secondary boycotts conducted by the
Teamsters Union, which ordinarily represents employees not of
manufacturers, but of motor carriers. There is nothing in the legislative history which suggests that the protection of the proviso
was intended to be any narrower in coverage than the prohibition
to which it is an exception, and we see no basis for attributing such
an incongruous purpose to Congress.

The term "produced" in other labor laws was not unfamiliar to Congress. Under the Fair Labor Standards Act, the term is defined as "produced, manufactured, mined, handled, or in any other manner worked on . . . ," 29 U.S.C. § 203(j), and has always been held to apply to the wholesale distribution of goods. The term "production" in the War Labor Disputes Act has been similarly applied to a general retail department and mail-order business. The Court of Appeals' restrictive reading of "producer" was prompted in part by the language of § 8(b)(4)(B), which names as a proscribed object of the conduct defined in subsections (i) and (ii) "forcing or requiring any person to cease . . . dealing in the products of any other *producer, processor,* or *manufacturer.*" (Italics supplied.) In its decision in *Great Western Broadcasting Corp.* v. *Labor Board*, supra, the Court of Appeals reasoned that since a "processor" and a "manufacturer" are engaged in the physical creation of goods, the word "producer" must be read as limited to one who performs similar functions. On the contrary, we think that "producer" must be given a broader reach, else it is rendered virtually superfluous.

Finally, the warnings that handbills would be distributed in front of noncooperating stores are not prohibited as "threats" with subsection (ii). The statutory protection for the distribution of handbills would be undermined if a threat to engage in protected conduct were not itself protected.

Reversed.

In another case, a fruit and vegetable packers union was on strike against warehousemen who sold apples to retail stores. A consumer boycott against the apples was instituted by the labor organization. Pickets were sent to the stores involved, but only after store managers were told that this was going to be done. The managers were also told that the purpose of the picketing was only to make an appeal to customers not to buy Washington State apples. Delivery entrances were not to be interfered with in any way, nor were the employees of the store. A complaint charging a violation of Section 8(b)(4) was issued and the National Labor Relations Board declared the union was guilty of an unfair labor practice. On appeal the order was set aside as the Court of Appeals maintained that in order to have a violation there must be an actual or likely substantial economic impact on the stores involved. The Supreme Court then vacated the judgment of the lower court and directed it to enter a judgment setting aside the order of the Board. In the opinion of the court, legislative history did not indicate that it had been the intent of Congress to place a ban on all peaceful picketing at secondary sites and particularly when the purpose was limited to boycotting only the primary employer's goods.[2] The Court distinguished between the primary nature of an activity that resulted in persuading customers not to buy a struck product, even though the site included the premises of a secondary employer and resulted in a decrease in purchases by customers of this secondary firm, and an activity that was directed at persuading the customers to cease from any trading with the secondary employer:

> . . . the latter stops buying the struck product, not because of a falling demand, but in response to pressure designed to inflict injury on his business generally. In such case, the union does more than merely follow the struck product; it creates a separate dispute with the secondary employer. . . . A violation of Sec. 8(b)(4)(ii)(B) would not be established, merely because respondents' picketing was effective to reduce Safeway's sales of Washington State apples, even if this led or might lead Safeway to drop the item as a poor seller.[3]

The "Notice to Managers" and the "Instructions to Pickets" which were distributed during the picketing in this case are included as Appendices 11 A and 11 B respectively so that the reader may see more clearly those things that are merely to "inform" or "publicize" rather than to "threaten," "coerce," or "restrain."

These two cases illustrate the extremely fine line that is drawn to distinguish between legal and illegal strike and boycott activity. It is of interest to note the criteria used by the court: legislative history, the legislation itself, congressional intent, established precedent, the basis of the lower court's decision, constitutional guarantees, and of course the facts unique to the issue at hand.

RECOGNITION OR ORGANIZATIONAL PICKETING

Picketing for the purpose of forcing or requiring an employer to recognize or bargain with a union was made unlawful under certain circumstances by the amendments to the National Labor Relations Act. This issue came before the National Labor Relations Board in 1961.[4] In this case the final order of the Board found that an unfair

[2] *National Labor Relations Board v. Fruit and Vegetable Packers and Warehousemen*, Local 760, 377 U.S. 58 (1964).

[3] *Ibid.*, pp. 72–73.

[4] Local Joint Executive Board of Hotel and Restaurant Employees and Bartenders International Union of Long Beach and Orange County; Culinary

labor practice did occur. The reasoning of the board is presented for analysis:

LOCAL JOINT EXECUTIVE BOARD OF HOTEL AND RESTAURANT EMPLOYEES AND BARTENDERS INTERNATIONAL UNION OF LONG BEACH AND ORANGE COUNTY: CULINARY ALLIANCE LOCAL No. 681
Leonard Smitly and Joseph W. Dunn d/b/a/ Crown Cafeteria, a copartnership and Pete Irwin. Case No. 21-CP-4, February 20, 1961. 130 NLRB 570:1961

Briefly, union representatives in April and May 1959 asked Crown to operate its cafeteria by hiring its employees through the union hiring hall and signing the standard union contract. Crown refused to do so, and employed nonunion employees instead. Beginning on May 5, 1959, the Respondents accordingly picketed the public entrance of Crown Cafeteria, with signs addressed to "members of organized labor and their friends," stating that the cafeteria was nonunion, and asking them not to patronize the cafeteria. This recognition or organizational picketing continued without the filing of a petition for more than a reasonable period of time after November 13, 1959, the effective date of Section 8(b)(7)(c).

On these facts the trial examiner concluded that the picketing, even though for an object of recognition or organization, fell within the protection of the publicity proviso to Section 8(b)(7)(c) because it did not have an effect of inducing any stoppage of goods or services.

We cannot agree with the Trial Examiners unduly narrow construction of the Act. Congress in Section 8(b)(7) expressed the general objective of prohibiting picketing by uncertified labor organizations where *an* object was recognition or organization, even though the picketing may also have had other objects as well. The subsections then particularize the prohibition in various factual situations: for example, such picketing is wholly banned under subsection (a) where another labor organization is entitled to continued recognition; and under subsection (B) it is banned when within a year a valid election has been conducted. Under subsec-

Alliance Local No. 681 [Leonard Smitley and Joseph W. Dunn d/b/a/ Crown Cafeteria, a copartnership] and Peter Irwin, Case No. 21-CP-4, February 20, 1961, 130 NLRB 570.

tion (C) the ban against picketing exists when a reasonable period of time not to exceed 30 days has elapsed after the commencement of picketing, except when a representation petition is filed. However, none of these qualifications applies to the facts of the present case, as the Trial Examiner and the parties all conceded.

We regard the Trial Examiner's and our dissenting colleagues' construction of the Act as undermining the carefully worked out program established by Congress in Section 8(b)(7). We cannot believe that Congress meant to permit recognition picketing merely because the picketing also takes the form of truthfully advising the public that the employer is nonunion, or does not have a union contract. Rather, we believe that Congress was careful to state that picketing will be permitted only if it is for "the" purpose of so advising the public. Indeed the ban against picketing is particularly applicable in the present situation, where the Union did not represent the majority of the employees, and the only lawful course for Crown to follow was to refuse to recognize the Union, as it did. See *Stork Restaurant, Inc.*, 130 NLRB 543.

We are satisfied that Congress added the proviso only to make clear that purely informational picketing, which publicizes the lack of a union contract or the lack of union organization, and which has no present object of recognition, should not be curtailed ". . . unless an effect of such picketing is to induce any individual employed by any other person in the course of his employment not to pick up, deliver or transport any goods or not to perform any services." But that is not the situation in this case. As the Trial Examiner found, apart from the picketing, the Union was in fact demanding present recognition from Crown. Indeed, under established doctrine, even if the Union had disclaimed any object of recognition which, of course, it did not do—but had engaged in the picketing here present, the Board would clearly have entertained a representation petition filed by Crown, apart from the specific provisions of Section 8(b)(7)(C). For a demand for recognition accompanied by picketing would not be deemed, under the Board's normal representation procedures, to have been removed by a disclaimer, where, as here, the picketing continues and the picket signs refer only to the lack of union organization. . . .

Consideration of the result of the Trial Examiner's, and our dissenting colleagues', contrary construction of the proviso convinces us of their error. They would permit present recognition picketing whenever the labor organization is careful to indicate by its picket signs only an ostensible purpose of advising the public. However, this would render meaningless, at the whim of a picketing union, the stated objective of Section 8(b)(7). The resulting nullification of the whole of Section 8(b)(7)(C) would most certainly result in an absurd situation. Clearly, under the established rules of statutory construction, the intention of the Congress to outlaw recognitional and organizational picketing is best effectuated by confining the second proviso of 8(b)(7)(C) to picketing where the sole object is dissemination of information divorced from a present object of recognition.

Moreover, the legislative history, if it were needed to explain what seems to us to be clear statutory language, supports this construction of the Act. As Senator Kennedy stated in the significant items of legislative history referred to by the Trial Examiner, the proviso applies only to "purely" informational picketing.

Accordingly, giving due weight to the terms of the proviso to Section 8(b)(7)(C), we find the instant picketing unlawful and not protected by the proviso because it was not for the sole purpose permitted in the proviso, namely, that of truthfully advising the public that Crown did not employ union members or have a union contract.

We conclude, contrary to the Trial Examiner, that the Respondents' picketing for more than a reasonable period of time after November 13, 1959, violated Section 8(b)(7)(C) of the Act, as alleged.

THE EFFECT OF THE UNFAIR LABOR PRACTICES UPON COMMERCE

The activities of the Respondents which we have found to constitute unfair labor practices, occurring in connection with the operations of Crown Cafeteria as described in the Intermediate Report, have a close, intimate, and substantial relationship to trade, traffic, and commerce among the several States and tend to lead to labor disputes burdening and obstructing commerce and the free flow of commerce.

THE REMEDY

Having found that the Respondents have engaged in certain unfair labor practices, we shall order them to cease and desist therefrom and to take certain affirmative action, which the Board finds is necessary to effectuate the policies of the Act.

Upon the basis of the foregoing and the entire record, we hereby reject the Trial Examiner's conclusion of law No. 3 and in its stead make the following:

CONCLUSIONS OF LAW

3. By picketing Crown after November 13, 1959, with an object of forcing or requiring Crown to recognize or bargain with the Respondents as the representative of Crown's employees without filing a petition under Section 9(c) within a reasonable period of time, the Respondents have engaged in unfair labor practices within the meaning of Section 8(b)(7)(C) of the Act.

4. The aforesaid labor practices are unfair labor practices affecting commerce within the meaning of Section 2(6) and (7) of the Act.

ORDER

Cease and desist from picketing or causing to be picketed. Here again the issue of informational picketing is brought under close scrutiny and an effort is made to establish a clear distinction between picketing for informative purposes and that which is intended to institute some action on the part of the employer.

"HOT CARGO"

Our final consideration of cases that illustrate rulings made on the basis of the Landrum-Griffin Amendments to the National Labor Relations Act is directed toward the "hot-cargo" issue. This case came before the National Labor Relations Board in 1967 and involved an agreement that contained a provision which prohibited union members from handling prefitted doors. A summary of the issue and the opinion of the United States Supreme Court follows:

NATIONAL WOODWORK MANUFACTURERS ASSOCIATION ET AL. V.
NATIONAL LABOR RELATIONS BOARD (NO. 110): 1967
(386 U.S. 612)

A general contractor, which had contracted with the Carpenters' International Union to be bound by the rules and regulations agreed upon by local unions with contractors in areas where the general contractor had jobs, became the general contractor on a housing project in Philadelphia, when a local collective bargaining agreement provided that no union member would handle any pre-fitted doors. The general contractor contracted for the purchase of premachined doors, which the union ordered its carpenter members not to hang. The NLRB dismissed secondary boycott charges brought against the union under 29 USC §§ 158(b)(4)(B) and 158(e), finding that the objective of the provision was preservation of work traditionally performed by jobsite carpenters and that the union's conduct related solely to work preservation. (149 NLRB 646.) The United States Court of Appeals for the Seventh Circuit sustained the dismissal of the charge under § 158(b)(4)(B), but reversed as to the charge under § 158(e).

On certiorari, the Supreme Court of the United States affirmed as to the charge under § 158(b)(4)(B), but reversed as to the charge under § 158 (e). In an opinion by Brennan, J., expressing the views of five members of the court, it was held that since the union's objective was preservation of work for the general contractors, and its conduct was not tactically calculated to satisfy union objectives elsewhere, it had not engaged in secondary activities proscribed by the statute.

It can be readily seen from the foregoing that the modifications made by the Landrum-Griffin Act resulted in tightening up those areas in the Taft-Hartley Act that had resulted in rather broad interpretations of picketing and secondary boycott activities as well as the "no man's land" jurisdictional issue.

The Scope of the Collective Bargaining Process

The need for bargaining on a collective basis was probably one of the strongest forces that motivated workingmen to join unions as early as two centuries before the Landrum-Griffin Act. As we have seen previously, a single employee or even a small group of employees could not effectively exert enough pressure on an employer to acquire even modest concessions, or even be an influential party in the setting of wages, hours, or working conditions. The National Labor Relations Act, as amended, corrected this situation by requiring collective bargaining on the part of the employer and the properly chosen representative of the employees. Parties are required to bargain together in good faith, and refusal to comply in this respect can result in an unfair labor practice charge being filed. It should be noted, however, that the requirement to bargain collectively and in good faith does not carry with it a requirement to agree or concede in order to reach an agreement. It is our purpose in this section to look at the constituents in the bargaining process and the role each of them plays in the negotiation procedure.

CONSTITUENTS

MANAGEMENT

Existing legislation does not precisely stipulate the environment that must surround the collective bargaining process, but it does impose a mutual obligation on the part of both management and employee representatives to meet at reasonable times. The employer or his management representatives must bargain with the individual selected by his employees and cannot refuse to negotiate because of personal preferences or bias or because the representative is not an employee. The employer is required to enter negotiations with an open mind and with the objective of reaching an agreement. Representatives of management at the collective bargaining table technically are authorized to make binding agreements on the part of the employer. There is no standard method for the selection of management representatives or the tactics they may employ during the bargaining. Usually, though, there is a top management officer present. Management negotiators may vary depending on the size of the organization, the expected issues, and the bargaining power of the union. However, one of the representatives is usually designated as spokesman so that the pattern of bargaining may be consistent. This individual is prepared to concede or agree to certain issues and can better judge the import of concessions on items that will emerge later in the negotiations. In addition to company officers, parties who typically participate in bargaining are plant superintendents or managers, directors of personnel and industrial relations, and the company attorney. Throughout negotiations, management seeks to protect its prerogatives or rights [5] and the financial position of the company.

THE UNION

The union is under the same general legislative requirements as the employer when participating in the collective bargaining process.

[5] See *NLRB* v. *American National Insurance Co.*, 343 U.S. 395 (1952).

Negotiations must be entered into in good faith and with the intent of reaching an agreement. They may be attended by persons from either the national organization, if the union is affiliated with one, or the local, if it is a small single-employer unit. The men who participate in this bargaining process are often highly skilled and experienced negotiators and in many cases professional negotiators, particularly in the case of national representatives. It is no longer true that management enters the negotiations with the advantages of experience in skill and tactics; frequently management finds itself in a defensive rather than offensive position, pitted against an astute and highly proficient opposition. The primary purpose of the union negotiator is, of course, to rectify conditions that appear undesirable, to gain as many advantages and concessions for union members as possible, and in so doing strengthen employee support for the union organization.

GOVERNMENT

There are other parties involved in the collective bargaining process in addition to management and the union. Government is directly involved when the National Labor Relations Board is included in the process. This occurs when an unfair labor practice charge is filed for a refusal to bargain, as was the case in Administrative Ruling No. SR-1142 (1961) when the General Counsel authorized the issuance of a complaint after an employer charged a violation of Section 8(b)(3), refusal to bargain, and stated:

> . . . Substantial basis exists for finding that the union attitude from the outset was that the company could "take it or leave it," that is, the company could sign a contract negotiated by major concerns with whom the company was not associated, in whose deliberations it had not participated, and whose operations differed from its own to a substantial degree or suffer a strike.[6]

In addition, and as we have seen in our analyses of labor legislation dealing with collective bargaining, the Federal Mediation and Conciliation Service can also be brought in when a labor dispute is threatened or exists and there may be a substantial effect on interstate commerce. The Service does not settle the dispute but merely recommends solutions to the parties. It should be emphasized that the Federal Mediation and Conciliation Service is not an arbitrator and

[6] *Labor Relations Cumulative Digest and Index* (Washington: Bureau of National Affairs, Inc., 1966), XLVI–LX, Part II, 348.

has no inherent authority to act in that capacity. The government is also indirectly involved in the collective bargaining process by the fact that the law does stipulate what is appropriate conduct.

BARGAINING UNITS

The types of units recognized for the purpose of collective bargaining can be single or multi-employer or plant, or smaller units such as a single department or craft. On the side of the employer there may also be employer associations that represent their members. The National Labor Relations Board has the authority to designate the kind of unit that is appropriate and does so according to the circumstances of each case. Legislation provides the manner by which the Board will establish the bargaining unit and declares that in making this designation it may not: (a) declare a unit appropriate if it contains both professional and nonprofessional employees unless the former vote to be a part of the unit; (b) declare craft units appropriate because any other designation had been found inappropriate by prior board rulings, unless separate representation had been voted upon; and (c) that a unit cannot be declared an appropriate unit if it contains plant guards as well as other employees. When deciding on appropriate units the Board takes several things into consideration. These include past practices of the employer, the kind of work done by the employees, the interests of the employees, and whether or not the employees are highly skilled craftsmen or semi-skilled industrial workers. The extent of organization cannot be the deciding factor according to the legislation but it may be a consideration. The following references to cases serve to illustrate these considerations.

The size of the unit was significant in an issue involving Denver-Colorado Springs-Pueblo Motor Way.[7] The Board had been petitioned to certify a bargaining unit that consisted of one full-time waitress and one part-time hostess. In refusing to certify the Board declared that because the part-time hostess spent more than half of her time engaged in another activity she did not qualify as a part of the unit ". . . and the Board does not certify bargaining representatives for units composed of one employee only." [8]

The interests and duties of employees was a deciding factor in a bargaining unit issue at J. W. Mays, Inc.[9] The Board held here that an appropriate unit could be made up of nonselling and selling em-

[7] 129 NLRB 1184 (1961).
[8] *Ibid.*
[9] 147 NLRB 968 (1964).

ployees because the counselling employees were not an homogenous group and in this self-service operation most of the employees not only perform the same functions but have the same interests.

Single-plant units are generally found to be appropriate when there are recognized differences in plant operations, geographic location, supervisory personnel, and interaction of employees. In the case of John C. Stalfort and Sons, Inc.,[10] the Board ruled that a single plant unit was appropriate even though the employer had a similar plant some miles away. The Board also added that this was true even though a two-plant unit could also be appropriate.

The inappropriateness of a multi-plant unit was declared when the Board refused to permit some in-store bakers to combine with the bakers of the wholesale bakery department who were at a different location and with whom they had no contact. The board declared: ". . . these employees constitute an integral part of the operating personnel of stores whose employees are currently represented as part of the multi-store units." [11] Multi-plants units are deemed appropriate, however, when the plants are in close proximity, there is a centralization of management and labor relations policy, and an interchange of employees.[12]

Single and multi-employer bargaining units have also been subject to Board rulings. The criteria used by the Board in determining the appropriateness of these kinds of units is set forth in the instance of Research Craft Manufacturing Corporation, where the Board ruled:

> . . . Production and maintenance employees of phonograph record manufacturer and record distributing company may constitute appropriate unit, in view of four-year bargaining history. Unrepresented employees of new manufacturing company may be included, in view of common management and integrated operations of these firms. Separate unit of such unrepresented employees also may be appropriate, since (1) plastic compound which they use in pressing records requires production process and machinery which is dissimilar from that ordinarily used in pressing records, (2) current bargaining representative never claimed that it represented employees of new company, and (3) employees engaged in new operation normally are allowed to decide whether they wish to be represented separately, even when new operation is integrated with old.[13]

[10] 156 NLRB No. 7 (1965).
[11] 137 NLRB 1741 (1962).
[12] 145 NLRB 1665 (1964).
[13] 129 NLRB 723 (1960).

Various kinds of special groups have wished to participate in bargaining as separate units, and as a result determination of the appropriateness of this activity has also been brought to the National Labor Relations Board for clarification and ruling. The legislation, as noted above, has given special treatment to three of these groups: professional workers, plant guards, and craftsmen. Others who have been subject to Board rulings are clerical or white collar personnel, managerial employees, and technicians. The Board, in deciding whether or not a group of workers could be separated to constitute a separate unit for purposes of bargaining, expressed a general attitude in an issue involving the Kalamazoo Paper Box Corporation when it ruled:

> . . . Sub-group of employees, such as truck drivers, will not be automatically severed from larger unit merely on basis of this traditional job classification and request for separate unit encompassing such classification; before severance is allowed, determination must first be made as to whether in reality, such employees constitute functionally distinct group and whether, as a group, they have overriding special interests, and this determination must be made upon factual situation existing in each case and not upon title, tradition, or practices. To extent that this approach is inconsistent with that applied in prior determinations, such cases are hereby overruled.[14]

It can readily be seen that determination of an appropriate bargaining unit is neither a simple nor an automatic process. Furthermore, the fact that a bargaining unit has been established does not mean that the issue will not emerge at a later date. Changes in production processes or organization structure can easily reactivate the issue and result in modifications in employee representation.

CONTRACT CONSIDERATIONS

For each bargaining unit that has been appropriately established, the employer and the union must negotiate an agreement. The process of negotiating an agreement can be a very simple and uncomplicated one. Not infrequently, however, the procedure is one that is extremely involved, incorporating various strategies and tactics, traditions and protocol, as well as compromises and concessions by both

[14] 136 NLRB 134 (1962).

parties. The discussion here is limited to those aspects of this process that generally are included as subjects of collective bargaining and which may become a part of the final agreement.

The law requires the parties to bargain on matters of wages and hours as well as other conditions of employment. The requirement to bargain also extends to the negotiation of the agreement and to any question that may arise from an existing agreement. While it is not possible to say that all agreements have consistent or standard inclusions, there are several things that are commonly covered. These include an itemization of wage rates paid for each kind of activity that takes place in the industrial unit, the method to be used for figuring overtime pay and call-back pay,[15] as well as variances that are to be allowed for shift differentials. There may or may not be included an escalator clause (cost of living increase) depending upon the length of time the contract is to run. The method for computing hours worked will also be included either on a per day or per week basis. Normally, a recognition clause is also included, representing a formal statement declaring that the union negotiating the agreement is the certified representative of the described bargaining unit.

Having been recognized as the exclusive representative of a bargaining unit, the union will undoubtedly want a union security clause in the agreement. The most common kind of union security bargained for by the union is the union shop, which requires membership after employment as a condition of employment and is established through a maintenance-of-membership agreement. Frequently agreements state that those employees who are members of the union in good standing at the time the agreement is reached will maintain their membership for the period covered by the agreement that any new employees or non-member employees will join the union and maintain membership in good standing as a condition of their employment.[16] It is not uncommon to include an escape clause even though the law does not require one. This inclusion refers to the employee who is a member of the union but who has not maintained his membership according to the provisions of the agreement. Should this occur, the employee is given a stated number of days to rectify the situation before he is subject to dismissal by the employer. It should

[15] *Call back pay* refers to a provision that guarantees an employee pay for a minimum number of hours of work if he is called to work for other than his regularly scheduled hours.

[16] It should be remembered that the National Labor Relations Act requires that a thirty-day period must be allowed before membership becomes compulsory.

be noted here that an employer is not required to bargain on a union security clause if the kind of security sought by the labor organization is prohibited by the National Labor Relations Act (closed shop), or if it is prohibited by state statutory regulations. Union security agreements are frequently accompanied by checkoff provisions. As we saw in our consideration of the Taft-Hartley Act, this procedure is lawful when the employee voluntarily signs an agreement to permit the employer to deduct union dues and fees from his wages. When the employee agrees to this arrangement he does so for either one year or for the tenure of the collective bargaining agreement, whichever is shorter.

Procedures that are to be followed in the areas of promotions, demotions, suspensions, lay-offs, transfers, recall, and discharge are also commonly included as subjects for collective bargaining. Some of these may be affected by seniority provisions. The inclusion of seniority provisions can be an item that causes considerable difficulty during negotiations, not necessarily in terms of inclusion or exclusion of the provision, but rather in terms of the method that is to be used to determine seniority status. Management is opposed generally to seniority purely on the basis of length of service with the company, particularly with respect to the changes in employee status having to do with promotions, demotions, suspensions, transfer, and discharge. Understandably, the employer is concerned with the abilities of employees who are to be promoted or removed from the productive process and not simply with the length of time spent on a job. In many cases agreements give priority to seniority considerations when an organization is required to lay off or recall employees, and consideration is focused on merit and ability in other situations. Seniority determinations may be made on the basis of all jobs contained in the plant as a unit, some division thereof, or by individual department. As might be expected, employers frequently favor the latter while unions prefer the basis to be the entire unit. Final determination, however, rests on willingness of the parties to compromise and the individual characteristics of the organizations involved.

Bargaining negotiations also take place, as a rule, on the subjects of vacations and holidays, sick leave, leaves of absence, and safety programs and procedures. Vacations are usually influenced somewhat by the nature of the production processes. Bargaining on this issue is usually an attempt on the part of the union to improve or increase the number of days granted and to minimize eligibility requirements for employees. The employer, on the other hand, generally maintains that length of service or time worked should be the determining factor. The inclusion of holidays as a subject of collective bargaining has become fairly standardized. Over time, the number of paid holidays has increased substantially and the bargaining process also extends to the matter of premium pay for employees who work on these days. It is not uncommon to find stipulations that require an employee to work either the day immediately preceding or following a paid holiday in order to qualify for premium pay when he is required to work on a holiday. Safety programs, sick leave, and leaves of absence provisions are quite often unique to the industry and cannot be described in general terms other than to say that consideration of these topics and the inclusion of them as a part of the collective bargaining agreement is generally agreed upon by the parties.

Other items that are commonly considered during the collective bargaining process are those dealing with pension plans, welfare programs, and bonuses. Employers are required to bargain on these issues if they are requested to do so by the labor organization with whom they are negotiating. The subject of a no-strike clause and a clause calling for a strike vote may also be included. While the employer can insist on the inclusion of a no-strike clause, bargaining on the strike vote is not compulsory. The lawfulness of these two inclusions is illustrated in the cases that appear on the following pages.

The majority of collective bargaining agreements also cover grievance procedures, even though it is not a mandatory inclusion. The procedure typically requires a series of distinct steps to settle grievances at various levels within employer and union organizations. Not infrequently the final step in this procedure is arbitration. The following procedure is presented as being generally illustrative:

GRIEVANCE PROCEDURE

Section 1. Definition. For the purpose of this Agreement, the term "Grievance" means any dispute between the Employer and the Union; or between the Employer and any employee concerning the effect, interpretation, application, claim of breach or violation of this Agreement; or any dispute which may arise between the parties. All grievances not mentioned within fifteen (15) days after they occur, or first knowledge that a grievance exists, shall be outdated, thus preventing an accumulation of grievances.

Section 2. Method of Processing. All grievances shall be reduced to writing and settled in accordance with the following procedure:

(a) The dispute or grievance shall be taken up by the Shop Steward, the aggrieved employee, and the Foreman of the department involved within fifteen (15) days as provided in Section 1 above. The foreman must give his answer within two (2) working days. If no satisfactory settlement is reached between the Shop Steward and the Foreman, then,

(b) The Shop Steward shall within (2) days present the grievance to the Shop Committee, if any, which shall investigate, present and discuss such grievance with an authorized representative of the Employer. In the absence of a Shop Committee, the next step shall immediately be followed. If no satisfactory settlement is reached between them within two (2) working days, then

(c) The Shop Steward shall within two (2) days call in a representative of the Union who shall meet with the authorized representative of the Employer and the Shop Committee, if any. The authorized representative of the Employer shall give his answer within two (2) working days.

(d) In the event the grievance or dispute is not satisfactorily settled as processed in (a), (b), and (c) above, an authorized representative of the Union may notify the Employer and the Association of the Union's desire to submit the grievance to a Grievance Committee of Employer representatives, parties to this Agreement. Such notice shall be sent via Certified Mail and must be postmarked within seven (7) days.

(e) The Employer Committee as referred to in (d) above shall be known as an Industry Committee. It shall consist of not less than three (3) individuals. The Employer involved in the grievance shall not be a member of the committee. It is the responsibility of the Association to set a date, time and place for the hearing as promptly as possible after receipt of the notice of the grievance from the Union, but in no event shall such time exceed five (5) days. The industry committee shall give its decision and recommendation to the parties in writing. In any event, such decision and recommendation shall be given to the parties within two (2) days after the conclusion of the Industry Committee hearing. If no settlement is effected by the Industry Committee and recommendation, the matter may then be submitted by either party to Arbitration, as hereinafter provided, within five (5) days after the Industry Committee decision.

(f) The aggrieved employee or the Shop Steward shall have the right to call in the Union Representative at any step of the grievance or arbitration procedure.

Section 3. Either party to this agreement shall be permitted to call employee witnesses at each and every step of the grievance procedure beginning with Step (d); the Employer, on demand, will produce production, payroll, and other records for the purpose of substantiating the contentions or claims of the parties.

Section 4. The grievance procedure and arbitration provided for herein shall constiture [sic] the sole and exclusive method of determination, decision, adjustment or settlement between the parties of any and all grievances as herein defined; and the grievance procedure and arbitration provided herein shall constitute the sole and exclusive remedy to be utilized by the parties hereto for such determination, decision, adjustment, or settlement of any and all grievances as herein defined.

Section 5. Any time specified herein shall not include any time on any Saturday, Sunday, or holiday.[17]

When the final step in the grievance procedure is arbitration, provisions are usually made as to the manner and selection of an arbitrator. The method for doing this is not standardized, and may range from a single arbitrator who is agreed to by both parties to a board selected by the parties and consisting of representatives for both parties chaired by an impartial third party. The process of arbitration is considered in more detail later in this chapter.

The foregoing considerations are not all inclusive of those subjects that are considered during the collective bargaining process, but they are representative of standard inclusions. The cases that follow are included to illustrate the attitude of the Supreme Court toward the collective bargaining process and the rulings the Court has made on the lawfulness of certain clauses found in collective bargaining agreements.

The Supreme Court considered the issue of mandatory subjects of bargaining in *NLRB* v. *Wooster Division of Borg-Warner Corporation.*[18] In this case an impasse occurred in collective bargaining negotiations when the employer refused to accept the collective bargaining agreement unless a "ballot" clause was included that would permit his employees to vote by secret ballot prior to going out on strike.

[17] International Association of Machinists and Aerospace Workers, Western States Maintenance Agreement and Western Empire Operators Association Supplemental Agreement, For The Period May 1, 1965, to May 1, 1968, pp. 39–43.
[18] 356 U.S. 342 (1958).

The employer also insisted that the recognition clause be worded to exclude the International Union, already certified by the National Labor Relations Board as the representative of the employees, and that the name of its uncertified local affiliate appear in place of the International. The National Labor Relations Board held that the employer was in violation of Section 8(a)(5) of the National Labor Relations Act by insisting on the inclusion of these clauses. In considering the issue the Supreme Court agreed with the Board and indicated that ". . . the issue turns on whether either of these clauses comes within the scope of mandatory collective bargaining as defined in § 8(d) of the Act." [19] The Court reasoned as follows:

NLRB v. Wooster Division of Borg-Warner Corporation: 1958
(356 U.S. 342)

The Supreme Court of the United States, Mr. Justice Burton delivering the opinion of the court:

. . . Read together, these provisions establish the obligation of the employer and the representative of its employees to bargain with each other in good faith with respect to "wages, hours, and other terms and conditions of employment. . . ." The duty is limited to those subjects, and within that area neither party is legally obligated to yield. *NLRB v. American Nat. Ins. Co.* 343 U.S. 395.

The company's good faith has set the requirements of the statute as to the subjects of mandatory bargaining. But that good faith does not license the employer to refuse to enter into agreements on the ground that they do not include some proposal which is not a mandatory subject of bargaining. We agree with the Board that such conduct is, in substance, a refusal to bargain about the subjects that are within the scope of mandatory bargaining. This does not mean that bargaining is to be confined to the statutory subjects. Each of the two controversial clauses is lawful in itself. Each would be enforceable if agreed to by the unions. But it does not follow that, because the company may propose these clauses, it can lawfully insist upon them as a condition to any agreement.

Since it is lawful to insist upon matters within the scope of mandatory bargaining and unlawful to insist upon matters without, the

[19] *Ibid.*

issue here is whether either the "ballot" or the "recognition" clause is a subject within the phrase "wages, hours, and other terms and conditions of employment" which defines mandatory bargaining. The "ballot" clause is not within that definition. It relates only to the procedure to be followed by the employees among themselves before their representative may call a strike or refuse a final offer. It settles no term or condition of employment—it merely calls for an advisory vote of the employees. It is not a partial "no-strike" clause. A "no-strike" clause regulates the relations between the employer and the employees. See *Labor Board* v. *American Insurance Co. supra,* (at 408, n. 22). The "ballot" clause, on the other hand, deals only with relations between the employees and their unions. It substantially modifies the collective bargaining system provided for in the statute by weakening the independence of the "representative" chosen by the employees. It enables the employer, in effect, to deal with its employees rather than with their statutory representative. Cf. *Medo Photo Corp* v. *Labor Board,* 321 US 678.

The "recognition" clause likewise does not come within the definition of mandatory bargaining. The statute requires the company to bargain with the certified representative of its employees. It is an evasion of that duty to insist that the certified agent not be a party to the collective bargaining contract. The Act does not prohibit the voluntary addition of a party, but that does not authorize the employer to exclude the certified representative from the contract.

Accordingly, the judgment of the Court of Appeals in No. 53 is reversed and the case remanded for disposition consistent with this opinion.

The subject of bargaining in good faith came before the United States Supreme Court again in *Fibreboard Paper Products Corporation* v. *National Labor Relations Board.*[20] The rather lengthy opinion of the court is presented here because it gives a very good insight into the reasoning of the court in deciding this.

[20] 379 U.S. 203 (1964).

FIBREBOARD PAPER PRODUCTS CORPORATION V.
NATIONAL LABOR RELATIONS BOARD: 1964
(*379 U.S. 203*)

*The Supreme Court of the United States, Mr. Chief Justice Warren
delivering the opinion:*

This case involves the obligation of an employer and the representative of his employees under §§ 8(a)(5), 8(d) and 9(a) of the
National Labor Relations Act to "confer in good faith with respect
to wages, hours, and other terms and conditions of employment."
The primary issue is whether the "contracting out" of work being
performed by employees in the bargaining unit is a statutory subject of collective bargaining under those sections. Petitioner, Fibreboard Paper Products Corporation (the Company), has a manufacturing plant in Emeryville, California. Since 1937, the East Bay
Union Machinists, Local 1304, United Steelworkers of America,
AFL-CIO (the Union) has been the exclusive bargaining representative for a unit of the Company's maintenance employees. In September, 1958, the Union and the Company entered the latest of a
series of collective bargaining agreements which was to expire on
July 31, 1959. The agreement provided for automatic renewal for
another year unless one of the contracting parties gave 60 days' notice of a desire to modify or terminate the contract. On
May 25, 1959, the Union gave timely notice of its desire to
modify the contract and sought to arrange a bargaining session
with Company representatives. On June 2, the Company acknowledged receipt of the Union's notice and stated: "We will
contact you at a later date regarding a meeting for this
purpose." As required by the contract, the Union sent a list
of proposed modifications on June 15. Efforts by the Union to
schedule a bargaining session met with no success until July
27, four days before the expiration of the contract, when the
Company notified the Union of its desire to meet.

The Company, concerned with the high cost of its maintenance
operation, had undertaken a study of the possibility of effecting
cost savings by engaging an independent contractor to do the
maintenance work. At the July 27 meeting, the Company informed
the Union that it had determined that substantial savings could be
effected by contracting out the work upon expiration of its collective bargaining agreements with the various labor organizations

representing its maintenance employees. The Company delivered to the Union representatives a letter which stated in pertinent part:

"For some time we have been seriously considering the question of letting out our Emeryville maintenance work to an independent contractor, and have now reached a definite decision to do so effective August 1, 1959.

"In these circumstances, we are sure you will realize that negotiation of a new contract would be pointless. However, if you have any questions, we will be glad to discuss them with you."

After some discussion of the Company's right to enter a contract with a third party to do the work then being performed by employees in the bargaining unit, the meeting concluded with the understanding that the parties would meet again on July 30.

By July 30, the Company had selected Fluor Maintenance, Inc. to do the maintenance work. Fluor had assured the Company that maintenance costs could be curtailed by reducing the work force, decreasing fringe benefits and overtime payments, and by preplanning and scheduling the services to be performed. The contract provided that Fluor would: "furnish all labor, supervision, and office help required for the performance of maintenance work . . . at the Emeryville plant of Owner as Owner shall from time to time assign to Contractor during the period of this contract; and shall also furnish such tools, supplies and equipment in connection therewith as Owner shall order from Contractor, it being understood however that Owner shall ordinarily do its own purchasing of tools, supplies, and equipment."

The contract further provided that the Company would pay Fluor the costs of the operation plus a fixed fee of $2,250 per month.

At the July 30 meeting, the Company's representative, in explaining the decision to contract out the maintenance work, remarked that during bargaining negotiations in previous years the Company had endeavored to point out through the use of charts and statistical information "just how expensive and costly our maintenance work was and how it was creating quite a terrific burden upon the Emeryville plant." He further stated that unions representing other Company employees "had joined hands with management in an effort to bring about an economical and efficient operation," but "we had not been able to attain that in our discussions with this particular Local." The Company also distributed a letter stating that "since we will have no employees in the bargaining unit covered by our present Agreement, negotiation of a new or renewed Agreement would appear to us to be pointless." On July 31, the employment of the maintenance employees represented by the Union was terminated and Fluor employees took over. That evening the Union established a picket line at the Company's plant.

The Union filed unfair labor practice charges against the Company alleging violations of §§ 8(a)(1), 8(a)(3) and 8(a)(5). After hearings were held upon a complaint issued by the National Labor Relations Board's Regional Director, the Trial Examiner filed an Intermediate Report recommending dismissal of the complaint. The Board accepted the recommendation and dismissed the complaint. 130 NLRB 1558.

Petitions for reconsideration, filed by the General Counsel and the Union, were granted. Upon reconsideration, the Board adhered to the Trial Examiner's finding that the Company's motive in contracting out its maintenance work was economic rather than anti-union but found nonetheless that the Company's "failure to negotiate with . . . [the Union] concerning its decision to subcontract its maintenance work constituted a violation of Section 8(a)(5) of the Act." This ruling was based upon the doctrine established in *Town & Country Mfg. Co.* 136 NLRB 1022, 1027, enforcement granted, 316 F2d 846 (C.A. 5th Cir 1963), that contracting out work, "albeit for economic reasons, is a matter within the statutory phrase 'other terms and conditions of employment' and is a mandatory subject of collective bargaining within the meaning of Section 8(a)(5) of the Act."

The Board ordered the Company to reinstitute the maintenance operation previously performed by the employees represented by the Union, to reinstate the employees to their former or substantially equivalent positions with back pay computed from the date of the Board's supplemental decision, and to fulfill its statutory obligation to bargain.

On appeal, the Court of Appeals for the District of Columbia Circuit granted the Board's petition for enforcement. 116 U.S. App. D.C. 198, 322 F2d 411. Because of the importance of the issues and because of an alleged conflict among the courts of appeals, we granted certiorari limited to a consideration of the following questions:

"1. Was Petitioner required by the National Labor Relations Act to bargain with a union representing some of its employees about whether to let to an independent contractor for legitimate business reasons for performance of certain operations in which those employees had been engaged?

"3. Was the Board, in a case involving only a refusal to bargain, empowered to order the resumption of operations which had been discontinued for legitimate business reasons and reinstatement with back pay of the individuals formerly employed therein?"

We agree with the Court of Appeals that, on the facts of this case, the "contracting out" of the work previously performed by members of an existing bargaining unit is a subject about which the National Labor Relations Act requires employers and the representatives of their employees to bargain collectively. We also agree with the Court of Appeals that the Board did not exceed its remedial powers in directing the Company to resume its maintenance operations, reinstate the employees with back pay, and bargain with the Union.

Section 8(a)(5) of the National Labor Relations Act provides that it shall be an unfair labor practice for an employer "to refuse to bargain collectively with representatives of his employees." Collective bargaining is defined in § 8(d) as "the performance of the mutual obligation of the employer and the representative of its employees to meet at reasonable times and confer in good faith with respect to wages, hours, and other terms and conditions of employment."

"Read together, these provisions establish the obligation of the employer and the representative of its employees to bargain with each other in good faith with respect to 'wages, hours, and other terms and conditions of employment . . .' The duty is limited to those subjects, and within that area neither party is legally obligated to yield. *Labor Board* v. *American Ins. Co.* 343 US 395. As to other matters, however, each party is free to bargain or not to bargain. . . ." *Labor Board* v. *Wooster Div. of Borg-Warner Corp.* 356 US 342, 349. Because of the limited grant of certiorari, we are concerned here only with whether the subject

upon which the employer allegedly refused to bargain—
contracting out of plant maintenance work previously performed
by employees in the bargaining unit, which the employees were
capable of continuing to perform—is covered by the phrase
"terms and conditions of employment" within the meaning of
§ 8(d).

The subject matter of the present dispute is well within the literal meaning of the phrase "terms and conditions of employment."
See *Order of Railroad Telegraphers* v. *Chicago & N. W. R. Co.*
362 U.S. 330. A stipulation with respect to the contracting out of
work performed by members of the bargaining unit might appropriately be called a "condition of employment." The words even
more plainly cover termination of employment which, as the facts
of this case indicate, necessarily results from the contracting out
of work performed by members of the established bargaining unit.

The inclusion of "contracting out" within the statutory scope of
collective bargaining also seems well designed to effectuate the
purposes of the National Labor Relations Act. One of the primary
purposes of the Act is to promote the peaceful settlement of industrial disputes by subjecting labor-management controversies to
the mediatory influence of negotiation. The Act was framed with
an awareness that refusals to confer and negotiate had been one of
the most prolific causes of industrial strife. *Labor Board* v. *Jones
& Laughlin Steel Corp.* 301 US 1, 42–43. To hold, as the Board has
done, that contracting out is a mandatory subject of collective bargaining would promote the fundamental purpose of the Act by bringing a
problem of vital concern to labor and management within the
framework established by Congress as most conducive to industrial
peace.

The conclusion that "contracting out" is a statutory subject of
collective bargaining is further reinforced by industrial practices in
this country. While not determinative, it is appropriate to look to
industrial bargaining practices in appraising the propriety of including a particular subject within the scope of mandatory bargaining. *Labor Board* v. *American Nat. Ins. Co.* 343 US 395, 408.
Industrial experience is not only reflective of the interests of labor and
management in the subject matter but is also indicative of the amena-
bility of such subjects to the collective-bargaining process. Experience
illustrates that contracting out in one form or another has been brought
widely and successfully within the collective bargaining framework.

Provisions relating to contracting out exist in numerous collective-bargaining agreements, and "contracting out work is the basis of many grievances; and that type of claim is grist in the mills of the arbitrators." *United Steelworkers* v. *Warrior & Gulf Nav. Co.* 363 US 574, 584.

The situation here is not unlike that presented in *Local 24 Teamsters Union* v. *Oliver,* 358 US 283, where we held that conditions imposed upon contracting out work to prevent possible curtailment of jobs and the undermining of conditions of employment for members of the bargaining unit constituted a statutory subject of collective bargaining. The issue in that case was whether state antitrust laws could be applied to a provision of a collective bargaining agreement which fixed the minimum rental to be paid by the employer motor carrier who leased vehicles to be driven by their owners rather than the carrier's employees. We held that the agreement was upon a subject matter as to which federal law directed the parties to bargain and hence that state antitrust laws could not be applied to prevent the effectuation of the agreement. We pointed out that the agreement was a "direct frontal attack upon a problem thought to threaten the maintenance of the basic wage structure established by the collective-bargaining contract. The inadequacy of a rental which means that the owner makes up his excess costs from his driver's wages not only clearly bears a close relation to labor's efforts to improve working conditions but is in fact a vital concern to the carrier's employed drivers; an inadequate rental might mean the progressive curtailment of jobs through withdrawal of more and more carrier-owned vehicles from service." Id. at 294.

Thus, we concluded that such a matter is a subject of mandatory bargaining under § 8 (d). Id. at 294–295. The only difference between that case and the one at hand is that the work of the employees in the bargaining unit was let out piecemeal in *Oliver,* whereas here the work of the entire unit has been contracted out. In reaching the conclusion that the subject matter in *Oliver* was a mandatory subject of collective bargaining, we cited with approval *Timken Roller Bearing Co.* 70 NLRB 500, 518, *enforcement denied on other grounds,* 161 F2d 949 (C.A. 6th Cir 1947), where the Board in a situation factually similar to the present case held that §§ 8(a)(5) and 9(a) required the employer to bargain about contracting out work then being performed by members of the bargaining unit.

The facts of the present case illustrate the propriety of submitting the dispute to collective negotiation. The Company's decision to contract out the maintenance work did not alter the Company's basic operation. The maintenance work still had to be performed in the plant. No capital investment was contemplated; the Company merely replaced existing employees with those of an independent contractor to do the same work under similar conditions of employment. Therefore, to require the employer to bargain about the matter would not significantly abridge his freedom to manage the business.

The Company was concerned with the high cost of its maintenance operations. It was induced to contract out the work by assurances from independent contractors that economies could be derived by reducing the work force, decreasing fringe benefits, and eliminating overtime payments. These have long been regarded as matters peculiarly suitable for resolution within the collective-bargaining framework, and industrial experience demonstrates that collective negotiation has been highly successful in achieving peaceful accommodation of the conflicting interests. Yet, it is contended that when an employer can effect cost savings in these respects by contracting the work out, there is no need to attempt to achieve similar economies through negotiation with existing employees or to provide them with an opportunity to negotiate a mutually acceptable alternative. The short answer is that, although it is not possible to say whether a satisfactory solution could be reached, national labor policy is founded upon the congressional determination that the chances are good enough to warrant subjecting such issues to the process of collective negotiation.

The appropriateness of the collective bargaining process for resolving such issues was apparently recognized by the Company. In explaining its decision to contract out the maintenance work, the Company pointed out that in the same plant other unions "had joined hands with management in an effort to bring about an economical and efficient operation," but "we had not been able to attain that in our discussions with this particular Local." Accordingly, based on past bargaining experience with this union, the Company unilaterally contracted out the work. While "the Act does not encourage a party to engage in fruitless marathon discussions at the expense of frank statement and support of his position," *Labor Board* v. *American Nat. Ins. Co.* 343 US 395, 404, it at least demands that the issue be submitted to the mediatory influence of collective negotiations. As the Court of Appeals pointed out, "it is not necessary that it be likely or probable that the union be afforded an opportunity to meet management's legitimate complaints that its maintenance was unduly costly."

We are thus not expanding the scope of mandatory bargaining to hold, as we do now, that the type of "contracting out" involved in this case—the replacement of employees in the existing bargaining unit with those of an independent contractor to do the same work under similar conditions of employment—is a statutory subject of collective bargaining under § 8(d). Our decision need not and does not encompass other forms of "contracting out" or "sub-contracting" which arise daily in our complex economy.

The only question remaining is whether, upon a finding that the Company had refused to bargain about a matter which is a statutory subject of collective bargaining, the Board was empowered to order the resumption of maintenance operations and reinstatement with back pay. We believe that it was so empowered.

Section 10(c) provides that the Board, upon a finding that an unfair labor practice has been committed, "shall issue . . . an order requiring such person to cease and desist from such unfair labor practice, and to take such affirmative action including reinstatement of employees with or without back pay, as will effectuate the policies of this Act. . . ."

That section "charges the Board with the task of devising remedies to effectuate the policies of the Act." *Labor Board* v. *Seven-Up Bottling Co.* 344 US 344, 346. The Board's power is a broad discretionary one, subject to limited judicial review. Ibid. "The relation of a remedy to policy is peculiarly a matter for administrative competence. . . ." *Phelps Dodge Corp.* v. *Labor Board*, 313 US 177, 194. "In fashioning remedies to undo the effects of violations of the Act, the Board must draw on enlightenment gained from experience." *Labor Board* v. *Seven-Up Bottling Co.* 344 US 344, 346. The Board's order will not be disturbed "unless it can be shown that the order is a patent attempt to achieve ends other than those which can fairly be said to effectuate the policies of the Act." *Virginia Elec. & Power Co.* v. *Labor Board*, 319 US 533, 540. Such a showing has not been made in this case.

There has been no showing that the Board's order restoring the *status quo ante* to insure meaningful bargaining is not well designed to promote the policies of the Act. Nor is there evidence which would justify disturbing the Board's conclusion that the order would not impose an undue or unfair burden on the Company.

It is argued, nonetheless, that the award exceeds the Board's powers under § 10(c) in that it infringes the provision that "no order of the Board shall require the reinstatement of any individual as an employee who has been suspended or discharged, or the payment to him of any back pay, if such individual was suspended or discharged for cause. . . ." The legislative history of that provision indicates that it was designed to preclude the Board from reinstating an individual who had been discharged because of misconduct. There is no indication, however, that it was designed to curtail the Board's power in fashioning remedies when the loss of employment stems directly from an unfair labor practice as in the case at hand.

The judgment of the Court of Appeals is

Affirmed.

Alternatives to Agreement

Failure to reach an agreement in the interpretation or application of an existing contract or when negotiating a new collective-bargaining agreement can result in interruptions in the productive process through strikes and lockouts. There are, however, some alternatives available to the parties that can serve to prevent such things from taking place. Those that we shall consider here are conciliation, mediation, and arbitration.

CONCILIATION, MEDIATION, AND ARBITRATION

Frequently the terms *conciliation* and *mediation* are used interchangeably. However, they are distinguishable and for purposes of definition the differences should be noted. Conciliation is an attempt to reestablish contact between the parties to a dispute in an effort to have them discuss the points on which they have conflicting opinions. The conciliator attempts to show these parties the advantages of settlement but he does not make recommendations or provide them with solutions. When conciliation fails, mediation may take place. The mediator takes a more active role and offers suggestions or compromises to the parties in an effort to settle the controversy. Acceptance of the recommendations of the mediator results in a settlement, but it should be noted that neither party is bound to accept any of his recommendations nor does the acceptance by one party bind the other. An agreement to go to mediation is simply an agreement to listen.

Arbitration is generally a more formal procedure. When parties agree to arbitrate they agree to accept the decision of a third party, or a board, and both parties are bound to accept this decision as final.

There is no federal labor legislation that specifically provides for the compulsory arbitration of labor disputes.[21] However, the Taft-Hartley Act did lay the foundation for voluntary arbitration by establishing the Federal Mediation and Conciliation Service. It should be emphasized that this service does not take an active part in the arbitration process, but rather stands ready to provide assistance to parties to a dispute if they have mutually agreed to arbitration and request advice. This assistance takes the form of providing a list of arbitrators who are qualified to hear the issues. Final selection is made by agreement between the disputants. The arbitrators who are recommended by the Federal Mediation and Conciliation Service conform to the standards and the fee schedule that the Service has established. There is also a private organization, the American Arbitration Association, that provides services to parties seeking assistance in establishing or conducting arbitration procedures. Other methods for the selection or appointment of arbitrators may be established by the parties and is usually explained in the collective bargaining agreement. In some very large organizations arbitrators may be retained on a permanent basis.

Arbitration, then, is voluntary and there are no legislative requirements for the conduct of the proceedings. For these reasons and others there are advantages to both parties that should be recognized so that the process might be encouraged as a substitute for industrial conflict. Of major importance is the fact that arbitration is much more economical in terms of time as well as money. Not uncommonly, the expense of arbitration is shared by the parties and amounts to much less than the accumulations of expense that can accrue in the lengthy process of litigation and appeals or strikes. Of importance, too, is the fact that the hearings conducted by an arbitrator are private and can be much less legalistic in conduct and language. As a result, there is

[21] The U.S. Arbitration Act passed in 1925 exempts disputes arising out of contracts of employment.

more latitude as to the admissibility of evidence and an opportunity for a better understanding for both parties. Of equal significance is the fact that arbitration paves the way for future negotiations because the parties have voluntarily agreed to accept the arbitrator's decision. Furthermore, a contractual agreement to arbitrate can prevent interruptions in the productive process which can be of considerable economic significance to the parties involved.

Another alternative to agreement that should be considered briefly is the use of the national emergency strike procedure. While this process was discussed in the previous chapter, it is mentioned here to remind the reader that it can serve to delay a strike through its provisions for a "cooling-off" period and injunctive relief. It should be noted, however, that these provisions will not guarantee that a strike will be prevented unless the parties agree to arbitration or unless an agreement is reached voluntarily before the no-strike period expires.

The foregoing clearly illustrates that the federal government stands ready to assist in the collective bargaining process by providing the machinery that serves to motivate the parties toward agreement. At the same time the government has excluded itself from actively participating in the process and by so doing perpetuates the philosophy that excellence in labor-management relations can be best achieved by encouraging voluntary and mutual agreement between the parties.

Summary

A study of the Landrum-Griffin Act would not be complete without evaluating whether or not the Act and the amendments that were made to it were effective in closing the loopholes that resulted from judicial interpretations of some of the Taft-Hartley Act provisions.

EFFECT ON THE TAFT-HARTLEY ACT

The problem areas that were identified in our discussion of the Taft-Hartley Act in Chapter Nine included activities with respect to "hot-cargo" clauses and "no man's land." The legislation is quite explicit as to the identification and definition of the circumstances surrounding these activities. While secondary boycotts and recognition or organizational picketing received special attention in the Landrum-Griffin Act, there are still instances where precise interpretation of the law is difficult.

This legislation also has provided additional guidelines and modifications to the collective bargaining process through the identification of alternatives available when agreements are difficult to reach. In doing this, the Landrum-Griffin Act has reaffirmed the desirability of collective bargaining and strengthened the processes that enhance industrial peace. In conclusion, it appears that the legislative purpose and intent of the drafters of this law have been basically accomplished.

APPENDIX 11 A

Notice to Managers

Notice to Storage [sic] Manager and Store Employees.

We are advised that you are presently engaged in selling Washington State Apples.

The 1960 crop of Washington State Apples is being packed by non-union firms, including 26 firms in the Yakima Valley. Prior to this year, the 26 Yakima Valley firms had been parties to a collective-bargaining contract with Teamsters Union Local 760 of Yakima, Washington, but this year, when a new contract was being negotiated, the employers took the position that many of the basic provisions of the prior contract, such as seniority, overtime, protection against unjust discharge, grievance procedure, and union security, should be weakened or eliminated entirely. These extreme demands plus a refusal to bargain in good faith led to a strike against the employer. The union made all possible efforts to avoid this strike, as did outside agencies who were assisting in the negotiations. Even the Governor of the State of Washington, the Honorable Albert D. Rosellini, intervened and suggested that the parties agree to a fact finding committee or arbitration. The union agreed to these proposals but the employers declined.

The employer's refusal to bargain in good faith has caused the Seattle office of the National Labor Relations Board to prepare a complaint against the employers, charging them with unfair labor practices in violation of federal law.

The strike at Yakima is still continuing and in order to win this strike, we must ask the consuming public not to purchase Washington State Apples.

Therefore, we are going to place peaceful pickets at the entrances to your store for the purpose of trying to persuade the public not to buy Washington Apples. These pickets are being instructed to patrol peacefully in front of the store, to stay away from the delivery entrances and not to interfere with the work of your employees, or with deliveries to or pickups

from your store. A copy of the instructions which have been furnished to
the pickets is attached herewith.

We do not intend that any of your employees cease work as a result of
the picketing. We ask that you advise your employees of our intentions in
this respect, perhaps by posting this notice on your store bulletin board.

If any of your employees should stop work as a result of our program, or
if you should have any difficulties as far as pickups and deliveries are concerned, or if you observe any of the pickets disobeying the instructions
which they have been given, please notify the undersigned union representative at once and we will take steps to see that the situation is promptly
corrected.

As noted above, our information indicates that you are presently selling
Washington State Apples. If, however, this information is not correct and
you are selling apples exclusively from another state, please notify the undersigned and we will see that the pickets are transferred to another store
where Washington State Apples are actually being sold.

Thank you for your cooperation.

APPENDIX 11 B

Instructions to Pickets

Dear Picket:

You are being asked to help publicize a nationwide consumer boycott
aimed at non-union Washington State Apples. To make this program a success your cooperation is essential. Please read these instructions and follow
them carefully.

1. At all times you are to engage in peaceful picketing. You are forbidden to engage in any altercation, argument, or misconduct of any kind.

2. You are to walk back and forth on the sidewalk in front of the consumer entrances to the grocery stores. If a particular store is located toward
the rear of a parking lot, you are to ask the store manager for permission to
walk back and forth on the apron or sidewalk immediately in front of the
store; but if he denies you this permission, you are to picket only on the
public sidewalk at the entrances to the parking lot. As far as large shipping
centers are concerned, you will be given special instruction for picketing in
such locations.

3. You are not to picket in front of or in the area of any entrance to the
store which is apparently set aside for the use of store employees and delivery men. As noted above, you are to limit your picketing to the consumer
entrances to the store.

4. This union has no dispute with the grocery stores, and you are forbidden to make any statement to the effect that the store is unfair or on

strike. You are also forbidden to request that the customers not patronize the store. We are only asking that the customers not buy Washington State apples when they are shopping at the store.

5. Similarly, you are not to interfere with the work of any employees in the store. If you are asked by these employees what the picketing is about, you are to tell them it is an advertising or consumer picket and that they should keep working. Likewise if you are asked by any truck drivers who are making pickups or deliveries what the picket is about, you are to advise that it is an advertising or consumer picket and that it is not intended to interfere with pickups or deliveries (i.e., that they are free to go through).

6. If you are given handbills to distribute, please distribute these handbills in a courteous manner and if the customers throw them on the ground, please see that they are picked up at once and that the area is kept clean.

7. You are forbidden to use intoxicating beverages while on duty or to have such beverages on your person.

8. If a state official or any other private party should complain to you about the picketing, advise them you have your instructions and that their complaints should be registered with the undersigned union representative.

9. These instructions should answer most of your questions concerning this program. However, if you have any additional questions or if specific problems arise which require additional instructions, please call the undersigned.

12

PUBLIC EMPLOYEES: ISSUES AND THE LAW

A study of the law of labor relations would not be complete without considering employer-employee relations in the public sector of the economy. This sector has become of increasing importance in recent years and represents that part of organized labor which ". . . has grown faster over the past two decades than in other major industry sectors. It has more than doubled since 1947, increasing from 5.5 million to 11.6 million." [1]

Public Employee Defined

The public employee is found in almost every kind of employment and he has a significant place in the efficient functioning of the econ-

[1] These figures include state and local as well as federal employee membership, the former representing about 90% of the 6-million increase. Joseph

375

omy. Some classes of federal as well as state and local public employees can be identified as civil service workers, public health and hospital employees, civilians in the military, policemen, firemen, and all those employees performing the hundreds of functions that are essential to the continuous functioning of any level of government. Difficulty in distinguishing between the public and private employee arises when there are persons performing the same tasks according to the same job descriptions and perhaps in the same physical location, one of whom is classified as a public employee and the other as a private employee; for example, a regular police force employed by a state government but aided and assisted by a large complement of private citizens who are supported by a non-governmental agency. A similar situation can occur in other essential services performed by fire protection agencies, parks and recreational facilities, hospital services, and educational institutions. Identification of these persons as public or private employees depends upon the circumstances surrounding each individual situation. While situations such as those described are more likely to occur at the state and local level, they are not uncommon in the federal services.

Whether an employee is considered public or private usually depends on the activity of the employer. In *National Labor Relations Board* v. *Carroll*,[2] a case involving the transportation of mail to and from a United States Post Office, the question of classifying an employer came before the court. In this case the owner of a transportation service had a contract with the government to perform certain services. The party involved had four other persons in his employ who operated his trucks. The contract stipulated that the truck drivers were to meet certain standards, sign a Post Office Department oath, and wear a cap and badge that identified them as postal workers. While performing their duties these men were under the direct supervision of the postmaster or other postal representatives. Furthermore, the postmaster had the authority to require the suspension of a driver by the operator if he believed his performance on the job did not meet the standards required. However, the operator also had the freedom to hire and fire whomever he chose and the right to determine work schedules and pay rates. The court in this case held that the United States was not the employer of the drivers of the trucks.

In a later case, which was decided after the passage of the Taft-

P. Goldberg, U.S. Bureau of Labor Statistics, *Monthly Labor Review*, "Labor-Management Relations Law in Public Service," (1968), p. 48.

[2] 120 F 2d 457 (1941).

Hartley Act, the issue of employer classification also arose.[3] The Governor of Missouri issued an order under a Missouri statute that would allow the state to take over the operation of a transit company which operated in the states of Missouri and Kansas and against whom a strike had been called. A Missouri Circuit Court issued an injunction that would prevent the strike "against the State of Missouri" from continuing. This order was affirmed by the Missouri Supreme Court ". . . on the ground that the statute was constitutional as 'strictly emergency legislation' designed solely to authorize the use of the state's police power to protect the public from threatened breakdowns in vital community services." [4]

It will be recalled that the National Labor Relations Act includes public utilities as a part of the definition of employer and also that Congress rejected the idea of treating them differently from other employers. In this case the state had seized a transit company to prevent a strike that would result in a breakdown in service to the public. The opinion of the court follows:

DIVISION 1287 OF THE AMALGAMATED ASSOCIATION OF
STREET, ELECTRIC RAILWAY AND MOTOR COACH
EMPLOYEES OF AMERICA ET AL., APPELLANTS,

v.

STATE OF MISSOURI: 1963
(374 U.S. 74)

The Supreme Court of the United States, opinion by Mr. Justice Stewart, announced by Mr. Justice White:

The appellant union is the certified representative of a majority of the employees of Kansas City Transit, Inc., a Missouri corporation which operates a public transit business in Kansas and Missouri. A collective bargaining agreement between the appellant and the company was due to expire on October 31, 1961, and in August of that year, after appropriate notices, the parties commenced the negotiation of an amended agreement. An impasse in these negotiations was reached, and in early November the appellant's members voted to strike. The strike was called on November 13.

[3] *Division 1287 of the Amalgamated Association of Street, Electric Railway and Motor Coach Employees of America v. State of Missouri,* 374 U.S. 74 (1963).

[4] *Ibid.*

The same day the Governor of Missouri, acting under the authority of a state law known as the King-Thompson Act issued a proclamation that the public interest, health, and welfare were jeopardized by the threatened interruption of the company's operations, and by an executive order purported to take possession "of the plants, equipment, and all facilities of the Kansas City Transit, Inc., located in the State of Missouri, for the use and operation by the State of Missouri in the public interest." A second executive order provided in part that "All rules and regulations . . . governing the internal management and organization of the company, and its duties and responsibilities, shall remain in force and effect throughout the term of operation by the State of Missouri."

Pursuant to a provision of the Act which makes unlawful any strike or concerted refusal to work as a means of enforcing demands against the utility or the State after possession has been taken by the State, the State petitioned the Circuit Court of Jackson County for an injunction on November 15, 1961. A temporary restraining order was issued on that day, and the strike and picketing were discontinued that evening. After a two-day trial, the order was continued in effect, and the Circuit Court later entered a permanent injunction barring the continuation of the strike "against the State of Missouri."

On appeal to the Supreme Court of Missouri, the appellants argued that the King-Thompson Act is in conflict with and is preempted by federal labor legislation, and that it abridges rights guaranteed by the First, Thirteenth, and Fourteenth Amendments. Reaffirming its earlier decisions in cases arising under the Act, the Supreme Court of Missouri rejected these arguments and affirmed the issuance of the injunction. 361 SW2d 33. We noted probable jurisdiction. 371 US 961.

We are met at the threshold with the claim that this controversy has become moot, and that we are accordingly foreclosed from considering the merits of the appeal. The basis for this contention is the fact that, after the appellants' jurisdictional statement was filed in this Court, the Governor of Missouri issued an executive order which, although reciting that the labor dispute between Kansas City Transit, Inc., and the appellant union "remains unresolved," nevertheless terminated the outstanding seizure order, upon the finding that "continued exercise by me of such authority is not justified in the circumstances of the aforesaid labor dispute."

Reliance for the claim of mootness is placed upon this Court's decisions in *Harris* v. *Battle*, 348 US 803, and *Oil, Chemical & Atomic Workers International Union* v. *Missouri*, 361 US 363. In the Oil Workers Case the Court declined to consider constitutional challenges to the King-Thompson Act, and in the *Harris* case declined to rule on the constitutionality of a similar Virginia statute, on the ground that the controversies had become moot. In both of those cases, however, the underlying labor dispute had been settled and new collective-bargaining agreements concluded by the time the litigation reached this Court. Here, by contrast the labor dispute remains unresolved. There thus exists in the present case not merely the speculative possibility of invocation of the King-Thompson Act in some future labor dispute, but the presence of an existing unresolved dispute which continues subject to all the provisions of the Act. . . . The situation here is thus quite different from that presented in the *Harris* and *Oil Workers Unions* cases, and we hold that the merits of this controversy are before us and must be decided.

The King-Thompson Act defines certain public utilities as "life essentials of the people" and declares it to be the policy of the State that "the possibility of labor strife in utilities operating under governmental franchise or permit or under governmental ownership and control is a threat to the welfare and health of the people." The Act imposes requirements in connection with the duration and renewal of collective bargaining agreements, and creates a State Board of Mediation and public hearing panels whose services are to be invoked whenever the parties cannot themselves agree upon the terms to be included in a new agreement. And where, as here, the recommendations of these agencies are not accepted, and the continued operation of the utility is threatened as a result, the Governor is empowered to "take immediate possession of" the utility "for the use and operation by the state of Missouri in the public interest."

In *Bus Employees* v. *Wisconsin Board*, 340 US 383, this Court held that the Wisconsin Public Utility Anti-Strike Law, which made it a misdemeanor for public utility employees to engage in a strike which would cause an interruption of an essential public utility service, conflicted with the National Labor Relations Act and was therefore invalid under the Supremacy Clause of the Constitution. The Supreme Court of Missouri in the present case rejected the appellants' argument that the Wisconsin Board decision was determinative of the unconstitutionality of the Missouri statute here in issue. The court held that the provisions of the King-Thompson Act dealing with the mediation board and public hearing panels were severable from the remainder of the statute, and refused to pass on any but those provisions which authorize the seizure and the issuance of injunctions against strikes taking place after seizure has been imposed. These provisions, the court ruled, do not—as in the *Wisconsin Board* Case—provide a comprehensive labor code conflicting with federal legislation, but rather represent "strictly emergency legislation" designed solely to authorize use of the State's police power to protect the public from threatened breakdowns in vital community services. Emphasizing that the company was not a party to the injunction suit, the court concluded that, although the State did not actively participate in the management of the utility's operations, the Governor's executive order had been sufficient to convert the strike into one against the State, and that an injunction barring such a strike is therefore not barred by the provisions of federal labor legislation. 361 SW 2d, at 44, 46, 48–52.

We disagree. None of the distinctions drawn by the Missouri court between the King-Thompson Act, and the legislation involved in *Wisconsin Board* seem to us to be apposite. First, whatever the status of the title to the properties of Kansas City Transit, Inc., acquired by the State as a result of the Governor's executive order, the record shows that the State's involvement fell far short of creating a state-owned and operated utility whose labor relations are by definition excluded from the coverage of the National Labor Relations Act. The employees of the company did not become employees of Missouri. Missouri did not pay their wages, and did not direct or supervise their duties. No property of the company was actually conveyed, transferred, or otherwise turned over to the State. Missouri did not participate in any way in the actual management of the company, and there was no change of any kind in the conduct of the company's business. As summed up by the Chairman of the State Mediation Board: "So far as I know the company is operating now just as it was two weeks ago before the strike."

Secondly, the *Wisconsin Board* Case decisively rejected the proposition that a state enactment affecting a public utility operating in interstate commerce could be saved from a challenge based upon a demonstrated conflict with the standards embodied in federal law simply by designating it as "emergency legislation." There the Court said that where "the state seeks to deny entirely a federally guaranteed right which Congress itself restricted only to a limited extent in case of national emergencies, however serious, it is manifest that the state legislation is in conflict with federal law." 340 US, at 394.

The short of the matter is that Missouri, through the fiction of "seizure" by the State, has made a peaceful strike against a public utility unlawful, in direct conflict with federal legislation which guarantees the right to strike against a public utility, as against any employer engaged in interstate commerce. In forbidding a strike against an employer covered by the National Labor Relations Act, Missouri has forbidden the exercise of rights explicitly protected by § 7 of that Act. Collective bargaining, with the right to strike at its core, is the essence of the federal scheme. As in *Wisconsin Board,* a state law which denies that right cannot stand under the Supremacy Clause of the Constitution.

It is hardly necessary to add that nothing we have said even remotely affects the right of a State to own or operate a public utility or any other business, nor the right or duty of the chief executive or legislature of a State to deal with emergency conditions of public danger, violence, or disaster under appropriate provisions of the State's organic or statutory law.

Reversed.

The Law as It Applies to Public Employees

Historically, various programs have been proposed that would serve to clearly establish the position of the public employee and his rights in the conduct of labor-management relations. To appreciate the pattern of the social and political attitude prior to a consideration of what are now established as the public employee's rights, a few of the proposals will be considered briefly.

As early as 1902, lobbying by factions working to acquire improvements for persons in the federal service was so intensive President Theodore Roosevelt issued a "gag order" to quell the activity. Again in 1906, President Roosevelt issued an executive order that prohibited:

. . . all officers and employees of the United States . . . individually or through their associations to solicit an increase in pay, or to
influence . . . any other legislation whatever, either before the
Congress or its Committee . . . save through the heads of the Departments . . . in or under which they serve, on penalty of dismissal from the Government Service.[5]

This was followed by even more stringent executive orders in 1910
and 1912 which were issued by President William Taft. These orders
did not prohibit the organization of employees but were quite explicit in identifying the appropriate machinery for the airing of
grievances. These "gag orders" did not effectively subdue the determination of either the public employees or their representatives from continuing efforts to achieve a legislative enactment that would provide
them with some recourse against the arbitrary decision-making of administrative heads.

The postal employees were affected by the passage of the Lloyd-
La Follette Act on August 12, 1912, which provided:

. . . membership in any society, association . . . or any other
form of labor organization of postal employees not affiliated with
any outside organization imposing an obligation or duty on them
to engage in any strike or proposing to assist them in any strike,
against the United States, having for its objects, among other
things, improvements in the condition of labor or its members, including hours of labor and compensation therefor and leave of absence, by any person or groups of persons in said postal service, or
by the presenting by any such person or groups of persons of any
grievance or grievances to Congress or any member thereof shall
not constitute or be cause for reduction in rank or compensation or
removal . . . from said service.[6]

This legislation then gave sanction to the organization of public employees and made lobbying activity on their behalf lawful, but it did
not establish a real employer-employee relationship for those who
were in the public service.

Unceasing attempts have been made ever since on behalf of public
employees to establish an acceptable collective bargaining climate for

[5] Morton Robert Godine, *The Labor Problem in the Public Service*
(New York: Russell and Russell, 1967), p. 195.

[6] U.S., *Statutes at Large*, XXXVII, 539–560.

them and one that would parallel that enjoyed by employees in the private sector. We need not review here the advances made in employer-employee relationships in private industry, that having been the subject of preceding chapters; however, it is important to emphasize that no such program can be associated with the public employee. Some achievements were made after long and arduous efforts on the part of lobbyists and employee representatives. Advances in wages and an improvement in hours and working conditions were accomplished. That the position of the public employee was improved cannot be denied, however, the hoped for goals were not achieved.

Between 1912 and the passage of the Taft-Hartley Act, strikes were by no means nonexistent in the public employee arena even though Presidential pronouncements kept reminding those involved, as well as the public, that this was not allowed.[7] In the years 1958–1961 eleven out of every one million days of public employment were lost because of strike activity. In all of these strikes the major issues were economic, with disputes regarding union organization and working conditions being of less significance as a major issue.[8] During this period notable progress was also being made among the employees within the Government Printing Office and the Tennessee Valley Authority. By 1943 labor union membership of public employees had reached significant size and the problem of employee unrest had not abated. When the Taft-Hartley Act was passed, this legislation included an explicit statement with regard to labor disputes and government employees that stated:

> . . . It shall be unlawful for any individual employed by the United States or any agency thereof including wholly owned Government corporations to participate in any strike. Any individual employed by the United States or by any such agency who strikes shall be discharged immediately from his employment, and shall forfeit his civil service status, if any, and shall not be eligible for re-employment for three years by the United States or any such agency.[9]

This statement was later modified in 1955 and stronger restraints were placed on lawful activity:

[7] See David Ziskind, *One Thousand Strikes of Government Employees,* (New York: Columbia University Press, 1940).

[8] Loretto R. Nolan and James T. Hall, Jr., U.S. Bureau of Labor Statistics, *Monthly Labor Review,* "Strikes of Government Employees," (1963), pp. 52, 54.

[9] U.S., *Statutes at Large,* LXI, Part 1, 160.

. . . no person shall accept or hold office or employment in the government of the United States . . . , who . . . participates in any strike or asserts the right to strike against the Government . . . ; or is a member of an organization of Government employees that asserts the right to strike . . . , knowing that such an organization asserts such rights.[10]

From 1949 on additional efforts were made to secure passage of legislation dealing with government employees. Generally, these proposals would have permitted unions or their officers to (a) represent members in presenting grievances, (b) consult with agency heads in policy matters dealing with safety, grievances, transfers, and working conditions, and (c) be protected when performing any lawful activity. Moreover, when agreement could not be reached on policies the matter would be sent to an arbitration board for decision. The authority to enforce the law would lie with the Civil Service Commission. None of these efforts, however, resulted in the passage of any specific legislation although some measures were favorably reported out of committee and received public support from some senators.

Programs for Public Employees

In an effort to resolve this problem for workers in the federal service, a Task Force on Employee-Management Relations in the Federal Service was established by President Kennedy in 1961. After extensive investigations this group found that the manner in which the various agencies handled labor relations differed considerably and that of fifty-seven agencies, representing ninety-three percent of the employees of the Federal Government, one-third of these employees were members of an employee organization. The Task Force concluded: "Whenever any considerable number of employees have organized for the purpose of collective dealing the attitude of the Government should be an affirmative willingness to enter such relations." [11]

[10] 5 U.S. Code, Sect. 118.
[11] U.S., Civil Service Commission, *Employee-Management Cooperation in The Federal Service* (Washington: U.S. Government Printing Office, 1962), pp. 1.01, 3.01, 3.02.

EXECUTIVE ORDER 10987

In January of 1962, as a result of the Task Force investigations, Executive Order 10987 was issued to deal with agency systems for Appeals from Adverse Action. The issuance of Executive Order 10988 coincided with this and was developed to deal with employee-management cooperation in the Federal Service.[12] Executive Order 10987 orders agency and department heads to establish ". . . a system for the reconsideration of administrative decisions to take adverse action against employees." [13] Furthermore, the order also requires that an appeals system be established through which adverse decisions can receive consideration and review should a former or present employee so wish. Also, the employee involved is to be given the right to present his appeal with the advice and/or by a representative of his own choosing. The order excludes from coverage the Central Intelligence Agency, National Security Administration, the Federal Bureau of Investigation, the Atomic Energy Commission, and the Tennessee Valley Authority. Moreover, the order further provides that upon the recommendation of agency heads, the Civil Service Commission may also exclude certain classes of employees.[14]

EXECUTIVE ORDER 10988

Executive Order 10988 marks a significant step forward in the movement for the organization of employees in the public service. In Section 1 of the order, federal employees are given the right to join or refrain from joining an employee organization, and the language here is similar to that in the National Labor Relations Act which applies to employees in the private sector. The type of labor union that is acceptable to the terms of the order is described in Section 2. This section specifically excludes any organization ". . . which asserts the right to strike against the Government of the United States or any agency thereof, or to assist or participate in any such strike. . . ." [15]

Acceptable forms of recognition are covered by Sections 3 through 6 of the order. Differences as well as similarities between public and private regulations are present here. In the matter of recognition, it

[12] Each of these may be found in Appendix 12 A and 12 B respectively.

[13] *Federal Register*, XXVII, No. 13 (Washington: U.S. Government Printing Office, January 19, 1962), p. 550.

[14] *Ibid.*, pp. 550–551.

[15] *Ibid.*

will be recalled that under the Taft-Hartley Act the twelve-month period for recognition and bargaining status started from the date on which the collective-bargaining agreement was executed. In the Federal Service the twelve-month period for exclusive recognition extends from the time the organization is initially recognized.

Three kinds of recognition are available under the order. The first of these is similar to that which existed prior to the issuance of this order and is identified as "informal" recognition. This form of recognition may be granted to any employee organization that cannot qualify for one of the other forms whether or not any other employee organization has acquired "formal" or "exclusive" status. When informal recognition is given, the organization may offer its views and recommendations to the agency involved. The agency, however, is in no way obliged to solicit the advice of an organization recognized in this way when establishing policy. Recognition of this type then does not provide for an opportunity to execute a signed collective bargaining agreement.

The second form of recognition covered by the order is identified as "formal" recognition. This kind of recognition is granted when the following conditions are met: (1) no other organization has acquired "exclusive" status, (2) at least ten percent of the employees in the unit are members, and (3) the names of officers and representatives must be submitted to the agency as must a statement of the organization's objectives, constitution, and by-laws. Under this form of recognition the agency is required to consult with the employee organization on matters affecting its membership. This form of recognition also does not result in a written agreement between the agency and the employee organization.

The third kind of recognition described in the order is "exclusive" recognition. In addition to meeting the requirements for formal recognition, an employee organization seeking exclusive recognition must be designated as the representative by a majority of the employees in the unit. Exclusive recognition for the most part is not available to employees who are classified as performing executive, personnel (other than clerical), or supervisory-evaluation duties. Units also may not consist of both professional and nonprofessional personnel unless the former vote to be a part of such a unit. Having achieved this kind of recognition, the employee organization becomes the representative of all the employees in the unit and as such may enter into collective bargaining negotiations with appropriate agencies on matters that have to do with working conditions of the employees in the unit.

Bargaining does not extend to policies and regulations that have been established by legislative or congressional action.

Management prerogatives are included in Section 7 of the order and to a large extent deal with established policies regarding promotion, transfers, training, discipline, and work methods. The responsibility for the execution of these policies remains with agency officials. Section 8 declares that contract terms are to be applied only to employees of the unit for whom the agreement was reached. Arbitration may be utilized when issues arise relative to the terms of the agreement; however, it must be made clear that this arbitration is advisory only and the decision of the arbitrator is subject to the approval of the head of the agency who is under no obligation to accept the decision as a mandatory order. Under Section 9, employee organizations are required to perform their business with members or potential members on off-duty hours. The next four sections are concerned with the implementation of the requirements of the order as well as carrying out its provisions. The procedures for the determination of exclusive recognition are also outlined in the Civil Service Commission. The Department of Labor is instructed to draft Standards of Conduct for Labor Organizations as well as to develop a Code of Fair Labor Practices. The rights of employees in the event of being subject to an adverse action case are given consideration in Section 14. Section 15 presents a savings clause preserving agreements that had been in existence at the time the Executive Order was issued.

The final consideration of Executive Order 10988 is concerned with exemptions. Specifically excluded are the Federal Bureau of Investigation and the Central Intelligency Agency or any other agency that may be involved with investigative, security, or intelligence operations. This section also permits an agency head to exempt other persons when he believes it is necessary to the national interest. Those employees who are generally exempt from this Executive Order are not exempt from Section 14.

In order to see whether or not Executive Order 10988 had any significant effect on union membership in the public sector the following figures are of interest:

*Membership of Federal, State, and Local
Government Employees in Labor Organizations
for years 1958, 1960, 1962, 1963*[a]

				UNION AFFILIATION				
	ALL UNIONS			AFL-CIO			UNAFFILIATED	
		Members[b]			Members[b]			Members[b]	
		Number			Number			Number	
Year	Number	Thousands	Percent[c]	Number	Thousands	Percent[c]	Number	Thousands	Percent[c]
1958	41	1,035	5.8	28	769	5.2	13	266	8.6
1960	41	1,070	5.9	30	824	5.5	11	247	8.1
1962	41	1,225	7.0	27	948	6.4	14	277	9.9
1963	59	1,453,309	8.1	35	1,116,014	7.4	24	337,295	12.0

a) U. S., Department of Labor, Bureau of Labor Statistics, *Handbook of Labor Statistics* (Washington: U. S. Government Printing Office, 1967), pp. 253–254.

b) Number of members computed by applying reported percentage figures of total membership, including membership outside continental United States. Total membership, moreover, may include retired and unemployed workers.

c) Percent of total union membership.

These figures suggest that there may be a significant relationship between the issuance of Executive Order 10988 and an increase in the numbers and size of membership in both affiliated and non-affiliated unions representing this particular class of employees. During the two-year period 1965–1967 growth of non-postal employees exceeded one hundred percent. In 1968 it was reported that employee organizations representing one and one quarter million employees had acquired exclusive recognition. Moreover, two hundred unions were then recognized with 811,000 employees on voluntary checkoff.[16]

STANDARDS OF CONDUCT

As directed by Section 13, the Standards of Conduct for Employee Organizations and the Code of Fair Labor Practices were drawn up and delivered by memorandum from the President to the Heads of Executive Departments and Agencies on May 21, 1963.[17] As stated by the President, the purpose of these documents is to:

[16] "The Objectives of Unionism in the Federal Service," from a speech delivered by W. V. Gill, Director, Office of Labor-Management Relations, at the National Conference of the Society for Personnel Administration, Washington, D.C., June 6, 1968, *Civil Service Journal,* IX (July–September 1968), p. 19.

[17] See Appendix 12 C.

. . . assist in securing the uniform and effective implementation of the policies, rights and responsibilities described in the Order. . . . by fixing more definitely the responsibility of employee organizations and agencies, providing more detailed criteria for the protection of rights secured under the Order and establishing procedures in both of these areas which will assure a necessary measure of uniformity within the Executive Branch of the Federal Government.[18]

The Standards of Conduct will not permit agencies to recognize any employee organization that does not: (a) subscribe to or maintain democratic practices and procedures; (b) prohibit persons who have affiliation or association with totalitarian, corrupt, or Communist organizations from holding office in the organization; (c) have internal accounting and financial control; and (d) make an effort to prevent a conflict of business or financial interests between the officers and the organization itself. Furthermore, should any agency believe that these requirements are not met, it cannot discontinue recognition without first consulting with the organization in question. When unable to resolve an issue, the agency is obliged to consult with the Secretary of Labor.

The second section of this document deals with the specific procedures that must be followed when an agency wishes to deny, suspend, or withdraw its recognition of an employee organization. Briefly, these procedures cannot be instituted when an organization has met the requirements of the preceding section unless an agency has evidence that indicates the employee organization has not complied with the requirements of the parent organization, or because it does not maintain the standards set forth in Executive Order 10988, or has been denied recognition under the requisites of that order. In any case, an opportunity must be allowed the employee organization to be heard and, if requested, an agency must provide this organization with a report on the results of investigations that have been made. Agencies may also consult with the Secretary of Labor before instituting denial or suspension procedures and are obliged to do so before making a final decision in such a matter. If an organization has been denied, suspended, or withdrawn from recognition by one agency, any other agency may also refuse to recognize the

[18] *Federal Register*, XXVIII, No. 101 (Washington: U.S. Government Printing Office, May 23, 1963), p. 5127.

same organization without pursuing the entire process after providing the organization an opportunity to be heard and after consulting with the Secretary of Labor.

CODE OF FAIR LABOR PRACTICES

The second portion of this Presidential memorandum deals with a Code of Fair Labor Practices applicable to all agencies and employees that are covered by the Executive Order. Several management practices are prohibited. Prohibited practices include: any intrusion by management on any of the rights granted employees by Executive Order 10988; any discrimination that would encourage or discourage employee membership in an organization; the offering of anything other than routine assistance and service to employees and/or their organizations; the taking of disciplinary or discriminatory action against any employee because he may have given testimony or filed a complaint under the Order; and refusing to recognize or negotiate with qualified organizations.

Employee organizations are also prohibited from taking certain actions. Interference with an employee when he is exercising the rights given him through Executive Order 10988, efforts to induce coercion of employees by management, or to coerce an employee, and thereby hindering him in the performance of his duty to the United States is prohibited. There can be no discrimination in granting membership to an employee because of race, creed, color, or national origin; and calling a strike, work stoppage, or slowdown against the United States Government (this latter also includes picketing when such is used in lieu of a strike). Furthermore, organizations which have attained exclusive recognition status cannot deny membership to any employee who has met reasonable occupational standards and has paid uniform initiation fees and dues. The organizations can, however, enforce established and approved disciplinary standards.

The final section of this Code of Fair Labor Practices sets forth the procedures that are appropriate for enforcement. Agencies are required to establish avenues through which employee's, agency's, or employee organization's complaints can be filed, investigated, and processed. Moreover, when such a complaint is made by a single employee or a group of employees and is subject to an applicable grievance procedure presently within the agency, the latter is the procedure that is to be followed. If an issue arises that comes without established procedures then the procedure set forth in this section of the memorandum is to apply requiring first a method for resolving the issue informally. Secondly, the appointment of an impartial hearing officer or a panel must be made, and thirdly, when informal settlement cannot be effected, provision for a hearing to be held before this panel or officer. The right to a hearing carries with it representation by council and the findings of fact and/or recommendations. Rehearings of issues that have been processed previously under the Standards of Conduct in the Order (Section 11) are not allowed. At the conclusion of the hearings, the findings of fact and the recommendations, if made, are to be available to the complainant or respondent. Furthermore, a summary or the entire report indicating the basis on which the agency intends to rely as well as a statement giving the reasons for the action taken by the agency is also made available to the complainant or respondent. Those cases involving strikes or other prohibited activities, as outlined above, are covered by the procedures and are subject to those legal remedies deemed appropriate by the agency head and are not subject to the limitations set forth in the memorandum.

The final decisions that are reached, as well as the reasoning which supports them, in complaints filed under the Code of Fair Labor Practices are to be made available to the national employee organization as well as to the affiliate directly involved in the issue. When the decision declares that the agency has been responsible for conduct prohibited by the Code, it is ordered to remedy the violation. If the decision is against the employee organization, the agency informs the organization of the violation and requests that appropriate corrective action be taken. If the employee organization does not comply with such a request, the agency head may withhold, suspend, or withdraw recognition, whichever he deems appropriate in the particular circumstance.[19]

The issuance of these executive orders, the code, and the standards of conduct has served to more clearly identify the status of the public employee and the part he may play in the collective bargaining process. Government employees now have some voice in affairs that affect the conditions surrounding their employment. To illustrate the attitude of the court after the issuance of Executive Order 10988, the case of *Harry J. Amell* v. *United States*[20] is presented. While the issue deals with back pay for government employees working on gov-

[19] It is of interest at this point to suggest to the reader that a comparison be made of the prohibited actions set forth in the Code of Fair Labor Practices and the Unfair Labor Practices for employers and employees contained in the National Labor Relations Act as amended.

[20] 345 U.S. 158 (1966).

ernment ships and the filing of a claim for payment of their wages as an appropriate action for the Court of Claims or the Federal District Courts, it is included here because the court opinion presents interesting dialogue on whether the parties should be classified as federal workers or as seamen.

HARRY J. AMELL ET AL., PETITIONERS,
v.
UNITED STATES: 1966
(384 U.S. 158)

The Supreme Court of the United States, Mr. Chief Justice Warren delivering the opinion of the court:

The case before us presents interesting problems of a jurisdictional nature. The Suits in Admiralty Act vests exclusive jurisdiction in the district courts when the suit is of a maritime nature. Under the Tucker Act, the Court of Claims has jurisdiction over contractual claims against the United States. This jurisdictional interaction presents itself here.

The petitioners are employees of various federal executive departments working aboard government vessels. They filed contractual actions in the Court of Claims, alleging they were entitled to back pay increases and overtime pay for their labors, invoking various federal pay statutes and regulations. In all these suits, the petitioners predicated jurisdiction on the Tucker Act, which has a generous six-year limitations period and provides a grace period as well, 28 U.S.C. § 2501 (1964 ed.). Their employer, the United States, filed motions to have the actions transferred to various federal district courts on the ground that the claims were of a maritime nature and justiciable exclusively under the Suits in Admiralty Act. This Act provides only two years for claimants to file suit, and also requires exhaustion of administrative remedies, 46 USC § 745 (1964 ed.). The Court of Claims granted the motions without opinion, simply citing to three unreported cases in which it had made similar dispositions. To uphold this transfer would bar those claims which accrued more than two years prior to the time the actions were filed. We granted certiorari, 382 US 810, and reverse.

On its face, the Tucker Act permits all individuals with contractual claims against the Government to sue in the Court of Claims.

The Suits in Admiralty Act similarly affords an open berth in the district courts, provided the claims are of maritime nature. The question is which Act should be applicable to the claims brought here, and this in turn depends on whether these seafaring petitioners are more appropriately classified as federal workers or as mere seamen.

The Government takes the position that these employees are to be deprived of the liberal benefits of the longer limitations period available to all other government employees under the Tucker Act. This is so, the Government reasons, because for purposes of wage claims the petitioners' status as seamen overrides their acknowledged role as federal workers. In assuming this posture, the Government seeks the best of both worlds. Congress is depicted as ambivalent in treating these petitioners either as seamen or as federal employees depending on which status may redound more to the benefit of the Government's proprietary interest.

The Government acknowledges that the petitioners are governed by a patchwork pattern of federal statutes which encompass many facets of their economic welfare. With regard to so-called fringe benefits, pervasive government schemes provide for sick leave and vacation pay, and for death, health, medical, and pension programs. The petitioners' potential recovery for personal injuries is limited strictly by a workmen's compensation statute governing them as federal workers to the exclusion of both the Public Vessels Act, *Johansen* v. *United States,* 343 US 427, and the Suits in Admiralty Act, *Paterson* v. *United States,* 359 US 495. By virtue of their governmental employment, the petitioners' right to join unions and to select bargaining representatives, unlike that of private seamen, exists only by express leave of the President, Exec. Order No. 10988, 27 Fed Reg 551 (1962), and they are forbidden, under pain of discharge, fine and imprisonment, from exercising or asserting the right to strike, 69 Stat. 624, 5 U.S.C. §§ 118p–118r (1964 ed.).

When it comes to wage claims the Government treats the petitioners, to their detriment, as seamen. The workers, however, have their wages fixed by federal statutes and regulations, like other federal employees. It is true that their rates of pay are geared to the prevailing wage scale in private shipping operations, but this factor diminishes upon analysis. A host of federal workers, like these seamen, have their rates of pay so adjusted. The petitioners, then, are essentially no different from the civil servants who deliver the mail, fight forest fires, construct public buildings, or who engage in countless other tasks which affect virtually every phase of the country's well-being. The wage scale of government-employed seamen is fixed by federal agencies; it is not automatically adjusted to the rate of pay prevalent in private industry, and in some cases the private pay rates are not easily ascertained. Further, these government employees—unlike normal seamen— benefit from wage pay increases won in the private industry only prospectively and to a limited degree. Often in the maritime industry, private contract negotiations continue beyond the terminal date set in a collective-bargaining agreement. When the agreement is signed, however, it generally provides that the private seamen receive the increased pay retroactively. The government seamen receive pay increases only from the actual date agreement is reached in the private sector. Therefore, the back pay claims are more appropriately catalogued on the government side of the ledger, although they may have a salty tang.

This inference as to congressional intent is reinforced in considering the claims for overtime pay. Here there is a specific provision—Section 205 of the Federal Employees Pay Act of 1945—which fixes the ratio of overtime pay to the employees' basic pay. Congress has thus explicitly prescribed that overtime pay should be fixed in a uniform manner for all government wage-board employees, whether seamen or not. Furthermore, in determining the applicability of this uniform statutory requirement, the court will be interpreting the pay regulation of an executive department. This task is typically within the province and expertise of the Court of Claims.

We think the foregoing indicates that with respect to these wage claims, Congress thought of these petitioners more as government employees who happened to be seamen than as seamen who by chance worked for the Government. The remaining problems relate to specific legislative amendments. The Government approaches this by noting that the Suits in Admiralty Act specifically repealed the Tucker Act so far as the two conflicted. This may readily be conceded, see, e.g., *Calmar S. S. Corp.* v. *United States,* 345 U.S. 446, 455–466; *Matson Navigation Co.* v. *United States,* 284 U.S. 352. Compare *Patterson* v. *United States,* 359 U.S. 495. From this proposition it adduces the principle that exclusive admiralty jurisdiction is now so deeply woven in the fabric of the law that congressional action is required to overturn it, cf. *State Bd. of Ins.* v. *Todd Shipyards,* 370 U.S. 451, 458. This principle is sound where applicable, but such is not the case here.

The evolution of the law, both statutory and judicial, indicates that at least until 1960, the jurisdiction of the Court of Claims over government seamen's wage claims was unchallenged. We do not understand the Government to dispute this fact. For example, wage claims by federal employees were found to be expressly within the ambit of the Tucker Act in *Bruner* v. *United States,* 343 U.S. 112, 115. In *United States* v. *Townsley,* 323 U.S. 557, this Court affirmed a judgment against the Government for overtime wages in favor of a government-employed operator of a dredge. The Court of Claims had assumed jurisdiction over the suit, 101 Ct. Cl. 237, and the Government never disputed the issue. Subsequent cases are to the same effect. It was on this line of precedent that the petitioners relied in bringing suit. This fact is worthy of mention to illustrate the impact upon claimants whose suits would otherwise be time-barred if we were now to hold that the Suits in Admiralty Act restricted all suits in cases like the present to the district courts, cf. *Brady* v. *Roosevelt S. S. Co.,* 317 U.S. 575, 581.

In 1960, Congress addressed itself in the jurisdictional overlap between the Tucker Act and the Suits in Admiralty Act. Its major aim was to empower the Court of Claims to transfer suits to the district courts when the latter had exclusive jurisdiction over them. This it accomplished by providing that when the transfer was made, the original filing in the Court of Claims would tell the applicable limitations period, Act of Sept. 13, 1960, Pub. L. 86–770, 74 Stat. 912, 28 U.S.C. § 1506. Simultaneously, Congress abolished the distinction between public and merchant vessels, a matter which had sorely confused attorneys and had caused misfilings in the past, S. Rep. No. 1894 86th Cong., 2d Sess, pp. 3, 6. In amending the Suits in Admiralty Act, Congress also wanted to affirm the existing law that suits which were justiciable exclusively under it would be brought only in the district courts. The new § 2 of the Act, 46 U.S.C. § 742, in the words of the Senate Report, S. Rep. No. 1894, *supra,* at p. 2, "restates in brief and simple language the now existing exclusive jurisdiction conferred on the district courts, both on their admiralty and law sides, over cases against the United States which could be sued on in admiralty if private vessels, persons, or property were involved."

The Government would have us believe that this oblique reference to private "persons" was designed to make inroads on the right of government employees to sue in the Court of Claims. We reject this argument. The legislative history surrounding this enactment contains no discussion whatever concerning claims brought by government-employed seamen. This is highly significant because of the active interest in nautical legislation generally taken by the maritime labor unions. If Congress had meant to lower the limitations period from six to two years, surely these unions would have been privy to the decision; this is all the more true when one considers that seamen are often stationed far away from their home ports and need a lengthy period in which to register their claims. If they were governed by the maritime Act, they would be required not only to sue but to exhaust administrative remedies as well within the shorter period, 46 U.S.C. § 745 (1964 ed.).

In effect, the Government asks us to repeal the former practice by implication. We have held in numerous cases that such a request bears a heavy burden of persuasion, e.g., *Bulova Watch Co.* v. *United States,* 365 U.S. 753, 758; *Fourco Glass Co.* v. *Transmirra Corp.,* 353 U.S. 222, 228–229. Further, Congress had the opportunity in 1964 to deprive government-employed claimants of their rights when it amended the Tucker Act itself. Instead, Congress broadened the forums available to plaintiffs suing the Government for fees, salary or compensation for official services, giving the district courts concurrent jurisdiction with the Court of Claims in matters of less than $10,000, 78 Stat. 699, 28 U.S.C. § 1346(d) (1964 ed.).

As in other jurisdictional questions involving intersecting statutes, there is no positive answer. We can do no more than to exercise our best judgment in interpreting the will of Congress. In this instance, we believe the traditional treatment of federal employees by the Government tips the balance in favor of Court of Claims jurisdiction. The Court of Claims possesses the expertise necessary to adjudicate government wage claims. It also serves as a centralized forum for developing the law, particularly in large wage claim suits. These tasks have been its responsibility since 1887. In multiparty wage suits of large amounts, having one forum eliminates any problem of transferring venue from several district courts to one locale, see 28 U.S.C. § 1406 (1964 ed.). If we are here mis-construing the intent of Congress, it can easily set the matter to rest by explicit language. We therefore reverse and remand the suits to the Court of Claims for further proceedings.

It is so ordered.

It should be mentioned that many state and local government employees are subject also to legislation enacted by the various states and not infrequently these statutes have been patterned after the federal legislation. The following illustrations are typi-cal of state attitude. In *McAlen* v. *Jersey City Incinerator Au-thority,* (N. J. Sup. Ct. App. Div. 1963), the New Jersey court de-clared that a strike against the Jersey City Incinerator Authority was not legal. The Jersey City Incinerator Authority had been developed by the municipal government to administer the city's garbage removal operation. This being the case, the strike was actually against the municipal government.[21] An Illinois court in *Board of Education of Community Unit School District 2* v. *Redding* (Illinois Sup. Ct., 1965), held that the peaceful picketing done by cus-todians at public school sites was not a lawful exercise of free speech under either the federal or state Constitutions.[22]

Each of the statutes in those states that have enacted legislation with respect to the public employee have similarities as well as differ-ences which we need not discuss here; it is sufficient to say that strike activity is also prohibited in all statutes at the state and local levels.

There have been numerous instances of public employees partici-pating in many forms of work stoppages or slowdowns at the state and local levels. Since the issuance of Executive Order 10988, how-ever, there have been only fifteen occasions in the Federal Service when a strike, work stoppage, or slowdown seemed imminent. Twelve of these were averted, however, and only three actually resulted in a violation of the law. A strike took place at the Tennessee Valley Au-thority during August of 1962, and as a result some eighty-one em-ployees were fired. In 1968 there were two incidents, one in Newark, New Jersey, in which postal workers were involved in a walk-out and the other in New York when employees of the Weather Bureau engaged in picketing.[23]

[21] *Labor Relations Reference Manual, Cumulative Digest and Index, 1960–1965,* (Washington: Bureau of National Affairs, 1966), p. 1019.
[22] *Ibid.*
[23] Grill, *op. cit.*

Summary

In this chapter we have looked at the position of the public employee and the status afforded him through legislative enactment as compared to the position held by an employee working at a comparable job in the private sector. While Executive Orders 10987 and 10988 have resulted in giving the public employee a larger voice in the labor-management relationship, he is still without many of the bargaining advantages his counterpart enjoys in private industry. Perhaps the greatest disadvantage under which the public employee works is that which does not permit him to legally strike. The question of whether or not he should have this right is not at issue here. However, it has long been recognized that the strike is the most powerful weapon an employee possesses. To be without this weapon leaves a worker with very little leverage with which he can exert pressure on an employer to achieve any changes in conditions of work.

There are other matters on which the public employee cannot negotiate or bargain with management. In many cases the schedules of salaries and wages are established by legislative enactment and management has neither the authority nor the power to make or commit itself to modification. In the Federal service such things as retirement plans, promotions, transfers, fringe benefits, vacations, and seniority are established by Civil Service regulations and do not come within the scope of administrative decision-making.

One may conclude that the collective bargaining process, though recognized as desirable and lawful in the public sector, is only a poor reflection of that which exists in private industry. Basically, the process appears to be a willingness to accept employee rights to organize but having done this it becomes a matter of negotiating so that recommendations will be heard and passed on. This by itself does not provide the public employee with a collective bargaining climate in any way comparable to that which prevails in private industry. It does not seem likely that efforts to strengthen the public employee's position will decline in the future but, rather, will gain strength in an effort to extend to this sector the same advantages that have accrued to employees in the private sector.

APPENDIX 12 A

Executive Order 10987:1962

AGENCY SYSTEMS FOR APPEALS FROM ADVERSE ACTIONS

WHEREAS the public interest requires the maintenance of high standards of employee performance and integrity in the public service, prompt administrative action where such standards are not met, and safeguards to protect employees against arbitrary or unjust adverse actions; and

WHEREAS the prompt reconsideration of protested administrative decisions to take adverse actions against employees will promote the efficiency of the service, assist in maintaining a high level of employee morale, further the objective of improving employee-management relations, and insure timely correction of improper adverse actions;

Now, THEREFORE, by virtue of the authority vested in me by the Constitution of the United States, by Section 1753 of the Revised Statutes (5 U.S.C.631), by the Civil Service Act of 1883 (22 Stat. 403; 5 U.S.C. 632, et seq.), and as President of the United States, it is hereby ordered as follows:

SECTION 1. The head of each department and agency, in accord with the provisions of this order and regulations issued thereunder by the Civil Service Commission, and to the extent specified in such regulations, shall establish within the department or agency a system for the reconsideration of administrative decisions to take adverse action against employees. Information on the system shall be brought to the attention of all employees. Within the principles established by this order and subject to the broad guidelines contained in the regulations, each department and agency is authorized to develop such agency appeals procedures as may be appropriate to its own organizational requirements.

SEC. 2. (a) The Civil Service Commission shall, not later than April 1, 1962, issue regulations to put this order into effect and shall make a continuing review of the manner in which this order is being implemented by the departments and agencies.

(b) Nothing in this order shall be deemed to enlarge or restrict the authority of the Civil Service Commission to adjudicate appeals submitted in accordance with Chapter I of Title 5 of the Code of Federal Regulations.

SEC. 3. The Civil Service Commission in issuing regulations and the departments and agencies in developing an appeals system shall be guided by the following principles:

(1) The appeals system shall be a simple, orderly method through which an employee or former employee may seek timely administrative reconsideration of a decision to take adverse action against him.

(2) Employees and representatives of employee organizations shall have an opportunity to express their views as to the formulation and operation of the appeals procedures.

(3) An appeal shall be in writing and indicate clearly the corrective action sought and the reasons therefor.

(4) The system shall provide ordinarily for one level of appeal, except that it may include further administrative review when the delegations of authority or organizational arrangements of the agency so require.

(5) An employee who has not previously had an opportunity for a hearing in connection with the agency decision to take adverse action shall, on his request, be granted one hearing, except when the holding of a hearing is impracticable by reason of unusual location or other extraordinary circumstance.

(6) The employee shall be assured freedom from restraint, interference, coercion, discrimination, or reprisal in presenting his appeal.

(7) The employee shall have the right to be accompanied, represented, and advised by a representative of his own choosing in presenting his appeal.

(8) The employee shall be assured of a reasonable amount of official time to present his appeal.

(9) An appeal shall be resolved expeditiously. To this end, both the employee and the department or agency shall proceed with an appeal without undue delay.

SEC. 4. The head of each department and agency is authorized to include provision for advisory arbitration, where appropriate, in the agency appeals system.

SEC. 5. (a) This order shall not apply to the Central Intelligence Agency, the National Security Agency, the Federal Bureau of Investigation, the Atomic Energy Commission, and the Tennessee Valley Authority.

(b) The Civil Service Commission, on the recommendation of the heads of the agencies concerned, may exclude classes of employees the nature of whose work makes the application of the provisions of this order inappropriate.

SEC. 6. This order shall become effective as to all adverse actions commenced by issuance of a notification of proposed action on or after July 1, 1962.

JOHN F. KENNEDY

THE WHITE HOUSE
January 17, 1962.

(F.R. Doc. 62–699; Filed, Jan. 18, 1962; 10:18 a.m.)

APPENDIX 12 B

Executive Order 10988: 1962

EMPLOYEE-MANAGEMENT COOPERATION IN FEDERAL SERVICE

WHEREAS participation of employees in the formulation and implementation of personnel policies affecting them contributes to effective conduct of public business; and

WHEREAS the efficient administration of the Government and the well-being of employees require that orderly and constructive relationships be maintained between employee organizations and management officials; and

WHEREAS subject to law and the paramount requirements of the public service, employee-management relations within the Federal service should be improved by providing employees an opportunity for greater participation in the formulation and implementation of policies and procedures affecting the conditions of their employment; and

WHEREAS effective employee-management cooperation in the public service requires a clear statement of the respective rights and obligations of employee organizations and agency management:

Now, THEREFORE, by virtue of the authority vested in me by the Constitution of the United States, by section 1753 of the Revised Statutes (5 U.S.C. 631), and as President of the United States, I hereby direct that the following policies shall govern officers and agencies of the executive branch of the Government in all dealings with Federal employees and organizations representing such employees.

SECTION 1. (a) Employees of the Federal Government shall have, and shall be protected in the exercise of, the right, freely and without fear of penalty or reprisal, to form, join and assist any employee organization or to form, join and assist any employee organization or to refrain from any such activity. Except as hereinafter expressly provided, the freedom of such employees to assist any employee organization shall be recognized as extending to participation in the management of the organization and acting for the organization in the capacity of an organization representative, including presentation of its views to officials of the executive branch, the Congress or other appropriate authority. The head of each executive department and agency (hereinafter referred to as "agency") shall take such action, consistent with law, as may be required in order to assure that employees in the agency are apprised of the rights described in this section, and that no interference, restraint, coercion or discrimination is practiced within such agency to encourage or discourage membership in any employee organization.

(b) The rights described in this section do not extend to participation in the management of an employee organization, or acting as a representative of any such organization, where such participation or activity would result in a conflict of interest or otherwise be incompatible with law or with the official duties of an employee.

SEC. 2. When used in this order, the term "employee organization" means any lawful association, labor organization, federation, council, or brotherhood having as a primary purpose the improvement of working conditions among Federal employees, or any craft, trade, or industrial union whose membership includes both Federal employees and employees of private organizations; but such term shall not include any organization (1) which asserts the right to strike against the Government of the United States or any agency thereof, or to assist or participate in any such strike, or which imposes a duty or obligation to conduct, assist, or participate in any such strike, or (2) which advocates the overthrow of the constitutional form of Government in the United States, or (3) which discriminates with regard to the terms or conditions of membership because of race, color, creed, or national origin.

SEC. 3. (a) Agencies shall accord informal, formal, or exclusive recognition to employee organizations which requests such recognition in conformity with the requirements specified in sections 4, 5, and 6 of this order, except that no recognition shall be accorded to any employee organization which the head of the agency considers to be so subject to corrupt influences or influences opposed to basic democratic principles that recognition would be inconsistent with the objectives of this order.

(b) Recognition of an employee organization shall continue so long as such organization satisfies the criteria of this order applicable to such recognition; but nothing in this section shall require any agency to determine whether an organization should become or continue to be recognized as exclusive representative of the employees in any unit within 12 months after a prior determination of exclusive status with respect to such unit has been made pursuant to the provisions of this order.

(c) Recognition, in whatever form accorded, shall not—

preclude any employee, regardless of employee organization membership, from bringing matters of personal concern to the attention of appropriate officials in accordance with applicable law, rule, regulation, or established agency policy, or from choosing his own representative in a grievance or appellate action; or

preclude or restrict consultations and dealings between an agency and any veterans organization with respect to matters of particular interest to employees with veterans preference; or

preclude an agency from consulting or dealing with any religious, social, fraternal or other lawful association, not qualified as an employee organization, with respect to matters or policies which involve individual members of the association or are of particular applicability to it or its members, when such consultations or dealings are duly limited so as not to assume the character of formal consultation on matters of general employee-management policy or to extend to areas where recognition of the interests of one employee group may result in discrimination against or injury to the interests of other employees.

SEC. 4. (a) An agency shall accord an employee organization, which does not qualify for exclusive or formal recognition, informal recognition as representative of its member employees without regard to whether any other employee organization has been accorded formal or exclusive recognition as representative of some or all employees in any unit.

(b) When an employee organization has been informally recognized it shall, to the extent consistent with the efficient and orderly conduct of the public business, be permitted to present to appropriate officials its views on matters of concern to its members. The agency need not, however, consult with an employee organization so recognized in the formulation of personnel or other policies with respect to such matters.

SEC. 5. (a) An agency shall accord an employee organization formal recognition as the representative of its members in a unit as defined by the agency when (1) no other employee organization is qualified for exclusive recognition as representative of employees in the unit, (2) it is determined by the agency that the employee organization has a substantial and stable membership of no less than 10 per centum of the employees in the unit, and (3) the employee organization has submitted to the agency a roster of its officers and representatives, a copy of its constitution and by-laws, and a statement of objectives.

When, in the opinion of the head of an agency, an employee organization has a sufficient number of local organizations or a sufficient total membership within such agency, such organization may be accorded formal recognition at the national level, but such recognition shall not preclude the agency from dealing at the national level with any other employee organization on matters affecting its members.

(b) When an employee organization has been formally recognized, the agency, through appropriate officials, shall consult with such organization from time to time in the formulation and implementation of personnel policies and practices, and matters affecting working conditions that are of concern to its members. Any such organization shall be entitled from time to time to raise such matters for discussion with appropriate officials and at all times to present its views thereon in writing. In no case, however, shall an agency be required to consult with an employee organization which has been formally recognized with respect to any matter which, if the employee organization were one entitled to exclusive recognition, would not be included within the obligation to meet and confer, as described in section 6(b) of this order.

SEC. 6. (a) An agency shall recognize an employee organization as the exclusive representative of the employees in an appropriate unit when such organization is eligible for formal recognition pursuant to section 5 of this order, and has been designated or selected by a majority of the employees of such unit as the representative of such employees in such unit. Units may be established on any plant or installation, craft, functional or other basis which will ensure a clear and identifiable community of interest among the employees concerned, but no unit shall be established solely on the basis of the extent to which employees in the proposed unit have organized.

Except where otherwise required by established practice, prior agreement, or special circumstances, no unit shall be established for purposes of exclusive recognition which includes (1) any managerial executive, (2) any employee engaged in Federal personnel work in other than a purely clerical capacity, (3) both supervisors who officially evaluate the performance of employees and the employees whom they supervise, or (4) both professional employees and nonprofessional employees unless a majority of such professional employees vote for inclusion in such unit.

(b) When an employee organization has been recognized as the exclusive representative of employees of an appropriate unit it shall be entitled to act for and to negotiate agreements covering all employees in the unit and shall be responsible for representing the interests of all such employees without discrimination and without regard to employee organization membership. Such employee organization shall be given the opportunity to be represented at discussions between management and employees or employee representatives concerning grievances, personnel policies and practices, or other matters affecting general working conditions of employees in the unit.

The agency and such employee organization, through appropriate officials and representatives, shall meet at reasonable times and confer with respect to personnel policy and practices and matters affecting working conditions, so far as may be appropriate subject to law and policy requirements. This extends to the negotiation of an agreement, or any question arising thereunder, the determination of appropriate techniques, consistent with the terms and purposes of this order, to assist in such negotiation, and the execution of a written memorandum of agreement or understanding incorporating any agreement reached by the parties. In exercising authority to make rules and regulations relating to personnel policies and practices and working conditions, agencies shall have due regard for the obligation imposed by this section, but such obligation shall not be construed to extend to such areas of discretion and policy as the mission of an agency, its budget, its organization and the assignment of its personnel, or the technology of performing its work.

SEC. 7. Any basic or initial agreement entered into with an employee organization as the exclusive representative of employees in a unit must be approved by the head of the agency or any official designated by him. All agreements with such employee organizations shall also be subject to the following requirements, which shall be expressly stated in the initial or basic agreement and shall be applicable to all supplemental, implementing, subsidiary or informal agreements between the agency and the organization:

(1) In the administration of all matters covered by the agreement officials and employees are governed by the provisions of any existing or future laws and regulations, including policies set forth in the Federal Personnel Manual and agency regulations, which may be applicable, and the agreement shall at all times be applied subject to such laws, regulations and policies;

(2) Management officials of the agency retain the right, in accordance with applicable laws and regulations, (a) to direct employees of the agency, (b) to hire, promote, transfer, assign, and retain employees in positions within the agency, and to suspend, demote, discharge, or take other disciplinary action against employees, (c) to relieve employees from duties because of lack of work or for other legitimate reasons, (d) to maintain the efficiency of the Government operations entrusted to them, (e) to determine the methods, means, and personnel by which such operations are to be conducted; and (f) to take whatever actions may be necessary to carry out the mission of the agency in situations of emergency.

SEC. 8. (a) Agreements entered into or negotiated in accordance with this order with an employee organization which is the exclusive representative of employees in an appropriate unit may contain provisions, applicable only to employees in the unit, concerning procedures for consideration of grievances. Such procedures (1) shall conform to standards issued by the Civil Service Commission, and (2) may not in any manner diminish or impair any rights which would otherwise be available to any employee in the absence of an agreement providing for such procedures.

(b) Procedures established by an agreement which are otherwise in conformity with this section may include provisions for the arbitration of grievances. Such arbitration (1) shall be advisory in nature with any decisions or recommendations subject to the approval of the agency head; (2) shall extend only to the interpretation or application of agreements or agency policy and not to changes in or proposed changes in agreements or agency policy; and (3) shall be invoked only with the approval of the individual employee or employees concerned.

SEC. 9. Solicitation of memberships, dues, or other internal employee organization business shall be conducted during the non-duty hours of the employees concerned. Officially requested or approved consultations and meetings between management officials and representatives of recognized employee organizations shall, whenever practicable, be conducted on official time, but any agency may require that negotiations with an employee organization which has been accorded exclusive recognition be conducted during the non-duty hours of the employee organization representatives involved in such negotiations.

SEC. 10. No later than July 1, 1962, the head of each agency shall issue appropriate policies, rules, and regulations for the implementation of this order, including: A clear statement of the rights of its employees under the order; policies and procedures with respect to recognition of employee organizations; procedures for determining appropriate employee units; policies and practices regarding consultation with representatives of employee organizations, other organizations and individual employees; and policies with respect to the use of agency facilities by employee organizations. Insofar as may be practicable and appropriate, agencies shall consult with representatives of employee organizations in the formulation of these policies, rules, and regulations.

SEC. 11. Each agency shall be responsible for determining in accordance with this order whether a unit is appropriate for purposes of exclusive recognition and, by an election or other appropriate means, whether an employee organization represents a majority of the employees in such a unit so as to be entitled to such recognition. Upon the request of any agency, or of any employee organization which is seeking exclusive recognition and which qualifies for or has been accorded formal recognition, the Secretary of Labor, subject to such necessary rules as he may prescribe, shall nominate from the National Panel of Arbitrators maintained by the Federal Mediation and Conciliation Service one or more qualified arbitrators who will be available for employment by the agency concerned for either or both of the following purposes, as may be required:

to investigate the facts and issue an advisory decision as to the appropriateness of a unit for purposes of exclusive recognition and as to related issues submitted for consideration;

to conduct or supervise an election or otherwise determine by such means as may be appropriate, and on an advisory basis, whether an employee organization represents the majority of the employees in a unit. Consonant with law, the Secretary of Labor shall render such assistance as may be appropriate in connection with advisory decisions or determinations under this section, but the necessary costs of such assistance shall be paid by the agency to which it relates. In the event questions as to the appropriateness of a unit or the majority status of an employee organization shall arise in the Department of Labor, the duties described in this section which would otherwise be the responsibility of the Secretary of Labor shall be performed by the Civil Service Commission.

SEC. 12. The Civil Service Commission shall establish and maintain a program to assist in carrying out the objectives of this order. The Commission shall develop a program for the guidance of agencies in employee-management relations in the Federal service; provide technical advice to the agencies in employee-management programs for training agency personnel in the principles and procedures of consultation, negotiation, and the settlement of disputes in the Federal service, and for the training of management officials in the discharge of their employee-management relations responsibilities in the public interest; provide for continuous study and review of the Federal employee-management relations program and, from time to time, make recommendations to the President for its improvement.

SEC. 13. (a) The Civil Service Commission and the Department of Labor shall jointly prepare (1) proposed standards of conduct for employee organizations and (2) a proposed code of fair labor practices in employee-management relations in the Federal service appropriate to assist in securing the uniform and effective implementation of the policies, rights, and responsibilities described in this order.

(b) There is hereby established the President's Temporary Committee on the implementation of the Federal Employee-Management Relations Program. The Committee shall consist of the Secretary of Labor, who shall be chairman of the Committee, the Secretary of Defense, the Postmaster General, and the Chairman of the Civil Service Commission. In addition to such other matters relating to the implementation of this order as may be referred to it by the President, the Committee shall advise the President with respect to any problems arising out of completion of agreements pursuant to sections 6 and 7, and shall receive the proposed standards of conduct for employee organizations and proposed code of fair labor practices in the Federal service, as described in this section, and report thereon to the President with such recommendations or amendments as it may deem appropriate. Consonant with law, the departments and agencies represented on the Committee shall, as may be necessary for the effectuation of this section, furnish assistance to the Committee in accordance with section 214 of the Act of May 3, 1945, 59 Stat. 134 (31 U.S.C. 691). Unless otherwise directed by the President, the Committee shall cease to exist 30 days after the date on which it submits its report to the President pursuant to this section.

SEC. 14. The head of each agency, in accordance with the provisions of this order and regulations prescribed by the Civil Service Commission, shall extend to all employees in the competitive civil service rights identical in adverse action cases to those provided preference eligibles under section 14 of the Veterans' Preference Act of 1944, as amended. Each employee in the competitive service shall have the right to appeal to the Civil Service Commission from an adverse decision of the administrative officer so acting, such appeal to be processed in an identical manner to that provided for appeals under section 14 of the Veterans' Preference Act. Any recommendation by the Civil Service Commission submitted to the head of an agency on the basis of an appeal by an employee in the competitive service shall be complied with by the head of the agency. This section shall become effective as to all adverse actions commenced by issuance of a notification of proposed action on or after July 1, 1962.

SEC. 15. Nothing in this order shall be construed to annul or modify, or to preclude the renewal or continuation of, any lawful agreement heretofore entered into between any agency and any representative of its employ-

ees. Nor shall this order preclude any agency from continuing to consult or
deal with any representative of its employees or other organization prior to
the time that the status and representation rights of such representative or
organization are determined in conformity with this order.

SEC. 16. This order (except section 14) shall not apply to the Federal Bureau of Investigation, the Central Intelligence Agency, or any other
agency, or to any office, bureau, or entity within an agency, primarily performing intelligence, investigative, or security functions if the head of the
agency determines that the provisions of this order cannot be applied in a
manner consistent with national security requirements and considerations.
When he deems it necessary in the national interest, and subject to such
conditions as he may prescribe, the head of any agency may suspend any
provision of this order (except section 14) with respect to any agency installation or activity which is located outside of the United States.

APPENDIX 12 C

Presidential Documents: Title 3—The President
Memorandum of May 21, 1963
(Standards of conduct for employee organizations and
code of fair labor practices)

Memorandum for the Heads of Executive Departments and Agencies

On January 17, 1962, I issued Executive Order No. 10988, which gives
effect to a new and affirmative Executive Branch policy looking toward participation by employee organizations in the formulation and implementation
of personnel policies affecting the well-being of Federal employees. If this
policy is to be truly effective, not only must the Executive agencies carry
out their duties in a manner consistent with the terms and spirit of Executive Order No. 10988, but the employee organizations must also conduct
their own affairs in a way which will promote orderly and constructive relationships with management officials and satisfy their inherent commitments
to high standards of ethical and democratic conduct.

It is, therefore, in the public interest to require that such organizations
adhere to standards of conduct which will insure the administration of their
internal affairs in a manner consistent with this public trust, while at the
same time recognizing their right to independence in the internal management of their affairs.

Accordingly, there is hereby prescribed, pursuant to Executive Order
10988, for application by all agencies subject to the Order, the Standards of
Conduct for Employee Organizations and the Code of Fair Labor Practices
in the Federal Service. They are designed to assist in securing the uniform
and effective implementation of the policies, rights, and responsibilities de-

scribed in the Order. The Standards and Code will assist in the implementation of the Order by fixing more definitely the responsibility of employee organizations and agencies, providing more detailed criteria for the protection of rights secured under the Order and establishing procedures in both of these areas which will assure a necessary measure of uniformity within the Executive Branch of the Federal Government.

In keeping with the spirit and intent of the Executive Order to promote cooperation in the conduct of relationships between agencies and employee organizations in the Federal service, it should, of course, be emphasized that primary reliance must be placed on informal settlement of differences and disputes by discussions between the parties. The procedures provided in the Standards and Code are intended to supplement such informal discussions and procedures, not to replace them.

This memorandum, including the Standards of Conduct for Employee Organizations and the Code of Fair Labor Practices, will be published in the *Federal Register*.

John F. Kennedy

STANDARDS OF CONDUCT FOR EMPLOYEE ORGANIZATIONS AND CODE OF FAIR LABOR PRACTICES

SECTION 1.1 *Purpose and scope.* These Standards of Conduct for Employee Organizations and the Code of Fair Labor Practices in Employee-Management Cooperation in the Federal Service are issued pursuant to Executive Order No. 10988. Their purpose is to assist in securing the uniform and effective implementation of the policies, rights, and responsibilities described in the Order by fixing more definitely the responsibilities of employee organizations and agencies, providing more detailed criteria for the protection of rights secured under the Order, and establishing procedures in both of these areas which will assure a necessary measure of uniformity within the Executive Branch of the Federal Government.

SEC. 1.2 *Definitions.*

(a) "Order" means Executive Order No. 10988.

(b) "Agency," "employee organization," and "employee" have the same meaning as in the Order.

(c) "Agency management" includes the agency head, and all management officials and representatives of management having authority to act for the agency on any matters relating to the implementation of the agency employee-management cooperation program as established under the Order.

(d) "Recognition" means recognition which is or may be accorded to an employee organization pursuant to the provisions of the Order.

SEC. 1.3 *General Responsibilities of the Civil Service Commission.* The Civil Service Commission, in accordance with the provisions of section 12 of the Order, shall be responsible for the dissemination of information with respect to the Standards of Conduct and Code of Fair Labor Practices, and shall insure an adequate exchange of information between agencies as to its application and enforcement.

Part a
Standards of Conduct for Employee Organizations

SEC. 2.1 *Application*. The provisions of this Part are applicable to all agencies subject to the provisions of the Order and to all employee organizations accorded recognition under the Order.

SEC. 2.2 *Standards of Conduct*. No agency shall accord recognition to any employee organization unless the employee organization is subject to governing requirements, adopted by the organization or by a national or international employee organization or federation of employee organizations with which it is affiliated or in which it participates, containing explicit and detailed provisions to which it subscribes calling for the following:

(a) The maintenance of democratic procedures and practices, including provisions for periodic elections to be conducted subject to recognized safeguards and provisions defining and securing the right of individual members to participation in the affairs of the organization, to fair and equal treatment under the governing rules of the organization, and to fair process in disciplinary proceedings;

(b) The exclusion from office in the organization of persons affiliated with Communist or other totalitarian movements and persons identified with corrupt influences;

(c) The prohibition of business or financial interests on the part of organization officers and agents which conflict with their duty to the organization and its members; and

(d) The maintenance of fiscal integrity in the conduct of the affairs of the organization, including provision for accounting and financial controls and regular financial reports or summaries to be made available to members.

SEC. 2.3 *Adoption of Standards*. No agency shall deny, suspend, or withdraw recognition by reason of any alleged failure to adopt or subscribe to standards of conduct as provided in section 2.2 of this Part unless it has first notified the organization and the national or international organization with which it is affiliated of such alleged deficiency and has afforded the organization a reasonable opportunity to make any amendments or modifications or take any action that may be required. In the event that any question arising under any provision of section 2.2 is not resolved in a mutually acceptable manner, the agency shall consult with the Secretary of Labor prior to making a final determination that an organization has failed to comply with such provisions.

SEC. 2.4 *Procedure for Denial, Suspension, or Withdrawal of Recognition.*

(a) An employee organization which has adopted or subscribed to standards of conduct as provided in section 2.2 of this Part shall not be required to furnish other evidence of its freedom from influences described in section 3(a) of the Order unless (1) the agency has cause to believe that the organization has been suspended or expelled from or is subject to other sanction by a parent employee organization or labor organization or federation of such organizations with which it had been affiliated because it has demonstrated an unwillingness or inability to comply with governing requirements comparable in purpose to those required by section 2.2 of this Part, or (2) recognition in any form has been denied, suspended, or withdrawn by any other agency pursuant to this Part or section 3(a) of the Order and such denial, suspension, or withdrawal remains in effect, or (3) there is reasonable cause to believe that the organization, notwithstanding its compliance with section 2.2, is in fact subject to influences such as would preclude recognition pursuant to the Order.

(b) In any case where additional evidence is required pursuant to (1), (2), or (3) of subsection (a) of this section, the agency shall not deny, suspend, or withdraw recognition on the basis of the exception stated in section 3(a) of the Order unless it has afforded the employee organization an opportunity to present to the agency such reasons or considerations as it has to offer relating to why recognition should not be denied, suspended, or withdrawn. If this opportunity is requested, the agency shall promptly hold a hearing. Upon request the agency shall make available to the employee organization for use in the hearing a concise and accurate summary of the facts on which the agency intends to rely in reaching its decision, together with a statement of the reasons for the agency action. In lieu of a summary statement, the agency may make available to the employee organization the entire report of the agency investigation. In any dispute over the accuracy or sufficiency of information so provided, the final determination shall be made by the agency head. The employee organization shall have an opportunity to be present at the hearing, to be represented by counsel, and to offer such oral and documentary evidence as may be relevant to the issue or issues in controversy. Any determination to deny, suspend, or withdraw recognition shall be made in writing by the agency head.

(c) The agency may consult with the Secretary of Labor before instituting any proceedings pursuant to clause (3) of subsection (a) of this section and shall consult with the Secretary of Labor prior to taking any final action with respect to the denial, suspension, or withdrawal of recognition.

(d) Where an agency determination denying, suspending, or withdrawing recognition of an employee organization is made in accordance with subsections (b) and (c) of this section after consultation with the Secretary of Labor, any other agency may thereafter deny, suspend, or withdraw recognition as to such employee organization or subordinate affiliate thereof, without regard to the procedures prescribed in subsection (b) if such other agency has afforded such employee organization or subordinate affiliate thereof an opportunity to present such reasons and consideration as it may have to offer as to why such prior determination should not be followed, and such agency, on the basis of such submission and after consultation with the Secretary of Labor, finds that further procedures are unnecessary.

SEC. 2.5 *Effective Dates.*

(a) The provisions of this part, other than section 2.4(b) and (c) as hereinafter provided, shall become effective immediately. No later than 6 months from such effective date, each agency shall adopt such permanent procedures as may be necessary to implement this Part. Insofar as may be practicable and appropriate, agencies shall consult with representatives of recognized employee organizations in the formulation of such procedures. Copies of any implementing regulations shall be made available to recognized employee organizations upon request.

(b) Prior to the adoption of such permanent procedures, in making determinations under the Order with respect to employee organizations which seek or have been accorded recognition, no agency shall deny, suspend, or withdraw such recognition on the basis of the exception stated in the Order except in accordance with procedures conforming as nearly as possible to the requirements of section 2.4(b) and (c) of this Part.

PART B
CODE OF FAIR LABOR PRACTICES

SEC. 3.1 *Application.* The provisions of this Part are applicable to all agencies subject to the provisions of the Order and to all employee organizations accorded recognition under the Order.

SEC. 3.2 *Prohibited Practices.*

(a) Agency management is prohibited from:

(1) Interfering with, restraining or coercing any employee in the exercise of the rights assured by Executive Order No. 10988, including those set forth in section 1 of the Order;

(2) Encouraging or discouraging membership in any employee organization, by discrimination in regard to hiring, tenure, promotion, or other conditions of employment;

(3) Sponsoring, controlling, or otherwise assisting any employee organization, except that an agency may furnish customary and routine services and facilities pursuant to section 10 of the Order where consistent with the best interests of the agency, its employees and the organization, and where such services and facilities are furnished, if requested, on an impartial basis;

(4) Disciplining or otherwise discriminating against any employee because he has filed a complaint or given testimony under the Order or under the Standards of Conduct for Employee Organizations or Code of Fair Labor Practices;

(5) Refusing to accord appropriate recognition to an employee organization qualified for such recognition;

(6) Refusing to hear, consult, confer, or negotiate with an employee organization as required by the Order.

(b) Employee organizations are prohibited from:

(1) Interfering with, restraining, or coercing any employee in the exercise of the rights assured by Executive Order No. 10988, including those set forth in section 1 of the Order;

(2) Attempting to induce agency management to coerce any employee in the enjoyment of his rights under the Order;

(3) Coercing or attempting to coerce, or disciplining, any member of the organization as punishment or reprisal for, or for the purpose of hindering or impeding his discharge of his duties owed as an officer or employee of the United States;

(4) Calling or engaging in any strike, work stoppage, slowdown, or related picketing engaged in as a substitute for any such strike, work stoppage, or slowdown, against the Government of the United States;

(5) Discriminating against any employee with regard to the terms or conditions of membership because of race, color, creed, or national origin.

(c) No employee organization which is accorded exclusive recognition shall deny membership to any employee in the appropriate unit except for failure to meet reasonable occupational standards uniformly required for admission, or for failure to tender initiation fees and dues uniformly required as a condition of acquiring and retaining membership, but nothing contained in this subsection shall preclude an employee organization from enforcing discipline in accordance with procedures under its constitution or bylaws which conform to the requirements set forth in section 2.2(a) of the Standards of Conduct for Employee Organizations.

Sec. 3.3 *General Procedures for Enforcement.*

(a) Each agency shall provide fair and adequate procedures for the filing, investigation, and processing of complaints or violations of section 3.2 which will cover all cases, except as provided in subsection (c) of this section, whether initiated by employees, an agency, or an employee organization, as follows:

(1) In cases initiated by an employee or several employees with the same complaint, in which the matter in issue is subject to an applicable grievance, or appeals procedure within the agency, such procedure shall be the exclusive procedure used.

(2) All cases not covered by subsection (a)(1) and (c) of this section shall be processed under procedures which shall include provisions for the informal resolution or adjustment of complaints where possible; for the designation of an impartial hearing officer or panel of such officers; and, in cases where it appears that there is substantial basis for a complaint and the matter is not informally adjusted, for an opportunity for a hearing before a hearing officer or panel of such officers upon notice, for the right to be rep-

resented by counsel, and for findings of fact, or for findings of fact and recommendations, by such officers or panel. Such procedures shall not, however, be available for the rehearing of issues processed under the provisions
of the Standards of Conduct or Section 11 of the Order. In performing the
function provided for in this subsection, hearing officers shall be responsible
directly to the agency head.

(b) Hearings held pursuant to subsection (a)(2) shall be informal, but
rights of confrontation and cross-examination shall be preserved so far as
may be necessary for the development of the facts, and the findings of fact
or findings of fact and recommendations of the hearing officer or panel shall
be based upon the record developed in the hearing. Copies of such findings
of fact or findings of fact and recommendations shall be made available to
the parties. In any proceeding under this section, the complainant or respondent shall be entitled to receive a concise and accurate summary of the
facts relating to the complaint, and upon which the agency intends to rely,
together with a statement of the reasons for the agency's action. The agency
may, in lieu of a summary statement, make available to the complainant or
respondent the entire report of the agency's investigation of the complaint.
In a case in which the complainant or respondent is provided with a summary statement, the hearing officer shall have the right, upon request, to
examine the entire record in such case, including all data gathered pursuant
to an investigation, to determine that the summary is fair and accurate.

(c) Cases involving any strike, work stoppage, slowdown, or related
picketing engaged in as a substitute for any such strike, work stoppage, or
slowdown, shall be covered by such procedures and subject to such remedies and sanctions consistent with law as the agency head determines to be
appropriate to the situation without regard to the limitations of this section
or section 3.4.

SEC. 3.4. *Final Decision and Notice.* All final decisions shall be in writing and shall be furnished to the organization and the national or international organization with which it is affiliated. Such decisions shall include a
statement of the findings and reasons in support of the decision. If the decision is that agency management has engaged in a prohibited practice, the
agency shall immediately take necessary action in accordance with the decision to remedy the violation. If the decision is that an employee organization has engaged in a prohibited practice, the agency head shall notify the
employee organization of the existence of such violation and request appropriate corrective action. Failure of an employee organization to comply
with such request after the date on which it becomes effective shall be
grounds for the withholding or suspension of recognition until the violation
has been remedied, or for the withdrawal of recognition in appropriate
cases as determined by the agency head.

SEC. 3.5 *Effective Date.*

(a) The provisions of section 3.2 of this Part shall be effective immediately. No later than six months from such effective date, each agency shall

adopt permanent procedures to implement this Part. Insofar as may be practicable and appropriate, agencies shall consult with representatives of employee organizations in the formulation of such procedures. Copies of any implementing regulations shall be made available to recognized employee organizations upon request.

(b) In making determinations under section 3.2 prior to the adoption of such permanent procedures, agencies shall as nearly as possible conform to the basic procedural requirements of this Part, and in no case where an opportunity for hearing, or a final notice as described in section 3.4, is required under this Part shall an agency withhold, suspend, or withdraw recognition without an opportunity for such hearing or without such a final notice.

13

HUMAN RESOURCE
UTILIZATION AND
THE LAW

Some of the most profound changes in business practices, economic welfare and security, and public policy resulted from the development of laws related to working conditions and manpower utilization. A different dimension of the trade union movement and a more general category of public policy and law are applicable to this subject, which nevertheless remains an integral part of the contemporary industrial relations scene.

Labor markets were not organized in the United States until well into the early part of the twentieth century. Working conditions for the average American during the nineteenth century were difficult in terms of hours, wages, and industrial hazards. The prevailing economic philosophy was oriented toward a free and unfettered competitive market economy, a philosophy which simply implied worker exploitation. Tactics that retarded social progress in the general area of working conditions, such as judicial and legal control of the union

417

movement throughout the eighteenth and nineteenth centuries, were based on the laissez faire philosophy. We have seen how the conspiracy doctrine, injunctions, anti-trust rulings, and the yellow-dog contracts were used to "manage" the laboring masses.

Dissension and strife within the labor union movement in its early years also retarded the improvement of working conditions. Still another factor contributing to what would now be regarded as undesirable working conditions was a burgeoning population fed by immigration. Industrialization, accompanied by rapidly changing technology and considerably less affluence than is now an expected norm, is still another factor that distinguishes working conditions of the past from contemporary conditions. Finally, economic depressions and inflationary periods combined with domestic and international difficulties also contributed to the maintenance of substandard working conditions in the United States economy in its early years of development.

Public policy related to labor and management bargaining processes has been complemented by the numerous other laws affecting human resources in a broader context. The first portion of this chapter traces the development of public policy and employment of child labor. Another area of dominant public policy concern for several decades in this century has been the development of laws regulating hours of work, minimum wages, and hazardous working conditions —also treated in this chapter. While these subjects are of less importance as contemporary issues, a considerable history and much progress undergirds the enlightened attitude of management on these issues today. The final portion of this chapter emphasizes still other contemporary dimensions to the economic welfare of workers. In the brief period of some three decades, a vast array of legislation has emerged on a broad front covering such diverse issues as federal wage and hour regulations, economic security, full employment and unemployment, and manpower development and utilization policies.

Child Labor Legislation

Society was not oblivious to the many undesirable working circumstances existing in the growing industrialized sector of the United States' economy. During the mid-nineteenth century, the federal government started to establish working standards applying to federal employees and employees working under contracts granted by the federal government. Soon after the close of the Civil War, Congress reduced the maximum working day to ten hours for employees under federal contract, and appropriately a quarter of a century later such employees were granted an eight-hour day.

The use of women and children in the labor force as employees of mine and manufacturing firms represented one of the more distressing abuses. Although we do not recognize child labor as a problem today, it was a serious problem one-half century ago—so serious that it became a national political issue. In 1910, for example, nearly two million persons under fifteen years of age were reported as gainful employees. This represented *one-fifth* of the total number of children between the ages of ten and fifteen.[1] It was not until the 1920's that the regulation of very hazardous work and long hours in factories were subjected to significant restraint.

COMMERCE AS A SOURCE OF AUTHORITY

Right after the Civil War, the state of Massachusetts passed statutes limiting the use of child labor. These laws stated that children under ten years of age could not be employed by manufacturing firms, and youths under fifteen years of age were not to be worked in excess of sixty hours per week in manufacturing industries. Although some of the other states followed the Massachusetts lead during the next 40 years, for the most part limitations on the use of child labor were weakly enforced. Between 1870 and 1920 the number of children employed under fifteen years of age nearly tripled, in part because of rapid industrialization. By 1916 the federal government became concerned and enacted the Owen-Keating Act, which prohibited the use of employed children for goods shipped in interstate commerce. This bill outlawed labor for youths under fourteen years of age and those between fourteen and sixteen could not work more than eight hours daily, six days a week. Within less than two years the Act of 1916 was challenged and brought to the Supreme Court on the grounds that the legislation was an illegal exercise of the power of the federal government to regulate interstate commerce.[2]

Essentially, the Supreme Court refused to sanction congressional regulation of child labor under the power granted to the federal government to regulate interstate commerce. As the decision of Justice Day reveals below, regulation of child labor was then viewed as a matter properly left to the states. Even though the Supreme Court had found it proper to allow Congress similar power to forbid the shipment of impure food or drugs, child labor was not then regarded

[1] *U.S. Census of Population,* 1910.

[2] *Hammer v. Dagenhart,* 247 U.S. 251 (1918).

as a legitimate item for federal regulation. Rather, the prevailing view was that the inherent police power of the states could and should be used to control abusive employment of child labor.

HAMMER v. DAGENHART: 1918
(247 U.S. 251)

Mr. Justice Day delivered the opinion of the court:

A bill was filed in the United States district court for the western district of North Carolina by a father in his own behalf and as next friend of his two minor sons, one under the age of fourteen years and the other between the ages of fourteen and sixteen years, employees in a cotton mill at Charlotte, North Carolina, to enjoin the enforcement of the act of Congress intended to prevent interstate commerce in the products of child labor. . . . The district court held the act unconstitutional and entered a decree enjoining its enforcement. This appeal brings the case here.

The controlling question for decision is: Is it within the authority of Congress in regulating commerce among the states to prohibit the transportation in interstate commerce of manufactured goods, the product of a factory in which, within thirty days prior to the removal therefrom, children under the age of fourteen have been employed or permitted to work, or children between the ages of fourteen and sixteen years have been employed or permitted to work, more than eight hours in any day, or more than six days in any week, or after the hour of 7 o'clock P. M. or before the hour of 6 o'clock A. M.?

The power essential to the passage of this act, the government contends, is found in the commerce clause of the Constitution, which authorizes Congress to regulate commerce with foreign nations and among the states. . . . The thing intended to be accomplished by this statute is the denial of the facilities of interstate commerce to those manufacturers in the states who employ children within the prohibited ages. The act in its effect does not regulate transportation among the states, but aims to standardize the ages at which children may be employed in mining and manufacturing within the states. The goods shipped are of themselves harmless. The act permits them to be freely shipped after thirty days from the time of their removal from the factory. When offered for shipment, and before transportation begins, the labor of their production is over, and the mere fact that they were intended for interstate commerce transportation does not make their production subject to Federal control under the commerce power. . . .

In interpreting the Constitution it must never be forgotten that the nation is made up of states, to which are entrusted the powers of local government. And to them and to the people the powers not expressly delegated to the national government are reserved, . . . The grant of authority over a purely Federal matter was not intended to destroy the local power always existing and carefully reserved to the states in the 10th Amendment to the Constitution.

In our view the necessary effect of this act is, by means of a prohibition against the movement in interstate commerce of ordinary commercial commodities, to regulate the hours of labor of children in factories and mines within the states,—a purely state authority. Thus the act in a twofold sense is repugnant to the Constitution. It not only transcends the authority delegated to Congress over commerce, but also exerts a power as to a purely local matter to which the Federal authority does not extend. The far-reaching result of upholding the act cannot be more plainly indicated than by pointing out that if Congress can thus regulate matters entrusted to local authority by prohibition of the movement of commodities in interstate commerce, all freedom of commerce will be at an end, and the power of the states over local matters may be eliminated, and thus our system of government be practically destroyed.

For these reasons we hold that this law exceeds the constitutional authority of Congress. . . .

It is apparent from this five-to-four decision that the majority of justices were willing to allow restrictions to be placed on a freely competitive economy under only limited circumstances that met vague criteria related to the "intrinsic" harm of goods shipped between states. The nebulous position of the Court majority was clearly observed in the dissent registered by Justice Holmes, who noted that the statute confined itself to prohibiting the shipment of goods produced by child labor and in interstate commerce as a proper exercise of the federal government's power. Justice Holmes' dissent on behalf of the minority opinion of the Court further defended the 1916 statute on the grounds that it clearly pursued the general welfare of all people of the nation and was within the constitutional powers granted to the federal government. Such an enlightened viewpoint was not to prevail, however, for some two decades.

THE TAX POWER

Proponents of national child labor laws, dismayed over the Supreme Court ruling in the *Hammer* decision, next attempted to control child labor by passage of a law in 1918 that taxed the use of child labor. This statute did not overtly forbid the use of child labor, but rather it levied a ten percent profit tax upon all employers who utilized child labor in the production of goods and services. The Drexel Furniture Company had employed child labor for some time and, upon the passage of the new tax law, refused to pay the assessment. In 1922 the case of *Baily* v. *Drexel Furniture* reached the Supreme Court of the United States.[3] The constitutional power to tax was a long-accepted power, based upon implied authority of the federal government to raise those revenues necessary to carry out its functions. The decision of the Supreme Court in the *Baily* case, however, was that the 1918 Act did not have the purpose of raising revenues. In contrast, the Supreme Court ruled that the statute was intended to penalize employers of child labor, and for that reason it was an invalid exercise of the constitutional power of the federal government.

After this unfavorable reaction by the Supreme Court, Congress sought remedial control of child labor in the only remaining way, constitutional amendment. In 1924 a congressional resolution was passed that would have given Congress control of the labor of all persons under eighteen years of age, and declared that the power of the states was not to be construed as being impaired by this resolution. The proposed constitutional amendment was also doomed to fail, in part, because its wording was such that the labor of all persons under eighteen could have been prohibited. Opposition quickly formed, particularly by agricultural groups who effectively lobbied against ratification of the proposed amendment in numerous state legislatures. At that time, ratification by 36 states was necessary for the resolution to be adopted as a constitutional amendment. Even today, however, the necessary number of states have not ratified the 1924 resolution.

Ratification of the proposed amendment of 1924 is no longer necessary because of the legislative changes that did occur in the 1930's. Even though the National Industrial Recovery Act of 1933 was later declared unconstitutional, as we noted earlier, the Act reflected social concern for child labor by forbidding the employment of children under sixteen years of age. Moreover, the difficulty of securing employment for adults during the early 1930's eroded the practice of em-

[3] 259 U.S. 20 (1922).

ploying child labor. The distinction between manufacturing and commerce that was so tenuously drawn in *Hammer* v. *Dagenhart* was completely forgotten with the passage of the Fair Labor Standards Act in 1938. The Fair Labor Standards Act, which is examined in greater detail later, remains the basic legislation limiting the use of child labor in this country today. Essentially, this Act reiterated earlier congressional limits to employing child labor in commerce or production designed for interstate commerce. For the most part, child labor under fourteen years of age is regulated or prohibited, and an eighteen-year-old age minimum has been declared for jobs that are demonstrated to be hazardous. In addition, hours of work are limited and conditions of work as specified by the Department of Labor must be complied with for persons between fourteen and sixteen years of age. Exemptions are possible for theatrical performers, parental employment of youth, and so forth. As a consequence of the Fair Labor Standards Act, child labor is no longer a contemporary problem. More recently, the emphasis placed upon education as a labor market entry requirement has also had great impact on child labor practices. As a matter of fact, the problem facing teenage youth today is largely one of inadequate job opportunities for those desiring employment. Abusive employment and long hours, so customary less than a half century ago, are history today.

Regulation of Working Hours and Wages

One of the major issues contributing to disputes between employers and employees throughout their long struggle centered upon the hours of work required per day and week. Prior to the beginning of the twentieth century the so-called standard work period typically consisted of a sunup to sundown 12-hour day, usually six days a week. With the exception of the steel industry, which continued a 12-hour day well into the 1900's, most American workers had achieved a 10-hour day by the turn of the century—an hour standard that prevailed for the first two decades of the 1900's. Other major matters that came before Congress during the early 1900's were the regulation of hazardous working conditions and the conditions under which female labor was employed. Advocates of social progress increasingly pressed for relief on these issues as well as for regulation of minimum wages.

As was true for the child labor movement, many abusive practices related to lengthy hours, hazardous working conditions, working conditions for females, and employment at substandard wages were checked by the Fair Labor Standards Act of 1938. The path of progress in these areas between the end of the nineteenth century and 1938 is documented by several major decisions of the Supreme Court that deserve further consideration.

HAZARDOUS WORKING CONDITIONS

Much of the progressive federal legislation that did appear during the early twentieth century was preceded by state legislation of labor relations and working conditions. However, a variety of inconsistencies in enforcement and accepted conditions prevailed.

Utah enacted legislation restricting the terms of employment in underground mines or smelter works to eight hours a day in 1896. The Utah statute was challenged in 1898 when it was appealed to the Supreme Court of the United States.[4] The basis of the challenge was that workers and employers had been deprived of the right to freely contract for mutually acceptable terms of work. The mining company, which had been convicted under the statute, further argued that their property rights had been deprived without due process of law and that the Utah statute did not apply fully to *all* persons but rather was "class legislation." The Supreme Court sustained this conviction and thus sanctioned the limitation of working hours under hazardous working conditions as specified in the Utah statute. This reasoning was predicated upon the recognition that working conditions in mining operations were potentially hazardous if exposure over prolonged periods of time were common.

HOLDEN v. HARDY: 1898
(169 U.S. 366)

Mr. Justice Brown speaking for the majority opinion of the Court:

This case involves the constitutionality of an act of the legislature of Utah of March 30, 1896, entitled "An Act Regulating the Hours of Employment in Underground Mines and in Smelters and Ore Reduction Works." The following are the material provisions:

"SECTION 1. The period of employment of workingmen in all underground mines or workings shall be eight hours per day, except in cases of emergency where life or property is in imminent danger.

[4] 169 U.S. 336 (1898).

"SEC. 2. The period of employment of workingmen in smelters and all other institutions for the reduction of refining of ores or metals shall be eight hours per day, except in cases of emergency where life or property is in imminent danger.

"SEC. 3. Any person, body corporate, agent, manager, or employer who shall violate any of the provisions of sections one and two of this act, shall be guilty of a misdemeanor. . . ."

The validity of the statute in question is, however, challenged upon the ground of an alleged violation of the Fourteenth Amendment to the Constitution of the United States, in that it abridges the privileges or immunities of citizens of the United States, deprives both the employer and the laborer of his property without due process of law, and denies to them the equal protection of the laws. . . .

This court has never attempted to define with precision the words "due process of law," nor is it necessary to do so in this case. It is sufficient to say that there are certain immutable principles of justice which inhere in the very idea of free government which no member of the Union may disregard, as that no man shall be condemned in his person or property without due notice and an opportunity of being heard in his defense. . . .

Recognizing the difficulty in defining, with exactness, the phrase "due process of law," it is certain that these words imply a conformity with natural and inherent principles of justice and forbid that one man's property, or right to property, shall be taken for the benefit of another, or for the benefit of a state, without compensation; and that no one shall be condemned in his person or property without an opportunity of being heard in his own defense. As the possession of property, of which a person cannot be deprived, doubtless implies that such property may be acquired, it is safe to say that a state law, which undertakes to deprive any class of persons of the general power to acquire property, would also be obnoxious to the same provision. Indeed, we may go a step further, and say that as property can only be legally acquired as between living persons by contract, that a general prohibition against entering into contracts with respect to property, or having as their object the acquisition of property, would be equally invalid. . . .

This right of contract, however, is itself subject to certain limitations which the state may lawfully impose in the exercise of its police powers. While this power is inherent in all governments, it has doubtless been greatly expanded in its application during the past century, owing to an enormous increase in the number of occupations which are dangerous or so far detrimental to the health of employees as to demand special precaution for their well-being and protection, or the safety of the adjacent property. While this court has held that the police power cannot be put forward as an excuse for oppressive and unjust legislation, it may be lawfully resorted to for the purpose of preserving the public health, safety, or morals, or the abatement of public nuisances, and a large discretion "is necessarily vested in the legislature to determine, not only what the interests of the public require, but what measures are necessary for the protection of such interests." (*Lawton* v. *Steele*, 152 U.S. 133).

We do not wish, however, to be understood as holding that this power is unlimited. While the people of the state may doubtless adopt such systems of laws as best conform to their own traditions and customs, the people of the entire country have laid down in the Constitution of the United States certain fundamental principles to which each member of the Union is bound to accede as a condition of its admission as a state. Thus, the United States are bound to guarantee to each state a republican form of government and the 10th section of the 1st article contains certain other specified limitations upon the power of the several states, the object of which was to secure to Congress paramount authority with respect to matters of universal concern. In addition, the Fourteenth Amendment contains a sweeping provision forbidding the states from abridging the privileges and immunities of citizens of the United States, and denying them the benefit of due process or equal protection of the laws.

It is as much for the interest of the state that the public health should be preserved as that life should be made secure. With this end in view quarantine laws have been enacted, in most if not all of the states; insane asylums, public hospitals, and institutions for the care and education of the blind established, and special measures taken for the exclusion of infected cattle, rags, and decayed fruit. In other states laws have been enacted limiting the hours during which women and children shall be employed in factories; and while their constitutionality applied to women has been doubted in some of the states, they have been generally upheld; thus, in the case of *Commonwealth* v. *Hamilton Manufacturing Co.*, 120 Mass. 383, it was held that a statute prohibiting the employment of all persons under the age of eighteen, and of all women laboring in any manufacturing establishment more than sixty hours per week, violates no contract of the commonwealth implied in the granting of a charter to a manufacturing company nor any right reserved under the Constitution to any individual citizen, and may be maintained as a health or police regulation.

Upon the principles above stated, we think the act in question may be sustained as a valid exercise of the police power of the state. The enactment does not profess to limit the hours of all workmen, but merely those who are employed in the underground mines, or in the smelting, reduction, or refining of ores or metals. These employments when too long pursued, the legislature has judged to be detrimental to the health of the employees, and, so long as there are reasonable grounds for believing that this is so, its decision upon this subject cannot be reviewed by the Federal courts. . . .

The legislature has also recognized the fact, which the experience of legislators in many states has corroborated, that the proprietors of these establishments and their operatives do not stand upon an equality, and that their interests are, to a certain extent, conflicting. The former naturally desire to obtain as much labor as possible from their employees, while the latter are often induced by the fear of discharge to conform to regulations which their judgment, fairly exercised, would pronounce to be detrimental to their health or strength. In other words, the proprietors lay down the rules and the laborers are practically constrained to obey them. In such cases self-interest is often an unsafe guide, and the legislature may promptly interpose its authority. . . .

We are of opinion that the act in question was a valid exercise of the police power of the state, and *the judgments of the Supreme Court of Utah are therefore affirmed.*

Subsequently another court decision on hazardous working conditions was rendered in New York. In the case *Lochner* v. *New York,* the Supreme Court invalidated a New York statute fixing the maximum hours of work in the bakery industry.[5] In this instance, the New York legislature had established a maximum 10-hour day for bakers because of health hazards—a statute overturned by the Supreme Court in a narrow five-to-four decision. Essentially, the majority of justices in the high court decided that the New York law attempted

[5] 198 U.S. 45 (1905).

to regulate hours of work in an industry seldom regarded as being hazardous. Furthermore, the Court argued that, in essence, the New York law unduly restricted individual rights to *liberty and property* protected in the Fourteenth Amendment to the Constitution. Justice Peckham's decision to restrict the residual police powers given to the states is expressed as follows:

> It must, of course, be conceded that there is a limit to the valid exercise of the police power by the State. The question whether this act is valid as a labor law, pure and simple may be dismissed in a few words. Clean and wholesome bread does not depend upon whether the baker works but ten hours a day or sixty hours a week. There is no contention that bakers are not able to assert their rights and care for themselves without the protecting arm of the state interfering with their independent judgment. It is a question of which of two rights shall prevail: the power of the state to legislate, or the right of the individual to liberty of person and freedom of contract. We think the limit of the police power has been reached and passed in this case. The limitation of the hours of labor of the statute has no direct relation to employee health.[6]

This reasoning prevailed in spite of the fact that the legislature of New York deemed working conditions to be undesirable. Furthermore, according to the dissent submitted by Justice Holmes, his fellow jurors had decided the case on the basis of their individual "economic theories" of free enterprise, which were inconsistent with the view of a large portion of the populace as well as the philosophy of most lawmakers.

HOURS OF WORK

Control of hazardous working conditions and regulation of hours presented grave difficulties to the Supreme Court of the United States. Interpreting the "proper" exercise of police power, which was restricted by the Fourteenth Amendment protection of the right to contract, was the source of this problem. Between 1908 and 1915, two decisions that were appealed from Oregon further revealed the Court's position on regulation of hours. In *Muller* v. *Oregon*, the Supreme Court supported an Oregon law that restricted the employment of women in selected industries in excess of ten hours during any given day.[7]

[6] *Ibid.*
[7] 208 U.S. 412 (1908).

The basic issue in this case was whether or not the 1903 statute limiting hours of work to a maximum of ten hours per day for women was an allowable area of state control. The Supreme Court ruled that this was a legitimate area of authority for state regulation under the police power. Moreover, the Court also argued that the Oregon legislation existed for the benefit of society at large since women were not equal competitors with men in the job market and the general welfare of mothers was essential to all of society. Justice Brewer's celebrated opinion on behalf of the majority of the Court observed:

> It is undoubtedly true, as more than once declared by this Court, the right of contract in relation to one's business is part of the liberty of the individual protected by the Fourteenth Amendment to the Federal Constitution; yet it is equally well settled that this liberty is not absolute in extending to all contracts. . . .[8]

Needless to say, this represents a rather unusual digression from the legal customs of those times—a situation prompted in no small way by the "sociological" brief submitted by Justice Louis Brandeis.[9] The Court also recognized:

> . . . that woman's physical structure and the performance of maternal functions place her in the disadvantage in the struggle for subsistence is obvious. This is especially true when the burdens of motherhood are upon her. Even when they are not, by abundant testimony of the medical fraternity, continuance for a long time on her feet at work, repeating this from day to day, tends to have injurious effects on the body and . . . the physical wellbeing of woman becomes an object of public interest and care in order to preserve the strength and vigor of the race. . . . The limitations which this statute places on her contractual powers, upon her right to agree with her employers as to the time she shall labor, are not imposed solely for her benefit, but also largely for the benefit of all. This difference justifies a difference in legislation and upholds that which is designed to compensate for some of the burdens which rest upon her.[10]

The *Muller* decision clearly validated the regulation of working hours insofar as labor that was harmful to females was concerned.

[8] *Ibid.*

[9] See Sanford Cohen, *Labor Law* (Columbus, Ohio: Charles E. Merrill Books, Inc., 1964).

[10] 208 U.S. 412 (1908).

Subsequently, the Supreme Court reached a comparable decision in the case of *Hunting* v. *Oregon* in 1917.[11]

Once again a statute passed in the state of Oregon was under question—in this case the law limited the hours of work for men employed in factory establishments to no more than ten hours per day. The statute further provided that three additional hours per day could be worked, but only if overtime was paid at the rate of one and one-half times the regular hourly wage. One striking feature of the Supreme Court's decision to validate this Oregon statute in the *Bunting* decision was its failure to take cognizance of the *Lochner* v. *New York* ruling that represented a contrary but potential precedent which could have been used to void this statute. The *Lochner* decision may have been ignored in part because of popular political opinion. National sentiment was modestly critical of the judicial climate established by the Supreme Court in other decisions which had made it difficult to regulate working conditions. Well-known legal authorities had also voiced their dissent with judicial rulings between the years separating the *Lochner* and *Bunting* decisions. In addition, talk of popularly rescinding judicial decisions was circulating which also may have contributed to the Court's more liberal acceptance of the Oregon law. In any event, the Court recognized the statute as a proper exercise of state police powers, in spite of the fact that opponents contended that the law was an attempt to regulate wages. Later the Fair Labor Standards Act of 1938 again superceded such judicial tribulation. Nevertheless, it is apparent that social and economic issues related to child labor and hours of work did create considerable duress during the period 1900–1930.

REGULATION OF MINIMUM WAGES

The development of public policy toward wages, particularly the establishment of minimum wage levels, experienced as stormy a history as did the child labor and hours laws discussed previously. The conventional economic theory of the early twentieth century as postulated by Smith, Ricardo, and other neoclassical economists such as Marshall and Clark philosophically supported the argument that a free labor market was inherently superior to a market with any controls. According to these views, competitive interaction between buyers and sellers for labor resources as well as goods and services leads to efficient performance in an economic system. This, of course, was a

11 243 U.S. 246 (1917).

viewpoint that happened to support the corporate and property interest groups of the times. With the advent of industrialization, increasing awareness of poor working conditions, and very low wage levels
for certain workers, the number of groups seeking regulatory action
multiplied. In some instances, states appointed investigatory commissions or passed laws determining the minimum wage, particularly for
female workers employed in the textile industry.

One of the earliest and more notable Supreme Court decisions
concerning minimum wage legislation was delivered in 1923 in the
Adkins v. *Children's Hospital* case.[12] The issue centered around the
validity of the District of Columbia's action concerning the establishment of legal wage minimums for female employees. As was true for
such controversial public manpower policy developed in the early
twentieth century, this statute was questioned on the grounds that it
authorized unconstitutional interference with the right to freely contract.

Justice Sutherland, who delivered the majority opinion for the
Court, recognized that there was no such thing as absolute freedom of
contract. However, he also pointed out that freedom was the general
rule and restraints on this freedom should be recognized as exceptions to the rule. In addition, Justice Sutherland buttressed his decision to invalidate the District of Columbia's regulation by noting that
earlier decisions rendered on the subject of working conditions pi-
voted around improvements in general health and welfare. In content, the District of Columbia law was described as

> . . . not for the protection of persons under legal disability or
> for the prevention of fraud. It is simply and exclusively a price-
> fixing law, confined to adult women . . . who are legally as capa-
> ble of contracting for themselves as men. It forbids two parties
> having lawful capacity . . . to freely contract with one another.
> The feature of this statute . . . is that it exacts from the employer
> an arbitrary payment for the purposes and upon the basis of hav-
> ing no casual connection with his business, or the contract or the
> work the employee engages to do. The law . . . ignores the neces-
> sities of the employer by compelling him to pay not less than a cer-
> tain sum, not only whether the employee is capable of earning it,
> but irrespective of the ability of an employer's business to sustain
> the burden. . . . The ethical right of every worker, man or woman,
> to a living wage may be conceded . . . but the fallacy of the pro-
> posed method of attaining it assumes that every employer is bound

[12] 261 U.S. 525 (1923).

at all events to furnish it. Certainly the employer by paying a fair equivalent for the service rendered, though not sufficient to support the employee, has neither caused nor contributed to her poverty. On the contrary, to the extent of what he pays he has relieved it. In principle, there can be no difference between the case of selling labor and the case of selling goods.[13]

Justice Sutherland also observed that the argument in support of the District of Columbia law would be understandable if it required an employer to pay in money instead of script, to pay at prescribed intervals, or to pay the value of the services rendered. The existing statute did not do this, however. Rather, the statute prescribed payment without regard to any of those relationships critical to the employment contract and the work performed under it. Therefore, Justice Sutherland declared that the statute was ". . . a naked, arbitrary exercise of power that cannot be allowed to stand under the Constitution of the United States." [14]

Chief Justice Taft of the Supreme Court submitted a dissent in this decision that was based on the fact that female employees frequently did not possess equal bargaining power with the employer and that it was quite appropriate for the legislature in such an instance to limit the freedom of contract between employees and employer under the police power. Taft also recognized that it may or may not be preferred economic practice to establish minimum wages, but this was an issue quite beyond the judicial authority and the competence of the Court to determine. Justice Holmes also supplied a dissent that noted that the statute

. . . simply forbids employment at rates below those fixed as the minimum required for health and right living. This statute does not compel anybody to pay anything. In short, the law in its character and operation is like hundreds of so-called police laws that have been upheld.[15]

The *Adkins* decision sharply restrained future progress in the area of minimum wage legislation. That the majority opinion of the Supreme Court was still strongly tied to the popular laissez faire doctrine of political economy was apparent to all.

The advent of the depression of the 1930's with widespread and

[13] *Ibid.*
[14] *Ibid.*
[15] *Ibid.*

persistent unemployment and severe wage cuts revitalized an interest in minimum wage legislation. The now famous threat to pack the Supreme Court of the United States, issued by President Roosevelt after his landslide victory in 1936, shifted the attitude of the Court from a conservative majority to a majority in support of more progressive and liberal action concerning manpower laws and working conditions. Even so, the *Morehead* v. *Tipaldo* case, which was heard by the Supreme Court in 1936, still did not clear the way for minimum wage legislation.[16] In this decision, the Supreme Court ruled in a narrow five-to-four decision that a New York minimum wage statute did not differ from the District of Columbia law and therefore the previous ruling rendered in the *Adkins* decision applied.

These developments were completely overshadowed in a landmark decision rendered in 1937 by the Supreme Court, with Chief Justice Hughes speaking for the majority.[17] This decision involved the minimum wage law passed by the state of Washington and resulted in a complete reversal of the *Morehead* and *Adkins* decisions. The striking reliance of Chief Justice Hughes on the point that the right to freedom of contract was qualified and protection of female workers was legitimate, contrasts markedly with the earlier decisions above and poignantly reveals how significant value judgments are in judicial matters.

WEST COAST HOTEL COMPANY v. PARRISH: 1936
(300 U.S. 386)

Mr. Chief Justice Hughes delivered the opinion of the Court:

This case presents the question of the constitutional validity of the minimum wage law of the state of Washington. The Act, entitled "Minimum Wages for Women," authorizes the fixing of minimum wages for women and miners.

The appellant conducts a hotel. The appellee Elsie Parrish was employed as a chambermaid and (with her husband) brought this suit to recover the difference between the wages paid her and the minimum wage fixed pursuant to the state law. The minimum wage was $14.50 per week of 48 hours. The appellant challenged the act as repugnant to the due process clause of the Fourteenth Amendment of the Constitution of the United States. The Supreme Court of the state, reversing the trial court, sustained the statute

---

16 298 U.S. 587 (1936).
17 *West Coast Hotel* v. *Parrish*, 300 U.S. 379 (1937).

and directed judgment for the plaintiffs. *Parrish* v. *West Coast Hotel Co.* (185 Wash. 581). The case is here on appeal.

The Supreme Court of Washington has upheld the minimum wage statute of that state. It has decided that the statute is a reasonable exercise of the police power of the state. In reaching that conclusion the state court has invoked principles long established by this Court in the application of the Fourteenth Amendment. The state court has refused to regard the decision in the *Adkins* case as determinative and has pointed to our decisions both before and since that case as justifying its position. We are of the opinion that this ruling of the state court demands on our part a reexamination of the *Adkins* case. The importance of the question, in which many states having similar laws are concerned, the close division by which the decision in the *Adkins* case was reached, and the economic conditions which have supervened, and in the light of which the reasonableness of the exercise of the protective power of the state must be considered, make it not only appropriate, but we think imperative, that in deciding the present case the subject should receive fresh consideration.

The principle which must control our decision is not in doubt. The constitutional provision invoked is the due process clause of the Fourteenth Amendment governing the states, as the due process clause invoked in the *Adkins* case governed Congress. In each case the violation alleged by those attacking minimum wage regulation for women is deprivation of freedom of contract. What is this freedom? The Constitution does not speak of freedom of contract. It speaks of liberty and prohibits the deprivation of liberty without due process of law. In prohibiting that deprivation the Constitution does not recognize an absolute and uncontrollable liberty. Liberty in each of its phases has its history and connotation. But the liberty safe-guarded is liberty in a social organization which requires the protection of law against the evils which menace the health, safety, morals and welfare of the people. Liberty under the Constitution is thus necessarily subject to the restraints of due process, and regulation which is reasonable in relation to its subject and is adopted in the interests of the community is due process.

This essential limitation of liberty in general governs freedom of contract in particular. More than twenty-five years ago we set forth the applicable principle in these words, after referring to the cases where the liberty guaranteed by the Fourteenth Amendment had been broadly described: "But it was recognized in the cases cited, as in many others, that freedom of contract is a qualified and not an absolute right. There is no absolute freedom to do as one wills or to contract as one chooses. The guaranty of liberty does not withdraw from legislative supervision that wide department of activity which consists of the making of contracts, or deny to government the power to provide restrictive safeguards. Liberty implies the absence of arbitrary restraint, not immunity from reasonable regulations and prohibitions imposed in the interests of the community." The minimum wage to be paid under the Washington statute is fixed after full consideration by representatives of employers, employees, and the public. It may be assumed that the minimum wage is fixed in consideration of the services that are performed in the particular occupations under normal conditions. Provision is made for special licenses at less wages in the case of women who are incapable of full service. The statement of Mr. Justice Holmes in the *Adkins* case is pertinent: "This statute does not compel anybody to pay anything. It simply forbids employment at rates below those fixed as the minimum requirement of health and right living. It is safe to assume that women will not be employed at even the lowest wages allowed unless they earn them, or unless the employer's business can sustain the burden. In short the law in its character and operation is like hundreds of so-called police laws that have been upheld." And Chief Justice Taft forcibly pointed out the consideration which is basic in a statute of this character: "Legislatures which adopt a requirement of maximum hours or minimum wages may be presumed to believe that when employers are prevented from paying unduly low wages by positive law they will continue their business, abating that part of their profits, which were wrung from the necessities of their employees, and will concede the better terms required by law; and that while in individual cases hardship may result, the restriction will ensure to the benefit of the general class of employees in whose interest the law is passed and so to that of the community at large." We think that the views thus expressed are sound and that the decision in the *Adkins* case was a departure from the true application of the principles governing the regulation by the state of the relation of employer and employed. . . .

What can be closer to the public interest than the health of women and their protection from unscrupulous and overreaching

employers? And if the protection of women is a legitimate end of
the exercise of state power, how can it be said that the requirement of the payment of a minimum wage fairly fixed in order to
meet the very necessities of existence is not an admissible means to
that end? The legislature of the state was clearly entitled to consider the situation of women in employment, the fact that they are
in the class receiving the least pay, that their bargaining power is
relatively weak, and that they are the ready victims of those who
would take advantage of their necessitous circumstances. The legislature was entitled to adopt measures to reduce the evils of the
"sweating system," the exploitation of workers at wages so low as
to be insufficient to meet the bare cost of living, thus making their
very helplessness the occasion of a most injurious competition. The
legislature had the right to consider that its minimum wage requirements would be an important aid in carrying out its policy of
protection. The adoption of similar requirements by many states
evidences a deep-seated conviction both as to the presence of the
evil and as to the means adopted to check it. Legislative response
to that conviction cannot be regarded as arbitrary or capricious
and that is all we have to decide. Even if the wisdom of the policy
be regarded as debatable and its effects uncertain, still the legislature is entitled to its judgment.

There is an additional and compelling consideration which recent economic experience has brought into a strong light. The exploitation of a class of workers who are in an unequal position
with respect to bargaining power and are thus relatively defense-
less against the denial of a living wage is not only detrimental to
their health and well-being but casts a direct burden for their support upon the community. What these workers lose in wages the
taxpayers are called upon to pay. The bare cost of living must be
met. We may take judicial notice of the unparalleled demands for
relief which arose during the recent period of depression and still
continue to an alarming extent despite the degree of economic recovery which has been achieved. It is unnecessary to cite official
statistics to establish what is of common knowledge through the
length and breadth of the land. While in the instant case no factual brief has been presented, there is no reason to doubt that the
State of Washington has encountered the same social problem that
is present elsewhere. . . .

The judgment of the Supreme Court of the State of Washington
is affirmed.

The importance of the *West Coast* decision was recognized across the nation, in large measure because the Supreme Court had expressly overruled the *Adkins* decision and, in this way, opened the door for fresh consideration of manpower policies and working conditions.

THE FAIR LABOR STANDARDS ACT

Although the history of manpower policy in the areas of wages, hours, and working conditions was very stormy, a dramatic reversal occurred in 1938. The severity of the depression, widespread poverty, intense economic insecurity, rampant unemployment, and generally declining standards of living had been the lot of millions of Americans for nearly a decade. With the favorable *West Coast* decision, the President of the United States in his 1938 congressional address called for the establishment of legal minimum wages as well as ceilings on working hours. The Seventy-fifth Congress moved promptly on this Presidential request and enacted the Fair Labor Standards Act in 1938.

The Fair Labor Standards Act was concerned with three major areas: (a) establishment of minimum wages, (b) specification of maximum working hours, and (c) federal control and discouragement of the employment of children. Numerous amendments have since been passed to update the Fair Labor Standards Act. Coverage under the Fair Labor Standards Act has been extended to encompass larger proportions of American workers irrespective of the size and circumstances of business enterprises involved.

The Fair Labor Standards Act was validated in a number of decisions rendered in the courts including *United States* v. *Darby Lumber Company* which was decided in 1941.[18] Although coverage and regulation has been extended repeatedly in the three decades since its passage, the basic accomplishment of this Act remains a national recognition that the federal government has a responsibility to monitor working conditions. This responsibility is firmly entrenched in the customs of business firms in our society as well as in the economic philosophy of the typical working man.

The administration of the Act has created modest problems in the areas of a minimum wage and child labor working standards. However, a good deal of serious questioning has repeatedly appeared in

[18] 312 U.S. 100 (1941). Also see *Opp. Cotton Mills, Inc.* v. *Administrator*, 312 U.S. 126 (1941), as well as *Mabee* v. *White Plains Publishing Company*, 327 U.S. 178 (1946).

the last three decades concerning the desirability of the minimum wage aspect of the law. Debate has centered around the desirability of establishing minimum wage levels today which reduce job opportunities for youth. In addition, there is a considerable amount of controversy about whether or not minimum wages mitigate or perpetuate the poverty conditions that encompass the some twenty million Americans living in poverty even in the affluence of the early 1970's. Finally, it should also be noted that the regulation of working hours, and particularly the overtime features of the Act, creates serious and highly technical industrial relations problems. While we cannot delve into these in any detail here, it is sufficient to note that determination of the basis for overtime payment as well as the basis for establishing a "40-hour work week" have been the subject of repeated arbitration decisions as well as National Labor Relations Board decisions. Administration of the law to contemporary industrial relations problems remains a difficult subject even today.

Contemporary Manpower Problems and Policy

Concern for employment security and conditions extends beyond the areas of the laws of collective bargaining or simple wage and hour laws. Public policy developments in the areas of human resource economics and manpower management embrace broad subject areas, each of which well might constitute a separate area of inquiry. Unlike much of the policy discussed previously, the courts have not played a major role. Actually, much of the policy in areas such as manpower development and utilization, equal opportunity, or unemployment compensation extends into social and economic problem areas that we are not prepared to evaluate. For this reason, we shall briefly touch upon some of the highlights and leave the task of complete inquiry to others.[19]

Passage of the Social Security Act in 1935 constitutes one major development in the area of employment and economic security. This legislation is most noteworthy as a *social* or *public* insurance system that embraces many of the different features of economic security of importance today. As is commonly known, the Social Security Act does facilitate retirement by providing retirement benefits to qualified workers. The purpose of these retirement benefits is to provide mini-

[19] The interested reader should consult United States Department of Labor, *Manpower Report of the President*, 1970 or other years.

mal economic security, financed through employee and employer contributions, for all aged workers.

During the 1960's the concept of public insurance was extended to the field of medical care and hospitalization for the aged, now also carried out under the same administrative provisions initially established in 1935. The variety of economic security programs spawned by the Social Security Act also includes coverage for disabled persons, relief for the blind and other disabled workers, and nominal life insurance-annuity security for dependent families.

Still another area covered by the broad umbrella of social and economic security includes workman's compensation for injury and death. Even today, hundreds of thousands of disabling accidents occur on the job, and permanent injuries and deaths number in the tens of thousands annually. Although a concerted effort has been made in recent years to reduce the probability of injury or death on the job, it is apparent that workman's compensation as well as injury prevention policies are appropriate. Currently, workman's compensation laws vary from state to state, and are compulsory in the majority of states. In nearly all instances workman's compensation programs are employer-financed. There is a wide variation in benefits, in terms of the proportion of a wage compensated for, weekly and monthly maximums, and the length of time for which benefits are available. Compensation benefits are generally meager in terms of the value of a working man's life, covering on the average 5 to 20 percent of a younger worker's earning power. The small lifetime protection is largely attributable to the fact that a number of states have maximum benefit periods or amounts that typically cannot exceed ten years or $30,000 to $40,000. When we compare this to the average high school graduate's lifetime earning capacity from age twenty to retirement, which is in the area of $300,000 to $500,000, the problem is all too apparent. As a consequence, disability and death cases are increasingly being brought to court and settlement in excess of what is presently allowed by compensation laws is common, provided that states have no statutory limits.

Unemployment compensation programs, currently a joint federal-state effort, represent still another dimension to the Social Security Act of 1935. This Act did not finance unemployment compensation programs directly, but it did encourage states to adopt unemployment compensation systems by allowing funds to be obtained from taxes levied under the 1935 Act. It is necessary, however, that the state establish an unemployment system under the guidelines provided for by federal procedures. Again, as with the workman's compensation programs, there is some question about the adequacy of unemployment compensation programs, maximum benefit periods, the exclusion of some firms, qualification in terms of work experience, and the dollar amount of benefits provided tend to limit coverage to about 35 percent of lost wages. In many instances, the union has negotiated with management for supplementary unemployment benefits that are designed to remedy inadequacies in public sponsored unemployment compensation systems. Unfortunately, hundreds of thousands of workers are long-run unemployables and benefit little from the existing unemployment compensation system.

As a consequence, numerous additional steps have been taken since 1958 to more effectively develop and utilize manpower. In 1958, for example, Congress passed the National Defence Education Act, which has since been expanded to provide federal assistance to education for needed skills and disadvantaged socioeconomic groups. After reexamining the problem of the geographic distribution of unemployment in 1961, Congress supported and developed the Area Redevelopment Act of 1961. This legislation, primarily directed towards depressed economic areas, focused upon stimulating economic growth by providing financial and technical assistance to business firms. In addition, the Area Redevelopment Act furnished manpower policy makers with limited experimental capability in manpower training. In 1962, the Manpower Development and Training Act was established as a first step towards formulating a broad, encompassing national manpower policy. This Act called for the establishment of national occupational training, and devoted attention to manpower development for the unemployed and underemployed workers living in depressed areas and under poverty conditions. In the eight years since the passage of the Manpower Development and Training Act, over one and one-half million workers have enrolled in occupational training and manpower development programs designed to update their skills, often made obsolete by a rapidly changing technology.

Numerous satellite manpower programs have been developed from the general philosophy embraced by the Manpower Development and Training Act. One of the more recent and widely heralded programs is Job Opportunities in the Business Sector (JOBS), which was launched in 1968 and has since been expanded. Essentially this program encourages private business and government to work together to train disadvantaged workers by compensating business firms for additional training expenses. Vocational education programs have also been strengthened, particularly since the passage of the 1963 and 1968 Vocational Education Acts. Furthermore, these Acts changed the direction of vocational education programs in the United States. Another notable piece of legislation launched in 1964 was directed at disadvantaged and poverty-stricken Americans. The Economic Opportunity Act, which has included such programs as Operation Headstart, is designed to strengthen the cultural and scholastic capabilities of the disadvantaged. Adult basic education programs are also a by-product of the Economic Opportunity Act of 1964. Adult training in basic education for persons over the age of eighteen may represent one of the greatest needs of the 1970's. Other manpower legislation and programs are almost too numerous to mention. Neighborhood Youth Corps, the Job Corps, and the Work Incentive Program similarly have been directed to manpower development and the maintenance of appropriate economic opportunities and standards of living for poverty-stricken Americans, who currently number over twenty million individuals.

In recent years, most of the public manpower policy has been directed towards the disadvantaged who tend to be members of minority ethnic groups, undereducated, either very young or very old, and residents of depressed areas. Increasing recognition of the economic plight of the poor, whose per capita income is approximately one-third that of the average American, has been heightened by the tensions and increasingly probable socioeconomic uprisings that characterized this nation in the late 1960's. Even though most disadvantaged and under-utilized manpower in this country consists of white Americans, the circumstances surrounding nonwhites have been bleak until very recently. The Equal Employment Opportunity title of the Civil Rights Law of 1964, and the law itself, constituted a major step forward in dealing with the problems of minority workers. There is little doubt that the nonwhite unemployment rates, which are at least twice as great as whites, must be remedied. Attention also must be focused on those factors causing nonwhite incomes to be only 60 to 75 percent of white family incomes. Discrimination on the job, employment discrimination, and unequal opportunities have plagued our nation for decades. These problems are now the object of increasingly effective state and federal pressures in a manpower and human resource context.

Many changes have appeared in the areas of labor, manpower, and public policy in the some two centuries since the earliest working men's associations gathered in this nation to promote their own interests. Indeed, one might well conclude that these dynamic adjustments that occurred in the area of human resources as a product of the democratic political process, represent the very strength of the economy in which we live today. Examining the economy decade by decade reveals a legal lag in relation to contemporary social and economic problems, which is much less apparent if one views progress over the course of the past two centuries.

Summary

The working conditions for labor have changed markedly over the course of the 1900's and new labor economic problems are emerging as the nation enters the decade of the 1970's. Child labor ultimately succumbed to corrective legislation, the form of the Fair Labor Standards Act of 1938, even though *Hammer* v. *Dagenhart* represented a serious setback for those who supported restricting the conditions and hours of work for minors. Hazardous working conditions, restriction on the number of hours of straight-time work for females and males, and regulation of minimum wages represented important issues that were resolved through the legal process prior to mid-century. This struggle to remedy working conditions is recorded in several court decisions such as *Holden* v. *Hardy* (1898), *Lochner* v. *New York* (1905), *Muller* v. *Oregon* (1908), *Adkins* v. *Children's Hospital* (1923), and the *West Coast Hotel* decision (1936), all of which are cited above. The Fair Labor Standards Act of 1938 represents one of the most comprehensive pieces of legislation to affect labor and working conditions.

Contemporary manpower problems such as poverty, unemployment, inadequate training, economic inequality, and insecurity have attracted considerable attention from public policy makers, particularly during the decade of the 1960's. These new challenges demand new answers and processes—a challenge that requires long-run changes in the work world as dramatic as those that occurred in this nation in relation to the union movement which we have recorded here.

INDEX

INDEX OF CASES CITED

449

DATE DUE

NO 24 '74			
AG 19 '76			
DEC - 6 1976			
APR 28 '86			
credited 5-19-86 BF NOV 17 '91			
DEC 08 '93			
		PRINTED IN U.S.A.